T. W. Allies

The Formation Of Christendom Vol. 5

The Throne of the Fisherman Built by the Carpenter's Son, the Root, the Bond and

the Crown of Christendom

T. W. Allies

The Formation Of Christendom Vol. 5
The Throne of the Fisherman Built by the Carpenter's Son, the Root, the Bond and the Crown of Christendom

ISBN/EAN: 9783742835772

Manufactured in Europe, USA, Canada, Australia, Japa

Cover: Foto ©Lupo / pixelio.de

Manufactured and distributed by brebook publishing software (www.brebook.com)

T. W. Allies

The Formation Of Christendom Vol. 5

THE THRONE

OF

THE FISHERMAN

BUILT BY THE CARPENTER'S SON,

THE ROOT, THE BOND, AND THE CROWN

OF CHRISTENDOM.

BY

THOMAS W. ALLIES, K.C.S.G.,

AUTHOR OF "THE FORMATION OF CHRISTENDOM"; "CHURCH AND STATE AS
SEEN IN THE FORMATION OF CHRISTENDOM"; "A LIFE'S DECISION";
"PER CRUCEM AD LUCEM, THE RESULT OF A LIFE"; "JOURNAL
IN FRANCE AND LETTERS FROM ITALY".

LONDON: BURNS & OATES, LIMITED.
NEW YORK: CATHOLIC PUBLICATION SOCIETY CO.
1887.

TO

HIS HOLINESS LEO XIII.,

ON WHOM NOW LIES THE CHARGE OF OUR LORD TO ST. PETER,

IS

Humbly Dedicated

THIS EFFORT TO TRACE ITS OUTCOME FROM THE BEGINNING

TO THE TIME OF ST. LEO THE GREAT.

Extract from Brief of His Holiness to the Author.

To our dear Son, Thos. Wm. Allies, Secretary of the Catholic Poor School Committee, London.

LEO PP. XIII.

Dear Son,

HEALTH AND APOSTOLICAL BENEDICTION.

We embrace with much charity, and joyously select for distinguished honour, men who to a skill and knowledge in studies of the highest import add a well-deserved reputation for piety and virtue, while they dedicate themselves to the service of religion. Now we are well assured that you, dear Son, are of approved piety and conduct; and being of keen and active mind, are distinguished in the higher and more difficult branches of human knowledge, while you have gained great merit by earnest action and by esteemed writings on behalf of the Catholic Faith. On account of these deserts it is our pleasure to bestow on you a title of great honour, in token of our exceeding goodwill towards you, and as an encouragement to you to advance daily in zeal for the Catholic cause. Desiring then to shew you a special benevolence and distinction, and absolving you on this mere account from whatever sentences of excommunication or interdict or other ecclesiastical sentences, censures, and penalties, which in any way or for any cause you may have incurred, if haply you have incurred, and deeming you so absolved, We by Our Apostolical Authority in virtue of this letter make you a Knight Commander of the Order of St. Gregory the Great, of the civil class. We institute, declare, and number you in the most distinguished rank and roll of the aforesaid Knights.

> Given at Rome, at St. Peter's, under the Ring of the Fisherman, on the 13th day of November, 1885, in the eighth year of our Pontificate.

M. CARD. LEDÓCHOWSKI.

FULL TITLES OF WORKS QUOTED.

The following works have been used by the Author, and being quoted by the name alone, the full title of them is here given :—

The Greek and Latin Fathers generally quoted from the old Benedictine edition, sometimes from that of Migne.
Newman, Cardinal, Arians of the Fourth Century, 3rd edition.
„ Notes on St. Athanasius, 2nd volume.
„ Causes of the Rise and Success of Arianism.
Hergenröther, Cardinal, Handbuch der allgemeinen Kirchengeschichte, 3 vols. 1876-1880.
„ Photius, sein Leben, &c., 3 vols. 1867.
Coustant, Epistolæ Pontif. Roman. Paris, 1721.
Hefele, Concilien-geschichte, 7 vols. 1855, &c.
Phillips, Kirchenrecht, 7 vols. 1845-1872.
Reumont, Geschichte der Stadt Rom, 3 vols. 1867-1870.
Gregorovius, Geschichte der Stadt Rom, 8 vols.
Niehues, Geschichte des Verhältnisses zwischen Kaiserthum und Papstthum. Münster, 1863.
Tillemont, Histoire des Empereurs, 6 vols. Paris, 1690.
„ Histoire Ecclesiastique, 16 vols. Paris, 1693.
Möhler, Patrologie. Regensburg, 1840.
„ Kirchengeschichte (Gams), 3 vols. Regensburg, 1867.
Arendt, Leo der Grosse.
Nirschl, Lehrbuch der Patrologie und Patristik, 3 vols. 1881-5.
Riffel, Geschichtliche Darstellung des Verhältnisses zwischen Kirche und Staat, &c. Mainz, 1836.
Broglie, Duc de, L'Eglise et l'Empire Romain, 6 vol. 1856-66.
Mansi, Sacrorum Conciliorum nova et amplissima collectiô: 1759, 31 vols.
Matthieu, le Cardinal Archevêque de Besançon; Le Pouvoir Temporel des Papes justifié par l'histoire. 1863.

TABLE OF CONTENTS.

CHAPTER I.

The Witness of Eighteen Centuries to the See of Peter.

	PAGE
The Throne of the Fisherman founded on three words,	1
The first word,	1
The second word,	2
The third word,	2
Coinherence of the several charges contained in them,	3
Effect of the three words through eighteen centuries,	4
They contain a direct divine institution,	5
The Church's recognition of the divine institution a second Factor,	6
One instance of such recognition to stand for all,	7
The council of Chalcedon and Pope St. Leo,	8
St. Leo's office as conceived by himself, and as expressed by the council,	9
A third Factor, the Divine Providence,	11
Action of this Factor between A.D. 325 and 600,	12
Further action in mediæval times,	13
And in modern times,	14
Exemplified in the most absolute of modern rulers,	15
Remark on the conjunction of the three Factors,	16
The subject of this volume, the evolution of the three Factors,	19
The first period,	20
The second period,	20
The third period,	21
The fourth period,	22
The fifth period,	23

	PAGE
The sixth period,	23
The seventh period,	24
The eighth period in which we live,	25
Action of the three Factors in the diversity of the periods,	26
Error frames its attacks upon isolated acts: truth contemplates the whole evolution of history,	27

CHAPTER II.

From St. Peter to St. Sylvester, No. 1.

The first General Council makes an epoch in itself,	29
How the subscriptions of bishops stand in the lists of the Council,	31
Importance of the cause for which it met,	32
The period A.D. 29-325 a complete one with special characteristics,	33
Aspect of the Church at the convocation of the Nicene Council,	34
Force of the emperor's recognition of the Council,	35
The Council viewed as proof of the existence of a Christian people,	36
The hierarchy exhibits the idea which made the people,	37
The marvel which this people presented,	38
The effect on the mind of Constantine,	40
How the Church speaks of her own existence,	42
The Council as a witness of the Church's previous history,	43
Dearth of early Christian history,	44
For which the Council in some degree makes up,	45
The constitution of Church government at the time of the Nicene Council,	46
How the Apostles divided the earth,	47
The episcopate universal, complete, subordinated, and one,	48
The triple Petrine Patriarchate,	49
Other primatial sees,	51
Great preponderance of St. Peter's authority in this hierarchy,	52

St. Gregory the Great, on the See of Peter at Rome, Alexandria, and Antioch, ...	53
St. Innocent I. on the see of Antioch, ...	54
The whole system of episcopal subordination and unity recognised and sanctioned by the Council, . . .	56
What this organic distribution of authority indicates, . .	57
St. Peter alone of the Apostles stands at the head of an episcopal line, ...	58
The meaning and range of the sixth Nicene canon, . .	61
What Pope Nicolas I. deduces from the three patriarchates,	63
Neither the Nicene nor any council gave its authority to the Roman church, ...	65
He quotes Pope Boniface I. to this effect, ...	66
Exposition of the Nicene Constitution by Pope Boniface, .	67
In which historic fact and theoretic principle are united, .	69

CHAPTER III.

From St. Peter to St. Sylvester, No. 2.

Lesson as to the government of the whole Church given by the Nicene Council, ...	71
The hierarchy answers to the unity of the one Christian people, ...	72
Four bands of this unity :	
1. Litteræ formatæ, ...	73
2. The system of mother and daughter churches, .	74
3. Provincial synods, ...	75
4. The universal recognition of the Primacy, . .	76
Growth of the hierarchy during a state of persecution, .	77
And of the Primacy in particular, ...	78
The office of bishop maintained by the willing obedience of its subjects, ...	79
Which denotes its source from a power recognised by them,	80
This is even more marked in the Primacy than in the Episcopate, ...	81

TABLE OF CONTENTS.

	PAGE
The martyrdom of five successive Popes in eight years,	82
The bishop of the second see called to account by the Roman bishop,	84
The emperor and the bishops equally acknowledge the Primacy at the cessation of heathen persecution,	85
Fixity and definiteness of functions in all the ranks of the hierarchy,	86
Key to the formation of the hierarchy supplied by Leo I.,	87
Testimony of Pope Innocent I. in the year 416,	89
Pope Julius in 342 sets forth the rule of tradition and custom,	91
Claims the year before the council of Sardica what its canon gave to him,	92
His letter shews throughout the original Primacy and the Church's constitution,	93
The Pope specially the judge of the bishop of Alexandria,	94
The Principate of Peter the fountainhead of "ecclesiastical rule,"	95
Political circumstances of the time give this letter still greater force,	96
Connection between the letters of Pope Julius I. and Pope Clement I.,	96
Completeness of the hierarchy in fact and theory at the Nicene Council,	97
Exercise of the Primacy proportionate to the condition of the Church,	98
How the Primacy was exercised in the first three centuries,	99
Connection between concentered authority and extent and complexity of dominion,	100
The Church's history without the Primacy inexplicable,	101
Infallibility demanded and exercised in the first centuries,	102
The Primacy in these centuries at once the Root, the Bond, and the Crown of the hierarchy,	104
The parallel course of the Empire and the Church from the birth of Christ to Constantine,	106
St. Leo the Great on the Providence of God in bringing St. Peter and St. Paul to Rome,	109

CHAPTER IV.

Constantine and the Church.

A new alliance of the State with the Church marks the contrast of this period with the Antenicene period,	116
Heathen persecution had hitherto protected internal autonomy,	117
Which was a traditional system of doctrine, government, and daily life,	118
The tradition of St. Peter and St. Paul maintained at Rome especially,	119
Alluded to by St. Ignatius of Antioch,	120
Urged by Popes Anicetus, Stephen, and Liberius,	121
The same tradition followed by Alexandria and Antioch,	122
Why the Primacy is latent in the period of persecution,	123
Circumstances which mark the fifty years between the first and second General Councils,	124
They act together, but must be treated consecutively,	126
1. Constantine's position and design when he becomes sole emperor,	127
He allies the empire with the Church,	128
Scope of his legislation,	129
The Christian hierarchy acknowledged in the extent to which it had grown up of itself,	131
Civil jurisdiction given to episcopal decisions,	132
Constantine's idea of the relation between Church and State,	133
Which prevails from his time,	135
2. The form of Roman sovereignty under Constantine,	136
The emperor held not an usurped but a legitimate power,	139
Which the chief Fathers expressly attest,	140
All the military force in the emperor's hand,	141
Civil office separated from military command,	141
The Consistorium Sacrum,	142
The emperor sole legislator and taxer,	142
The bureaucratic nobility,	142

TABLE OF CONTENTS.

	PAGE
The empire of Constantine and that of the Russian Peter identical,	143
The prefectures, dioceses, and provinces of the empire,	144
Constantine exercises absolute power in the State, while he acknowledges a divine authority inherent in the Church,	145
He sets in motion powers the action of which he cannot foresee,	146
3. Movement of the imperial residence from Rome,	147
4. Constantinople consecrated as Nova Roma,	149
The emperor's withdrawal exalts the position of the Pope,	151
5. The bishop of Byzantium becomes bishop of Constantinople,	152
His see becomes forthwith the most coveted see of the East,	153
And likewise the central field of heresy from the death of Constantine to Theodosius,	154
Rise of the "Resident Synod,"	155
6. The new connection between the emperor and the bishop of the city in which he resided,	156
7. Degradation from their original rank of other bishops,	158

CHAPTER V.

CONSTANTINE AND HIS SONS, JULIAN, VALENTINIAN, VALENS.

Constantine visits Rome, leaves it for good, and founds a new capital,	160
Recalls Eusebius of Nicomedia and Theognis of Nicæa to their sees,	162
Conduct of Constantine under influence of Eusebius,	163
How Eusebius manages to depose St. Eustathius of Antioch,	164
How he attacks Athanasius, who is threatened by Constantine,	165
Athanasius refuses to attend a council at Cæsarea,	167

TABLE OF CONTENTS. xvii

	PAGE
Constantine summons a council at Tyre to judge Athanasius,	167
His instructions to the council, and the synod of Egypt's comment on it,	168
Contrast between the council of Tyre and that of Nicæa,	170
Athanasius attends it, and is deposed by it,	170
Appeals to Constantine; is banished by him to Treves,	171
Constantine in the thirteen years of his sole government,	172
The weapon devised by Eusebius against the hierarchy,	173
How he led Constantine to infringe the hitherto subsisting order,	174
Constantine's government in his last years a foretaste of all subsequent evils,	175
The three emperors, Constantine II., Constans, and Constantius,	177
Eusebius of Nicomedia model of the court-bishop for after ages,	178
Athanasius returns, and is attacked by Eusebius,	179
He flies for refuge to Rome, and is acquitted by the Pope in council,	179
The Eusebians hold the council of the Encænia at Antioch against him,	180
Letter of Pope Julius in defence of the old order of the Church,	181
Pope Julius moves the emperors to call the council of Sardica,	182
Its acts, and the retirement of the Eusebians to Philippopolis,	182
The question of the Church's unity and independence raised by these councils,	183
The East and West in opposite camps after the council of Sardica,	185
Persecution of orthodox bishops returning from Sardica by Constantius,	185
Athanasius returns in 346 after his second exile of six years,	186
Deplorable state of Antioch upon his visit there,	186
Constantius sole emperor in 350: his person and character,	187
He is swayed by the Arian Valens, and by his Arian empress,	188

b

TABLE OF CONTENTS.

	PAGE
Especially hates Athanasius,	189
Attacks him through the synod of Arles and that of Milan,	189
Tyrannises over the bishops at the council of Milan,	190
His attack on Pope Liberius described by Athanasius,	193
Theodoret describes how Liberius is banished by Constantius,	196
The judgment of Athanasius respecting Pope Liberius,	197
His dictum: the party of Arius have no king but Cæsar,	198
Constantius drives Athanasius from Alexandria,	199
The night attack described by Athanasius,	200
The Alexandrians appeal to the emperor, who justifies the act,	201
Hosius denounces the tyranny of Constantius,	201
Athanasius declares the Church's independence of the emperor,	202
Is an outlawed fugitive during the remaining five years of Constantius,	203
Is brought back in virtue of the decree of the apostate emperor Julian,	203
Later councils in the reign of Constantius,	204
St. Hilary describes the councils of his time,	204
And St. Gregory of Nazianzum,	205
Constantius receives clinical baptism from an Arian bishop and dies of fever,	206
The twenty months of Julian,	207
Four emperors in twenty-eight months, and division of the East and West,	207
Valentinian's upright government in the West,	208
Valens oppresses the Catholics in the East,	209
Athanasius is banished for the fifth time, but is soon restored,	210
Basil writes that the sight of him would compensate for all evils,	211
Valens causes eighty ecclesiastics to be set adrift in a burning ship,	211
After a tyranny of eleven years he is burnt in a Thracian cottage,	212
Theodosius made emperor in the East by Gratian,	213
His law of February 28, 380,	214

CHAPTER VI.

FROM CONSTANTINE AT NICÆA TO THEODOSIUS AT CONSTANTINOPLE.

	PAGE
Ecclesiastical retrospect of the period, 325-381,	216
Alexandria and Antioch at Nicæa,	217
The position of Rome in regard to them,	219
Beginning of the Eusebian attack on the Church's constitution,	220
Heresy and schism at Antioch during fifty years,	220
Constantinople in Arian hands for forty years,	221
The five banishments of Athanasius and the sufferings of Alexandria,	223
What the banishment of bishops meant,	226
Applied to the bishops of Antioch, Constantinople, Milan, Poitiers,	227
And to Pope Liberius,	228
How this punishment exceeded any inflicted by heathens,	230
St. Basil's cry of distress in 373 under the persecution of Valens,	231
St. Gregory of Nazianzum on episcopal councils in his time,	234
And on the bishops at the council of Constantinople in 381,	235
His words express to the life the Arian tyranny,	236
Deterioration of the Eastern episcopate marked by these bishops,	237
The instrument by which Eusebius violated the Church's constitution,	238
The council of Constantinople in 381 received only as to its creed, not as to its canons,	241
Development of the papal dignity in 325-381,	242-274
1. The splendour of Rome when visited by Constantius in 357,	243
Rome in the fourth century deserted by her emperors,	244
Still in Constantine's time the stronghold of heathenism,	245
Advance of the faith and decline of its opponents through the century,	246
Spiritual life advances as temporal power decays in Rome,	248

xx   TABLE OF CONTENTS.

                                                                   PAGE

2. Arian action on the great Eastern sees and the Eastern episcopate, ... 249
Contrast in succession to the Roman See, . . 251
3. The Arian heresy in connection with the founding of Constantinople, ... 253
Arian servility and imperial domination, . . . 254
4. Synod of Aquileia a contrast to that of Constantinople, ... 256
Innovation in the third canon passed at Constantinople, ... 257
Causes from which it sprung, ... 259
Every Byzantine emperor seeks to exalt his bishop, 261
The canon rejected by Alexandria, and unknown to the West, ... 262
St. Gregory of Nazianzum on the faith of Rome and Constantinople, ... 264
5. Church and State under Constantine, Constantius, and Valens, ... 265
6. Acts done in 330-380 against the Papacy which turned to its increase in influence, . . . 268
7. The frustration of Constantine's purposes in founding Constantinople, ... 271
The greatest favour Constantine conferred on Rome was the leaving it, ... 273

CHAPTER VII.

CHURCH AND STATE UNDER THE THEODOSIAN HOUSE.

The Church advances by the defeat of heresy, . . . 275
Her doctrine and her government built up simultaneously, 276
The difficulties of Theodosius, ... 277
He strives as a statesman to undo the evil wrought by heresy, ... 278
The imperial letter of 430 sets forth the union of the Empire and the Church, ... 281
And expresses the conviction both of emperors and Fathers, 282
Heretical emperors themselves not indifferent to truth, . 284

	PAGE
In what capacity emperors convoked general councils,	285
The letter explains the conduct and the legislation of the emperors from 380 to 430,	286
The statement as to the natural order of human society being based upon the appointment of God,	286
And as to the supernatural order embodied in the Church,	287
The imperial power guardian of the union of the two,	287
Belief of the Christian hierarchy on this point,	288
St. Augustine as its exponent,	289
His answer to Macedonius,	290
His larger answer to Count Boniface,	292
Actions of Jewish and heathen kings praised in Scripture,	293
All things have their proper times,	294
Our Lord converted St. Paul by force,	296
Guests, first invited, then compelled, to the supper,	297
But one view in the laws of the two powers as to their union,	298
The transformation from the First to the Second Council,	299
The Empire as looked at by the Church,	300
The Church as looked at by the empire,	302
Their reciprocal attitude thus brought about,	304
Different effect of this attitude produced in East and West,	305
Rise of the bishop of Constantinople,	305
Episcopate of St. Chrysostome and of Atticus,	306
Of Nestorius, and the opposition of Alexandria in St. Cyril,	309
Position of the great sees at the council of Ephesus,	311
Striking recognition of the Roman Primacy at the second Ecumenical Council,	312
Force given to this recognition by the temporal circumstance of the time,	314
The point of authority reached by the bishops Proclus and Flavian,	317
The dress and surroundings of an Eastern Roman emperor,	318
Internal administration of the diocese of Constantinople,	319
The Church's independence acknowledged by the emperors from Constantine to Leo I.,	321
In the East the alliance between Church and State had produced a State-made patriarch overshadowing the patriarchs of the original hierarchy,	322

CHAPTER VIII.

CHURCH AND STATE AND THE PRIMACY FROM 380 TO 440.

	PAGE
Contrast of the Papacy based on the succession from St. Peter to the State-made patriarch,	324
Loss of the papal letters from St. Clement I. to St. Julius I.,	325
Letter of Pope Damasus to the bishops governing the East,	326
Series of decretal letters beginning with Pope Siricius,	327
Letter to Himerius of Tarragona based on the person of St. Peter,	328
Whose authority as vested in the Pope is acknowledged by St. Ambrose,	329
Universal authority claimed in the single letter of Anastasius,	330
Pontificate of Innocent I.: his various letters,	331
His action in the case of two African councils,	332
Which refer their judgment on a matter of faith to him,	333
Rescripts of the Pope welcomed by St. Augustine,	335
Principate of the Apostolic See as understood by St. Augustine:	337
1. An authority including and corroborating acts of local councils,	338
2. Based upon the promises made in the Scriptures to St. Peter,	338
3. Who is set by Christ as form and beginning of the episcopate,	339
4. It existed from the beginning,	340
5. Acknowledged as not of ecclesiastical but divine institution,	340
6. The power indicated in its own nature supreme as a Principate,	341
Creation of the bishop of Thessalonica Apostolic Vicar over ten provinces,	342
A personal relation renewed by each Pope at his accession and at the death of each vicar,	344
The double process of decretal letters and establishment of vicariates parts of "the administration of Peter,"	345
The combination of faith and discipline in these letters,	347

The "*compages*" of the Church strengthened,	348
Letter of Pope Innocent to the patriarch of Antioch,	349
The temporal condition of the empire in the reign of Theodosius,	351
Barbarian chiefs placed by him in Roman commands,	353
Civil condition of the Roman city,	354
The place of the absent emperor filled by the present Pope,	356
Agony of the Western empire following the death of Theodosius,	357
Capture of Rome in 410 a landmark,	359
It serves to render visible the City of God in the world,	360
The Roman Primacy after the fall of the city as defined by Pope Boniface,	362
Contrast of the Eastern empire and its extent,	364
Political condition of things when the council is convoked at Ephesus,	365
General characteristics of the papal letters from Siricius to Sixtus;	366
1. The point on which the whole papal authority is grounded,	366
2. An institution divine, not political,	370
3. Of spiritual, not of imperial descent,	371
4. Inherited from the preceding centuries,	372
5. Unaggressive and conservative,	373
6. Has all the past of the Church at its back,	374
7. Established on spiritual basis by the break up of the empire,	375
8. Political prostration of the city of Rome,	376
9. Spiritual power emerging from political ruin,	377
The epoch of the second council in 431,	378
What had passed between A.D. 325 and 431,	381

CHAPTER IX.

The Flowering of Patristic Literature, No. 1.

The Nicene Council a great epoch,	383
From six points of view:	

TABLE OF CONTENTS.

	PAGE
1. The union of the two powers, ...	384
2. Freedom of the Church to meet in general council,	384
3. Freedom of the Papacy to exert its authority, . .	385
4. Freedom *ab extra* to all to preach the Gospel, . .	385
5. Public introduction of the monastic life, . . .	386
6. Heresy and schism in their action on the formation of doctrine, ...	387
The brilliant period of Greek literature compared with that of patristic literature, ...	388
The Church more than renews a greater Hellas, . . .	390
And a greater Rome, ...	391
The patristic literature possesses a unifying spirit of which the Greek, the Roman, and the present literature is destitute, ...	392
An effect of heresy in promoting theology, ...	393
A contest for life or death, ...	394
Carried on through the fourth and fifth centuries from the preceding, ...	395
The faith passing from historical tradition into theology, .	398
Unity of the dogmatic struggle from Nicæa to Chalcedon, .	400
" The gates of hell shall not prevail,"	403
The universal study of the Scriptures by Fathers at this time, whereby they sought support for the great tradition on which the Church had hitherto rested, ...	404
The ecclesiastical sense accounted the key to the meaning of Scripture, ...	406
The triad of Egypt, Gaul, and Syria, ...	410
St. Athanasius, his life, character, and style, . . .	411
St. Hilary, his time of confession, and his work, . .	413
St. Ephraem, his life and writings, ...	417
His testimony to St. Peter's Primacy, ...	419
The triad of Cappadocia; St. Basil, his life and works, .	421
St. Gregory of Nazianzum, ...	423
St. Gregory of Nyssa, ...	424
St. Cyril of Jerusalem, his catechetic doctrine, . . .	426
His words upon the Eucharistic Sacrifice, ...	427
St. Epiphanius, his life and witness, ...	428
St. John Chrysostome, his birth, life, and writings, . .	429

CHAPTER X.

THE FLOWERING OF PATRISTIC LITERATURE, No. 2.

	PAGE
St. Ambrose elected bishop when a catechumen,	432
His daily life described by St. Augustine,	434
The wide range of his influence and his writings,	435
St. Jerome: his life, writings, and opinion of contemporaries about him,	437
The conversion, life, and works of St. Augustine,	440
St. Cyril of Alexandria : his time, character, and works,	446
Theodoret : his life and works,	447
The works of St. Leo postponed to the treatment of his government,	449
What the Tradition was from which the Fathers entered on the study of Scripture,	449
The principles of interpretation in the schools of Alexandria and Antioch,	452
Illustrated by Diodorus of Tarsus and his pupils Theodore and Chrysostome,	454
Theodore, St. Chrysostome, St. Augustine, three parallels,	458
Number of Scriptural commentators,	459
Treatises on Christian doctrine and catechesis,	460
Defence against Judaism,	461
Exposure of heathenism,	461
Praise of the cloistral and virginal life,	462
Point of time at which the virginal and monastic life appeared as a public factor,	463
The Fathers practised and praised it solely for its spiritual beauty,	465
Its political and social importance upon the fall of the empire,	467
The virginal life described by St. Anthony,	468
And by St. Athanasius,	469
Masters of the eremitic and cloistral life,	470
The mystical life, Markarius and the so-called Dionysius,	470
Histories of Eusebius, Sozomen, Socrates, Theodoret, Rufinus,	471

xxvi   TABLE OF CONTENTS.

	PAGE
History of heresies, by Theodoret, Epiphanius, Philastrius, Augustine,	471
The treasure of letters left by the Fathers,	472
The verses of St. Gregory of Nazianzum,	473
Prudentius compared with Claudian,	474
His encomium on the Roman Peace preparing the way for Christ,	475
His prayer for Rome in the hymn to St. Laurence,	476
His hymn describing his own life,	477
His description of Rome on the feast of her two patrons,	478
St. Eulalia buried "under the feet of God,"	480
Sixty unnamed martyrs, whose names are known to Christ,	480
Concurrence of Prudentius, Claudian, and Rutilius, as to the position of Rome,	481
Reumont on the attachment to the Roman empire,	481
The whole intellectual movement from Nicæa to Chalcedon,	482
Ideas magnified in the Church, corrupted and lost in heresy,	485
Development as described in the fifth century,	487
Vincent of Lerius gives a picture of the Church's course down to his time,	487-491

CHAPTER XI.

ST. LEO THE GREAT.

The times at St. Leo's accession, A.D. 440,	492
Political circumstances in the West,	493
And in the East,	495
Ecclesiastical circumstances and position of the Pope,	498
The Council of Ephesus in 431 when held was the first ecumenical council after the Nicene,	498
Definite acknowledgment by it of the Primacy,	499
Leo elected Pope during his absence in August, 440,	501
His sermons and letters acts of a ruler who knows not fear,	503
They indicate his supreme authority,	504
He speaks in Latin as Athanasius or Basil speaks in Greek,	505

TABLE OF CONTENTS.

	PAGE
He exposes in a few lines the Nestorian and Eutychean heresies,	505
Authority with which he writes to the patriarch of Alexandria,	506
Position of Proclus and Flavian as archbishops of Constantinople,	507
Eutyches starts his heresy at Constantinople under Flavian,	507
Who invites St. Leo to terminate the heresy by his letter,	507
The great dogmatic letter of St. Leo,	508
The council called the Latrocinium shews the absolute need of the Primacy,	509
Appeal of Theodoret to Pope Leo,	510
Leo rejects the decrees of the Council and annuls it,	511
Theodosius II. supports the Council and Dioscorus,	513
And dies suddenly by a fall from horseback,	514
Marcian and Pulcheria succeed and support the Pope,	514
Leo accepts the convocation of the council of Chalcedon by Marcian,	516
Acts of the council of Chalcedon,	518
Recognition of the Primacy in its synodical letter,	519
The 9th, 17th, and 28th canons attempted to be passed,	520
What was aimed at in these canons,	521
The legates reject them: they are passed under protest,	524
The Pope's consent to the canons solicited,	526
The Pope refuses: his reasons given,	527
Annuls the canons in his letter to the empress Pulcheria,	529
The emperor accepts St. Leo's decision, and the canons are expunged,	530
Recapitulation of what passed at Chalcedon,	531
The Primacy exercised by Leo, between his saving Rome from Attila and Genseric,	533
What was the salvation wrought by Leo,	534
The days of Leo,	535
The Primacy under Leo is become the Church's centre of gravity and of life,	535
Internal causes leading to this,	536
The Roman bishops in the strain of the Arian heresy,	538
Again, in the Pelagian heresy and the Donatist schism,	538

	PAGE
Again, in the Nestorian heresy,	539
Again, in the Eutychean heresy,	539
External events co-operating with the same result,	540
Loosening of imperial power in the West, tension in the East,	541
The bishop of Constantinople exalted as the emperor's tool,	542
And is put forth in the East as a balance to the Pope in the West,	543
The imperial power unequally matched by the patriarchates,	544
St. Leo exercised no power but what his predecessors claimed,	546
What St. Leo did for his own and all succeeding time,	547

THE THRONE OF THE FISHERMAN.

CHAPTER I.

THE CONTINUOUS WITNESS OF HISTORY THROUGH EIGHTEEN CENTURIES TO THE SEE OF ST. PETER.

A.D. 29.   Ποίμαινε τὰ πρόβατά μου. *Be Shepherd of My Sheep.*
A.D. 1880.   *The Sacred Majesty of the Supreme Pontificate.*
Leo. XIII. Allocutio, 20. Aug.

AT this moment a power exists in the world which goes back in undisputed succession for eighteen centuries and a half. Its origin was in this wise. A Man was walking attended by twelve other men in that mountain region under Hermon and Lebanon, which looks down upon the land of Judea. The men were disciples of One who called himself by the mysterious title "Son of Man," and He asked His disciples, "Whom do men say that the Son of Man is?" They answered, "Some say that He is John the Baptist, others that He is Elias, others that He is Jeremias, or one of the prophets". Then the Man said to His disciples, "But whom say you that I am?" And one of the disciples thereupon answering said, "Thou art the Christ, the Son of the living God". Then the Man, turning to him who had answered His question, not only for himself, but for the whole company of twelve, said to him: "Blessed art thou, Simon Bar-jona; because flesh and blood have not revealed it to thee, but my Father, who is in heaven. And I say to thee, that thou art Peter, and upon this rock I will build my Church, and the gates of hell shall not prevail against it. And I will give to thee the keys of the kingdom of heaven, and whatsoever thou shalt bind on earth shall be bound in heaven; and whatsoever thou shalt loose on earth, it shall be loosed also in heaven."

A year had passed away, and the same Man was sitting at table with these same twelve men. The time of His passion was instant, and in view of it He had instituted the rite in which He created the chiefs of His kingdom, and He spoke to them of the kingdom which He was disposing to them, described the nature of its rule, and indicated the character of the person who should exercise it. And then, singling from among the Twelve the same one of His disciples as in the instance just recorded, He said to that one: "Simon, Simon, behold Satan hath desired to have *you* that he may sift you as wheat. But I have prayed for *thee*, that thy faith fail not, and thou, being once converted, confirm thy brethren."

On the same night, the Man who had thus twice conferred a special charge on the same disciple was taken by the Chief Priest of his nation, delivered over to the secular power, and put to death by the procurator of the Roman emperor, as one who claimed to be king of the Jews. After dying on the cross, He was buried, but His disciples said that He rose again and appeared to them. And in one of these appearances, as seven of the chief were fishing in the Lake of Galilee, they saw Him standing on the shore. And He called to them, and invited them to dine with Him. And after the dinner He said to the same disciple whom He had twice before distinguished in the company of his brethren by giving him a singular charge: "Simon, son of John, lovest thou Me more than these?" He saith to Him, "Yea, Lord, Thou knowest that I love Thee". He saith to him, "Feed My lambs". He saith to him again, "Simon, son of John, lovest thou Me?" He saith to Him, "Yea, Lord, Thou knowest that I love Thee". He saith to him, "Be Shepherd over My sheep". He saith to him the third time, "Simon, son of John, lovest thou Me?" Peter was grieved because He said unto him the third time, "Lovest thou Me?" And he said to Him, "Lord, Thou knowest all things; Thou knowest that I love Thee". Jesus saith to him, "Feed My sheep".

Many men of many nations in many times have written on these three words, and they have written more volumes on them than the letters which they contain. Here we will only say that in them has been found to dwell a living spirit which binds together and interpenetrates them all, so that the power indicated by one of the words dwells also in each. The images which express the power vary, but the variation serves to complete the idea of the thing indicated. Each of them involves the other two : the charge promised or bestowed in each is equal in its range to that contained in the other two. Each is indispensable, and all are indivisible. If the office which is contained in any one of the three were severed and bestowed on another person, the effect would be to create a rival and antagonistic power. In short, there is in them a true coinherence ; and that which is especially the test[1] of orthodoxy in expressing the doctrine of the Holy Trinity is found to belong to the creation of the Primacy as instituted by the sole act of the Church's Founder for the government of his kingdom, and expressed in the three several investments or charges.

Accordingly, the effect accomplished by these three words, which are likewise one, corresponds to the mysterious grandeur of the institution which they convey. The Lord of all power formed in them a new sovereignty, the reflex of His own Person. And never have words been spoken on earth which have had a greater and more continuous efficacy. Through the eighteen centuries and a half they have never been silent ; they have never ceased to work upon the hearts of men ; and their working has not diminished, but increased with each succeeding age. And now, as in all past centuries, they draw men from all parts of the earth before the chair of a man like themselves, save that in him they recognise the bearer of a singular com-

---

[1] See Card. Newman, *Athanasius*, xi. 72-4.

mission, the holder of an unrivalled dignity, the Ruler, the Confirmer, the Shepherd of His brethren, and all this because he is the successor of him who was so made by that "Son of Man," the Christ, whom he had himself confessed to be "the Son of the Living God".

This power, then, thus existing, after an unbroken succession of eighteen centuries and a half, claims to have in the eyes of all those who believe in "the Son of Man," as "the Christ, the Son of the Living God," a direct divine institution. It is not of men, nor given by men, but it stands at the head of the Christian religion as founded by the author of that religion, as founded moreover to be its support and bearer: for the Rock precedes the structure which is built upon it ; and the Shepherd exists before the flock which he gathers into the fold ; and the Confirmer is prior to those whom he confirms. In all this we see not a power which ascends from below, but a power which comes from above : which comes complete and entire from One in whom all power is seated.

In virtue of the commission bestowed in these three words, and in virtue of that alone, we behold a single man the fountain of mission throughout the whole world to one Episcopate, which diffuses the same doctrine, and exercises the same priesthood in the perpetual daily offering of the same sacrifice, and has done so continuously without break, without faltering, "unresting, unhasting," from the Day of Pentecost to the present day. That one man speaks a word : bishops from all the world listen to it ; attend upon him ; fill the most august temple in the world with their presence, in which they who in their civil condition speak naturally the languages of the north and south, the east and the west, renew the Pentecostal miracle by uttering in one voice and language what they believed with one faith concerning "the Son of Man," who is "the Christ, the Son of the Living God," and concerning the power which He has set up on earth, and to which they bear witness by their coming.

This is that "sacred majesty of the Supreme Pontificate" which rests upon the Divine Institution as its sole origin.

But that which is the chief factor of this power which we are contemplating is not the only one.

The Church's recognition of this divine institution is a second and distinct factor.

I speak to those who believe that there is in the world "the Catholic and Apostolic Church," as they believe that there is the one God, Creator of heaven and earth: who believe that this Church has traversed eighteen centuries and a half of human history with an organic unity, a steadfast and unchangeable doctrine, an uninterrupted life: as being, in short, the Body of Him who grows through the ages from His first coming to redeem His world until His second to judge it and reward it.

This Church's recognition, therefore, of a Power is a factor in the maintenance of that Power distinct from the divine institution on which it primarily rests. Such recognition does not create it, but bears witness to it, as already created. Such is precisely the demeanour of the great councils of the Church, which have met during these eighteen centuries and a half, towards the See of Peter. They declare, and the Church, by their mouth, declares, that Peter speaks in that See, that perpetual Peter who is doorkeeper of the kingdom of heaven, and bearer of the keys, and shepherd of the sheep, and confirmer of his brethren. The Church does not make him all this in declaring him to be this. He who made him this is the Maker of the Church herself. She is only recognising the voice of her Lord in the person of His disciple as her Lord has made him.

And here I content myself with quoting a single instance of such declaration, because it seems to me to fulfil all the conditions which the most exacting critic could impose for the establishment of its value, that is, its convincing force, to all those who believe in the Church and her Maker.

I take, therefore, a point in history, the middle of the fifth century. At this point the Church had passed through three centuries of persecution, the upshot of which was that the great world-empire, by the voice of the remarkable chief who was her head, acknowledged her to be the divine kingdom of Christ upon earth. She had, moreover, passed through a hundred and twenty-five years, four full generations of men, in which the empire, through the perverse conduct and misbelief of the son or successors of the very man who had acknowledged her paramount dignity as the kingdom of Christ, had suffered what was, in fact, a most grievous persecution, that in which a large number of her own bishops, seduced by Court favour and worldly interests, surrendered or compromised her most sacred and cardinal doctrine, the Godhead of her Founder. And in these four generations she had witnessed the perpetual decline in political power and influence of that great city, mother of so many daughters, the original seat of the world-empire, and the queen of its provinces, until Rome actually fell under a barbarous invader, and the rulers of the empire created by her ceased to inhabit her walls. The Church had, likewise, in this time produced the most illustrious of her ancient fathers, Ambrose, Jerome, Hilary, and Augustine in the west: the great Athanasius, Basil, also the great; the two Gregories, the peerless orator whose eloquence became attached to his name, as his greatness afterwards was to the conquering Charles; Cyril also, the special doctor of the Incarnation. And last of all, worthy for his power of word and force of doctrine, to be ranged with these, but eminent above them all as speaking from the See of Peter, the great St. Leo.

That age, beginning with the Nicene Council, and ending with St. Leo himself, is conspicuous among all the ages of the Church, even to the present day, for the learning, ability, fervour, and success of the Church's great writers. They were the blessings which God gave to His Church as the fruit of its first great Council: in them the Son of God manifested that divine power which the Council had proclaimed to belong to Him.

If there be, then, any voice which the student of the ancient Church may recognise as carrying with it the collective testimony of the first four hundred years, it is the voice of the Council of Chalcedon. That Council beheld the Church presided over by the most eminent man who, from the time of the Apostles, had filled the See of Peter: the man also who has put forth in language so definite and lucid the power which his See then exercised as the See of Peter, that there is no possibility of mistaking his meaning. St. Leo[1] had written to the bishop of Thessalonica, in the very act of giving him authority over metropolitans and bishops, "that the structure of our unity cannot completely cohere unless the bond of charity bind us into a solid mass"; for as "we have many members in one body, but all the members have not the same office, so, we being many, are one body in Christ, and every one members one of another". It is the connection of the whole body which makes one soundness and one beauty; and this connection, as it requires unanimity in the whole body, so especially demands concord among bishops. For though these have a common dignity, yet have they not a general jurisdiction: since even among the most blessed Apostles, as there was a likeness of honour, so was there a certain distinction of power, and the election of all being equal, pre-eminence over the rest was given to one. From which type the distinction also among bishops has arisen; and it was provided by a great disposition that all should not claim to themselves all things, but that in every province there should be one whose sentence should be considered the first among his

[1] Ep. xiv. c. 11.

brethren. And others, again, seated in the greater cities, should undertake a larger care, through whom the direction of the universal Church should converge to the one See of Peter, and nothing anywhere disagree from its head.

Thus St. Leo conceived and expressed his office. When, five years after this expression of it by him, the great Council met, it not only spoke of St. Peter "as the rock and foundation of the Catholic Church, and the basis of the orthodox faith," but addressed St. Leo himself as " the very person entrusted by the Saviour with the guardianship of the vine," " whose anxiety is to preserve in unity the body of the Church," and who, " as a head, presided over them as members ".

Thus the largest Council of the ancient Church recognised that St. Leo was not only successor of St. Peter, but that his conception of his office as St. Peter's successor was true and legitimate, and that conception is exactly the same with what, after the lapse of fourteen hundred years, is in practice carried out now.

It is useless for my present purpose to repeat a testimony which every great Council affords, and which can be seen drawn out with the utmost accuracy, and with the appeal to the invariable tradition of all the preceding centuries in the last Council, that of the Vatican.

The point, therefore, on which I am treating, that the recognition of the Church is the second factor in the existence of St. Peter's See, and its function in the whole body, I conceive to be sufficiently established. For if the synodical action of a General Council addressed to the Pope himself, which attests the rights of his See, and the position which he occupied as successor of St. Peter, cannot be trusted as expressing the mind of the Church in the whole preceding period, then neither can the attestation of that same Church to any doctrine, however sacred and primary, be accepted. It is not open to any one to take the Council's witness as to the Person of Christ, and to reject it as to the Primacy which Christ instituted. Or, at least, any one who so acts shows that he bends the facts of history to meet his private wishes ; that he follows the Church and the Fathers when they bear witness to what he likes, but deserts the Church and the Fathers when they bear witness to that which he is resolved for other reasons, by an act of private judgment, not to accept.

From the divine institution of the Primacy, which is its first factor, and of the Church's recognition of it, which is the second, I pass to a third, which is distinct from both. I mean the action of the First Agent both of doctrine and of life working through His Providence in a vast connection of times and of peoples. A great writer [1] has alluded to "that concentration of the Church's powers which history brings before us". He adds: "The progress of concentration was not the work of the Pope: it was brought about by the changes of times and the vicissitudes of nations".

Let us take one out of manifold instances.

From the Day of Pentecost to the decree of toleration by Constantine, a period of 284 years, the Church was

[1] Card. Newman's letter to the Duke of Norfolk, 1875.

in a state of either active persecution, or at least repression—material, social, and intellectual,—such as the power of the civilised world could exert against it. Its Episcopate grew up in a condition of large autonomy, which defined the action of each see, wherein great isolation was produced by distance when locomotion was difficult, and common action interfered with by the sleepless jealousy of a hostile civil power; wherein, likewise, another jealousy, that of the Eastern mind against Western domination, was perpetually at work; wherein, still more, the extreme jealousy of the Roman State suspecting anything like a polity, while it would act against any single bishop in his see, would be incomparably more opposed to the primatial action of one, the bishop of the capital. These causes did actually prevent the assembling of any meeting of bishops more extensive than provincial councils. We find at the end of this epoch the Egyptian church, under the bishop of Alexandria; the Eastern churches, under the see of Antioch; the churches of Western Asia Minor, under the see of Ephesus; the African churches, with Carthage at their head, as it were, great and powerful members of the Christian body. They do not obscure the Primacy of Rome, but they form an equipoise to it, holding vigorously to their several traditions and their local habits, a strong instance of which is afforded by the Ephesine province in its time of celebrating the Easter festival. This is the state of things at the era of the Church's peace. Go on a similar period of three hundred years, and what do we see? The same writer says : "It was not the Pope's fault that the Vandals swept away the African sees, and the Saracens those of Syria and Asia Minor, or that Constantinople and its dependencies became the creatures of imperialism". And certainly we may add that it was no fault of the Pope that the ruthless sword of the false prophet and his successors well-nigh exterminated the Alexandrine and Antiochene churches. But it is a fact that the Kalifate of the false prophet conspired, by its very construction, as well as its violence, to aid the Petrine monarchy ; and that as the great anti-Christian religion seized upon the eastern and southern shores of the Mediterranean, the Pastorship of Peter united the north and the west against it.

Thus, the churches of Alexandria and Antioch, coeval with that of Rome, and having Peter for their founder ; those also of Africa and Asia Minor, which all were the chief columns of episcopal autonomy, at the same time that they were illustrations of the hierarchical order in the Church, of which St. Peter's See was the crown and complement, all disappear before the beginning of the mediæval Church, and leave Rome alone in her original greatness. The second and third sees, with their dependent metropolitans and bishops, almost vanish ; the first towers at a still loftier eminence over those which remain.

And of what ensued when that mediæval Church had begun, the same writer proceeds to say : "Nor was it the Pope's fault that France, England, and Germany would obey none but the author of their own Christianity, or that clergy and people at a distance were obstinate in sheltering themselves under the majesty of Rome against their own fierce kings and nobles or imperious bishops, even to the imposing forgeries on the world and on the Pope in justification of their proceedings. All this will be fact, whether the Popes were ambitious or not; and still it will be fact that the issue of that great change was a great benefit to the whole of Europe. No one but a master, who was a thousand bishops in himself at once, could have tamed and controlled, as the Pope did, the great and little tyrants of the middle age."

Again, to come nearer to our own times, there was a great monarchy, the most splendid which arose at the termination of the middle age, in the country which, as it was most completely moulded into a nation, was the stronghold of nationalism in its modern form. And in that country the sovereign, reducing all the powers of the State well-nigh into his single person, had woven so skilfully a net round the divine power of the Church that it was fettered in all its action by the civil power. Not only did the sovereign bestow its bishoprics, but he imposed in countless instances superiors upon its religious houses; and the Pope himself was not free to communicate with the very prelates to whom he had himself given spiritual jurisdiction. Thus Peter in that realm seemed to be fast bound in chains of gold. Even his doctrinal decrees had to wait for their promulgation on the placet of the government. So it went on for a century and a-half, when suddenly that prodigious fabric of pampered and presumptuous despotism fell to the ground, dragging with it in its ruin, as it seemed, for a time, the divine fabric itself, whose ruler it had enlaced with countless ligatures. But, behold, within ten years a conquering chief picked up, as he said himself, with the point of his sword, the crown of Clovis which lay on the ground, and applied himself to the Pope to restore the fallen church. And this was done, at the request of the civil ruler, the despot of all others most jealous of spiritual power, by the exercise on the Pope's part of that spiritual power in a degree of which the preceding centuries had seen no adequate example. It was not the Pope's doing that Napoleon eradicated Gallicanism, nor that a Corsican upstart, the very antithesis of Charlemagne, accomplished what Charlemagne would never have attempted to execute.

But, once more, there is an action of Divine Providence, if possible, still more striking. The very man who had called forth this extreme exercise of spiritual power in the Pope, drunk with success, and conceiving that all things were lawful to one who had ridden over the necks of kings and confiscated kingdoms, turned against the Pope, dethroned him from the possession of his own city, held him in captivity, encompassed him with ignominies. And when the successor of Peter threatened to use spiritual arms against him, "What does the Pope mean," said he, "by the threat of excommunicating me? Does he think the world has gone back a thousand years? Does he suppose that the arms will fall from the hands of my soldiers?" Within two years after these remarkable words were written, the Pope did excommunicate him, in return for the confiscation of his whole dominions, and in less than four years more the arms did fall from the hands of his soldiers; and the hosts, apparently invincible, which he had collected, were dispersed and ruined by the blasts of winter. On which the same writer says : " Gregory was considered to have done an astounding deed in the middle ages, when he brought Henry, the German emperor, to do penance and shiver in the snow at Canossa; but Napoleon had his snow-penance too, and that with an actual interposition of Providence in the infliction of it".

These are but specimens in the course of eighteen centuries, exhibiting that action of the Prime Agent which I have termed the third Factor in the Primacy of the Pope. The eighteen centuries are full of them. Here I take only sufficient to make my meaning plain. This continued action of the Divine Providence over a number of ages, amid the most diverse peoples, an action in the several instances not foreseen, not desired by the Popes themselves, often accompanied by great calamities to the Church, exerted in circumstances which the Popes themselves have done their utmost to prevent, yet removing impediments to the full action of the Primacy in its proper sphere; this is to be taken into account as superadded to the Divine Institution, and to the Church's recognition of it as Divine.

On the conjunction of these three Factors I make two remarks. The first, that nothing can be more opposed to the notion that the Primacy, as regards its origin, is an usurping power, and, as regards its exercise, is a grasping power, than the fact of its result being the common effect of these three agents. The second is that no greater security for the authenticity of such a creation as the Apostolic See can be afforded than the concurrence of the three Factors in producing the result.

Let us take a parallel case.[1] The sense of sight conveys images to the mind, by means of which it exercises its inherent power of generalising. Another sense, that of touch, exercised in like manner, corroborates the conclusions which the former sense had drawn. Thus the two senses, sight and touch, are joint guarantees for the facts from which, again, a multitude of different minds draw conclusions, and these, when noted and arranged, go to frame a science. I select the science of astronomy, wherein the fact of gravitation being once discovered enables the observer to foretell, as the result of a long series of calculations, the motions of the heavenly bodies. Thus he foresees that a small body, such as the moon, will cover at a particular moment the main disk of the sun, and produce, for the space of a minute, in particular regions of the earth, an annular eclipse. Or, again, he foresees the precise periods when the most beautiful of planets, twice in the course of a hundred and ten years, will

[1] *Cf.* Duke of Argyll, *Unity of Nature*, p. 64. "Throughout the whole of this vast series (of animal life) the very life of every creature depends on the unity which exists between its sense-impressions and those realities of the external world which are specially related to them," &c.

enter to our sight, in a certain zone of the earth, as a small dark spot upon the disk of the sun; and the moment of its ingress and egress, after being calculated beforehand with the utmost nicety, will serve to measure the distance of the earth in describing its orbit round the sun, which itself is to be the unit of measure for the vastness of that universe revealed by the telescope to human eyes. A man would be deemed devoid of reason who refused credence to the science, which is attested by the exact fulfilment of the times specified in such observations.

But would not the reason be equally blind which could contemplate persistently these three Factors of the Church's Primacy, first its Divine Institution, resting upon the words and acts of the Founder of the Christian faith; secondly, the recognition of it by the continued testimony of the Christian people, from the earliest time; and thirdly, the action of the Divine Providence, through a long series of times and nations, supporting it in the most unexpected ways: who could view it, I say, as a result of these three, and then fail to acknowledge it? Such blindness would be equivalent to asserting that the astronomer who had calculated the exact moment of a solar eclipse, or of a transit of Venus over the sun, had no ground for his calculations.

It is true that the similitude in one important point fails to convey the force which the concurrence of the three just named Factors is calculated to produce on the mind. For the motions of the heavenly bodies, when the facts summed up in the word gravitation were once ascertained, are stable and unchanging. Still the foretelling them is sufficient to prove the reality of the science which connotes them, and the trustworthiness of the senses upon whose testimony the science must rely to obtain its facts. But the result of the three Factors above-mentioned, repeated through a long series of ages, and a sequence of the most unforeseen changes affecting nations and governments, arts and human conduct, and the interminable maze of human successes and defeats, arising from actions which themselves are free,—such a result which yet is ever issuing in the maintenance of a power such as naturally could not subsist for a single generation, this, I say, constitutes a proof in support of the origin, the exercise, and the authenticity of this power, which gives, in those three respects, a certainty far beyond that of the science to the reflecting mind and unprejudiced will.

My subject, then, in the following pages is how three constituents—the first, a Divine Institution on the part of the Founder of the Church; the second, the life of faith in the Church, that is the recognition by the Church of her Lord's action; and the third, the external world in the hands of the Divine Providence, which is the guidance of Him who made and maintains both world and Church—elucidate and support each other, and thus] produce a common result through the eight great periods which have hitherto constituted the history of the Church in the eighteen centuries and a half as yet traversed by her. This common result I call "The Throne of the Fisherman, built by the Carpenter's Son," by which I mean the continuous and the ever-increasing influence and work of St. Peter's See, as the instrument by which the Divine Kingdom is begun, propagated, and maintained.

I divide the eight periods as follows :—

The first is that from the Day of Pentecost, A.D. 29, to the Nicene Council in 325. This is the period in which the Church contends for its existence as the Divine Kingdom with the enmity of the heathen State, embodied in the greatest of the world-empires which has hitherto existed. It is fitly terminated by the recognition in the Council on the part of the heathen State that the Christian Episcopate constituted a kingdom bearing a doctrine, having its own unity and essential independence in its three constituents of priesthood, teaching, and jurisdiction.

The second period lasts from the Nicene Council to the Episcopate of St. Leo the Great, and the fall of the Western Roman empire. It embraces on the one hand the action of the Roman State towards the Christian Church after recognising its divine authority; and on the other hand the spontaneous and emphatic acknowledgment of the Roman Church's " Superior Principate" by the whole Episcopate during the period of its greatest Doctors. The Pope, as the supreme holder of the Church's Priesthood, Teaching Office, and Jurisdiction, comes into complete prominence, while the empire still subsists in unbroken power and dignity; and the East gives its testimony to the Papacy in the person of Pope Leo by the voice of its most numerous Synod, the Fourth General Council, held at Chalcedon.

The advance in power and influence which fell to the Roman See in the period which runs from Pope Sylvester to Pope Leo is one of the most remarkable events in history. It was made while the empire still existed in force, and during that first time of the Church's liberty from heathen persecution, which ran between the empire's recognition and the age of barbarian inundation. Nor can any outward change be greater than the condition of the Church such as it was from the Day of Pentecost to the peace of Constantine, and its condition more especially from the time at which Constantine became sole emperor to the fall of the Western empire.

The third period lasts from the fall of the Western empire to the proclamation of Charlemagne as head of a renewed empire by Pope Leo III. in 800. In this period old Rome perishes, as St. Gregory I. describes the perishing which went on before his eyes; and by the single force of the divine Primacy the Rome reduced by the Gothic war, by, its re-conquest under Justinian, and by the Lombard settlement in Italy to a mere provincial city, which was not even the capital of the province in which it lay, is raised to be the capital of a new Christendom by Leo's crowning the head of the Teuton invaders to be sovereign of the Christian people which was in process of making out of these invaders. In this period also the Eastern empire is crippled. There rises an internecine struggle between a new anti-Christian religion and the Christian faith, in which a great portion of the Eastern Church is laid waste and destroyed. The wandering of the nations in the West is succeeded by their settlement in the conquered provinces. It is the rise of a new state of things in the accession of a great sovereign who seems for a time to restore the majesty of the Roman name.

This is a period with characteristics of its own, as distinct as those of the two preceding periods, while the power exhibited by the Primacy is as striking as in either of them. The change of the world between A.D. 476 and 800 is vast in every point of view.

I mark the fourth period as dating from the commencement of Charlemagne, as Emperor of the Romans, in 800, to the decision of the question of Investiture under Calixtus II. in 1122. This period includes the creation of Christian Europe, a beginning of Christendom as a community of Christian States civilly independent, but joined in unity of belief over against four great enemies—(1) the Eastern imperial despotism, the perpetual fosterer and ultimate head of schism ; (2) the spurious Mahometan theocracy founded on force; (3) barbaric violence of nations yet in process of formation, and the corruption of manners mixed with it; and (4) the perpetual strain of the Western imperial power, coveting the absolute power of the old Roman monarchy, which had its root in heathenism, which the Christian faith had sought to tame, and had really checked and reduced within bounds.

In all this the Divine Primacy is seen working in a

world very different as to its moral forces and gravitation from the world in either of the former periods.

The fifth period I mark from Pope Calixtus II. to Pope Boniface VIII. It is the completion of Christian Europe : a group of nations educated out of barbarism by the Church, in which the civil polity of each was based upon the religion of the Cross.} [A conquest of Christian principles as to government, but an imperfect conquest, the age indeed of faith, but scarcely that of love. The skill of the artificer certainly was not wanting, but

> Vero è che forma non s' accorda
> Molte fiate all' intenzion dell' arte,
> Perchè a risponder la materia è sorda.
> —Dante, *Paradiso*, i. 127.

The matter was still barbaric, Christianised but not thoroughly digested. This new Christian Europe was cut out of the Teutonic rock, firm indeed and grand, but rough likewise and angular; and here the Roman Pontiff both formed the design and laid the blocks, but the defective will of the subordinate masons marred the workmanship.

The sixth period I give from Pope Boniface VIII. in 1303 to the conclusion of the Council of Trent in 1564. Its device is Christendom in combat with an ever advancing material wealth, and a parallel advance in the corruption of discipline, the effect of which is seen in the great schism of the West. And this intestine struggle, which upheaves Christendom, proceeds until at length the vast fabric, reared with divine wisdom on one part, and the labour of so many nations on the other, is rent by the intractable and conflicting elements which had been embraced, but not fused nor tempered to Christian perfectness. This period is fitly closed by that great Council of Trent, larger in the field of doctrine which it traversed, more thorough in its effects than any which preceded it. Accordingly, from it springs a reformation of manners, an elucidation and harmonising of doctrine; in short, a new age of Christian learning, which, in its results, more than recalls the splendours of the most prolific Christian antiquity.

The seventh period I count from the Council of Trent to the French Revolution. Its character is, on the one hand, the defection of nations from the Christian faith, and from the bond of Christendom which is the result of that faith ; while, on the other hand, the great Council is succeeded by a century during which the Church's discipline is purified, her inward life is strengthened, her doctrine is built up and perfected by a vast array of learned writers which no previous age could show.[1] But in the second portion of this period, all the elements of evil which have marred the Church's action and partially defeated her influence during two centuries, at length came to a head, and by attempting to overthrow the Christian faith itself in the greatest of the Christian family of nations, cast the world back into a new heathenism. Great powers of destruction are let loose. Not only is the empire, begun in Charlemagne, after a

---

[1] As an illustration of this, reference may be made to Backer's history of authors belonging only to the Company of Jesuits, and again to Hurter's *Nomenclator Literarius*.

long secularisation, finally swept away, but the union between the spiritual and the civil authorities, of which that empire was the symbol and seal, is vehemently shaken throughout the whole Christian world, and with it the civilization which was the fruit of that union risks being changed into the corrupt civilization of the old heathen world.

This great convulsion marks the entrance of the eighth era, a new and greater as well as a more formidable one, in the midst of which we stand and of which the Vatican Council betokens the character. If the Church ceases to be the Church of the old Roman empire and the head of an European Christendom, it is that she may become the Church of the four quarters of the world and the head of a truly ecumenical Christendom. As an earnest of this we have beheld a scene to which past times offer no parallel. In the great hall, under the noblest dome in the universe, which receives her Fathers, the princes of her provinces come from India and from China, from America and Africa. It is a glory which Nicea and Chalcedon did not see; which the Lateran also under one of the greatest Popes was not given to enjoy, for the world to which Innocent III. spoke was narrow in comparison with the world which the word of Pius IX. called around him. It is the seed-time of future conquests. It is the building of the wall wherein the mason works with the sword in one hand and the trowel in the other, but in which the glory of the later temple is to exceed that of the former. For so the Divine Builder constructs His work, causing the impediments which hinder its advance to strengthen and mature the ultimate result, so that the rent which tore Europe asunder shall end in uniting the world.

My intention is to give eight distinct pictures of the action of the Holy See in these several epochs. The concurrence of the three Factors, the Divine Institution, the Church's recognition of it, the action of Providence ruling the events of the outer world, will be shown equally in all. The variety of circumstances in these epochs is so great as to make a marvel of that action of the Holy See, resulting as it does from three constituents, which persists in them all. For instance, how vast the dissimilarity between the first period of persecution by the civil authority of the empire, in which the Primacy was founded, and the second of establishment in the same empire, when it was indisputably recognised. Again, between the second of an establishment in an empire which tried to be Christian, and that third condition of ruin, dissolution, and isolation through the inroad of barbarian hordes, destitute in themselves of cohesion, but hurling their wild force on the degenerate empire: when the Primacy on these troubled waters laid the foundation of a new spiritual kingdom. Again, between the education of barbarians, which made Christian kings out of raiders and pirates in the fourth period, and that great and terrible contest with wealth and internal corruption of manners and discipline in the sixth period. Again, what a contrast between the Europe which was led in crusades by the Popes against the false prophet in the fifth period, and the Europe which could listen to teachers of moral corruption and intellectual negation, such as Voltaire and Rousseau, springing up in its own bosom, during the seventh. And finally, the eighth period in which we live is one wherein the world, which from the time of Constantine had acknowledged its safety to lie in union with the Church, has turned almost completely against the Church; and the City of God in the midst of nations, corrupt and hostile, burns like the fiery bush in the desert. The action of the Holy See in all these periods has been necessary, has been incessant, has been decisive, and moreover a particular action of the Divine Providence upon human affairs has been requisite in each of them to maintain it.

It is customary with anti-Catholic writers to deal separately, with these periods, or, rather, to view the events contained in each, not as forming parts of one connected history, but as isolated events, and to attack the Holy See in each of them by singling out abuses as if they had destroyed the society in which they were tolerated. But these writers are never found to consider the cumulation of proof which the persistency of its action throughout them all exhibits, nor the power of that action for good. It is as if a French historian were to direct his whole attention to point out and exaggerate the private faults committed by individual kings of France, while he disregarded the action of the monarchy in forming out of antagonistic fragments a great realm, and giving it cohesion and unity. But this illustration affords no adequate parallel to the action of the Papacy. The one is the force of an institution in a single State, whereas the continuance of such a power as the Papacy through so vast a range of centuries, amid changes of race, manners, and tempers so multiform, and upon a crowd of nations, is an instance which gives the full force of Cicero's words, supplying the Christian expression of "God" for the heathen one of "nature": "Opinionum commenta delet dies; Dei judicia confirmat".

That it lasts throughout them all; that in each and all of them it forms the centre, bond, and crown of the Divine Kingdom, in which it acts as the sun in the solar system,—these are proofs of its divine institution to which the course of earthly empires supplies no parallel. It has shown itself to be the Rock through the 1850 years in which Peter has fed the flock of Christ.

CHAPTER II.

FROM ST. PETER TO ST. SYLVESTER.

THERE is scarcely, in the long history of the Christian Church, a point of time to be found at which the kingdom of Christ appeared before the world in greater grandeur than at the convocation of the first General Council. They who, for ten generations, had been treated as the outcasts of the earth, in whom the Roman ruler had persistently persecuted the members as he had begun by crucifying the Head, upon the charge of usurping Cæsar's sovereignty, were now invited by Cæsar to meet in his palace, and to exercise there, as free agents, the most sacred functions, for the maintenance of which they had so long suffered. He appeared before them as the Church's sword and shield, not interfering with their deliberations, not himself either making with them or subscribing their decrees, but proclaiming them when made as laws of the empire, and declaring repeatedly, with the official voice of the empire's head, that God spoke in His bishops, and a divine inspiration[1] had guided their judgments.[2]

---

[1] Hefele, *Concilien-geschichte*, i. 420.—i. 258.

[2] Socrates, *Hist.*, i. 9, gives Constantine's letter to the Church of Alexandria, in which he says: "That which has commended itself to the judgment of three hundred bishops cannot be other than the doctrine of God; seeing that the Holy

The bishops who sat in this Council were 318, a number which speedily became very famous, and as to which St. Ambrose first, and after him many others, compared the servants of God at the Council with the servants of Abraham in his battle with the kings. Of the 318, five only came from the Latin provinces of the Church, and all the rest from the Eastern. Among them were eminent confessors of the faith, who had suffered in the last and greatest persecution: such as Potamon, bishop of Heraclea in Egypt, who had lost an eye; Paphnutius, of the Upper Thebais, who had both lost an eye and been maimed in the knee, and was renowned for his miracles, as were also Spiridion of Cyprus and James of Nisibis; Paulus of Neocæsarea, lamed in both hands by the hot irons of the emperor Licinius; Leontius of Cæsarea, endued with the gift of prophecy; and St. Nicholas of Myra. "Some," says the contemporary historian Eusebius, "were distinguished for their wisdom, others for ascetic life and endurance, others as sharing both these qualities. There were those who were honoured for the length of their days, others in the bloom of youth, some that had but just attained episcopal rank. To all of them the emperor had ordered abundance of provision to be supplied day by day." "Not a few," adds Theodoret, "were eminent

Spirit dwelling in the minds of such men has disclosed to them the divine will". And in the circular letter sent round to all Churches, preserved by Eusebius, *Life of Constantine*, iii. 20, he says: "Receive then with all willingness this truly divine injunction, and regard it as the gift of God. For whatever is determined in the holy assemblies of the bishops is to be regarded as indicative of the divine will."

for apostolic gifts, and many bore the marks of Christ on their body."[1]

The acts of the Council have not been preserved; only its creed, its canons, and its synodal letter; but the subscriptions remain in several lists, all of which preserve one order. The first signature is that of Hosius, bishop of Corduba, and of the two Roman priests, Vitus and Vicentius, legates of the absent Sylvester, bishop of Rome; then the two Eastern patriarchs who were present, Alexander of Alexandria, and Eustathius of Antioch; Makarius, bishop of Jerusalem. Then follow the signatures of the other bishops, province after province, so that the metropolitan is always followed by his suffragans. "To each group of subscriptions," says Hefele, "the name of the ecclesiastical province is also expressly prefixed: only in the case of Hosius and the two priests this is wanting. They subscribed first, and without the naming of any diocese. That, in his case and theirs, no province was prefixed to their subscription points to the fact that they acted not in any particular capacity, as representatives of a particular Church, but as Presidents of the whole Synod, and that we have to recognize in them the $\pi\rho\delta\epsilon\delta\rho o\iota$ of Eusebius. The analogy, likewise, of the other General Councils speaks for their presiding, specially of the Ephesinian, where also, outside and before the other legates who came from Italy, a bishop of very great dignity himself, Cyril of Alexandria, as in

---

[1] Eusebius and Theodoret.

this case Hosius, acted as Papal Legate."[1] So, again, at the Fourth Council, the Emperor Mariean, accompanied by the Empress Pulcheria, when he attends, assures the bishops, "We have wished to take part in the Council for the purpose of confirming the faith, not of exercising any authority, after the example of the religious prince Constantine":[2] words which, coming from the mouth of an Eastern emperor, absolutely exclude the notion, which some uncatholic writers have attempted to set up, that Constantine either presided at the Council or named its presidents.

The importance of the cause for which they met equalled the grandeur of the meeting itself. The occasion was the denial of the Godhead of the Son by Arius; and the decision of the Council proclaiming in its creed that the Son is of one substance with the Father was received throughout the world as the voice of the whole Church, though all the bishops present from the Western half of the Church were but five. But the legates of the Pope presided over the Council, gave their subscription at the head, and its decrees were transmitted to the bishops of the West by Pope Sylvester, according to the canon[3] of the Church at that time, which forbade councils to be held and decrees to be passed save with the consent of the bishop of Rome, who occupied the

---

[1] Hefele, *Concilien-geschichte*, i. 36, 37. See also, Niehues, *Kaiserthum und Papstthum*, p. 255, for the position of the Roman Legates in the five extant lists of subscriptions.

[2] Quoted by Riffel, p. 394, from Acts of the Council, vi. p. 466.

[3] See the last paragraph of Pope Julius' letter, A.D. 342, with respect to the church of Alexandria: for the general rule, Socrates, ii. 17, and Sozomen, iii. 10.

see "wherein," to use the words of the Council of Arles, held in the year 314, "the Apostles (Peter and Paul) sit for ever, and their blood without intermission bears witness to the glory of God".[1]

St. Athanasius, present at this Council as Deacon of the Alexandrine patriarch, and the ablest of all in setting forth the doctrine which formed the subject of its chief deliberation, proclaimed it to be "a pillar and standard of victory against every heresy". St. Leo declared that its laws would last to the end of the world. The Eastern Christians so honoured it that Greeks, Syrians, and Egyptians had each a special feast to commemorate yearly the 318 Nicene bishops. "The list," says Tillemont, "would be endless were one to attempt enumerating the witnesses to the rank of the Nicene Council; and in all centuries no one, except a few heretics, has spoken of this holy assembly save in terms of the highest veneration."[2]

Thus for the first time after three hundred years the Church of Christ met in General Council, and solemnly proclaimed its faith in the Godhead of that Lord from whom it had begun to be, and in whose power alone it subsisted: wherein the heresy which denied the Head gave occasion to the Body to appear before the eyes of all men manifest to sight and touch.

This point of time is for ever memorable, but likewise there is no portion of the Church's history which forms a more complete period with special character-

---

[1] Synodal letter of the Council of Arles to Pope Sylvester in 314: the greatest Council before the Nicene.   [2] Hefele, i. 421

istics than that which commences with the day of Pentecost and terminates with the conversion of the Emperor Constantine, as seen in the great recognition of the Christian kingdom, betokened by the convocation at his request of the first General Council. Of course this period, as the time of the Church's beginning, when its faith was first preached and its spiritual government planted through the whole Roman world and beyond it, when by a divine birth it sprung from the womb of the Jewish synagogue, when it fought its first fight with imperial paganism, possesses a singular interest and importance. There must be within its range everything, at least in germ, which can afterwards arise. All the Church's faith, all her government, all her divine power, all her claim over individual man and over human society, must be there at least potentially, if not in actual exercise, just as the power shown in the Nicene Council of determining the doctrine of the Godhead of Christ covers every possible determination of doctrine which the Church can make. Of the many aspects presented by the Church in this period I am about to choose one in particular, and in doing so I shall consider the period, for better elucidation of the subject, as if it were one day of the divine government, and review it looking backwards from its termination. The aspect under which I shall regard it is the action of St. Peter's See in the period ended by the Nicene Council.

And first the outcome of this whole period is that at its termination the Church appears as a hierarchy consisting of a priesthood, a teaching and a jurisdiction possessed in solidarity by that hierarchy, and a people yielding it spontaneous and complete trust and obedience. The hierarchy therefore bears in itself the authority and the doctrine of Christ. It is a Body corporate which offers sacrifice, teaches, and rules over the souls and bodies which belong to it in the name of Christ. The conversion of Constantine consists in the fact that he owns Jesus to be the Christ, the Saviour of the world, and owns this hierarchy to be His kingdom on earth, within which the Christian people lives and works. Strictly speaking, he is not yet a Christian, for he is not baptised. But his[1] causing the Church to meet in General Council by moving the spiritual authority to convoke it, by authorising its members, the prelates, who are his civil subjects, to attend it, by even placing the public posts at their disposal for this purpose, and when they meet by receiving them in his palace and supporting them bounteously, by appearing before their assembly as one who, albeit he is the Roman emperor holding in his single person the whole legislative, judicial, and administrative authority of the Roman empire, yet receives the decision of this Council as the voice of God—all this action of his makes the most com-

---

[1] Rufinus, E. i. 1: "Sermo usque ad aures religiosi principis, quippe qui omni studio et diligentia curaret qua nostra sunt, pervenit. Tum ille *ex sacerdotum sententia* apud urbem Nicænam episcopale concilium convocat." Pope Damasus, who was himself of man's estate at the convocation of the Council, says it was held by direction of the Roman See. At a Synod of 93 bishops, held probably in the year 369 (see Hefele, i. 714), that Pope, Valerian of Aquileia, and the other bishops wrote to the Eastern bishops; in their letter the words occur: "Majores nostri CCCXVIII. episcopi, atque ex urbe sanctissimi episcopi urbis Romæ directi, apud Nicæam confecto concilio hunc murum adversus arma diabolica statuerunt. —Migne, vol. xiii. p. 348.

plete recognition of the Church as the kingdom of Christ, and of her hierarchy as the government of that kingdom which a Roman emperor could give. And this it is which in spite of errors in government and defects in personal conduct, such as appear especially in his later years, after this Council, have conferred on the name of Constantine,[1] as the first Christian emperor, an imperishable and even unique distinction.

Further, the meeting of a General Council is the proof of another very wonderful fact, which one may call the great work accomplished in these three centuries. The act is this, and I call it very wonderful because when Augustus three hundred years before was ruling the same empire which Constantine ruled, in the time when Virgil sung of him that he should restore the golden age to Latium and stretch his empire to the confines of Asia and Africa, no glimpse of such an event was apparent to poet, philosopher, or ruler. That event is, that a singular people had come into existence and was spread through all its cities and provinces, a people the whole mind of which was ruled by the idea of the Church's unity as the Family, the House, the Fold, the Kingdom, and finally the Body of Christ. It formed but a part of the population, taking one here and another there, according to no visible rule of selection, embracing at once learned and ignorant, rich and poor, young and

---

[1] *Cf.* St. Ambrose in his sermon on the death of Theodosius, 40: "Cui licet baptismatis gratia in ultimis constituto omnia peccata dimiserit, tamen quod primus imperatorum credidit, et post se hereditatem fidei principibus dereliquit, magni meriti locum reperit." The striking testimony of St. Ambrose to the baptism of Constantine on his deathbed is to be noted.

old, the master or his slave, even those who had been corrupt and those who had been pure in their previous life; and where it was most numerous, no doubt, only a minority belonged to it. It was scattered through great distances. It spoke many languages. It was composed of many races. Its rulers as a whole had never before met together, had never seen each others' faces. Its books were few, and multiplied only by laborious and costly transcription. It had no newspapers, and locomotion was slow and toilsome. Notwithstanding all these impediments, the idea which occupied in chief the mind of this Christian people was the sense that it was one, the sense of the unity of Christ's kingdom on earth.

The hierarchy is the realisation of this idea. The Christian people, however locally scattered, was knit together by its one Episcopate. The Family, House, Fold, Kingdom, and Body of Christ are expressed in the sacerdotal, doctrinal, and jurisdictional power which our Lord set up, which in its whole and every derivation came from His own Person, from the Body crucified on Calvary, the same Body in which He gave the paschal salutation, "Peace be with you," on the following Easter day. This triple power was possessed by every bishop, not as an independent ruler, but in the solidarity of the Episcopate. This Episcopate was seen acting as a whole in the Nicene Council. The distribution of power within the Church is subordinate to the capital idea of the Church herself, as that which possesses this triple power: a power which depends on her unity and is conditioned by it, because it is the power of one Person, the God-man.

If we reflect that what we call in one word the Roman empire was not a nation like to any of the great nations which now make up the Christian world, but a vast confederacy of most dissimilar races and peoples, held down as well as held together by the force of successive conquests, which stretched over hundreds of years, under the dominion of one city alien in temper and spirit from many of its subjects, the formation of this one people in its bosom will exhibit something of its marvellous character. That such a jointing together of the most dissimilar materials as the empire presented should exist at all was a great wonder in the eyes of Rome's most philosophic historian.[1] The work, says Tacitus, speaking by the mouth of a Roman general in the convulsion which followed Nero's death, was the fruit of Rome's practical wisdom, valour, and discipline exercised through eight hundred years. He viewed with dismay the prospect of its disruption: a dismay amply justified when four hundred years after he spoke the disruption came. What then was the marvel that by the sole power of persuasion, against every material interest, a people was seen to arise through the vast extent of this confederacy, a people stretching from Newcastle in the North to Babylon in the East, from the deserts of Atlas to the Scythian steppes, a people one in heart and mind, in belief and conduct, in spiritual government and manners?

---

[1] Tacitus, *Hist.* v. 73, Speech of Cerialis: "Pulsis, quod Dii prohibeant, Romanis quid aliud quam bella omnium inter se gentium existent? Octingentorum annorum fortuna disciplinaque compages hæc couvaluit, quæ convelli sine exitio convellentium, non potest."

And in speaking of this creation we must remember also that from the times of the Apostles themselves—whose letters are full of exhortations against false teachers—the Church encountered the whole force of heresy, solely by the superior power of unity and the attraction of truth which made itself felt in her own bosom. Her Fathers have drawn up lists of the most divers opinions, which they called heresies, in order to mark that they were the offspring of human choice, not of divine authority, and which in every generation during this period of persecution sought either to draw away her own children from her fold, or to pervert the minds of the heathens who were approaching her. From three sources especially a fertile crop of errors sprang up: from Judaic opinions or prejudices, from notions derived out of Greek philosophy, and again from Eastern religious systems. Amid all these the Church held on her way, propagating her faith, and maintaining her government by the sole power of the divine Word in her; and she, who was subject to every force of material repression from the Gentile empire and society in the midst of which she was rising, could use no such force against false brethren, or half believing converts, or impostors who professed to be Christians, whilst they held a thousand varying fancies of their own. And it was noted that heathen persecution did not light upon heretics. A secret sympathy made the world which hated the Church take part with them as the Church's most dangerous enemies, and its own best friends and most efficient allies.

But to none of these was Constantine attracted. It was the one organised Christian Church which alone he acknowledged. It was the double fact of its unity in doctrine and government which he admired. It was the fact of the great Christian people which he beheld, and which subdued the proud mind of the Roman ruler to humble belief in the power of the crucified God. For Constantine was nearly the last of a series of able military captains who began to rise in the second half of the third century, and saved by their energy the Roman empire from dissolution. The whole course of his life, up to the time when the imperial power was centred at last in his single hand, which took place in the year preceding the Nicene Council, led him to appreciate the enormous difficulty of maintaining unity of government in a frame so composite. And proportionate to this sense of the difficulty which civil government in so unevenly tempered a mass presented, was his admiration of that spiritual power which had created before his eyes the Church's spiritual unity, that is, the Christian people. The first expressions of Constantine to the Christian Church, his frank homage and profession of obedience to her laws and dictates, betoken this admiration. There can be no doubt that the service which he expected from the Church in maintaining the unity of the empire by the unity of her doctrine, discipline, and government, was one great motive which moved him to become a Christian, and not only so, but to make the empire, so far as in him lay, Christian also. He wished to communicate to the civil power, which seemed ready to fall to pieces under his hand, that tenacity of life, that unity of purpose, that most simple yet wonderful constructive skill, which the Church's history for three hundred years presented to him. And he greeted Pope Sylvester with awe as the chief Bishop of such a power. He bestowed upon him the Lateran palace, which originally belonged to the Plautian family, was confiscated by Nero, and then belonged to his empress, Fausta; and he began, within the precincts of the palace, a church, dedicated to the Saviour, the world-famous Lateran Basilica. Thus, out of the palace of a distinguished Roman family, sprung the Patriarchium of the Roman See, which to the beginning of the fourteenth century, continued to be the proper residence of the Popes; whilst the church constructed by Constantine became the Mother Church of Christendom.

And no less at the opposite north-western end of Rome rose at the request of Pope Sylvester, by Constantine's hand, over the bones of the Fisher of Galilee, the Basilica with double aisles, and ninety-six pillars, partly of Parian marble and partly of granite, which became the centre of devotion to all the Christian world. And the emperor showed his personal homage to St. Peter by the gift of a coffin of gilded brass, covered with a cross of the purest gold as long as the coffin itself, bearing the words: "Constantine Emperor and Helena Empress. This dwelling a royal court surrounds, bright with equal lustre." The dwelling being the coffin, and the court the church; and the first Christian emperor built the shrine of the chief Apostle on the spot where his predecessor, Nero, had exposed Christians to the foulest outrage, and near where the nightly oriental mysteries of Cybele continued to pollute the earth.[1]

Such were the outward actions of the emperor towards the papacy, while his inward thought was to infuse the unity[2] of the Christian Church into the Roman state, when he had made it Christian. By this we may judge of the greatness which that achievement of the Church conveyed to his mind.[3]

But its greatness is attested by the Church herself, for immediately after the confession of Almighty God Himself in the Creed, the Father, the Son, and the Holy Ghost, and the confession of what the Second Person has done in becoming incarnate for us, and the confession of the Third Person as proceeding from both; the Church confesses her own existence, as the special work of the Third Person, to be one, holy, catholic, and apostolic for ever. Thus, in the order of divine truths which make up the Christian inheritance, next to the being of God and the Redemption itself, stands the being of the Church. The fact which struck with such force the mind of the first Christian emperor is to the Christian mind all through the ages second in rank only to the Being of God and the Passion of God, being their chief result as concerns us, and as such is put in the

---

[1] Reumont, i. 637-8; Gregorovius, i. 92.

[2] See the picture of this unity given from the letter to Diognetus, in *Formation of Christendom*, vol. i. 218-23.

[3] Reumont, i. 615, well expresses his purpose: "Er hoffte den Staat durch das Christenthum zu retten".

mouth of her children as their daily confession, the ground of their hope and perseverance, the oath by which they are enrolled as soldiers in the Christian warfare.

In the review, then, of the first three centuries, we come first of all to the exhibition of the Church herself as the kingdom of God, which is contained in her recognition as such under Constantine. And thus I am brought to the special function of St. Peter's See in accomplishing this existence of the Church as the kingdom of God during this period.

We possess in the hierarchy, as it is presented to us in the Nicene Council, a testimony of incomparable value to the history of the Church in the centuries preceding it. The value of the testimony is heightened by the fact that we have no continuous and detailed history of Christian things in those times. They who search the earliest extant history, for instance, that of Eusebius, published in the year preceding the Council's convocation, will have to lament how bare and scant are its notices of the most important events and institutions, how very little in detail is recorded concerning the labours and preaching even of the Apostles. Of St. Paul we know most, and this is due to his own letters and St. Luke's epitome of some apostolic acts. Yet from these not a tithe of the work done in this one Apostle's ministry, from his conversion to his martyrdom, can be drawn. And to this knowledge authentic history adds very little indeed. Concerning nine of the Twelve " whose sound went out into all the earth, and their words to the end of the world," and who helped to build up so vast a structure of churches in many various lands, we know next to nothing. No history could equal in interest an authentic and detailed record of the apostolic preaching during the first seventy years. But we possess none. The first twelve chapters of the Acts gives us a sketch of St. Peter's guidance of the infant Church at Jerusalem: concerning the remaining deeds which filled up his long pontificate of thirty-eight years no detailed history exists. We may estimate the loss thus sustained by a single contrast. The planting of the Anglo-Saxon Church, with the chief incidents belonging to it, has been recorded for us by one of its earliest sons, and the providence of God has allowed his record to come down to us. And it is enough to shew how absolutely identical the Church in which Bede lived and laboured in the eighth century was in all its doctrines, sacraments, and discipline with the Church of the nineteenth. But no Bede exists for the history of the Church during the hundred years following the Day of Pentecost; nor for the next century; nor for the third. We have only preserved for us certain acts and incidents, such as the succession of bishops in the three great patriarchal Sees, and in that of Jerusalem; fragmentary accounts of persecutions and martyrdoms; visits of bishops to Rome; here and there a letter; a heathen historian's scornful reference to a "huge multitude" who gave up their lives for the faith at Rome in the time of St. Peter and St. Paul (but for which the modern spirit of denial would have reduced to insignificance that first persecution altogether). Such notices as these make up all that we know of the Church's history before the peace of Constantine. Christian writers were few in those times. Missionaries rather laboured and suffered than wrote. Men of leisure and learning there were none, at least among Christians. But, likewise, the greater persecutions of the third century destroyed many records, and particularly the local records of their martyrs made by their own churches, for which, in the Roman Church, special provision was made by appointing from the beginning a notary for each of the seven regions. It seems that no acts of the proceedings in the Nicene Council were compiled by its authority. We have only three documents of it, its creed, its twenty canons, and its synodal decree, with various lists of the subscriptions to it. Most precious, therefore, is the knowledge concerning the hierarchy of the Church which the meeting of this Council conveys to us, because that hierarchy gives us the result of the whole period of three centuries as to the government which had grown up in the Church from the time of the Apostles, by their institution, in which they carried out the commands of their Lord. "For neither," says Tertullian,[1] a witness writing 130 years before the Council, "did they choose to bring in anything of their own arbitrament, but faithfully gave over to the nations the discipline which they had received from Christ." And another, the personal friend of St. Peter and St. Paul, and the third successor of St. Peter, says "the offerings and liturgic acts Christ

---

[1] Tertullian, *de Præs.* 6; St. Clement, i. 40-44.

commanded to be performed with care, and not to be done rashly or in disorder, but at fixed times and seasons. And where and by whom He would have them performed He himself fixed by His supreme will, that all things being done with piety according to His good pleasure might be acceptable to His will." But especially, he adds, they established by express order of our Lord the succession of bishops.

Thus the Nicene hierarchy emerges from the waters of the persecution like a great pyramid from the midst of a lake, being the visible embodiment of those divine communications made to the Apostles in the great forty days from His Resurrection to His Ascension, as they were realised to human life through ten generations of men at the cost of lifelong labours, trials, watches, martyrdoms innumerable. We have here in its collected mass the work thus accomplished, the government by which the Church had taken possession of the earth, when "instead of her fathers children were born to her, whom she had made princes in all lands". Nothing here was the effect of court favour; nothing of human ambition. It is the Church's free development of her own powers; her execution of her Lord's purpose, inspired by Himself; the words of His mouth carried into act. A palace has been built, not in a night by magic powers, but in three hundred years, by the unwearied toil of numberless masons, all instinct with one purpose. Often and often they have not only toiled, but cemented the work with their blood. We cannot trace each portion of it as it was built up part by part, which it might have been granted us to do; but the completed temple we are allowed to see, and, what is more, it stands for all generations to come. The Twelve,[1] with Peter at their head, divided the earth, and their mode of division lasts good unto the end.

They divided it in this wise:

The intention of the Apostles uniformly carried out by them, and proclaiming by this uniformity that it was the command of their Lord, was, after the foundation of the Church in Jerusalem and the lapse of the prescribed time of priority for offering the divine kingdom to the acceptance of the Jews, to plant it in the great cities of the Roman empire. There were three of prominent rank: Rome, the seat of the empire itself, and up to the time of the faith's promulgation holding in herself "the secret of empire";[2] Alexandria, the capital of Egypt, a place of vast commerce, and of immense mental activity as common ground between the East and West, as also the adopted country of a great Jewish population; and Antioch, the capital of the East, and the seat of the most important military

---

[1] Mamachi, vol. i. 313-4, thinks the time when the Apostles left Jerusalem cannot be absolutely determined; it is impossible to reconcile the twelve years which some have supposed to have been assigned by our Lord for preaching to the Jews with other parts of history, such, *e.g.*, as Peter's sitting for seven years at Antioch. But he thinks that it cannot be denied that the Apostles, before their separation, met and determined together on the mode of imparting Christian doctrine, so that there should be complete agreement in what was to be professed and practised.

[2] "Evulgato imperii arcano posse principem alibi quam Romæ fieri."—Tacitus, *His.* i. 1. This secret was divulged in the convulsion following Nero's death, when a general commanding in a province became emperor by the choice of his soldiers rather than by election of the Senate at Rome.

command in the Eastern portion of the empire. Now, the Apostle Peter was the first bishop of Antioch, and the first bishop of Rome; and scarcely had he begun to plant the Church in Rome when he sent his disciple Mark to found the Church in Alexandria. In like manner the Apostle Paul founded bishops' sees in Ephesus, in Philippi, in Thessalonica, in Corinth, in Athens, in Crete, and other places. That the other Apostles did the like in the countries wherein they laboured as missionaries, there is no doubt. I do not dwell on this, because I have only to deal with the result as it is apparent at the Nicene Council. The first General Council meeting in 325 shews the Church everywhere on the earth governed by bishops. This episcopal government has four qualities which it is important to note when we are regarding the hierarchy itself, as it bears upon the creation of the Christian people. It is universal in extent; it is complete in character; it has subordination in its members; while the whole body of rulers is one. It is universal in that it covers the whole ground which the Church herself occupies, so that there are no outlying territories in which no bishop rules. As a government it is complete, because it is uniform, complete, and entire in itself, comprising in every case the priesthood, diaconate, and inferior ranks of clergy, with the faithful people, whether they be few or many; possessing and exercising for these the fullness of the sacraments, the same order of worship and discipline. So far as this, each diocese is a whole. But no one diocese stands by itself. There is likewise subordination between the several dioceses. Every bishop belongs to a province, in which there is a metropolitan; and as the bishop has a council of presbyters in his diocese, so the metropolitan has a council of bishops co-extensive with his province. Nor does the subordination stop here. For many metropolitans again are under the bishops of the more important cities. And, finally, there is a supreme see, which gathers together the bishops of the capital cities, and creates that bond of unity, in virtue of which the whole Church is in her government one, without which there would not be a kingdom at all.

What is actually seen at the Nicene Council is that the three greater metropolitans (who from the middle of the fifth century were called patriarchs, but long before possessed their prerogatives), the bishops of Rome, Alexandria, and Antioch, were in possession of a higher authority than the rest, an authority which had come down to them from the first origin of their sees, and which the Council did not create, but recognise. Though their sees were the most renowned cities of the empire, the higher authority of these bishops was carried back to the Apostle Peter, who had sat in person, first at Antioch and then at Rome, and had placed his disciple Mark at Alexandria. The name of Peter stood at the head of the episcopal catalogue in these three sees:[1] and the local tradition in all of them gave constant witness afterwards to Peter in many various ways. The Nicene Council knew only these three superior metropolitans, recognising their special rights

[1] Hergenröther, *Photius*, i. 26.

in the Sixth Canon,[1] which runs thus: "Let the ancient custom continue in force which subsists in Egypt, Libya, and Pentapolis, by which the bishop of Alexandria possesses authority over all these, since the like custom subsists also with the Roman bishop. In like manner also their privileges should be preserved to the churches, as to Antioch and the other provinces. And in general it is plain that if any one become a bishop without the consent of the metropolitan, the great Council decrees that he do not remain a bishop. But if two or three, through individual spirit of contention, resist the general choice of all, which is at once reasonable and according to ecclesiastical rule, let the voice of the majority prevail."

In these terms the Council admitted what were afterwards called the patriarchal rights of the bishop of Alexandria, over the three civil provinces of Egypt, Libya, and Pentapolis, which in the time of St. Athanasius had nearly a hundred bishops. It admitted a similar right in the see of Antioch over the metropolitans subject to it, in which patriarchate both metropolitans and bishops were much more numerous than those subject to the Alexandrine bishop. The Council in this Sixth Canon justified the prerogatives which it thus admitted in the see of Alexandria by reference to a similar right existing and exercised at Rome; and then by force of the same principle recognised the prerogative of Antioch and of metropolitans in general.

[1] Hergenröther, *Photius*, i. pp. 26-30, shews that the sixth Canon speaks of the rights of the great metropolitans over a complex of provinces.

In the previous history of the Church these three named sees, which were often called in a special sense "the Apostolic Sees," exercised a sort of hierarchical triumvirate,[1] which the Roman see, ever strenuous in its grasp of tradition, firmly maintained. They were the chief leaders of ecclesiastical matters, as to which they referred in the first instance to each other. Thus in the judgment deposing Paul of Samosata, the Synod of Antioch in 269 directed its letter to Dionysius of Rome and to Maximus of Alexandria. Before that, in the Novatian schism, and in the contest upon heretical baptism, these sees had carried on an active correspondence with each other.

Three sees, whose bishops were soon after called exarchs—those of Cæsarea in Cappadocia, of Ephesus, and of Heraclea in Thrace—had similar rights over metropolitans, as well as the primate of Carthage in Africa. The bishop of Rome stood at the head of all, universally recognised as the special successor of the Prince of the Apostles, and as the first of bishops. He exercised his supreme jurisdiction in the East only over patriarchs in the first instance, not over particular bishops; but he was the only patriarch in the whole West.[2]

Now, looking at this hierarchy as the recipient and inheritor of such apostolic power as was to continue in the Church—of that Apostolic College itself with which our Lord promised to be all days unto the consummation of the world—I think it cannot fail to

---

[1] Hergenröther's *Photius*, i. 80.   [2] *Photius*, pp. 26, 30.

strike any one who reflects upon the subject how great is the preponderance in it given to the authority of St. Peter. For not only the first and greatest see derives from him, all that authority which it exercises over and above that which belongs to every bishop in his diocese, and which is the same in all, whether the diocese be small or great, but likewise the second and the third, after the norm, so to say, of the first, as is intelligibly suggested in the terms of the Sixth Nicene Canon, exercise the rule of mothers over a large progeny of bishops, and all the three are sees of Peter. And the Council, in speaking of this prerogative as actually belonging to the three sees, does not claim to bestow it, but recognises it as existing from the beginning. "Let the ancient custom be maintained," are the words which it uses in mentioning that prerogative of the Alexandrine see which it is maintaining, but which it is not conferring, and which it justifies by reference to the practice of Rome as the rule and type, whilst it would have it maintained at Antioch also, with the privileges of metropolitans generally in the other provinces. The preeminence which has its norm in the Roman see, and its largest exercise after Rome in the other two sees of Peter, and which is further carried out in the connection of metropolitans with their suffragans through the various provinces of the Church, certainly suggests the conclusion that Peter is the source of whatever dignity, over and above the simple episcopate, belongs to the patriarchal, exarchal, or metropolitan rank.

And, in fact, from early times, the Popes recognised

the two bishops of Alexandria and Antioch as, conjointly with themselves, successors of Peter. Thus St. Gregory the Great wrote to the holder in his time of the see of Antioch in very remarkable terms: " Your Holiness has written to me much respecting the Chair of Peter, Prince of the Apostles, when you say that he sits there in person to this very time in his successors. I receive with pleasure what is said of the Chair of Peter by him who sits in it himself. For who does not know that the Holy Church has been established on the solidity of the Prince of the Apostles, who expressed in his name the firmness of his mind, being called Peter from the Rock (Petra)—to whom the Truth said, ' I will give to thee the keys of the kingdom of heaven'; and again, 'Thou, when thou art converted, confirm thy brethren'; and a third time, ' Simon, son of John, lovest thou me? Feed my sheep.' And, thus, though there be many Apostles, yet in virtue of its very principate, only the see of the Prince of the Apostles, which is the see of one in three places, received supreme authority. For he made that see sovereign, which he honoured by resting in it, and there ending the present life. He distinguished the see to which he sent his disciple, the Evangelist. He strengthened that in which he sat himself for seven years, though he was to leave it. This is why, the see upon which by divine authority three bishops now preside, being the one see of one, I appropriate to myself whatever good I learn from you. And if you believe any good of me, take it to your own merit, since we are one thing in Him who said 'that all may be one'."[1]

It may be asked why does St. Gregory in writing to the patriarch of Antioch on the unity of the three sees of Peter solemnly introduce the three great words of our Lord to Peter which contain the special grant of his primacy? Is it not because the Church from the beginning connected the metropolitan authority, in its highest degree, which is the patriarchal, immediately with the person of Peter? He intimates that the hierarchy itself, in which the patriarchs above all illustrated the principle of headship and subordination, was an emanation from the Primacy. The episcopal dignity being in itself equal in all who held it, its subordination in its various ranks, and the unity of the whole mass centred in its supreme holder, are the direct result of the grant made in these three words to Peter. For St. Gregory says: "*Though* there be many Apostles, yet in virtue of its very principate only the see of the Prince of the Apostles received supreme authority". Accordingly the reference to the three great words is most pertinent.

But we can trace this idea of St. Gregory the Great back through many generations. Pope Innocent,[2] nearly two hundred years earlier than St. Gregory, and

---

[1] St. Greg. I., Ep. vii. 40. "Itaque cum multi sint Apostoli, pro ipso tamen principatu sola Apostolorum Principis Sedes in auctoritate convaluit, quæ in tribus locis unius est. Ipse enim sublimavit Sedem in qua etiam quiescere et præsentem vitam finire dignatus est. Ipse decoravit Sedem in qua Evangelistam discipulum misit. Ipse firmavit Sedem in qua septem annuis quamvis discessurus sedit. Cum ergo unius atque una sit Sedes, cui ex auctoritate divina tres nunc Episcopi præsident, &c. [2] Ep. xxiv.

only ninety years after the Nicene Council, recognised the patriarchal right of the bishop of Antioch over his provinces by referring to this Canon of the Nicene Council, which, he says, "singly expresses the mind of all bishops throughout the world"; and he adds, "We note that this privilege was given to Antioch not so much on account of the city's magnificence as because it is known to be the first seat of the first Apostle where the Christian religion received its name, where a great meeting of Apostles was held, and which would not yield to the see of the city of Rome, except that the latter rejoices in having received and retained to the end that honour which the former obtained only in transition".

At the Nicene Council there are other sees founded by Apostles and in possession of great dignity. Of these we may take as a specimen the see of Ephesus, at the head of which St. Paul had placed St. Timotheus, which was the Mother Church of the province of Asia, and had exarchal dignity, intermediate, that is, between patriarchs and metropolitans. Moreover, the Sixth Canon of the Council recognised not only the special privileges of Alexandria, referring to the norm of Rome, and then those of Antioch, but with them the whole system of episcopal subordination, adding, "Likewise in the other provinces the privileges are to be preserved to the churches. And, indeed, as a general rule it is manifest that if any one become a bishop without the consent of the metropolitan, the great Council orders that he be not a bishop."

From this disposition of the Episcopate at the time of

the first General Council, as it was ranged, first under three great sees of Peter, which as Mother Churches comprehended many hundred bishops, and were set over many metropolitans; secondly, as it was found in a number of countries which were grouped in what became exarchal complexes of provinces under the sees of Ephesus, Cæsarea in Cappadocia, and Heraclea in Thrace; thirdly, as existing in other provinces outside of these, we see that the hierarchy of the Church did not consist of independent bishops, but of bishops closely bound together, the unity of the province lying in the metropolitan, of metropolitans in their patriarch, of patriarchs in the chief see of Peter. Some of these names were indeed posterior, but the tie which they denoted was from the beginning. And that the see of Peter at Rome dealt in the first instance, as far as regarded the Eastern portion of the Church, only with patriarchs, counting them as responsible for the metropolitans and bishops who belonged to their several circles of authority, by no means lessens its sovereign principate, but bears witness to that genuine love of legitimate rule, blended with autonomy, which characterises the Church from her birth through the whole period of her struggle with the pagan empire. But in the whole West, comprising Italy, Africa, eastern and western Illyricum, the Gauls, Spain, Britain, the bishop of Rome was the sole patriarch; and these would seem to be the "greater dioceses,"[1]

---

[1] Placuit a te qui majores dioceses tenes, per te potissimum omnibus insinuari. —Mansi, xi. 469. The term $διοίκησις$ at this time expressed the complex of provinces contained in a great prefecture of the empire; a diocese was $παροικία$, a province $ἐπαρχία$.

the holding of which the Council of Arles in 314 attributed to Pope Sylvester, and requested him to transmit their decrees to the several provinces.

As I have said, the least reflection upon the fact that at the first General Council of the Church only three patriarchal sees existed, all which ran up to Peter in their episcopal succession, coupled with the fact that the bishops comprised in these three patriarchates made up a large majority of the whole number of bishops in the Church, would of itself shew the preponderance of St. Peter's authority in that constitution of the Church which comes before us as the result of that period when the Church, unconnected with the heathen State, and continually assaulted by it, established the distribution of spiritual power within herself, in the words of St. Leo, " according as the one spirit prompted her from one fountain of grace".[1]

But the organic distribution of authority under this system of patriarchs, metropolitans, and bishops shewn by the Nicene Council indicated more than this preponderance.

And the better to understand what it does indicate, reflect how different would have been the aspect which the internal relation to each other of the chief members of this hierarchy would have presented to us if, for instance, while the first see, that of Rome, had descended from St. Peter as its first bishop, the second see, that of Alexandria, had descended from St. Andrew as its first

---

[1] St. Leo, Ep. ix., speaking of St. Peter and St. Mark: "Quum sine dubio de eodem fonte gratiæ unus spiritus fuerit et discipuli et magistri".

bishop, and the third see, that of Antioch, had descended from St. John as its first bishop. Nor need we stop at this supposition. The Apostles had, each of them, power to found sees wherever they taught. They did actually so found them. What would have prevented the twelve Apostles from each founding a patriarchal see in the chief city of the country which he evangelised, such as Rome, Alexandria, and Antioch actually were? And each of them might have become the first bishop of the see so founded. Whereas at the Nicene Council we find the more than remarkable fact that not a single bishop existed who could claim an Apostle as the first bishop of his see except the bishops of the three sees of Peter. St. Paul appointed St. Timotheus to be not only a bishop, but a metropolitan at Ephesus; and St. Titus to be not only a bishop, but a metropolitan in Crete, for the purpose of establishing bishops in the several cities of the island. He founded also the see of Thessalonica, which became afterwards a great metropolitan see, and many other sees, but in no one did he sit as bishop. The other Apostles did likewise. St. John in his latter years lived at Ephesus, and exercised apostolical authority over the Asiatic churches, but he became bishop of no see. It is true that the see of Jerusalem had for its first bishop St. James, who is generally accounted one of the Twelve. But the succession to this see was interrupted by the destruction of the city and the events following it; so that when Jerusalem once more appeared as the name of a Christian see, its bishop took rank not as the successor of an Apostle, but as suffragan of the metropolitan of Cæsarea, and though sitting with distinction at the Nicene Council,[1] it was only in the fifth century that he received patriarchal rank from the fourth General Council in honour of the original founding of the Church at Jerusalem.

Thus at the Nicene Council there were many apostolic sees in the sense that they had been founded by Apostles, but not one whose bishop could claim by unbroken episcopal descent from an Apostle to be the representative of that Apostle, and so to be the depositary of his apostolic power, except the three patriarchs, who, in the language of St. Gregory the Great, held the one see of the one Peter at Rome, Alexandria, and Antioch. This is a historical fact. What is the meaning of it?

What meaning is there but that Divine Providence carried out in the whole period of the Church's planting and the three centuries of heathen persecution the promise and grant of our Lord to St. Peter to be the bearer of the keys in His house and the shepherd of His people? And this is done by causing the whole organisation of the Church to proceed from Peter as the bishop in the highest degree, by making his See of Rome "the origin and principle of unity," "the root and matrix of the Church," as St. Cyprian called it, while none of the other Apostles stand at the head of an episcopal line.

---

[1] Constant. *Præfatio*, xiv., observes: "Tacemus de Hierosolymitana cui licet proprium honorem servari voluerit Nicæna Synodus, tamen ei *ne metropoliticum quidem jus dignitatemque concessit.*

Again, this is exactly what Pope Innocent I. meant when, in answering the reference of the African bishops to him, he said that "in questions of faith I consider that all our brethren and fellow-bishops should refer to no other than to Peter, who is, in fact, the author of their own name and honour". This was Peter's special privilege among the Apostles, that the episcopate radiated from his person. This was what St. Ambrose meant when he wrote in the name of the Council of Aquileia to the emperors Gratian, Valentinian, and Theodosius, not to allow "the Roman Church, the head of the whole Roman world, to be disturbed, for this is the fountain-head whence the laws of our venerable communion flow forth to all men".[1] Again, St. Optatus has assigned a specific reason for this fact in his well-known words to a Donatist adversary: "You cannot deny that you know that the Chair of Peter first of all was fixed in the city of Rome, in which Peter, the head of all the Apostles, sat, whence, too, he was named Cephas: in which single Chair unity was to be observed by all, so that the rest of the Apostles should not each maintain a Chair to themselves, but that forthwith he should be a schismatic and a sinner who against that singular Chair sets up another".

And to make this result the more marked, the most distinguished Apostle after St. Peter is associated with him as a sort of second founder of the Roman see, from which every document of supreme importance has run during the long ages of the Christian faith in the name

---

[1] St. Innocent, Ep. xxx.; St. Ambrose, Ep. xi.

of St. Peter and St. Paul. But no other see claims the Apostle who founded so many sees as the head of its line, nor was St. Paul himself bishop of Rome.

And in this connection we must recur to the fact that the Nicene Council grounded its recognition of the privilege of the Alexandrine see to preside over several provinces upon ancient custom, which it justified by the practice of the Roman see. Then it went on to extend that recognition to the whole hierarchical organisation exemplified in the instance of Alexandria. Thus it recognised this order of subordination as pre-existing to itself, as something which it was not creating, but maintaining, because it came down from ancient times, which means, of course, the original institution of the Apostles. The Council added nothing and changed nothing in this state of things: and thus this organisation is not the work of the Council, but rather the Council itself a result of the organisation.

For in this Canon is contained that whole organic and graduated distribution of power by which the Church in her hierarchy presented that subordination which makes the unity and beauty of a kingdom; and this being so, most significant is the reference to Rome as the type, standard, and example of patriarchal power. There can be no subordination without headship; and where the headship lay is sufficiently plain from the fact that at the end of the first three centuries of the Church's existence, the See of Peter—the episcopal succession springing from Peter—had generated the whole order of bishops, metropolitans, and patriarchs, of which it stood at the head : so absolutely at the head, that there was no other bishop who could claim episcopal successsion from an Apostle.

The structure of the Church, as a well-ordered kingdom, is based upon the limitation of every individual bishop's authority to a certain prescribed territory. This had been the original teaching and practice of the Apostles. At the Nicene Council this limitation appears, is acknowledged, and maintained by the Council. But the kingdom of Christ required the principle of supreme authority, which was the bond of unity. So necessary was this, that even among twelve apostles, who were given authority over all the earth, a Primate was made to cause that authority to be exercised in unity.[1] How much more was such a Primacy requisite, when the Apostolic College of Twelve was succeeded by an Episcopate containing hundreds or thousands of members. But I am not here stating a doctrine ; I am only noting a fact. The fact is, that after three centuries of struggle with the pagan State, the result of the independence won, at the cost of incessant persecution, presents us with a constitution in which the episcopate spread through the whole world so far as it is occupied by the Church, having sprung from the womb of Peter's see, has its only patriarchs in the successors of that see ; its type of the episcopal power itself in Peter, and the subordination of its members in a structure of which he is the legitimate, acknowledged, undisputed head.

The Popes often declared—and I am about to cite a

[1] St. Jerome.

remarkable instance of it—that the Nicene Council bestowed nothing on the Roman see, being aware that by the word of Christ it already had the Primacy, a supreme authority to which nothing was wanting. We may remark a singular corroboration of the fact declared by the Popes in the latent recognition of the Primacy which the Canon contains. For the privileges indicated, acknowledged, and ratified in it comprehend all that authority which one bishop has over another, short of the Primacy itself. Of such authority the patriarchal is the highest derivation; and it is here referred back to Rome. If the Alexandrine bishop governed three provinces with their metropolitans, it was an ancient custom derived from the same exertion of power at Rome. But in all this the Council grants nothing new; it only recognises an existing fact. And the fact is, that episcopal power being in itself equal in each recipient, whatever authority one bishop exercised over another is, in the last resort, a derivation from the Primacy. Nothing is here conferred upon Rome; but a great deal is suggested as belonging to Rome.

In the middle of the ninth century a very great Pope, Nicolas I., addressed from his sick-bed at Rome a letter to the Eastern emperor Michael, in which he draws these same conclusions from the acts of the Nicene Council.[1] In answer to the insults of the emperor, he wrote: " God give you grace to know the greatness and the nature of the Roman Church's privileges; from whom they took their rise, and who was

[1] Nicolas I., Ep. viii.; Mansi, xv. 204.

the author of its supreme authority. If you will ask this of us, as the ministers of Christ and the dispensers of His mysteries, we will do our best to shew it you; if you scorn the knowing it, and only direct your efforts against the privileges of the Roman Church, beware lest they turn against you. It is hard for you to kick against the goad. If you will not hear us, all that remains for us is to esteem you as our Lord Jesus Christ commanded in the case of those who despise listening to the Church of God. Especially the privileges of the Roman Church, founded by the mouth of Christ in St. Peter, carried out in the Church's own disposition, observed from antiquity, celebrated by the General Councils, and continuously venerated by the whole Church, can in no respect be lessened, in no respect infringed, in no respect changed. For the foundation laid by God cannot be removed by human effort; what God has established remains firm and strong, and he sins before all who attempts to resist the ordinance of God. The privileges, I repeat, of that See or Church are perpetual. They were rooted and planted by God. They may be attacked but not transferred, assaulted but not removed.[1] They were before your empire; they remain, thank God, as yet uninfringed. They will last after you, and so long as the Christian name shall be preached, they will continue entire.

"These privileges were given to this holy Church by

---

[1] This points, says Cardinal Hergenröther, to the attempted translation by the Greeks of the Primacy from Old Rome to New Rome, after the removal of the imperial residence thither.

Christ; they were not given by Councils, but only celebrated and venerated by them. Through them it is not so much an honour as a burden which lies upon us, though we gained that honour not by our own merits, but by the ordination of God's grace through and in the person of the blessed Peter. They enjoin and compel us to bear the solicitude of all the churches of God. For the society of St. Paul, the vessel of election and teacher of the truth, was added to St. Peter: and they, like two great luminaries in heaven, divinely fixed in the Roman Church, filled the world with the splendour of their shining. Nor were they, after their death,[1] brought to Rome by princes to confer on the Roman Church greater privileges, as you rather stretched power than used reason in doing, so as to strip other churches of their patrons, and enrich Constantinople with their spoils; but coming to Rome in the flesh, preaching the word of life, removing from her the darkness of error, beaming on men's minds with the light of truth, and consummating their martyrdom on one and the same day, they consecrated that Church with their blood, and dedicated it to God without spot or wrinkle, or any such thing. Thus they made the Church of Alexandria their own, as that of the son and disciple of one of them, since the son's inheritance lies in the parent's power, and the disciple's glory belongs to his master. Now Peter had already made the Church of Antioch his own by his corporal presence,

---

[1] An allusion to the translation to Constantinople of the relics of St. Andrew, St. Luke, and St. Timothy.

which, as St. Innocent says, only yielded to Rome because it possessed but in transition that which Rome kept. Therefore, through these three chief Churches, the care of all the Churches looks for the guidance of the chief Apostles, Peter and Paul. In the place of these fathers, we, by divine aid, have become sons, and, however unequal to them in merit, are appointed princes over all the earth." . "Observe, moreover, that neither the Nicene Council, nor any other, conferred any privilege upon the Roman Church, because it knew that it had received the fullness of all rights in the person of Peter, and the government of all Christ's sheep." Then Pope Nicolas quotes his predecessor, Boniface I., who sat from 418 to 422, for that precise interpretation of the Nicene Council which I have given above. "This," he says, "is attested by Pope Boniface in writing to all the bishops of Thessaly. The institution of the whole Church from the beginning was derived from the rank given to St. Peter, in whom its government and whole sum consists; for, as the culture of religion increased, the fountain of ecclesiastical discipline which he established diffused itself through all churches. The precepts of the Nicene Council bear witness to this, so that it did not venture to make any appointment over him, seeing that nothing could be conferred above his merit. In fact it was aware that everything was given to him by the word of the Lord."[1]

---

[1] St. Boniface, Ep. xiv.; Constant. 1087. "Institutio universalis nascentis Ecclesiæ de beati Petri sumpsit honore principium, in quo regimen ejus et summa consistit. Ex ejus enim ecclesiastica disciplina, per omnes ecclesias, religionis

On which Pope Nicolas comments, "If everything, then nothing was wanting in that grant. And if you carefully examine the regulations of the Nicene Council, you will find that it conferred no increase on the Roman Church, but rather derived from its form the particular privilege which it admitted in the Alexandrine Church."

This great letter of Pope Nicolas is in fact a summing up of the testimony afforded by the eight preceding centuries to the government of the Church, as it was instituted in the beginning, and as it was recognised by the first General Council. And as Pope Innocent, ruling eighty years after it was celebrated, said of it that it "conveyed in itself the mind of the bishops throughout the whole world,"[1] so Pope Boniface, ten years later, observed that the Nicene Canons, in recognising the existing government of the Church, as it was then arranged in provinces, under metropolitans and patriarchs, bore witness to that government as springing from the person of St. Peter, the type and standard of the bishop, in whose Primacy the whole Church-government was summed up and consisted. That is a declaration, among other things, that all power exercised by an individual bishop over another bishop is a derivation from the Primacy. This was the fountain-head, out of which the whole constitution

---

jam crescente cultura, fonte manavit. Nicænæ Synodi non aliud præcepta testantur ; adeo ut non aliquid super eum ausa sit constituere, cum videret nihil supra meritum suum posse conferri. Omnia denique hinc noverat Domini sermone concessa."

[1] "Revolventes auctoritatem Nicænæ Synodi quæ una omnium per orbem terrarum mentem explicat sacerdotum."—Ep. xxiv. ; Constant., col. 851.

of the Church, in its subordination and autonomy, flowed. The Pope in every bishop, and more especially in the tenants of the great sees, respected an authority of which he was the supreme holder. It is to be remembered that this "disposition of authority" is not a development, but the form which the Church took at her birth. It is not something which the Nicene Council created, but that which it recognised as existing from the beginning, that of which it found the norm in the See of Rome, and acknowledged as valid because it was found there. There is no constitution of the Church before the Nicene. The "three Sees of the one Peter" were rooted in the apostolic order of things; and Peter was the source of the Episcopate from the beginning. It is history in its most rigid declarations on which we here rest. There is only one class of persons which can consistently deny the force of this fact. It is those who do not believe in the Church's existence from the beginning, with a corporate life, as the kingdom of God; and who, therefore, do not believe in the continuance of that corporate life. Those who believe in *no* Church, and those only, are not touched by these facts. But these words of Pope Boniface, written in the year 422 to the bishops of the Illyrian province, who since the time of Gratian had ceased to belong to the Western empire, are of such importance that we may dwell on them a moment longer. They state the constitution of the Nicene Church to be the evolution of the power stored up in the person of Peter by the direct gift of Christ; a power not given by the Church, but by the author of the Church for the purpose of making her. In this case, therefore, historical fact and theoretical principle are at one. In historic fact the Sixth Canon of the Council delineates the Church outspread before it in the arrangement of its provinces; metropolitan over bishops; patriarch over metropolitan; and the first See of Peter over all: a disposition of power eminently legitimate, autonomous, subordinated, and, in fine, springing from unity and maintaining unity. The theoretic principle of this fact is luminously expounded by Pope Boniface, addressing a province of Greek bishops. He derives from Peter's person the whole authority thus drawn out in its graduated arrangement during the Church's conflict with the heathen world in three hundred years. What he says amounts to this. The chief bishop—he who held the episcopal authority in Capite—has generated the Episcopate in its various ranks. The tree, which already overshadowed the earth, had grown up from the root of Peter. The solicitude of all the Churches had flowed over from the Church of St. Peter and St. Paul to the various bishops of the world in various degrees. The episcopal authority, itself the same in all, in the least diocese of the Church as in its greatest, was by that wonderful word and gift of Christ derived in the first instance from Peter, inasmuch as he was created Pastor of the Church on the shore of the lake of Galilee, and, while it remained full and entire in him, yet had been dispensed without diminution to his brethren throughout the world. "The government and its entirety consist in him." Such is the fact attested, and such the doctrine given to the Greek bishops, less than a hundred years after the Nicene Council, and accepted by those bishops, both as fact and doctrine, when St. Augustine was in the greatness of his genius the first Doctor of the Church.

It was no innovation, but perpetually repeated in the decretal letters of the Popes, of which we begin to have a series from the time of Siricius, who himself wrote in 386 from the shrine of St. Peter; "through whom," he says, "sprung the beginning both of the Apostolate and the Episcopate in Christ". And in this he was only expressing the tradition of the Apostolic See from the beginning, which was the foundation of all its acts, and alone could justify them. The learned editor [1] of these letters, so far as they have been preserved in the first four centuries, makes a double remark here, which I will cite. Of so many Pontiffs famous for doctrine and sanctity, whom even to suspect of claiming what did not belong to them would be the height of rashness, not a single one can be found who did not believe that the prerogative had been granted to him or to his church to be head of the whole Church; while among all the churches founded by the Apostles or their successors, no single one can be found who ventured to call himself the head of the whole Church. Either the Popes claimed what was their right, by the gift of Christ, or they were one and all impostors from the beginning.

[1] Constant. *Epistolæ Romanorum Pontificum*, p. 111.

CHAPTER III.

FROM ST. PETER TO ST. SYLVESTER, PART II.

WHAT great lesson of Church government have I drawn in the preceding treatment of my subject from the fact of the Nicene Council?

Instead of looking for exertions of extraordinary power by the Popes in the period antecedent to that Council let us weigh the constitution of the Church itself at the Council. What is the meaning of it as given to us by the Popes from the very time of the Council, by Siricius, Innocent, Boniface I., Leo the Great, Gregory the Great, and referred back to by Nicholas I., when writing to the Eastern emperor himself, who originated the Greek schism? They declare the Nicene constitution itself to be an emanation of the Papacy; the whole ecclesiastical discipline itself to have issued from the fountain of Peter; the whole principle in the Episcopate of order, subordination, and headship, in its various degrees, to be but the carrying out by the Apostolic College of the words, "Feed my sheep," and the charge conveyed in them. According to their tradition, which is invariable and unbroken, and animates every action of their ministry, not only did the great "Shepherd and Bishop" (1 Pet. i.), as His first vicar terms Him, cause the episcopal power itself to spring from the person of Peter, but the hierarchical order of that power, by which alone one kingdom of Christ could be and was maintained, was no less an emanation of his Primacy. That is, a power was given first, and in universal extension, to him, which should afterwards be communicated in its several degrees to others.

The Nicene Council stands at the distance of 250 years from the action of the Apostles themselves, a time long enough to shew the issue of a great principle, the principle of hierarchy; further, a time of which the characteristic is either active persecution, or at least fundamental enmity, to the doctrine and government of the Church on the part of the world. The details of a continuous history are indeed wanting to us in large part when we treat of this period, but the result in the meeting, action, and constitution of the Council is quite unimpeachable.

If that constitution did not arise[1] in the way which the Popes before and from that time, and ever afterwards, declared it to have arisen, how did it come about? To this, I think, no answer can be given.

I now proceed to another point, which is the intimate correspondence between the hierarchy as seen in opera-

[1] What I am here stating as a fact of history, testified in the fourth century, is defined as a dogmatic truth by the Vatican Council de Ecclesia Christi:—" Ut vero episcopatus ipse unus et indivisus esset, et per coherentes sibi invicem sacerdotes credentium multitudo universa in fidei et communionis unitate conservaretur, beatum Petrum cœteris Apostolis proponens in ipso instituit perpetuum utriusque unitatis principium, ac visibile fundamentum, super cujus fortitudinem æternum exstrueretur templum, et Ecclesiæ cœlo inferenda sublimitas in hujus fidei firmitate consurgeret".

tion at the first General Council, and that profound consciousness of its own unity which filled the whole Christian people. The *Brotherhood*[1] was the name which it bore everywhere among its own members. But in the greatest Christian communities—as at Rome, Alexandria, Antioch, Ephesus, Carthage—it was not felt more keenly to be the brotherhood than in the smallest bishop's see which could be found through the vast extent of the Roman provinces. For the bishop of that small see was one of a mass of rulers, and the civil officer who ruled his people was not more completely pieced into the network of the State's organisation than he into that episcopal circle[2] which formed the Church's diadem. The springing up of this hierarchy throughout the earth by the force of an innate power is one of the marvels shewn by the Christian Church in this its first stage. The sense of isolation, which might naturally have fallen on those who formed but a small minority in so many towns and cities distant from each other, was thus overcome, and the meanest Christian in the least bishop's see was well aware that he belonged to a brotherhood which was everywhere. But there are four chief bonds of unity which deserve to be specified.[3]

1. Christians who travelled from one place to another

---

[1] Matt. xxiii. 8. πάντες ὑμεῖς ἀδελφοί ἐστε. 1 Pet. ii. 17. τὴν ἀδελφότητα τιμᾶτε. St. Cyprian, Fraternitatem universam meo nomine salutate. Mamachi i. 6 says:—"Invaluit præterea apud nostros nomen *fratrum*, quod est a Christo servatore in Ecclesiam introductum, itaque deinceps propagatum est, ut non modo ab Apostolis sed etiam a Christianis omnibus usurparetur".

[2] The constitution of Valentinian III., A.D. 445, says:—"Sancti Petri meritum, qui princeps est episcopalis coronæ".—St. Leo, vol. i., p. 642.

[3] Enumerated by Hergenröther, K.-g., i. 195-7.

were provided with letters from their own bishop, which testified their condition as Christians, and enabled them to take part in the rites of the Church, and to enjoy the blessings which it communicated wherever they went. They would naturally be the bearers of such tidings as it would be well for the brotherhood to receive. Thus the nomination of bishops was communicated : the glorious sufferings of martyrs were recorded in accounts sent by one church to another. Errors in doctrine likewise as they arose, and the censures which they drew down, thus became known. It was the special function of bishops to give these letters, so that even Confessors were not allowed the privilege of giving them. The church of Smyrna's record of the death of Polykarp sent to the church of Pontus, and that of the churches of Lyons and Vienna in Gaul, describing the great persecution in which St. Blandina and so many other martyrs suffered, sent to the churches of Asia Minor, are instances of letters intended not for individuals but whole communities.

2. Again, the family bond of churches, as mother and daughter, ran through the whole Church, having its most remarkable instances in the three patriarchal sees. This bond sprung as it were naturally out of that conduct of the Apostles and their first successors, which consisted in planting the faith in the chief cities. The civil metropolis thus often coincided with the spiritual, but it was not the civil pre-eminence which bestowed the spiritual rank ; it was the dignity of the founders. Thus churches founded immediately by an Apostle took

the first rank; then those which were mediately apostolic by derivation from these. Perhaps the authority of the Jewish synagogue over those depending on it suggested this arrangement to the Apostles; as Jerusalem itself was the Mother Church to Judæa, Samaria, and Galilee, until by its destruction the metropolitan dignity passed to Cæsarea. So strong was this hierarchical order that before the middle of the third century, Heraclas, the bishop of Alexandria, could depose Ammonius, bishop of Thmuis, for disobedience, and consecrate a new bishop. In Africa the primate of Carthage stood over the metropolitans of provinces, in which the eldest bishop of each province became the first. The fabric of this gradation of metropolitans was complete before the Nicene Council.

3. Side by side with it was the operation of the government which it involved. With the second half of the second century the meetings of bishops in yearly or half-yearly synods of their respective provinces become more and more frequent, having their prototype in the meeting of the Apostles at Jerusalem. Here was a provision against the attacks of heresy; here accusations, if need were, against bishops themselves could be heard. The institution strongly marks the blending of autonomy with subordination, and testifies the compact fabric of the Church, so that the power of the bishop, which seems in his own sphere of action complete, is found subject to the higher authority of his brethren.

4. But over all, and that to which all converge, is the Primacy of St. Peter's See of Rome. As these several churches and ecclesiastical provinces sprung from its

bosom, so they need and live by its supreme authority, not an authority which interferes at every step, which is jealous of the bishop in his diocese, of the metropolitan in his province, of the patriarch in his complex of provinces, but a power which, as it first gave birth to this order, so maintains and regulates it from the top to the bottom. This patriarchal constitution of the Church, to which every existing record of antiquity bears witness, so far from being the antagonist of the Primacy, is its own creation. Exactly the same principle which made Alexandria, Antioch, Ephesus, and other great mother cities what they were, made Rome their head. Our Lord's own grant, and that alone, gave this power—the regimen and summa of which Pope Boniface speaks—to Peter, and his choosing to be bishop of Rome centred it at Rome, but it is identical in character from the least to the greatest bishop, and is the source at once of their ordinary power and of their subordination.

This is the state of things *inside* the Church; but we have now to cast a glance on the state of things *outside* it, while this great work was being done.

If we look at the hierarchy of the Church in its complete state, as assembled at the Nicene Council, we might suppose this work of three centuries to have been accomplished under the serene guardianship of the Roman peace, as the spontaneous growth of a people, and as the nursling of sovereigns chosen by itself. But in reality it was the work of a community, which, during the whole time, was exposed to the dislike, the suspicion, the hatred of the most powerful and most despotic empire which ever has existed. These feelings were not superficial, nor were they transient. The Church's spiritual government was the outcome as well as the bearer of a doctrine which supported it. Its sole source was the Person of a Man executed by servile punishment as a criminal who claimed rights which were said to interfere with the dominion of the Roman emperor. The doctrine which His Apostles derived from Him was as much opposed to the customs and habits of those to whom it was preached as the Person from whom it was derived was in their eyes contemptible. How is it possible now to convey an adequate sense of that "folly" which was imputed by the Gentile to the believers of a religion who worshipped for their God one who had been crucified as a slave. There was found not many years ago, on the wall of the imperial palace on the Palatine, an outline which may have been scratched by a soldier in the body-guard of Decius in an idle hour. It portrayed the crucifixion of a man with an ass's head, and it bore the legend, "Anaximenes worships his God". That soldier's scribble comes down to us through sixteen centuries as a photograph of the mind with which prince, philosopher, and people alike regarded the Author of the Christian faith. Tacitus and Pliny the younger, Trajan and Marcus Aurelius, the crowd which tortured St. Albina in the theatre of Lyons, and burnt St. Polykarp in the theatre of Smyrna, speak in that crucifix with the ass's head.

As to the hierarchy which sprung from the Crown of Thorns, its three great constituents—three, but so inti-

mately blended together that they formed one mass—
were a priesthood, a teaching, and a jurisdiction to which
the analogous powers in the gentile world could not but
feel a complete antagonism. The history of the three
centuries exemplifies this in every form of persecution.
It is true the gentile power used material force only
from time to time. But from the act of Nero persecuting the Christians of Rome and severing them from that
protection of the law which allowed Jews as Roman
subjects to profess an inherited religion down to Constantine's decree of tolerance Christians were ever liable
to penal prosecution, though they were not always
actually suffering from it. The times when the emperors
themselves set in action the powerful engine of Roman
law against them have been expressed in the number
of ten persecutions. But the spiritual opposition of
the vast gentile world through all its minor varieties of
the polytheistic creed never ceased. The Christians
during these centuries were ever as sheep among wolves.
We shall do scant justice indeed to that perfect form of
government which the Church at her first General
Council exhibited, unless we consider it as produced by
her while living in the midst of her enemies in a state
of conflict and of oppression. And in particular, as to
this Primacy before which Constantine bowed himself,
which he honoured with gifts, on which he bestowed the
Lateran Palace for its dwelling, whose chief church bore
his own name as the Basilica of Constantine, had not a
great predecessor seventy years before — one who
attached his name to that of Trajan, and claimed to

exhibit in its purest form the spirit of the old Roman rule—declared that he would sooner see a competitor for his throne arise, than the appointment of a bishop in the See of Peter. That one expression, preserved for us incidentally in a letter of Cyprian, is invaluable in throwing a broad beam of light over the relation between the Church and the Empire in the middle of the third century. It is like the light cast by the letter of Pliny to the emperor Trajan at the beginning of the second century, which reveals so much, both as to the number and innocence of Christians, and as to the profession of Christianity itself being liable to the punishment of death before any special decree made by that emperor. These two incidents, even taken alone, will serve to convey to us some notion, though a feeble one, of that rivalry to the empire under which the Christian Church not only propagated its doctrine, but unfolded its government.

By the time of Constantine every city and town over the immense Roman confederacy had a bishop, whose authority was as completely a magistracy (ἀρχή) as that of a civil or military officer under the emperor. Origen, indeed, draws an instructive parallel between the bishop and the prefect of a city. But this authority rested upon the spontaneous obedience of a Christian people. In no case had it legal support. That is saying little. Its existence was a matter of jealousy to every civil officer among those who were not Christians with whom it came in contact. No more certain proof that the episcopal authority was the result of a power which the

Christians themselves freely acknowledged can even be desired than this jealousy which it excited in those who were outside. Consider a moment its uniformity from this standing-point. It was not established partially, but everywhere. Had there been any usurpation of episcopal over presbyteral authority, the victory of the bishop could not have taken place everywhere. Such an authority, to be everywhere, must have come from a power which was everywhere recognised by Christians as decisive and supreme; as an ordinance, in fact, of the Apostles. We do not need an historical record of this, though such exists[1]—the fact is more than any record of it. Again, as regards the civil power, the known subjection of Christians to such an officer as their own bishop, deriving his authority from a consecration bestowed in the Christian society itself, was calculated to make it much more difficult for them to live unmolested among the heathen than if no such officer existed. In fact we have, in the martyrdom of St. Ignatius of Antioch, an instance of the wrath which his dignity awakened in Trajan. If that most able, cautious, and temperate of Roman emperors—who cited the spirit of his age as opposed to cruelty, just as if he had lived in the nineteenth century—could have seen his empire covered with a network of bishops in closest union and correspondence with each other! Would it not have moved him to attempt their extermination in mass? The successor who took his name *did* see this a

---

[1] As in the Epistle of St. Clement, those of St. Ignatius, in St. Irenæus, Tertullian, and St. Cyprian.

hundred and fifty years later, and did vow extermination; but the providence of God did not allow him to execute it.

We are, then, entitled to consider the state of persecution under which the Christian Episcopate arose and spread itself everywhere with a uniform and well-defined authority, as a certain proof that its institution was legitimate and unquestionable according to the principles which ruled the Christian people. It sprung from something which their convictions and their feelings acknowledged. It increased the enmity of the empire to them during a long period in which other causes rendered that enmity persevering and relentless. It added a hostile government to a hostile doctrine for the increase of hatred in the minds of the heathen. The stress of every persecution fell upon the officers of the Christian Church in proportion to the degree of their dignity.

But now the proof for the legitimacy of the episcopal order derived from its establishment everywhere during the period of persecution, forcible as it is, is far exceeded by the same proof when applied to the Primacy. The function of every bishop as a local governor, as chief of the Christian worship, as teacher of its people, as ruling the daily spiritual life in a city, was offensive to the heathen power, thought, and feeling; but the special function of St. Peter's See at Rome in those three particulars was a subject of intense dislike to the Roman State. Every act of this spiritual government had to take place in the face of this heathen jealousy. Certainly it could only be practised upon a willing community. The notion of a fictitious or an usurping Primacy growing up in these three centuries is utterly incompatible with the whole condition of things which then surrounded Christians. The heathen State proscribed them altogether—their doctrine, their worship, their manner of life. It objected to their withdrawal from secular employments. No doubt it was some time before the rulers of Rome thought of them at all as bound together in a wide extending *polity;* but when they came to the perception of this, they would be most prone to fasten the charge of treason upon it, and it should never be forgotten by Christians that this was the original charge for which our Lord suffered. But most of all that the Christians should have in Rome itself one to whom they looked up as their chief bishop would be to every one zealous for the maintenance of Roman power and sovereignty what it seemed in the eyes of Decius. Within the decade in which those words recorded by St. Cyprian were spoken by Decius, though he soon himself ceased to reign, five Popes suffered martyrdom. Pope Fabian having issued a letter against a criminal bishop, was executed by Decius in 250. So fierce was the persecution that the Roman See remained vacant eighteen months. This was the occasion on which the emperor denounced the appointment of a successor. In spite of this Pope Cornelius, descended from one of the noblest families in Rome, who had passed through all the offices of the church in gradation, was unanimously elected. In 252 the emperor Gallus banished him to Cività Vecchia, where he was martyred the 14th September, 252. The next Pope, Lucius, was banished in 253 and then martyred. The following Pope, Stephen, maintained, according to his contemporary, Dionysius of Alexandria, the ancient renown of his Chair in providing for the spiritual and temporal wants of the furthest churches. At the instance of Cyprian, he brought back peace in the church of Arles by deposing the schismatical bishop Marcian. He restored the Spanish bishop, Basilides, to his see, though in this case he was, as Cyprian thought, deceived by him. In the full consciousness of his Primacy and appealing to his descent from Peter, he maintained the Roman tradition as to baptism against the resistance of the bishops in Asia Minor and Africa. After four years he too died a martyr in 257. On the 6th of August, 258, his successor, Xystus II., followed him. A troop of heathen soldiers seized him as he was offering the Holy Sacrifice in the catacomb of Prætextatus, and beheaded him in his episcopal chair together with four of his deacons, and the Roman See remained vacant until July 21, 259.[1]

That is a leaf taken from the history of ten years in the Church's life at the middle of the third century. These five Popes, as many before and many after them, exercised their jurisdiction at the cost of their lives. But the acts by which they exercised it; the letters by which they deposed one bishop and re-established another in distant Gaul and Spain; the authority by which

---

[1] The preceding narrative is drawn from Hergenröther, K.-g., i. 199-200.

the very next Pontiff, Dionysius of Rome, called on his contemporary, Dionysius of Alexandria, to make clear his faith on the subject of the Blessed Trinity; these, and a great number of such acts, how could they take effect at all in a community unrecognised by Roman law, and often outlawed by it, save through the willing, the devoted obedience of the Christians to whom they were addressed. A messenger of the Roman church, whether priest, or deacon, or subdeacon, or lector, or acolyte, carried such mandates into distant lands, in the civil power's despite, and they were listened to and obeyed.

We have seen how Heraclas, bishop of Alexandria, was in virtue of the discipline which prevailed in the Alexandrine patriarchate[1] able to depose a bishop for disobedience to his directions. His successor some twenty years later, Dionysius, a man of high distinction, was a personal friend of the Roman bishop Dionysius, who followed next the five martyr Popes. He was however accused to the Pope of error in doctrine, and was called upon by the Pope for his answer, which was heard before a Roman Council. The patriarch corrected certain expressions, and the papal judgment still existing is said to exhibit such clearness and distinctness, such an accordance with faith and with science, as to make sensible the loss we have sustained in not possessing in general the judgments made by the Popes from

---

[1] This is two hundred years before that title was given to the bishop. The power long preceded the name, which dates from the Council of Chalcedon.

the time of St. Clement to the end of the persecution.[1] Pope Dionysius likewise consoled by letter the Christians in Cappadocia who had been sorely tried by barbarian irruptions. St. Basil, a hundred years later, bore witness how the Popes had ever supported the Orientals by their letters, and that his church of Cæsarea preserved in grateful remembrance that writing of St. Dionysius.

As all particulars regarding the preaching and acts of nine out of the twelve Apostles are wanting, so we have nothing like a continuous history of the acts of Popes from the death of St. Peter to the termination of the time of persecution. But what we see is the emergence at the end of this time of a power which the whole hierarchy recognises, to which no beginning can be given short of St. Peter himself; no warrant for its existence assigned save the authority given to him by our Lord. A power which in consequence of its own nature the heathen State would regard with the utmost jealousy. A power such as, in consequence of that same nature, the bishops of great cities would be tempted to regard with rivalry, if it had not been planted in the Christian mind from the beginning by Him who alone could originate it. Now, as to those without, we see that as soon as the heathen sovereign acknowledges the Church, he acknowledges its chief hierarch. And as to those within, the great Western Council of Arles, in the first year after the peace of the Church, speaks to

---

[1] Cardinal Newman's *Causes of the Rise and Successes of Arianism*, p. 282. " It is a great misfortune to us that we have not had preserved to us the dogmatic utterances of the ante-Nicene Popes," &c.

him with the utmost deference as the holder of the greater complexes of dioceses governed by the chief officers of State, and requests him to transmit their canons to the several bishops in virtue of his authority. Therefore the joint testimony from without and from within during the time of persecution and at the moment of its cessation is sufficient to prove that it was what it professed to be, the dignity conferred by our Lord on St. Peter for the maintenance of His kingdom on earth.

And here we must note another mark of the perfect legitimacy which this hierarchy presents to us in all its gradations up to the supreme throne of Peter at its head. This is the fixity and definiteness of functions in the bishop, the presbyter, the deacon, and in the inferior ranks of the clergy which formed as it were the substructure of the diaconate. It was spread, as we have often noted, among a vast variety of peoples and races, but it did not vary with the variations of their temperaments. The stable Roman, the fanatic Egyptian, the versatile Syrian, the fervid African, the unsettled barbarian, received alike the same government; the Christian priest was one in all; the Christian bishop ruled on the same lines his particular flock, whether he was a Greek, like Athanasius, or a descendant of the noblest Roman gens, like Cornelius, or a rhetorician of Carthage, like Cyprian, or a slave who once escaped from his master, like that Onesimus for whom the Apostle condescended to beg pardon. It is especially in the first three centuries that we see the spirit of the original institution, before court favour had made time-servers of any bishops, before ambition could be thought to have assaulted its higher ranks. There could not have been an Eusebius until there was a Constantine.

Now, in the period which closes with the Nicene Council, we find the hierarchy complete in all its parts, as it was born from the womb of the Roman See, and grew up to its full stature. A letter addressed by St. Leo to no less a person than the patriarch of Alexandria, bishop of the Church's second see, seems to me to give a lucid statement of the principle as well as the practice which effected this great work. The occasion is the ordering that the making of priests and deacons should take place on Sunday, according to the custom of the Roman church. The letter[1] runs: " Leo the Bishop to Dioscorus, bishop of the Alexandrine church, greeting.—Conference with one who is both Father and Brother is bound to be most acceptable to your Holiness, and to be received by you in the same temper with which you perceive it to proceed from us. For it is our duty to have one feeling and action, that, as we read, one heart and one mind may be shewn in us. For inasmuch as most blessed Peter received the Apostolic Principate from the Lord, and the Roman church abides in what he instituted, it is impious to believe that his holy disciple Mark, who first ruled the church of Alexandria, formed on any other rules the decrees which he handed down to his successors: since beyond doubt there was one spirit in the disciple and the master, drawn from the same fountain of grace; nor

[1] St. Leo, Ep. ix.

could he who was ordained hand anything down save what he had received from his ordainer. We therefore do not allow[1] that, confessing ourselves to be of one body and faith, we should have any discrepancy, and that the institutions of the master should be one and those of the disciple be other. The rule therefore which we know to have been observed with great care by our Fathers, it is our will should be maintained also by you.[2] For besides the authority of custom, which we know to proceed from apostolic teaching, the Holy Scripture also manifests it. We therefore with care and kindness admonish you, that you take pains not to neglect what has become fixed in our custom as derived from the form of paternal tradition, that so we may entirely agree both in our faith and in our acts. We have therefore given this letter to our Son, the presbyter Posidonius, on his return to carry to you. He has frequently been present at our processions and ordinations, and in his many missions to us has recognised how we hold to the apostolic authority in all things."

Now that which St. Leo here records in various expressions, as that "one spirit of the disciple (St. Mark) and the master (St. Peter) drawn from the same fountain of grace," "the institutions of the master," "the rule observed with great care by our Fathers," "the authority of custom which we know to proceed from apostolic teaching," "what has become fixed in our custom as derived from the form of paternal tradition," "the holding to the apostolic authority in all things "—

---

[1] Non ergo patimur. [2] A vobis quoque volumus custodiri.

all this denotes one thing, a living tradition respecting the whole Christian doctrine, government, and practice deposited by Peter in the Roman church, which each bishop received and handed down in turn, and from which he drew as the emergency arose what sufficed for every occasion. The whole of this rested upon the fact that " Peter received the Apostolic Principate from the Lord ". And it was notorious to the whole Church that he had so received it, or the warning would have been addressed in vain to an Eastern bishop. But the bishop of Alexandria knew well enough that his own authority over the metropolitans and bishops of his patriarchate, nay, his episcopal authority itself, rested on the same basis : the basis of an unvarying custom handed down from the Apostles.

But this principle of unswerving tradition, derived from the Principate of Peter deposited in the Roman church, has been set forth by one of his predecessors in the year 416, that is, twenty-four years before the accession of St. Leo, with at least equal explicitness. Nor is it irrelevant to remark that it was that bishop of Rome in whose pontificate the heathen majesty of Rome was first violated by the capture of the Queen of Nations under Alaric, a northern barbarian. St. Innocent, writing to a bishop, says,[1] " If the priests of the Lord had the will to preserve entire the institutions of the Church, as they are handed down from the

[1] Innocent I., Ep. xxv., *Sacerdotes Domini*. At this time this term, so strongly individualising the one in each diocese who offered the Divine Sacrifice for all, and dispensed the Divine Food in the Mother-Church, indicated the bishop by his great function.

blessed Apostles, there would be no diversity, no variation in the ranks and consecrations themselves. But while every one thinks himself bound to hold not what has been handed down, but what he likes best, from this, in different places or churches, different rites seem to be held or celebrated. And thus scandal arises in the population, who, in their ignorance that what has been handed down from ancient times has been corrupted by human presumption, suppose either that the churches do not agree with each other, or that this contradiction has been introduced by Apostles or apostolic men. For who is ignorant, or does not lay to mind, that what was delivered by Peter, Prince of the Apostles, to the Roman church, and is maintained to this very time, ought to be kept by all; and that nothing should be superinduced, or admitted, which has no authority, or seems to claim a precedent elsewhere. Especially since it is notorious that no one has established churches over all Italy, the Gauls, the Spains, Africa and Sicily, and the interjacent islands, save those whom the venerable Apostle Peter, or his successors, have appointed bishops. Or let them refer to history if in these provinces any other Apostle is found or recorded to have taught. If no such record can be found it is their duty to follow that practice which the Roman church maintains; the church from which there is no doubt that they received their beginning. Otherwise, in their willingness to pursue strange claims, they may appear to surrender the fountain-head of their institutions."[1]

---

[1] Ne dum peregrinis assertionibus student, caput institutionum videantur omittere.

If only these two passages from authorities so venerable as the first Innocent and the first Leo be considered, I think that the whole basis on which the Church of the first three centuries rested will be discerned.

But further, only seventeen years after the Nicene Council, A.D. 342, when the Western empire was ruled by Constans, and the Eastern by Constantius, a letter was addressed by Pope Julius to the Eusebian bishops at Antioch, which Athanasius has preserved for us and incorporated into his works. The Pope, from beginning to end of this great letter, refers to a certain rule of tradition and custom as guiding his own actions and the actions of those who had gone before him. Thus he remarks that the Eusebian bishops had sent to him a priest and two deacons to defend their conduct towards Athanasius. On his part Athanasius had sent members of his own clergy. The one and the other had been heard in Council, and the clergy from Alexandria had refuted those from Antioch. Whereupon the Antiochene legates had besought the Pope to convene a Council to consider these matters afresh. "If they had not done so,"[1] says the Pope, "but I had of my own accord advised a Council to detect those who had written to us, for the sake of the brethren who had complained that they had suffered injustice, my advice would have been reasonable and just. For it is according to the order of the Church and agreeable to God." The brethren here spoken of were chief bishops of the

[1] Julii, Ep. 1. The parts quoted are in sections 22, 33, 29, 35. St. Athanasius's *Apologia contra Arianos.*

Church in the East, whom the Arianising party was persecuting: Athanasius of Alexandria, Paul of Constantinople, Marcellus of Ancyra, and a great many others, from Thrace, Syria, Phœnicia, and Palestine, who had taken refuge at Rome and appealed to the Pope. The Pope here declares that he was in his right, according to the order of the Church, in requiring their cause to be reheard. That is, he attributes to the existing rule of the Church, coming down from the Apostles, that right belonging to himself, which in the next year in the Council of Sardica was expressly decreed at the instance of Hosius, to honour the memory of the Apostle Peter.[1]

This letter must be read and studied from beginning to end, in order to see how perpetual is the reference in it to the settled order of the Church as a rule coming down from antiquity, unwritten but ever acted upon. And in this we see a faithful picture of the Church's original constitution at the time when Eusebius of Nicomedia with the support of Constantius, now an Eastern emperor and practised upon by Eastern jealousies, began to break in upon it. It was a living government, not a paper charter. And so it had a reserve power for every difficulty which might arise.

Accordingly in this letter Pope Julius appears not merely the supporter of some persecuted bishops, but the upbearer of the true faith, the protector of the Church's order, the avenger of her laws. He tests the individual's belief by comparison with the undisturbed fountain-head, with the tradition of the Apostles, with

[1] Council of Sardes, Third Canon.

the sentence of the Nicene Fathers. Aud so we see communion with him to be the surest sign of communion with Christ, and that he who has it not is likewise severed from charity.[1]

Thus we see by this letter that the Pope, in virtue of his Primacy, had invited Athanasius, bishop of the Church's second see, and standing at the head of the hundred bishops of Egypt, Lybia, and Pentapolis, when oppressed by the bishops at Antioch, the instruments of a court intrigue, to come to Rome and defend himself. "What was it my duty to do," says the Pope, "or what does the ecclesiastical rule require? except not to condemn the man, but to hold him for a bishop, as we did. For besides all this he stayed here eighteen months, awaiting your coming, or those who were willing to come. And his presence shamed us, for he would not have been here, but for confidence in his cause. And he came not of himself, but cited by us."

If this "ecclesiastical rule," thus perpetually appealed to as the living law of the Church, had come down to us complete in a written form, the early discipline of the Church could not have been disputed as it has been by those whose minds have been nurtured in heresy and schism. Here, with regard to the second see of the Church in particular, the dependence upon Rome, in case the doctrine or conduct of its bishop is impugned, is specified as part of the ancient rule of the Church.

"If any fault had been committed," writes the Pope, "judgment should have been made, not thus, but

[1] Riffel, p. 562. Paragraph translated.

according to the rule of the Church. We should all have been written to" (he speaks as the head of the Council at Rome, for though the Pope wrote in his single name, everything which he wrote had passed in Council, which he ratified with his authority), "that thus justice might have been decreed by all. For it was bishops who were sufferers, and not ordinary churches either, but those which Apostles themselves had personally directed. But especially in the case of the church of Alexandria why did you not write to us? Know you not that this was the custom, first that we should be written to, and that the right judgment should go forth from this place? If any such thing was suspected against the bishop there, it behoved to write to the church here. But now, not having informed us, but having done themselves what they chose, they would have us who have taken no part in the condemnation to share their decision. Not such are the statutes of Paul; not so have our Fathers delivered down to us. This is another form, a novel mode of procedure. I beseech you bear this with good will. I write what is for the general good. For what we have received from the blessed Apostle Peter, this I also declare to you. And I would not have written deeming that this was manifest to all, save that what has happened has disturbed us. Bishops are seized upon and banished'; others are intruded from a distance; others are plotted against; so that their people grieve over those who are taken away, are compelled to take the intruders, may not ask for those whom they would like, and have to take those whom they dislike."

It is remarkable that the series of Papal letters from that of Pope Clement I. at the end of the first century to this of Pope Julius I. has been lost to us, as well as many other documents during the period of persecution. It is only the loss of these Decretal Letters which has permitted men to close their eyes to the subsistence of the Church as an historic fact in the form of a definite polity proceeding on a uniform plan: that is, the *rule* followed by the Apostles, the fountain-head of which lay in the Principate left by St. Peter in Rome. One letter of the third Pope from St. Peter, his fellow-worker St. Clement,[1] providentially remains as lately recovered in its entirety, to bear witness to this; and it lays down the propagation of churches by episcopal descent from the Apostles, who were simply carrying out therein the command of their Lord, as absolutely as the letters just quoted of St. Julius, St. Innocent, St. Boniface, and St. Leo refer their own conduct to the rule of the Church existing among them as inherited from St. Peter: and this letter of St. Clement likewise asserts and exercises the Roman Principate in the defence and judgment of bishops as distinctly as they do, while it dates from the lifetime of St. John the Evangelist.

If anything can add to the intrinsic force of this letter as a living witness of the Church's constitution at the time of the Nicene Council, and at the exact commencement of the division into separate governments of the East and West, it is the political

---

[1] The letter of St. Clement to the Corinthians; see especially sections 58, 59, 68.

circumstances of the times. The dearly prized unity wrought by Constantine was breaking up under his sons. The Eastern bishops were acting under the lead of Eusebius who had translated himself by the influence of the emperor Constantius from the See of Nicomedia to that of Constantinople, from which Paul, the lawful bishop, was banished. Constantius then held his court at Antioch, divided from his brother Constans, the Western emperor, by the strongest jealousy. Eusebius, the master spirit of the Arian faction, had already deposed Eustathius from Antioch, and Athanasius from Alexandria, and now moved the bishops at Antioch against the See of Rome, which was in the Western empire. The mild and dignified narration of the Pope in which he exhibits the highest prerogatives of his see as a place of refuge for the oppressed bishops of Eastern sees, and of the very highest rank, is the more telling because the ancient order of the Church appears in it as a matter of course. And he censures the illegal action of the bishops at the great Council of the Encœuia at Antioch as contrary to all that order which had come down to the Church from her foundation. He appeals to the statutes of Paul as household words, and to what he had received from the blessed Apostle Peter, which he deemed to be manifest to all, which only the extremity of the wrong done to Athanasius, Paul, and others forced him to cite.

The letter of St. Clement in A.D. 96, and the letter of St. Julius in A.D. 342, should be read together to judge adequately how they bridge over the intervening period, and unite the Primacy of the apostolic age with that of the fourth century, when the great age of persecution had passed over the Church.

Now, to return to the hierarchy as seen in action at the Nicene Council, an action which was to determine a controversy involving the very existence of the Church. I consider it to be complete, because it there represented the whole Church, and as a fact had been drawn out of that Apostolic Principate which had been received from St. Peter; and because, further, it was in all its gradations a fixed, legitimate, unvarying power, of which the Pope stood at the head, as careful not to lessen the respective rights which belonged to his brethren as to guard from infringement the "Principate" committed to himself—a Principate which preceded the body it was to govern, both in principle and in fact.

Thus the whole hierarchy was formed on a complete idea, which cannot be more tersely expressed than in the words of St. Leo applied to St. Peter and St. Mark: "There was one spirit of the disciple and the master drawn from the same fountain of grace".

It follows, from what has just been said, that while "the Apostolic Principate received by Peter from the Lord" was the root and womb of the whole hierarchy, not only in principle but in historic fact, the exercise of that Primacy was during these three centuries —as it has continued to be in every succeeding century —proportionate to the state and condition of the Church. Its action during the ages of persecution will be different from its action in a subsequent age, when the Roman State has acknowledged the Church; or again, from another period, when the whole order of civil government has been interfered with by the wandering of the nations.[1] Not everything which follows from the idea of the Primacy was actually drawn out in the first centuries, just as not every work which the Church was to do had then been actually done. An Episcopate in which the three great Sees of Peter exercised a sort of triumvirate[2] in the Church was sufficient for the needs of those times. Until the emperor had bowed his head to the Church there was no danger of bishops dwelling at his court, entering into intrigues for his favour, countenancing the introduction of spiritual privileges for the exaltation of a particular church which was not grounded on descent from Peter, but on proximity to the emperor. The Primacy grew with the Church. Nor were the Popes themselves careful to draw out all that was contained in their Primacy before the time which needed each particular exertion of it. In the great order of government, at the head of which they stood, the bishops throughout the world had, as a rule, been constant in their faith. Penetrated as they were with the sense of the divine origin of the magistracy which each of them administered, they were not tempted to encroach upon the territory of their brethren. They had enough to do to live in any peace with the pagan empire. The rules of their forefathers were scrupulously followed by them. These rules were their only charter. We have just seen how St. Leo describes the strict maintenance of apostolic tradition at Rome, as Pope

[1] Hergenröther, K.-g., i., p. 197, sec. 229.   [2] Idem, *Photius*, i., p. 30.

Julius had done a hundred years before him ; as Pope Clement I. had done at the end of the first century. There can be no doubt that such was the temper of the various churches throughout the world, while the world stood in open opposition. The band of union was not yet disturbed by ambitious struggles of individual bishops. A simple tone of brotherly affection prevailed in the letters of the foremost bishops, which was only endangered when, as in the case of Cyprian, they thought doctrine was in peril or the settled order of the Church disturbed. The divisions were mostly local, within a particular church, but did not sever churches from churches. We find no single instance which succeeded of a contest arising from a bishop exalting himself beyond the range of his jurisdiction, as was the case afterwards ; no hankering and hunting after external rank, such as formed the subject of lamentation so often from the fourth century onwards. Thus Paul of Samosata, besides his doctrinal error, was a strange appearance in the Episcopate of his day,[1] ill-omen as he was nevertheless of so many oriental bishops in the future.

The Popes neither found occasion nor duty to interfere with an order thus generally observed by their brethren. A supervision of the churches beyond their own patriarchate through their immediate superiors was sufficient, especially when the exercise of their authority in the patriarchate and at Rome itself was accompanied with the risk of life. Thus it is quite possible that at

[1] Compare Hergenröther, K.-g., i. 197, and *Photius*, i. 80-1, from whom the preceding page is drawn.

the time of the Nicene Council no individual bishop at a distance from Rome realised the power that was latent in St. Peter's See, because there had not been occasions to call it forth. The extent of that "superior Principate" to which St. Irenæus bore witness, and which St. Augustine[1] declared to have existed always in the Apostolic See, had not yet been defined, save by those words of the great Shepherd Himself, Feed my lambs, be Shepherd over my sheep: definition enough for the age of martyrdom and confessorship. The times were far distant, and the circumstances far different, when it would appear as "a thousand Bishops rolled into one" to meet the barbarism of half converted kings, and subdue the secular spirit of feudal bishops.

Thus we have to bear in mind in this first period of the Church, as in every succeeding period, the proportion between the Primacy and that kingdom over which it is set. St. Peter's headship over the Apostles was not less real, because they were guided by the Holy Spirit as well as he; rather the full force of St. Jerome's remark must be considered: If a head was required among those Twelve to avoid schism, divinely guided and inspired as they were, how much more when that College of Twelve was dilated to the Episcopate, whose members were *not* divinely guided as individuals save when they acted together in the unity of the Body, and *not* inspired, but only guaranteed the maintenance of what they had received by persevering in that unity.

[1] St. Aug., Ep. xlii.: "Romanæ Ecclesiæ in qua semper Apostolicæ Cathedræ viguit principatus".

Nay, we may apply the analogy of human government here, which suffices for the occasion. The polity of the city of Romulus was one thing and the polity of the empire of Augustus another: and the authority needed to govern the latter was greater, more peremptory, and more concentred than that which sufficed for the former. The condition is invariable in earthly kingdoms that concentred authority is required to maintain ample and intricate dominion; and as the one divine kingdom is still composed of men, how can it be otherwise in this respect?

I think if this consideration be fully pondered, all that species of objections to the proof of the Principate inherited from St. Peter, which has been symbolized by allowing a Primacy existing from the beginning and exercised in the first three centuries, yet refusing a Supremacy as a growth of a supposed usurpation from ambitious motives, in later times, will fall to the ground.

On the other hand, it is impossible to understand the history of the Church at all, unless we bear in mind the force of the three divine words spoken to Peter in the presence of his brethren, and living in the hearts and minds of all generations in the Church. "Who is ignorant," wrote St. Gregory the Great to the patriarch of Alexandria, "that the holy Church was established on the solidity of the Prince of the Apostles?" But here St. Gregory is only repeating the testimony of his predecessors for hundreds of years, who used the same language, and appealed to the same fact as notorious to all. If these three words be taken away, not merely from the text of three gospels, but from the consciousness of the Christian Church diffused through the world, then the conduct of the Church, her councils, and her acts for so many generations, are deprived of their support. It is like taking away the central pillar on which the whole roof of the chapterhouse rests. The only result to the student of history will be the effacement from his mind of the divine kingdom altogether. For with the idea contained in these great words of our Lord, who, as Redeemer, prefigures and creates His kingdom, the kingdom stands or falls with all its mass of wondrous deeds and superhuman sufferings, which without the idea of the kingdom have no reward nor even any meaning, and there remains no reason for that series of lives innumerable sustained above the standard of natural virtue, the least of which is the result of a power which the whole world cannot give.

But it must be remembered also, that in these three centuries the power existed in the Church's Principate to do all which the Church needed to do; and foremost among these things is the maintenance of its divine faith and doctrine amid all the dangers of material persecution and spiritual seduction. No kingdom of thought, above all a kingdom which dealt with the most awful problems that can touch the mind of man, could subsist for one generation, not to speak of ten, without the power to determine irrevocably and infallibly what was true and what false in its own belief. That power was exercised in the Nicene Council on a subject not exceeded in importance by any other, the Godhead of its Founder. No controversy which has been raised in the nineteen centuries goes more thoroughly down to the root of all belief than this, whether the Saviour of the world was God Himself or a creature. The Nicene Council determined that controversy. And the vast authority of the Roman See is seen not the least in the fact that its assent to the decision of the Council alone made it ecumenical. For while the 318 Fathers who sat in the Council fairly represented the various provinces of the Church in the East, five only of the whole number were Western bishops. These were Hosius of Corduba, Cæcilian of Carthage, Marcus in Calabria, Nicasius of Dijon, Domnus of Stridon in Pannonia. There were also two Roman Priests, Vitus and Vicentius, who together with Hosius were legates of Pope Sylvester, and their signatures are found in the lists of subscriptions next to that of Hosius and before those of the bishops of Alexandria and Antioch. And yet the decision of the Council was received without question by all the bishops of the West because the authority of the Pope transmitted it to them. Through all after ages it was esteemed the great and incomparable Council, and its decision accepted as the decision of the Church, for which no other reason can be assigned save the Principate of the Roman See, raising its character from an Eastern to an ecumenical Council.[1]

[1] Hefele, i. 47: "Aus dem Gesagten erhellt auch, dass und in wiefern ein allgemeines Concil der Bestätigung durch den Papst bedürfe. Solange nämlich der Papst die Beschlüsse einer noch so zahlreichen Synode nicht genehmigt hat und ihnen nicht beigetreten ist, so lange sind dieselben noch nicht Beschlüsse eines allgemeinen Concils, indem ja ein solches in der Trennung von dem Papste nicht möglich ist."

Thus we have seen that the Primacy of St. Peter's successor, as it was the foundation, so it was the keystone of the whole hierarchy; as it was the beginning, so also the crown and termination of the whole building. It was, as a matter of fact, what St. Cyprian called it, the "root and womb" of the Church, and this in a twofold respect, both as the ordinary power of the bishop had its prototype and starting-point in the person of Peter, and as the gradation of ranks in the Episcopate, in which precisely the hierarchy consists, was an emanation of the Primacy. It was owing to this "origin of unity" that the propagation of the Church went on, not at haphazard and without counsel, but with a settled design and order. Again, through the whole three centuries it was the bond, so that however the Episcopate might increase in material extent, it remained tied together in the Primacy, and the origin of unity subserved its maintenance. And this bond of the Primacy was seen in "the one See of the one Peter"[1] existing in the only three original patriarchates. And further, at the conclusion, in a period of time so momentous as that in which the spiritual and civil powers were entering upon a course of joint-action after centuries of strife, in this most remarkable decision of the Council when all the provinces of the Church for the first time came together as well as in previous controversies where they only assembled partially in local synods, it was the crown which set the seal on their proceedings. For, from the beginning,

---

[1] St. Gregory the Great quoted above, p. 53.

it had been a part of "the ecclesiastical rule"[1] that without the assent and consent of the first bishop of the Church the votes of an assembly of his brethren, however numerous, remained without force as a decision of the Church. The power of confirmation alone made them one structure.[2] And in every case of doctrine this power is of supreme importance. But in such a case as the heresy of Arius, the Church without such a power would have been a helpless prey to an error overthrowing Christianity itself.

To be the root, the bond, and the crown of government in the Church are three distinct things. The concentration of three such privileges in a single person, and their maintenance in that person from generation to generation, shew a marvellous exhibition of divine power. The three so united cumulate each other's force, they run into and complete each other, so that, distinct as they are in idea, in practice they cannot be severed from each other.

They were necessary for the building which was to be erected. It is one of the marvels of divine action in the world's history that such a building was constructed in troublous times, in the bosom of a society exposed to incessant persecution. This is a revelation of strength out of weakness, which the more it is contemplated the

---

[1] I do not suppose this "Rule," so often referred to by the Popes, to have been made by any Council, or to have been written. It was a principle of life deposited in the bosom of the Church, and descending from the action observed by the Apostles.

[2] *Compages*, the word so often used to express the whole mass of the Church: as used by Tacitus for the Roman empire itself.

more it creates astonishment. The Providence of God, before whom all things lay, not as tossed about in the turbid current of human struggles, but as the unrolling of a distinct, unfaltering purpose, led St. Peter to Rome at the moment when that queen of cities was the centre and the soul of a vast empire. The Providence is specially shewn in choosing the centre of human power, as the centre likewise from which a divine action should be carried out. The high-priesthood of the Church is set up in Cæsar's capital; neither the great city of the East, nor the great city of Egypt, would have been suitable for it; nor the soft Ionian capital of Diana; nor Athene's city, the parent of Greek culture. The city which had no peer in human grandeur had that grandeur made use of for a superhuman design. But the choice of Rome would have been fruitless unless Peter had been sent thither, charged with the divine powers stored up in the commission of the Eternal Shepherd to feed His flock. Two things utterly dissimilar were joined together: the human majesty of the seat of empire, the divine majesty of the Christian Pontificate. The latter alone enabled him to use the authority of the Queen-City as if it had been the pedestal on which he set his chair of teaching. He himself tended that flock from the beginning; he tended it there in weakness and obscurity. In this conduct St. Peter is the image of those successors, thirty-two in number, who followed him in his chair down to Pope Sylvester. In Rome they taught and suffered: five, as we have seen, once suffered martyrdom consecutively in eight years. And of the whole number half were martyrs. From Rome they sent their messengers through all the West, so that there was not a bishop's see which had not been founded by Peter or one of his successors. In this they were repeating Peter's example, since he had no sooner set foot in Rome than he founded the great Alexandrian patriarchate in his son Mark, and in doing this created the most perfect specimen of hierarchical discipline after Rome itself. But before he came to Rome he had founded the bishop's chair in Antioch, and become himself the first in that line of bishops who were to preside over the great oriental prefecture, a region in which it is probable that the Church flourished more than in any other during these first centuries. In Rome itself, in less than two centuries after St. Peter, the Church he planted had grown to such strength and in such order that the great general who had seized on the empire feared the appointment of its bishop more than the insurrection of a rival, because, no doubt, he who possessed among his titles that of sovereign Pontiff, recognised[1] in the Pope's universal jurisdiction over the Christian brotherhood a real competitor, so far as regarded his spiritual supremacy. One after another these Popes laboured, ruled, and died, and often a dim recess in the catacombs was the place where they offered the Holy Sacrifice, and where one of them at least is recorded to have been martyred in the act. In the meantime the empire of Augustus had culminated in Trajan; had begun to verge downwards after Marcus

[1] Bossuet.

Aurelius; had been saved from dissolution only by the courage of Decius and the military emperors who succeeded him. By the time of Diocletian,[1] Rome had ceased to be the seat of the emperors who ruled in its name, but were no longer chosen either by its people or its senate, and no longer even dated their edicts from its walls. Then began the last and fiercest persecution, and when it is passed, the Pope, emerging from the catacombs, receives from a willing emperor his Lateran Palace, that he may make it, by residing there, the seat and centre of ecclesiastical authority, and is found to stand at the head of a religious kingdom, and to occupy in it a position analogous to that of the emperor in the civil order. Truly a wonderful sequence and contrast. Our Lord chose to be born under Augustus as the empire was beginning; to die on Calvary by the authority of its second ruler; to crucify his first Vicegerent under the last scion of the family of Augustus; to destroy the deicide city, and break for his Church the mould of Judaism when his Apostles had preached his faith during forty years through the Roman world and beyond it; and then after two hundred and fifty years to draw his kingdom out of the catacombs, when its structure, having spread itself over the whole Roman dominion, shewed every proof of youth and strength before the waning empire. The last great military chief but one holding the concentrated authority of that vast empire, yet dreading that it would break to pieces under his hands, approached the kingdom of the despised and

[1] See Reumont, i. 534-543.

hated Galilean, seeking truth from its doctrine and unity from its discipline for his fainting peoples, and bowed his head before the voice of its bishops assembled in council as if it were the voice of God.

Thus, in three centuries, Jesus Christ made a kingdom for Himself by the action of St. Peter's See, and fixed the spiritual sovereign in Rome the head of heathendom, in the person of a Galilean fisherman, from whom the sovereignty descended, and as the Rome of the Cæsars waned, and the successors of Augustus no longer occupied his palace, the Rome of Christ grew, until its dominion was wider in virtue of His religion than it had ever been by the power of its armies, a dominion which it owed to the Apostolic Principate given to St. Peter. The grant made to Peter in the three great words had been realised and embodied in the actual history of the first three centuries.

But why do we say these things with poor words of our own in the nineteenth century, when, in the middle of the fifth, they have already been spoken in Rome itself by the great voice of him whom the ancient Church in her largest Council saluted as " the head of the members," "entrusted by the Saviour Himself with the guardianship of the vine". Can any voice equal in force his who drew out to the world of the old civilization, as it was on the point of perishing, the triumph of the Cross, a Roman in the midst of Romans, a successor of St. Peter upon the feast of his martyrdom, the chief bishop in the assembly of his brethren? He saw the line of the great Theodosius still sitting on the thrones

of the East and West, and he saw it descend from both.
He saw the capital of the world yet standing in the
glory of its buildings unimpaired,[1] and was soon himself
to save it from falling under Attila, and to break its fall
under Genseric. He addressed it, the not yet discovered head of the world-empire, which had already
become a sacerdotal city instead of an emperor's residence. And what he said is no less than the history of
three hundred years drawn by the inheritor of Peter's
authority in the very centre of its action.

On the 29th June, the Feast of St. Peter and St.
Paul, shortly before the fourth General Council, St. Leo
the Great spoke the following words to the bishops of
Italy, who were specially summoned on these anniversaries:—" In all sacred solemnities the whole world
is partaker: and the affection due to the One Faith
requires that to commemorate what has been done for
the universal salvation should call forth a general joy.
But the festival of to-day is to be venerated with a
special exultation belonging to this city, besides the
reverence which it claims from the whole world. The
spot which has been glorified by the end of the chief
Apostles should have the chief place of joy on the day
of their martyrdom. For they, O Rome, are the men
through whom the light of Christ's gospel shone upon

---

[1] Of Rome in the fifth century, Gregorovius (i. 110) says: " Denn nun war das
Heidenthum in Rom völlig erlöschen; die Stadt war christlich, durchdrungen
vom Cultus der neuen Religion, von dem völlig ausgebildeben System der
kirchlichen Verwaltung beherrscht, an deren Spitz der hoch angesehene Bischof
stand. Aber dennoch sah Rom völlig heidnisch aus, seine architektorische
Pracht dauerte, seine zahllosen Monumente standen aufrecht."

thee, when she who was the mistress of error became the disciple of truth. They are thy holy Fathers and thy true Pastors, having with better and happier omens founded thee for a place in the heavenly kingdom, than those who laid the first stones of thy walls, of whom the one who gave thee thy name stained thee with a brother's blood. They it is who have advanced thee to this glory, that being made by the sacred See of St. Peter the head of the world, as a holy nation, a chosen people, a priestly and a royal city, thy rule might be wider through a divine religion than an earthly domination. For far as, crowned with many victories, thou hast stretched thy empire by land and sea, the struggle of warfare has wrought thee a smaller realm than the Christian peace.

"For God, who is good, and just, and all-mighty, who has never denied His mercy to the human race, and has ever drawn all men in general to the knowledge of Him by innumerable blessings, with a yet more secret purpose and a yet profounder affection, took pity on those who were wandering in voluntary blindness, and sinking ever downwards in sin, by the mission of His Word, equal and co-eternal with Himself. And He, being made flesh, united the divine nature to the human nature on such terms that His bending down to the lowest became our exaltation to the highest. Now the Divine Providence had prepared the Roman empire in order that the effect of this unutterable grace might be diffused through the whole world, and to this end extended it so far that its borders might touch upon all nations. For it was an admirable disposition of the divine work that many realms should be confederated in one empire, and that the rule of a single city should open up vast populations to the rapid proclamation of the faith. But this city, being ignorant of Him who had made its power, while its rule was nearly universal, was in servitude to the errors of all, and thought itself the seat of great religion because there was no falsehood which it rejected. Thus its deliverance through Christ was marvellous in proportion to that diabolical bondage in which it had been held.

"For when the twelve Apostles, having received, through the Holy Spirit, the power to speak all tongues, undertook to teach the gospel to the world by dividing among themselves its several territories, blessed Peter, the chief of the apostolic order, received for his lot the citadel of the Roman empire. The purpose of this was that the light of truth, revealed for the salvation of all peoples, might be more efficaciously diffused through the whole body of the world from its head. For where was the nation which would not then have countrymen in this city? Or what people would be ignorant of that which was taught at Rome? That one spot in which the errors of the whole world had been studiously collected and incorporated was the place in which to overthrow the opinions of philosophy, to dissolve the vanity of earthly wisdom, to explode the worship of devils, to destroy the whole mass of impiety lodged in the various sacrifices.

"This, then, is the city to which, most blessed Apostle

Peter, thou didst not fear to come, while the Apostle Paul, the fellow-heir of thy glory, was still occupied in the ordering of other churches. Thou enterest that forest of howling beasts, that ocean whose abyss was swept by storms, with more assurance than when thou didst walk the water. You who, in the house of Caiaphas, trembled at the voice of a serving-maid, do not fear Rome, the mistress of the world. Had Claudius less power than the judgment of Pilate, or Nero less cruelty than the rage of the Jews? The force of your affection overcame what there was reason to dread, nor would you endure to fear those whom you had promised to love. Doubtless you had already conceived that affection of fearless charity, when the love to our Lord which you professed was confirmed by the mystery of His question thrice repeated. Nor had you any other intention than, in feeding the sheep of Him whom you loved, to spend that nutriment which was your own support.

"But your confidence was increased by the signs of so many miracles, by the gifts of so many special favours, by the experience of so many virtues. You had already instructed populations of the circumcision, which had believed. You had already founded the church of Antioch, where the dignity of the Christian name first arose. You had instructed in the gospel laws Pontus, Galatia, Cappadocia, Asia, Bithynia. You could neither be doubtful of the success of your work, nor ignorant as to the age[1] which you would reach

---

[1] Alluding to the words, "When thou shalt be old thou shalt stretch forth thy hands, and another shall gird thee".—John xxi. 18.

when you bore the standard of Christ's cross before Rome's citadel, where the divine preordination had assured you beforehand both the rank [of your power and the glory of your passion.[1]

"In this your blessed colleague as Apostle, Paul, the vessel of election and the special teacher of the gentiles, meeting you, was associated with you at a time when all innocence, all modesty, all liberty was at the last gasp under Nero's empire. His rage, enkindled by the excess of every vice, hurried him to such a degree of madness, that he was the first to inflict a general persecution on the Christian name, as if the grace of God could be extinguished by the murder of saints. For to them it was the very greatest gain that the contempt of this dying life was the perception of eternal happiness. Precious, then, in the sight of the Lord is the death of His saints; nor can any kind of cruelty destroy the religion which is founded on the mystery of Christ's cross. The Church is not lessened but rather increased by persecutions, and the Lord's field clothes itself in a richer harvest when the grains which are buried singly spring up multiplied. Thus thousands of blessed martyrs proclaim the vast progeny which has grown out of those two illustrious germs of the divine seed. And they, in rivalry of the Apostles' triumphs, girdle our city with the far and wide flashing of their empurpled ranks, forming for it a single diadem composed of many jewels.

[1] Quo te divinis præordinationibus anteibant et honor potestatis et gloria passionis.

"And when we commemorate all the saints, we must have a general joy in this guardianship, which God has prepared for an example to us of patience and a confirmation of faith. But we have a right to greater exultation in the excellence of these Fathers whom the grace of God has advanced to such a height among all the members of the Church, as to make them like the light of the two eyes in that Body the Head of which is Christ. And on their merits and virtues, which surpass all power of specch, we should think there is no diversity and no separation, for in their election they were paired, in their labour they were alike, and in their end they were equal to each other."

No moral evidence is demonstrative, for, if it were, there would be no merit in faith any more than in seeing a mathematical truth. But if any will not accept as historical truth the work of St. Peter and St. Paul, here set forth by the chief bishop of the Christian Church in the very place where the knowledge of what they had done was a household word in every Christian home, it may safely be said that they resist evidence which would be accepted in any case wherein some motive foreign to the desire of the truth did not intervene.

CHAPTER IV.

CONSTANTINE AND THE CHURCH.

THE period of five generations, one hundred and fifty years, which begins with the Nicene Council in 325, and extends to the fall of the Western empire in 476, forms a great contrast in the history of the Church with the period which ended with that Council. As distinctly as the first period ends, another begins, and it dates from the Council, which is a most striking embodiment of the Church's work in the three centuries preceding it, while it is no less striking as the memorable event, new and unheard of before, the first meeting of the States-General of the Church, from which her subsequent history descends. Doctrine, government, the most varied action and suffering, the action and suffering of individuals, the action and suffering of masses, the heaving of a vast empire, the reciprocal movements of its provinces on each other, the Eastern jealousy of the West, and again the antagonism of the Grecian mind with the Roman, excited into new force by the momentous act of Constantine in founding Nova Roma on the banks of the Bosphorus, enter into this most varied history. Its complexity baffles all adequate portraiture.

But among many characteristics of this new era one may be taken as having throughout the whole of it a vast and permanent influence. Whereas the previous time had been a period of persecution by the State, this is a period of alliance with the State. What sort of an alliance it is and with what sort of a State, and what is the effect of it on the Church's constitution, and on her doctrine, these are subjects for our consideration in detail. But we may take this new relation of amity between the two great Powers—the Spiritual and the Temporal—as a sort of common root from which a number of branches diverge. These will have to be dealt with separately, and then the general result must be drawn from their connection with each other.

Let us first cast a glance back upon the state of things which preceded this new alliance: that is, the whole condition of the Church as to government and as to doctrine, while it was under heathen persecution. That heathen enmity at least assured to the Church a great practical autonomy. Perhaps what I mean by this word would be better expressed as the development of the Church's own principle of tradition, in that wide and large sense of living upon that which is handed down.[1] "A traditional system of theology consistent with, but independent of, Scripture, has existed in the Church from the apostolic age." And not only a traditional system of theology but of government. Now I mean by tradition the practical union of these two, doctrine and government, as seen in the daily habits of life, and

[1] Newman's *Arians*, p. 226.

as contained in great institutions; for instance, the sacraments, and all that concerns their practice, and in worship. From the first instant of her existence the Church was a polity; and the handing down of this polity, undisturbed by the meddling of the civil power, is the autonomy of which I speak as the special character of the Antenicene Church. For this polity was most truly a law to itself in this period: a law in government, in interpretation of Scripture, in the tradition of the whole unwritten code of thought and precept. Upon this tradition the whole fabric of faith as well as the whole order of government alike rested. The Church in fact was built on this one principle from its centre to its circumference; not upon anything written *alone:* though no doubt the Scriptures, both of the Old and the New Testament, formed a part of this tradition. But St. Athanasius, the great Father who above all others represents this tradition of the Antenicene Church, because of the time in which he lived, and the combat which he maintained, "ever exalts the theological sense over the words, whether sacred or ecclesiastical, which are its vehicle".[1] Thus he speaks in his encyclical letter of the year 341, addressed to all bishops: "Let every one lend his aid, as feeling that he is himself a sufferer, lest shortly the ecclesiastical canons and the faith of the Church be corrupted. For both are in danger, unless God shall speedily by your hands amend what has been done amiss, and the Church be avenged on her enemies. For

---

[1] *History of the Arians,* p. 226.

our canons and our forms were not given to the churches at the present day, but were wisely and safely transmitted to us from our forefathers. Neither had our faith its beginning at this time, but it came down to us from the Lord through His disciples."[1] St. Athanasius was at this time taking refuge with Pope Julius at Rome from the Arian attack directed by the court-bishops at Antioch upon the constitution which he thus describes. And he held the second of the three great sees of Peter, the fortresses in which this traditionary and unwritten constitution was most jealously guarded. But above all, and at the head of all, the See of Rome.

The statutes of St. Peter and St. Paul had been from the beginning the heirloom of the church at Rome: the remembrance of their acts had filled the whole city, and were household words to Christians during the three centuries which preceded Constantine:[2] and the first act of the great emperor was to erect a church to the Saviour in the imperial palace, which he had given for a habitation to the successor of Peter, and two churches to the two great Apostles whom he found in possession of the highest reverence as the patron saints of the city, the one as founder and first bishop of the church there, the other as the teacher of the Gentiles, who for two years had laboured in the nascent church, and was joined

---

[1] St. Athanasius, *Historical Tracts*, p. 3, Oxford translation. See also pp. 45 and 55; and the whole letter of St. Julius to the Eusebians bears witness to this unwritten "Canon" or rule of the Church, as quoted in chapter iii.

[2] *Cf.* Beumont, i. 675.

there in martyrdom with his elder brother.[1] The bishops of Rome, in possession of this heirloom from the beginning, drew from it, as an inexhaustible treasure, the doctrine alike and the discipline which from that centre they diffused over the earth. They act from the beginning and throughout as men conscious of this treasure, as men charged with this deposit. There is no faltering in their accents. While the Apostle John yet lived, St. Clement spoke out his decision in full confidence as to the authority on which he rested, and called for obedience to it in the name of the Blessed Trinity,[2] and as the voice of the Holy Ghost. Looking back also on the fifty years of apostolic teaching which preceded his letter, he recorded the establishment of the episcopate throughout the world as the injunction of Christ carried out by those whom He had sent. He was the third from St. Peter in the See of Rome, and St. Ignatius, who was the second from the same St. Peter, in the See of Antioch, writing to the Romans, recognises this heirloom in the words he addressed to them: "I do not give you commands, like Peter and Paul: they Apostles, I one condemned".[3] In the middle of the second century St. Anicetus, resting upon this same force of tradition, urged upon St. Polykarp, a disciple of St. John, the observance of Easter after the Roman, and not after the Jewish custom. A hundred years later, in the middle of the third century, St. Stephen, in the matter of heretical baptism, resisted St. Cyprian, who was supported by the African bishops, with the words: "Let

[1] Gregorovius, i. 101. [2] St. Clement, i. 40, 44. [3] St. Ignatius ad Romanos, 4.

there be no innovation, but that which is handed down be maintained".[1] And these words may be said to express the whole conduct of the Popes in these three centuries. They carried on a living tradition, dating from St. Peter and St. Paul. So in the middle of the fourth century Liberius, treading in the footsteps of his predecessor Julius, addressed the unworthy son of Constantine, one of the worst persecutors of the Church, in the words:[2] "God is my witness, the whole Church with her members is my witness, that in faith and fear of my God I tread and have trodden under foot all human considerations, as the gospel and the apostolic rule require. Not with rash anger, but by the divine right as settled and observed, and, living in discharge of an ecclesiastical office, I have fulfilled what the law required, nothing through boastfulness, nothing through desire of honour. And God is my witness that I approached this office against my will : in which I desire, so long as I remain in the world, to continue without offence to God. And never was it my own statutes but those of the Apostles which I guarded and carried out. Following the custom and order of my predecessors, I suffered nothing to be added to the episcopate of the city of Rome, nothing to be taken from it. But preserving that faith, which has run down through the succession of bishops so great, many of whom were martyrs, I hope to guard it for ever without spot."

I believe that no more accurate statement of the basis on which the faith and discipline of the Antenicene

---

[1] Nihil innovetur nisi quod traditur. [2] Liberius, Ep. iv. 8.

Church rested can be given than in the words of Liberius thus cited, and the conduct of his predecessors.[1] And what the Roman bishop was in chief, the bishops of the Sees of Alexandria and Antioch were next to him, and the bishops of every metropolis, and of every city in their degree, during the whole period of persecution. They all lived upon this tradition of faith and discipline, down to the time when the Arian heresy arose, and before the alliance with the civil power.

The preceding period shews us no trace of such an ecclesiastical revolution as took place afterwards in the East.[2] It is easy to see that the time of persecution was utterly unsuited for attempts on the part of bishops to exalt their sees. The system of hierarchical order, to which the Sixth Canon of the Nicene Council bore witness, had grown up simply and naturally. But we must bear in mind that however great the autonomy of the provinces, when at its utmost development, was—a time which we may probably identify with that of the Nicene Council—the unity in faith and government of the Church, as the kingdom of Christ upon earth, was at all times and in all places a fixed and primary principle. All the ten generations of the Antenicene Church could no more conceive two kingdoms of God, separated from each other in faith or government, than two Gods, or two Christs. And again, this episcopal self-government

---

[1] The tenacity with which the Roman bishops held to this principle of tradition throughout their whole line in the first four centuries is set forth with much learning and lucidity by Constant. *Epistolæ Romanorum Pontificum*, Preface, pp. ii.-lv.

[2] Hergenröther, *Photius*, i. 30.

did not allow of independence in any particular bishop.
Such a notion is unknown to antiquity. Each bishop
spoke with the solidarity of the whole body of which he
formed a part: and that bishop of the third century,
who is distinguished for the force with which he expressed episcopal self-government, is the same who expressed the solidarity of the body, and its foundation in
the unity of St. Peter's See, in a sentence which has
become an adage.[1]

It is requisite to state this once more, before we pass
to the contemplation of a very different state of things.
But this natural and orderly growth of the Church in
its episcopate contains the key to the apparent latency
of the Primacy in the first period. "As long as the
family lives in peace and quiet, the father's authority is
hardly observed."[2] The ambitious struggling of bishops
with each other is subsequent to the alliance between
Church and State, which begins with the sole rule of
Constantine. Until that struggle arose the interference
of the Primate was not needed. The suffering from
without secured tranquillity from within. When a
bishopric involved confessorship or even martyrdom,
bishops were little fain to lord it over Christ's heritage.
Some words used by St. Gregory the Great, in the case
of a certain primate lying under accusation, will shed a
light over the whole period terminated by the Nicene

---

[1] St. Cyprian: Episcopatus unus est: cujus a singulis in solidum pars tenetur.
—Super illum unum ædificat ecclesiam suam.—Quicquid a matrice discesserit,
seorsum vivere et spirare non poterit; substantiam salutis amittit. De unitate
ecclesiæ.

[2] Möhler, K.-g., i. 589.

Council.[1] "As to what he says that he is subject to the Apostolic See, I know not what bishop is not subject to it, if any fault be found in bishops. But when no fault requires it, all are equal according to the estimation of humility." While the order of the hierarchy, which ran up to apostolic institution, remained unshaken, the bishop who stood at its head did not interfere. When "fault was found in bishops," the Primacy came out to repair it. And with this intimation we proceed to the history of the fifty years following the Council in respect both to government and doctrine.

I find that a consideration of the following circumstances must enter into a treatment of the period between the first General Council, that of Nicea, held in the year 325, and that Council of Constantinople held in 381, which, though it was composed exclusively of Eastern bishops, came afterwards, by the acceptance of its decisions on the faith by Pope Damasus, but by no means of its canons of discipline, to be reckoned the second General Council. They form together a sort of moral atmosphere in which as it were every breath of the Church is drawn during the hundred and fifty years. First, the new alliance between the Catholic Church and the Roman empire, heathen until Constantine's conversion, which took the place of the former enmity. Secondly, the power of the emperor, which in this its last form, the design of Diocletian completed by Constantine, was become unrestrictedly despotic, holding in its single hand the executive, legislative, judicial, and

[1] Ep. ix. 59.

military power. Thirdly, the corrupt condition of heathen society in general, and specially in the great cities, and its effect upon the Christian society, no longer divided from it by heathen persecution of the Christian faith. Fourthly, the definitive removal of the imperial residence from Rome, not only as a constantly recurring fact, arising from the military engagements of the emperor, but as a matter of determined policy. Fifthly, the embodiment of this policy in the foundation of a new city on the banks of the Thracian Bosphorus, with the title and privileges of a New Rome; the effect of which was to give a new head to the empire, and powerfully modify the position of the original capital, from whose womb the empire had sprung. Sixthly, as another effect of this, a rise of the bishop of the new capital, in influence first, and then in rank, which is totally unlike anything hitherto seen in the history of the Church. And, again, seventhly, the special connection which thus springs up between the emperor continually resident in his new capital, and the bishop of the city thus created; which, beginning in an episcopal relation between the sovereign and the bishop of the city in which he resides, tends from the first to become, and speedily issues in becoming, another and special relation, the results of which will be seen as our narrative proceeds. Eighthly, the progressive degradation of the second and third sees of Peter, at Alexandria and Antioch, from the rank which they had held since the beginning of the Church, and in full possession of which they are seen at the Council of Nicea, and the substitution of the bishop seated in the new capital, so that he takes the second rank, with the disturbance of the whole Antenicene hierarchy which thereupon ensued. Ninthly, there is the effect of the imperial despotism, as the form under which civil authority was then exercised, upon the Christian episcopate, more especially on the Eastern part of the empire.

Now not only do these nine great incidents act severally on this period, but they are all of them in simultaneous and continuous action. They can only be exhibited one after the other, but in real life their force was exercised together. And over against all these, in general contrast and antagonism to them, but occasionally strengthened, and as to the ultimate issue certainly corroborated by them, we have the development of the Pope's dignity in Rome, together with the maintenance of his independence. And these two great results will be found to follow in no small degree from the many bearings of the act of Constantine in founding Constantinople as Nova Roma.

In treating therefore these circumstances in order one after the other, as must of necessity be done, they must be understood to be not posterior in time to each other, but all progressing together; and having treated them separately we must attempt to draw some conclusions as to the effect of their joint operation, as making together the soil on which the Church was planted, and was striking her roots more strongly day by day in this fourth century.

I. From the moment in which by the defeat of Licinius in the year 324, the year before the Council of Nicea, Constantine became sole master of the empire, a great design appears to have taken full possession of his mind. From the fall of Maxentius,[1] eleven years before, he had been occupied in the work of placing by imperial legislation the Catholic Church on a par in privileges with that vast and heterogeneous mass of heathen worship over the whole of which as Pontifex Maximus he presided. But from the time he became sole emperor he went beyond this in the purpose of bestowing special rights and privileges upon the Church, with the intention of drawing from her all the support which the unity of her doctrinal belief and the impact of her hierarchical order could confer upon the empire. He was fifty years of age when all his competitors for a share in the empire had sunk before him, and he became sole master, with a halo of glory surrounding his head, which may be compared in modern times with that lustre of victory which rested on the head of the first Napoleon at forty years of age, just before the ill-fated Austrian marriage. No other position perhaps will convey an adequate impression of Constantine's grandeur when he called together the first General Council. He was still in the first fervour of his devotion to the Church, still in the original expectation of the benefit which his empire was to derive from being penetrated and restored by the spirit of Christian truth, peace, and unity. Master of all the Roman provinces, and of every department of government within them, he was not yet, he had not yet

[1] Treated by Reffel, pp. 76-83.

aspired to become, master of the Church; he frankly acknowledged both her divine origin and her independent authority as the kingdom of Jesus Christ; and when he acknowledged Jesus Christ, he did not seek to separate Him from His kingdom or his kingdom from Him. As emperor he proclaimed in no uncertain language that the voice of the Christian episcopate was the voice of Christ, and deserved his own obedience as well as that of his subjects.

It was therefore part of a settled plan that in his legislation from this time during all the remainder of his reign—that is, in the thirteen years of his sole monarchy—he bestowed upon the bishops, the clergy, and the Church, as one universal corporation, a civil status most strongly contrasting with the condition of all these in the centuries preceding his conversion.

Constantine named himself fellow-servant of the bishops, in the sense that he addressed the bishops,[1] as recorded by an eye-witness, his friend Eusebius of Cæsarea, "You are bishops of the things inside the Church, while I, being appointed by God over the things without, am bishop there"; shewing by these words that it did not belong to him ever to assume the functions of a bishop within the sanctuary of Christian doctrine and government, but to stand sword in hand at the door as Christian emperor, with the power of a ruler and the spirit of a son, and thus at once to receive and execute the decision of the Fathers. This position he faithfully and strictly occupied at the Council of Nicea.

[1] Eusebius, *Life of Constantine*, iv. 24.

He neither made nor took part in the decrees of the Council; but he received its members as emperor in his palace, he supported them so long as they were in consultation with the whole weight of his authority, and he promulgated immediately their decrees as laws of the empire, to which all owed not only interior obedience as Christians, but civil obedience as subjects. And by so acting he established the rule that whoever afterwards acted against the decrees of the Council committed also a civil offence against him as emperor.

In this lay the fullest recognition of the episcopate, according to the spontaneous order in which its hierarchy had grown up during the three preceding centuries, as the bearer of spiritual authority, in which episcopate the Pope, as the centre of unity, appeared with a perfect consistency over against the emperor, the one as the guardian of the supernatural, the other the guardian of the natural order. Constantine, it should be observed, entirely held the divine delegation in virtue of which he was emperor, as expressed in his own words, "appointed by God over the things without".

The place thus taken by Constantine ruled all the action of the empire towards the Church throughout the period of which we treat, except during the twenty months of Julian's monarchy. From the moment that the emperors acknowledged themselves to be sons of the Church, they could not possibly continue on the standing ground of simple toleration,[1] such as that taken by the decree dated from Milan in 313, when heathendom

---

[1] As set forth by Phillips, *Kirchen-recht*, iii. 18.

was accounted to have equal rights with the Christian Church. When the emperor became a son, his sonship involved obedience in spiritual things; and since the Church is, as the kingdom of Christ, intolerant of error which denies Christ, that character of intolerance could not fail to impress itself, though it might be gradually, on the legislation of a State whose authority was completely bound up with it.

Therefore with Constantine began the series of laws which forbade heathen sacrifices, closed or destroyed temples, or ordered them to be changed into churches.[1] Quick one upon another followed the edicts which established the Church in intimate relation with the empire. The freedom from taxation possessed by the imperial Patrimonium was granted to Christian churches. The manumission of slaves in the presence of a Christian priest received complete legal force. The decision of bishops in matters of law was made binding. The Christian clergy was granted exemption from public burdens and offices in the same degree as the heathen priesthood possessed it. The Church was empowered to receive inheritances in her proper character. Sunday was made a holy day. The punishment of crucifixion was abolished in honour of the Saviour. The penalties imposed on celibacy were removed. On the one hand the great services which Constantine rendered to Christianity, on the other hand the customary position of the emperor in regard to the worship of the whole realm,

[1] Reumont, i. 616.

explain his relation to the Christian clergy and to the Church's constitution.

Constantine made the position of the clergy privileged. We spoke of the civil burdens from which they were relieved in order that they might devote themselves entirely to their work. These burdens were very oppressive. Respectable burgesses could not decline municipal offices. These offices entailed a responsibility for the product of the taxes, the result of a constitution which originally guaranteed municipal independence, but afterwards was misused into a weapon of the fiscal system when carried out to its extreme, besides that in Rome particularly certain offices led to ruinous expenses.

But the force [1] which the civil power allowed to the Church's jurisdiction was among the most important of these privileges. The emperors recognised ecclesiastical jurisdiction in the same extent to which it had reached in the time before this union took place. Let us note how much is conveyed in this remark. The civil power had for nearly three hundred years entertained the strongest enmity against the Church. This struggle was needful for the Church herself, since in this way only could the separation between the temporal and eternal, which in heathendom had run into one, be effected, and the Church's independence be attained only through that thorough opposition which the State assumed to her. It was during this period that the whole life of the Church was developed in its fulness, and therefore this period precisely is of the greatest

[1] Phillips, *Kirchen-recht*, iii. 25, iii. 11.

importance in the formation of ecclesiastical law. A number of institutions belong to it, which come forth afterwards in legislation, the source of which is accordingly to be found not in that legislation itself, but in the unwritten law of Christian antiquity. One of these is the right of property, of which the Church in this period is seen to be the unrestricted possessor, though she was often robbed by violence of her children's gifts. So the Church's jurisdiction was formed in this period, and received its extension over civil matters of contention, especially because Christians followed the Apostle's advice,[1] to submit themselves to the bishop's arbitration rather than to judges who were hostile through their heathenism, and who sat in courts which gave a public sanction to idolatry. Accordingly when the Church had won the victory thus long delayed, the State accepted her whole system as she had formed it in the period of persecution and enmity. God had not given the making of that system to kings; only when it was complete from summit to base He called in the rulers of the world with the word: "And now, kings, understand: receive instruction, ye that are the judges of the earth". And so Constantine, thus called in, ordered as a civil law that all contentions of clergy with each other should be decided by the bishop: and also that his office of arbiter in matters of the laity should have legal force, and be introduced into civil process. The bishop remained the competent judge of clerical transgressions. If a bishop himself had transgressed, he was called to account before

---

[1] 1 Cor. vi. 1.

the provincial synod. Constantine formed the true conception of his position in that he did not think himself competent to pass sentence on bishops.

If we try to represent to ourselves the idea of Constantine with regard to the relation between the Church and the empire, as it may be collected from his acts, it would be this. His purpose and his act coincided in this that he admitted the one Christian and Catholic Church to that same intimate alliance with the Roman empire which had been held by the heathen religion, of which he found himself as emperor the Pontifex Maximus. But he admitted it to this alliance according to his conception of the one Church, as the kingdom of Jesus Christ, and of its episcopate as administering that system of belief and spiritual government of which he found it in undisputed possession. Thus he made its bishops magistrates of the empire, through its whole extent. But this was not all. He admitted them to that magistracy with the same relative position which they held in their own spiritual hierarchy. Thus the bishops of the great cities became at once men of high rank in the empire. In Constantine's own time the bishops of Rome, Alexandria, and Antioch took their place among the most considerable personages of the empire. He most fully recognised in them a power which he had neither created himself nor his predecessors before him. Nay, their possession of it, their administration of that joint system of belief and government, was the very thing which had attracted to them the ruler of men, the civil head and bond of a hundred and twenty discordant provinces over which he thought himself "appointed by God". His conception of their unity even exceeded the degree in which it practically existed, as his conduct at the first rise of the Arian heresy, and his language to the bishop of Alexandria and Arius testifies. Viewed from this side the legislation, in which he was so actively engaged during the years which succeeded the Council of Nicea, does him great honour. He saw the evils of the heathen society, and he fled for succour to the Church. The key to all this legislation is the wish to make the empire itself Christian in its principles of action. Himself as emperor in possession of despotic power, which he strove in theory to perfect and in action to carry out to its utmost limit, he yet fully recognised that it belonged to the Church,[1] as having deposited in her a teaching office created and maintained by the Holy Ghost, to decide all matters of faith, to inquire into and to determine errors as to such matters, when they arose, and to issue decrees as to what was and what was not the doctrine handed down in her tradition. When they were so issued, he gave them civil force; but the right to issue them he acknowledged as inherent in the bishops alone. No man was ever less disposed to surrender his civil authority: yet he viewed the Church distinctly as an immediate divine revelation, as an absolute religion, which excludes every other, which censures every addition or diminution of that which it holds to proceed from its own essence, counting the one and the other an attack upon the sanctuary of its life.

[1] Riffel, p. 280.

His conduct at the Council of Nicea manifestly betokened all this. And grievous as certain acts of his towards the end of his life, when he fell under wrong guidance, appear to be, it would not seem that he ever ceased to hold these principles. The burial of the great emperor by his sons in the vestibule of the church which he had built in honour of the Apostles at Constantinople strikingly exhibited the spirit of devotion to the Church in which he died. As if, said St. Chrysostome, to show that he was the servant of the Apostles, and that "what porters are to kings in their palaces, kings are at the tomb to fishermen".[1] Again, the way in which Athanasius ever speaks of him, and the homage to his unexampled success recorded by St. Augustine,[2] bear a concordant witness to his upright intention in his acts towards the Church.

The idea thus introduced into the empire by him who was its most brilliant ruler since Augustus and Trajan had an immense range and a permanent effect. From his time the joint action of the spiritual and the temporal power runs through everything, and this new Christian legislation of the empire itself creates an immense change in the whole position of things as compared with the preceding period. The period before Constantine is symbolised by the Pope saying mass over the body of a martyr in a chapel of the catacombs, with

---

[1] Hom. xxvi. on 2nd Cor.

[2] Nam bonus Deus Constantinum imperatorem, non supplicantem demonibus sed ipsum verum Deum colentem, tantis terrenis implevit muneribus quanta optare nullus auderet.—De Civ. D. v. 25.

the faithful watching lest soldiers should break in to terminate the sacrifice of the Body and Blood of Christ with the sacrifice of him who offered it, as in the case of Sixtus II. actually happened, while the period after Constantine is symbolised by the Pope seated in the Lateran Palace for well nigh a thousand years from Sylvester to the captivity of Avignon, and thence presiding over a world-wide Church, where papal and imperial rule jointly proclaimed that the church which Constantine built in the precincts of the palace thus conferred on the universal Primate was the Mother and Teacher of all churches.[1]

2. The next point is the nature of that sovereignty with which Constantine brought the Christian Church into so close a relation.

It had become under Constantine himself an absolute monarchy, in which all the rights which belong to the human society for self-preservation and maintenance were vested in the single person of the emperor. Originally Augustus had changed the republican constitution of Rome by uniting in himself the authority as to civil government of consul, tribune, and censor, with the imperial command over the army. With each transmission of this power it tended to become more complete, as the impossibility of governing the vast confederation of peoples under the system of mutual checks and divided functions, which is called a republic,

---

[1] Inscription on the Lateran Church—
"Dogmate papali datur ac simul imperiali
Quod sim cunctarum mater caput ecclesiarum".

impressed itself more and more on the minds of men.
By the end of the first century under the Antonine
emperors from Nerva to Marcus Aurelius it may be
said to have become not only legitimate but in a sense
constitutional. Four emperors successively chosen by
adoption had greatly raised its reputation. For it may
be observed that the natural descent from father to son
in the transmission of supreme power never seemed to
prosper at Rome; and the mighty trust of imperial
power was itself much more like that of a president for
life of a republic[1] than that of a king with settled
authority and dynastic rights, which are also limitations.
By the time of Septimius Severus the radical defect of
the empire, as being based rather on the will of the
soldiery than on civil right as implied in a choice by
the senate, had come clearly to view; and the history of
the third century shews the Roman power brought to
the verge of destruction "by an uncertain list of independent rivals who rose and fell in irregular succession
through the extent of a vast empire".[2]

From that most dangerous crisis Rome was saved at
length by a line of valiant and able generals who were
one after another invested with the purple. Then
Diocletian set himself to remould the shaken authority
of the empire on the basis of a pure monarchy, rather
according to Eastern notions of government than that of
the great republic to which the empire had succeeded.
And Constantine completed what Diocletian had begun.
Both had in view to terminate insurrection, and to bind

[1] As observed by Champagny.   [2] Gibbon, chap. x., on the 30 tyrants.

together all the powers of the commonwealth in self-defence. A gigantic body indeed, if only one life could pervade the whole. The chief external danger arose from the Teuton tribes along the whole northern frontier, a thunder-cloud ever ready to discharge itself, and the great rival monarchy of Persia in the East which had risen in fresh life and vigour in the third century. The Roman emperor of those days needed to unite bodily vigour sufficient to spend twelve hours a day in the saddle, with the military and organising genius of Alexander or Julius. Nor was Constantine unworthy to compare with either of them. Nor does he seem blamable for the extent of power which he wielded. He did not create the system of government which it was his endeavour to regularise, and so to modify and arrange its several functions that all might contribute to united action, and to discourage the wasting of forces by perpetual insurrection in the various provinces of so vast a body which were all needed against the two external foes. He reigned in fact for a longer time than any of his predecessors since Augustus, and many in his own day may have felt that he had united the good fortune of that emperor with the majesty of Trajan in whom the empire culminated.

In the hands of such a sovereign what was the bearing of an absolute temporal power towards the spiritual power which he was the first Roman emperor to acknowledge, and which he brought into intimate relation with himself?

Before I answer this question let me state as briefly

as possible the nature and extent of Constantine's power.

Let us bear in mind that this absolute temporal power was in no sense an usurpation. Viewed as the development of that power which Augustus had set up more than three centuries before it was entirely legitimate. The capitol and the provinces, the senate and the people, the needs of war and peace, the innumerable exigencies of a confederation which for vastness and complexity the world has never seen equalled, all had contributed to form it, to increase its attributions, and consolidate its exercise of them. Tacitus may give a picture of Roman history which suggests a perpetual contrast between the aristocratic liberty of republican Rome, and the servility of senate and people under a Nero or Domitian: but Tacitus himself would not have counselled that the government of the Roman empire in the fourth century should have been carried on under the constitution of which Cato witnessed the overthrow. I observe, further, that the great men, who were also great saints, who lived under this government, and suffered sometimes from the abuse of power, such men as St. Athanasius, St. Basil, St. Ambrose, St. Augustine, and St. Leo, never speak of the power as too great in itself. They continually express their reverence for it: they warn the holders against the ill-use of it: they call upon them in their own day to discharge its functions uprightly: they speak of it as an immense trust placed in human hands, and of the account to be rendered of it to a divine judge, but they nowhere attribute the evils of the time to the exaggeration of the power itself. They seem to have felt instinctively that if a Roman peace and a stable dominion in the face of Teuton barbarian valour and Persian force and fraud were to be maintained in a realm which stretched from Newcastle to Syene, from the Euxine to Morocco, it could only be done by the right use of such a power under a Constantine or a Theodosius. They bore the tyranny of a Constantius and a Valens; they were loyal under the incapacity of Arcadius and Honorius; but in no case did they rise against the imperial power itself, desiring only, and incessantly praying, that worthy possessors of it might be granted to the commonwealth. Accordingly the words in which St. Gregory [1] of Nazianzum addressed Theodosius when he terminated the long Arian usurpation of Constantinople and restored its churches to the Catholics, may be taken to express the sentiments of all the Fathers in regard to the imperial power. "You emperors venerate your purple, for my word shall supply the legislators themselves with a law. Understand the trust committed to you, the greatness of the mystery which surrounds you. The whole world is under your hand, mastered by the little circle of a diadem and the short compass of a robe. What is above is God's alone; what is below is yours also. Be gods then to those under you, for let the boldness of my word correspond to your power. We both hear and believe that the heart of the king is in the hand of God. Therein let your strength be; not in gold nor in armies."

[1] Orat. xxxvi. 11.

All the military forces of the empire were in the single hand of the sovereign. Constantine changed the very construction of the legion, and employed largely the barbarous tribes in the composition of his armies, and their chiefs in the service of the empire, a policy which was continued by Theodosius; so that Alaric the Goth was at the funeral of that emperor as a stipendiary Roman general; and no doubt had that emperor's life been prolonged for twenty years, Stilicho and Alaric would have been the right and left hand of the emperor, and would have saved that Rome for which under his son the one in vain gained victories, while the other avenged by its capture the refusal given to him of his demand to command its armies.

In reorganising the civil administration of the empire, Constantine separated the civil from the military authority. This was to undo a principle of Roman government, which came down from the earliest times of the city. The consul was at once magistrate, jurist, and commander. The proconsul carried these undivided powers into every province. But Constantine aimed at preventing the abuse of the powers of the State against its head. And while he created an administration which formed a wheelwork of civil powers moved by his own single touch from summit to base of the political machine, he divided these two great forces in order to hold them both in his own hands.[1]

The whole fabric of powers, civil and military, was crowned by a great council of state, over which the

[1] Broglie, ii. 209-210, 223.

emperor presided, and in which the heads of the several public services sat, together with a certain number of independent counsellors. Its name was "the Sacred Consistory". It replaced that deputation of senators which Augustus had at his side in the first times of the empire. It received appeals in all criminal, civil, and fiscal causes which were to come under the emperor's direct cognisance. It often formed in fact a cabinet council, in which however the emperor was his own prime minister, for in the emperor all the lines centred.

The legislative power was exercised by the emperor alone, in the form of edicts. Thus the whole power of imposing taxation, and regulating the repartition of the taxes, the power to increase, diminish, or alter them, lay in him; while the prefects of the prætorium, with all the array of public servants who were ranged under them, levied the taxes, estimated and apportioned the details of their incidence, and watched over their due collection.

A most characteristic institution of Constantine was the nobility which he created as a special support of the imperial throne. This bore no resemblance to the ancient Roman patriciate, being not a nobility of family, but a rank derived from the position held in the imperial service—a personal, not hereditary, nobility. A title was attached to each great public employment, rising with progressive rank in the service, and when the time of retreat came the last title was retained. The emperor therefore was the supreme commander, the supreme magistrate, the supreme judge, the sole legislator and taxer of the empire; and in all these capacities he had beneath him a bureaucratic nobility, whose rank as well as their subsistence depended on him, while an army of subordinate agents depended on them. The number of State servants thus maintained may be estimated from a single instance, that of the count who governed the diocese of the East, and who had six hundred subordinate officers, and wanted more.

In all the circumstances above enumerated, but specially in the sacred consistory, in the sort of cabinet sitting in it, and attending on the emperor, most of all, perhaps, in the very characteristic institution of a bureaucratic nobility, the actual Russian empire appears an exact transcript of the empire as settled by Constantine. This last institution indeed was introduced by Peter I. into an empire wherein the Boyards had formed a nobility of long descent and hereditary right parallel to the imperial family rather than derived from its grant, as the Roman patriciate, anterior to the empire itself, had preceded the Byzantine bureaucracy. But yet more than any particular institution, the spirit by which the empire founded at Constantinople was ruled seems to have been transferred to the empire ruled first from Moscow and now from Petersburgh; and the heiress of the Paleologi carried as her nuptial dowry to a northern husband all the rights which an interminable succession of Eastern emperors, changing in family but identical in spirit, had exercised from the foundation to the fall of Constantine's city.

The empire to which he gave this abiding form contained fourteen dioceses, which were ranged under four prætorian prefects, who governed respectively the East, Illyria, Italy, and Gaul. The prefecture of the East had five dioceses—the East properly so called, governed by a count, and containing fifteen provinces; Egyyt, containing five or six provinces; Asia, governed by a vicarius, or proconsul, containing eleven provinces; Pontus, governed by a vicarius, with eleven provinces; Thrace, governed by a vicarius, with six provinces.

The prefecture of Illyria contained three dioceses— Macedonia, under a vicarius, with six provinces; Dacia, with a vicarius, and five provinces; Illyria proper, with six provinces.

The prefecture of Italy contained three dioceses; that is, Italy properly so-called, governed by a vicarius, with seven provinces; the district of the city of Rome, containing ten provinces; Africa, governed by a vicarius or proconsul, with eight provinces.

The prefecture of the Gauls embraced three dioceses, each governed by a vicarius; that is, Spain divided into seven provinces; Gaul, whose old seven provinces formed now seventeen subdivisions; and Britain, containing five.

The whole made fourteen dioceses, and one hundred and nineteen or twenty provinces.

Besides these there were the prefects of the two imperial cities, Rome and Constantinople, independent of the prætorian prefects, forming an internal administration of these cities, which depended directly on the emperor.

To reduce this vast system of jurisdiction to perfect order, and to maintain that order, was the task on which Constantine was incessantly engaged.[1]

His words and his acts, the legislation in which he so largely indulged, and upon which he impressed an uniform character, all concur to assure us that his chief object, as one who had before him the long experience of his own reign and the terrible dangers undergone by the empire in the second half of the third century, was to move the empire, as one force, against pretenders to the imperial throne within, and disturbers of the Roman peace without, on the North and the East. A firm believer in the truth of the Christian faith, in which however he was far from being accurately instructed, and having moreover a strong conviction that the God of battles had twice—first in the case of Maxentius, and secondly in the case of Licinius—decided in his favour, as champion of Christ, and given the empire of the world into his hands as a Christian, he truly accepted the Christian Church as possessing in the decisions of its episcopate and its daily practice the doctrine of salvation. He divested himself of his office of Pontifex Maximus in regard to it, while he retained that office, as a potent instrument of government, in the case of that congeries of heathen rites, the falsehood of which his laws declared. In thus acknowledging the Christian Church he by no means meant to diminish his civil authority as emperor. Nothing could be further from his mind than any intention to create a limited monarchy instead of an

[1] Broglie, ii. 201-2.

absolute one, since the last was to his mind, as soldier and prince, a necessity for governing at all the vast and heterogeneous mass of the empire.

It would be no derogation to his political penetration to suppose that he had not sounded the whole depth of the questions which gathered round the relations of the two powers, nor seen all the conditions necessary for their harmonious co-operation. The relation he himself was making was a new one in Roman history, a new one likewise in the history of the Church. He was the first to call together, by divine inspiration, as he said, a general council: the first, therefore, to set in motion a spiritual power which would exercise an influence as yet unknown. He began, so to say, a new development in the Christian hierarchy itself; for the action of the head upon the hierarchy so called together, and the recognition by the hierarchy of its head in future times, and the long history thus to be wrought out, were things of the future, far beyond the ken of any mind, had it belonged to the greatest of conquerors, legislators, and rulers. That co-operation of Church and State which Constantine began was a most powerful lever in the joint history of both, the effects of which no one could foresee.

I conceive, then, that Constantine's own view of his relation to the Church was, that while he acknowledged her independent existence and spiritual authority, and without grudging looked upon her rulers as the depositaries of Christ's doctrine and power, he was disposed to use all his power, as emperor, in support of what he considered to be the true ecclesiastical decision. Thus his action appeared after the Council of Nicea. He banished Arius, Eusebius, and some others, to enforce its decision. Afterwards he recalled Eusebius, and, as to his judgment upon ecclesiastical affairs, fell almost under his dominion in the latter years of his reign. He threatened Athanasius with deposition if he did not consent to receive Arius back: he peremptorily commanded him to attend a Council at Tyre: and finally he died, leaving him in a banishment imposed by himself. And in all these proceedings he chose to think himself to be carrying out the sentence of the episcopate, and guarding the sanctuary of the Church as "bishop of the things without".

Such was the power of the Roman emperor, with which the Church had to deal in that whole period of 150 years from the Council of Nicea to the fall of the Western empire. Such a power exercised by a friend within the Church is very different in its effects from those which the same power exercised by an open enemy from without would produce. That the power is seated within the Church, and claims to be her defender, by no means removes the struggle between the Church and the world, but it alters the characteristics of the struggle. It is as an incident of the political and religious condition of things at that time that I have said thus much concerning this power.

3. Another act of Constantine was productive of the most important and long-continued consequences, which spread themselves out far beyond the foresight of its framer.

The emperors had for some time ceased to reside

habitually at Rome. The exigencies of warfare, the perpetual defence of the Northern and Eastern frontier, had led them to move continually their court, and with it the seat of government—Treves and Milan in the West, Antioch and Nicomedia in the East, Sirmium and Sardica in the North, became at times imperial residences. But Rome had hitherto been the one recognised capital, and in the name of Rome the emperors chosen by their own armies reigned. But with Constantine's purpose, from the time he became sole emperor, to make the Christian religion the religion of the empire, was intimately blent the purpose to consolidate and unite all the forces of the empire for its self-preservation. His rule of twenty years, the fierce conflicts with competitors over whom he had triumphed, the constant tendency to insurrections which he had witnessed, one may say all his experience, military and civil, had convinced him that the empire needed the utmost efforts of a vigilant and united government, ever ready at the menaced spot in time of danger, to be preserved from falling to pieces; while his genius as a great ruler told him that the position of Rome did not satisfy the requirements of the empire as a place for its supreme authority to dwell in. Moreover, it would seem that he was made painfully to feel during his last residence in Rome, which had been saddened by the terrible deaths of his eldest son Crispus and his wife Fausta, that Rome, its senate, its traditions, as centre of the heathen worship, as shrine of the Capitoline Jupiter, with whose worship the empire of the world was associated in Roman minds, offered the strongest opposition of any city in his dominions to his design of recognising the Christian religion as the religion of the State: part of which design was to use the great moral force of that religion for the tie and support of an empire which he felt to be in danger of collapse.

Thus, after making an imperial palace the seat of the Pope's authority, after building churches to the two great Apostles, whom he found recognised patrons of the Christian city, after endowing them with magnificent revenues, he left Rome in 326 never to return. And not only so, but he took steps to make the absence of the emperor from Rome, which had hitherto been as it were fortuitous, and the result of immediate circumstances of the time, to become perpetual. Only four years after his departure, the empire was startled by the solemn consecration of a new city on the banks of the Bosphorus, and found its centre and basis transferred from West to East.[1]

4. For Constantine, not content with bringing into existence a city which he stretched the whole power of his empire to make at once equal in extent and in grandeur of buildings, in statues, and works of art, to old Rome, conferred upon it likewise the name and privileges of a new Rome; and in so naming it declared his design that it should be for the future empire what the city on the Tiber had been for the past. Thence he and his successors after him would watch and ward off the Northern tempest which ever threatened to

[1] See Reumont, I. 610.

burst; thence they would defeat and repel the forces of the resuscitated Eastern monarchy, sole rival of the Roman empire. Rome's emperor would dwell henceforth by the waters of Europe and Asia, controlling both continents; and his city from its very birth should be Christian, and carry on, or at least maintain, the conquests of Rome under the banner of Christ. Chosen as a matchless military position, equally defencible by sea and land, it should also be enriched by the beauty of earth and heaven at once: radiant skies above, flowing waters around, magnificent mountains in the distance, richly-wooded hills crowning, not a meagre, muddy rivulet, but the ocean-like current of the Bosphorus; winds which tempered the heats of summer. He would give it at once churches to rival those of Rome; forums which should surpass Trajan's wonderwork; while the statue of the sun-god should bear the head of Constantine, and the cross in his hand be upheld as the token at once of religion and of empire.

Such, it may be conceived, was part of Constantine's design; how very different was the result which followed his design will be seen hereafter.

The consequences to Rome were immediate. One of them we may note here. Constantine left Rome in 326; a period of thirty-one years elapsed before another imperial visit—that of his son Constantius in 357. Another like period to the visit of Theodosius in 387. It would seem that Theodosius came again for a moment after his victory over Arbogastes in the months immediately preceding his premature decease in January, 395. This was all that Rome saw of the sovereigns from the departure of Constantine till the end of that fourth century, in which its conversion from a heathen to a Christian city took place.

But one effect of the imperial withdrawal from Rome, which Constantine had scarcely considered, took place and progressed in force through the whole century. Constantine had acknowledged the existing Primacy of the Roman church, had largely endowed it. In withdrawing he removed the presence of the only authority which could compete with it in the sight and feelings of men. Besides, in removing the seat of power definitively to the Eastern part of the empire, he reduced Rome to a municipal position,[1] which more and more brought out the dignity of her bishop. This result of course would be gradual. But from the moment that there was no emperor at Rome, her bishop, who was the first bishop of the Church throughout the world, became the first personage in dignity in the world's old capital. Moreover the gifts of the faithful had made him already, in St. Jerome's words, " a man of most costly poverty".[2] The same act which made a new Rome in discrowning old Rome of her temporal majesty began to create in her mind, as a city, the sense of another majesty; to make her feel herself the centre of another power, a spiritual power far surpassing in grandeur as well as extent the temporal rule of a Trajan. Within eighty years after

---

[1] This is dwelt upon by Gregorovius, vol. i.
[2] Vir ditissimæ paupertatis, Ep. cxxx, c. 16, said of Pope Anastasius, who sat A.D. 398-402.

Constantine's departure from Rome the greatest voices of retiring heathenism proclaimed this majesty of the discrowned city, and the Christian Prudentius scarcely surpassed the confessions of Claudian and Rutilius in the statement that Rome was the head of the whole human race by the power of that faith of which she contained the centre.

5. Let us take another result which did not come into Constantine's thought. When Byzantium by the choice of her new founder became Constantinople and New Rome, the rank of her bishop had been simply that of a suffragan to Heraclea, the see of the Thracian exarch. But the rise of the bishop of Nova Roma was as sudden and portentous as that of the new capital. Before the transfer of the imperial residence the bishopric of Byzantium was far too unimportant to have drawn any attention to itself, and only one bishop, Metrophanes, is known to have existed. He was succeeded by Alexander, who was bishop at the dedication of the imperial city, and who, six years afterwards, bravely resisted the reception of the triumphant Arius to communion—a resistance which succeeded through the terrible death of the heresiarch. The bishop Alexander died the next year, and from his death the see of Nova Roma, under Constantine's successors, became an object of vehement ambition to every courtier spirit in the Greek episcopate.

The whole subsequent history of the bishop of Constantinople is summed up in the fact that he was bishop of the see in which the emperor had his residence.

This was the beginning of his greatness, the cause of its increase, its unfailing support, the whole principle on which it rested. Through many hundred years the Eastern emperors worked unfailingly for the exaltation of that see, in order that, through its bishop, they might rule the Eastern episcopate ; and during all these centuries the bishops of that see subserved in turn the design of the emperors to subjugate the episcopate. At the birth-feast of Constantinople in May, 330, its bishop was suffragan of the metropolitan of Heraclea, without any precedence of honour or jurisdiction. Eight years after this, Eusebius, who originally was bishop of Berytus, and got himself translated against the canons to Nicomedia when the court sat there, thought it worth his while to compass the deposition of the orthodox bishop Paulus, and to take his place at Constantinople, as the court had left Nicomedia. In less than ten years the see where the emperor resided had become the most coveted post in the Eastern episcopate. Upon the death of Eusebius, the Arian party succeeded in placing Macedonius in his seat by help of the emperor Constantius. The orthodox bishop Paulus ended his life after exile by a cruel martyrdom ; and the episcopate of the wavering heretic, Macedonius, terminated in 360 by his fifth expulsion. Eudoxius, who had been bishop of Germanicia, and then of Antioch, took his place, following in this double violation of the canon the example of his predecessor, Eusebius ; and the see of the imperial residence, thirty years after its birth, was a greater object of desire than the apostolic throne of Antioch. Eudoxius inspired the emperor Valens, whom he baptised, with Arian sentiments, and supported him in his worst actions against the Catholics. Dying in 370, the Arian party elected Demophilus for his successor. He was bishop during the severest part of the Arian persecution. At length, after the death of the Emperor Valens, the Catholics' at Constantinople, scattered, without a head, and suffering the hardest oppression, cast their eyes upon the renowned champion of the faith, Gregory of Nazianzum. He gathered round him in a small oratory, which he called the church of the Resurrection, the few Catholics who, fifty years after its triumphant birth as a great Christian city, still remained. Here he preached his most famous discourses, and fought a battle with five sects: the Eunomians, Macedonians, Apollinarists, Photinians, and Novatians.

Thus, from the death of Constantine in 337 to the accession of Theodosius and the expulsion of Demophilus in 381, the see of Constantinople was in the hand of Arians and the centre of court intrigues, and likewise the most coveted of Eastern sees by worldly men. If not in this time already,[1] yet certainly from the episcopate of Nectarius onwards not merely the bishops but the metropolitans of Greece, Macedonia, and Thrace, and of Asia also, in the narrower sense, had begun to collect themselves round the bishop of Constantinople and look upon him as their superior. The bishops of the whole Eastern empire streamed to Constantinople, both for

[1] *Kirchen-lexicon*, iii. 994.

their private and their official affairs, which they had to settle with the emperor. He committed the enquiry and decision upon these affairs to his own bishop. The bishop was accustomed to hold counsel with the various bishops thus visiting the imperial city, and so to resolve the questions laid before him by the emperor. Thus arose a peculiar church-court—"the Resident Synod".[1] It was natural that the bishop of the place, who was agent at the court for his brethren far and near, should preside over this synod. It was most natural that the city, which was the practical capital of the empire, and gave laws to the world, should invest its bishop with a portion of its power. It was natural that the emperor should prefer a bishop created by himself in his own capital, who rested on nothing but the maxim that the ecclesiastical rank of a bishop depended on the civil rank of his city, to the distant bishops of Alexandria and Antioch, who sat as successors of St. Peter, and presided over comparatively independent patriarchates of metropolitans and bishops. And so this first period of fifty years, during which Constantinople was the centre and battle-place of heresy, was terminated by a canon of the Eastern synod held at Constantinople in 381, which raised the bishop who, in 330, had been a simple suffragan of Heraclea to take the second rank, at least of honour, after the bishop of Rome, "because Constantinople is New Rome". And the emperor Theodosius supported the canon.

The Pope when he ratified this Council's decrees of

[1] ἡ σύνοδος ἐνδημοῦσα (see *Photius*, i. 38).

faith, and so made it the second General Council, did not ratify this change in the order of the hierarchy, nor did the bishop of Alexandria accept it; but it held its ground in Eastern practice.

6. The emperor's connection with the bishop of his capital following at once upon the first alliance between the Church and the empire was a new thing in the history of the Church. The whole line of Roman bishops from St. Peter to St. Melchiades had been martyrs or confessors, their connection with the reigning emperor being one of pure repulsion, inasmuch as they held the office of all others most offensive to him, the supreme pontificate, which was an invasion to his mind of his own sacred authority. Every bishop as bishop was hateful to a heathen emperor; but towards the bishop of bishops there was unique enmity. With St. Sylvester, the first tenant of the Roman See after the alliance, Constantine's personal intercourse ceased, when he left Rome in the year 326. Moreover, Constantine, when appealed to by the Donatists, had recognised St. Sylvester's Primacy; had called the General Council at Nicea in union with him; had seated him for the exercise of his supreme authority in an imperial palace. His intercourse with St. Sylvester, therefore, as with the bishop of the ancient capital, was an intercourse of Christian emperor with the Primate of the Christian Church. Quite other would be his connection with the bishop of the new capital when, at its dedication in 330, Alexander, who had hitherto been bishop of Byzantium, became bishop of Constantinople. That connection,

which lasted seven years, until the death of both in 337, was one between an omnipotent emperor, who had become Christian, on one side, and on the other a simple bishop, who, by the act of that emperor, had become head of a very important instead of an insignificant city. Constantine could not anticipate the consequences which we have just very briefly mentioned—the flocking of Eastern bishops and metropolitans round the imperial throne in his new city, the forming of a Resident Council of such bishops, having for their president the bishop of that city; in short, the whole prodigious growth of influence which raised the prelate of a city, the very seat of heresy and intrigue during the forty-four years succeeding his own death, to be by virtue of its privileges as New Rome the second bishop in the Church, the imperial instrument for governing the Eastern episcopate to all future time. To no particle of this influence or rank was the bishop of the new capital entitled according to the hierarchy of the Church which Constantine recognised at the Nicene Council. It sprang from his act in founding the new capital; it was a most unexpected result of the connection of the emperors in the new city of their constant residence with the bishop of that city. The act which left the Roman bishop comparatively free to exercise the inherent powers of his Primacy was raising a sort of rival to him in the bishop of the new capital; and later on we shall see how the *servus natus* of imperialism, after dethroning the bishops of Alexandra and Antioch from their second and third place, which they had held from the beginning of the

Church by apostolic descent, was to develop into Ecumenical Patriarch over his brethren, who owed no deference to the suffragan of Heraclea, but were content to hold the train of the bishop of Constantinople.

7. Every step in the progressive exaltation of the bishop of Constantinople was at the same time a pure result of imperial power, and accompanied by the degradation of other bishops from their original rank. The first step, which dates from the rise of the Arian disturbances, and is confined to usage during their continuance, is that the bishop of the capital escapes from subordination to his metropolitan. With the Principate of Theodosius the custom becomes embodied in a public act, and the bishop of the capital takes the headship of the Thracian exarchate instead of the archbishop of Heraclea. In the episcopate of Nectarius he goes on to interfere with the archbishop of Ephesus and the bishops of his exarchate, then with the archbishop of Cæsarea in Pontus and his exarchate. This advance in jurisdiction, which was not given by the canon of 381, was done by the force of custom, by the action of the "Resident Council," in which he presided, by the emperor's perpetual reference to him, as presiding in that Council, of episcopal affairs from the neighbouring provinces. He constantly and silently advances under the imperial cover. The great emperor Theodosius, induced no doubt by his anxiety to restore order in the shattered Greek episcopate, was the chief mover in obtaining that canon which was passed in 381 at the first council of his reign by the bishops of the Eastern

empire alone, and which gave him the second rank, so far as precedence went, in the whole Church, "because Constantinople is New Rome". With that canon, never presented to Rome, and never accepted by Rome, and repudiated by Alexandria, the first stage of his advancement is completed. His power is wanted at the right hand of the emperor to restore to peace and order the Eastern episcopate, distracted and demoralised by the Arian convulsion of the preceding fifty years. And thus he assumed a precedence of rank over the bishops of Alexandria and Antioch, though he had not yet advanced so far as to invade their jurisdictional authority. Antioch, it may be remarked, since the deposition of its legitimate bishop Eustathius, by the action of Eusebius in 330, had been the constant prey of intrigue, heresy, schism, and contested elections; and Athanasius, the most illustrious champion of the faith, had been in this period five times driven from his see, though he died in possession of it in 373, eight years before this Council, which transferred to an upstart his original precedence in the hierarchy, as successor of St. Mark and St. Peter.

CHAPTER V.

CONSTANTINE AND HIS SONS—JULIAN, VALENTINIAN, AND VALENS.

WE proceed to a short narrative of events between the Council of Nicea and that of Constantinople in 381, which will illustrate the simultaneous working of the seven circumstances above summarised.

Constantine felt his prosperity crowned by the happy result of the Nicene Council. He considered himself to have through it restored peace and unity to the Church. At that moment his political, military, and religious success was complete. He was come in his own life to the point of triumph which is wont to turn the heads of great men. Having banished Eusebius of Nicomedia and Theognis of Nicea from their sees to a distant province, and caused successors to them to be appointed, he departed for Rome. He entered it on July, 328,[1] in the costume of an Asiatic monarch, his tunic covered with pearls, wearing on his head a closed crown, which confined the curls of his hair. A few days afterwards he refused to attend and take part in the great procession of the knights to the Capitol in scarlet robes and garlands of

[1] Broglie, ii. 73, 92, 96.

olive, to sacrifice to Jupiter. The heathen feeling in
the vast majority of the senate, of the higher classes
and of the common people, of which Rome was the
centre, then broke out against him. Moreover at this
time probably took place the terrible domestic tragedy
which deprived him by his own act first of his eldest son
and then of his wife, the empress Fausta, mother of his
remaining children. He left Rome in October, 326,
never to return; but he had already founded and muni-
ficently endowed her chief churches. He had not, as
was once believed, been baptised by St. Sylvester; that
act was deferred to the very end of his life, and was then
performed by one whose influence over Constantine was
every way disastrous—Eusebius of Nicomedia, the leader
of the Arian party.

The dislike of the senate and great families of Rome to
his person and to his project of establishing the Christian
religion seems to have confirmed his resolution to found
a new capital, which he viewed as the beginning of a
new empire. Upon his return to the East he threw
himself with the greatest ardour into this design, and
by the most unscrupulous use of his imperial power
Constantinople was built, and inaugurated as a new
capital and the Christian city of the future, in less than
four years. The rest of his life was given up to the
double purpose of reorganising his empire, according to
the idea of Diocletian, and that in union with a religion
which he professed with the utmost zeal, though he had
not become a member of it, while he thought himself,
and meant to be, a strenuous defender of its doctrines,

of which, to the end of his life, he had no accurate knowledge.

Constantine, attending his sister Constantia, widow of Licinius, on her death-bed, had received into his favour, at her request, a certain priest imbued with Arian opinions. This priest had the art to persuade him that Eusebius the banished bishop of Nicomedia, with his comrade, Theognis of Nicea, received the doctrine of the Nicene Council. Thereupon Constantine recalled the exiles and re-established them in their sees, to which others had been appointed by an uncanonical exercise of power. The court was still at Nicomedia, and there Eusebius had full opportunity to exercise the talent of delicate flattery with which he was endowed. In a few months he had recovered all the influence he had ever obtained over the emperor, and from that time to the end of Constantine's life was his chief adviser in ecclesiastical affairs.

"Eusebius and Arius," says Athanasius,[1] "like serpents coming out of their holes, have vomited forth the poison of this impiety; Arius daring to blaspheme openly, and Eusebius defending his blasphemy. H was not, however, able to support the heresy until he found a patron for it in the emperor. Our fathers called an Ecumenical Council, when three hundred of them, more or less, met together and condemned the Arian heresy, and all declared that it was alien and strange to the faith of the Church. Upon this its supporters, perceiv-

---

[1] *History of the Arians to the Monks*, written A.D. 358-360, sec. 66, Oxford translation.

ing that they were dishonoured, and had now no good ground of argument to insist upon, devised a different method, and attempted to vindicate it by means of external power. They have shewn that the other heresies are but their younger sisters, whom they surpass in impiety, emulating them all, and especially the Jews, in their iniquity. For as the Jews, when they were unable to prove the charges which they pretended to allege against Paul, straightway led him to the chief-captain and the governor; so likewise these men, who surpass the Jews in their devices, make use only of the power of the judges, and if anyone so much as speaks against them he is dragged before the governor or the general."

Thus wrote the great confessor and champion, when he had been for thirty years exposed to the violence which he describes; and in these words he has summed up the character of the Arian conflict during the whole fifty years from the time when Eusebius of Nicomedia was taken into the favour of Constantine, to the death of the emperor Valens in 378.

Constantine was in temper and character despotic, as a man who had risen to undivided empire by the most wonderful success as commander was likely to be; and he was most zealous to maintain the unity of the Church's doctrine and organisation as a support of the unity of the empire. He was also sincerely attached to the doctrine of the Church as determined at the Nicene Council, and so he continued to the end of his life. The art of Eusebius consisted in this, that he insinuated to the emperor a certain course of action, which to Constantine's mind appeared to unite these three things: absolute obsequiousness to his will, maintenance of the Church's doctrine and discipline, and union of the two powers in his own hand. We shall see instances of this in the acts which we have to record.

Thus when Eusebius was himself restored to favour and recalled from the banishment which had been inflicted on him as plotting against the faith, he was supposed by the emperor to be faithful to the Nicene Creed. When he persuaded the emperor to summon Arius to his court, it was that the emperor might assure himself that the doctrine of Arius was not irreconcilable with the decision of the Council; and the heresiarch presented Constantine with a creed, the deceptive language of which the emperor was unable to discern, and so he accepted the worst of the Church's enemies under the supposition that he was a faithful son,[1] and endeavoured to force him upon Athanasius in that character.

Then Eusebius set himself to depose the holders of the two great sees of Alexandria and Antioch. He began with Eustathius of Antioch. This bishop had obtained the name of a confessor under Diocletian and Licinius. He had been bishop of Berœa, and was appointed to Antioch in 325. Renowned at once for learning, eloquence, literary skill, as well as for a holy life, he had vigorously defended the faith at the Nicene Council. It is plain how unacceptable to the Arian faction such a person in so high a place must have been. Eusebius proceeded against him in this wise. He repre-

[1] Broglie, ii. 285.

sented to Constantine that he was most desirous to visit the great church which the emperor was building at Jerusalem to commemorate his mother's discovery of the Holy Cross. Forthwith the bishop of Nicomedia, with his friend Theognis of Nicea, was sent thither at the public cost. He returned in company with many bishops by way of Antioch; and there he contrived to hold a council of bishops, at which accusations were made against the faith and the morals of Eustathius, and he was deposed from his see. A deputation was sent to Constantine to inform him that a sedition was being raised in one of the chief cities of the empire by its bishop. The emperor sent the Count Musonianus to inquire into the matter, and upon his report the sentence of the council was carried out, and Eustathius was banished to Philippi, and submitted to deposition from his place as third bishop of the Church. Eusebius, however, did not succeed in his attempt to put his special friend and fellow-worker Eusebius of Cæsarea in the great see of the East, whose own refusal to change the see of Cæsarea for that of Antioch was highly praised and corroborated by Constantine.

This deposition of a patriarch was reckoned the first act of the Arian persecution. It was the beginning of a state of schism and heresy at Antioch, which lasted for more than eighty years, and paralysed the influence and authority of that great see, so that it yielded almost without an effort to the encroachments of the see of Constantinople.

To overthrow Athanasius, who had been elected in

328 to the headship of the Egyptian bishops at Alexandria, was not so easy a matter. The steps taken by Eusebius were these.

Arius having been received by the emperor at Constantinople, upon a dubious profession, to which the ignorance of Constantine led him to give an orthodox interpretation, Eusebius wrote a very flattering letter to Athanasius asking him to admit Arius to communion, with the suggestion that it would be agreeable to the emperor. Athanasius simply refused. Thereupon a second messenger came bearing a polite but imperative letter from Constantine. To this also Athanasius replied that it was impossible for him to do what was asked. The refusal made a great stir in the palace at Constantinople, and was followed by a much severer letter from the emperor, carried by two of his Palatine guards—Syncletius and Gaudentius. Athanasius has preserved a part of it, which runs thus:[1]—"Having therefore knowledge of my will, grant free admission to all who wish to enter into the Church. For, if I learn that you have hindered or excluded anyone who claims to be admitted into communion with the Church, I will immediately send some one who shall depose you by my command, and shall remove you from your place."

Upon this, says Athanasius, "I wrote and endeavoured to convince the emperor that that anti-Christian heresy had no communion with the Catholic Church".

After this an interval of some time passed, which was used by Eusebius to depose, as we have seen, the bishop

[1] Athanasius, *Historical Tracts*, p. 89.

of Antioch, and to foster the enemies of Athanasius in Egypt. False reports concerning the loyalty of Athanasius were carefully spread, and supported by the prefect Philagrius. Constantine consulted Eusebius, and was advised by him to recur to the method which had succeeded so well at Nicea. Only a meeting of bishops was competent to consider the conduct of one of the first bishops in the Church. In consequence Constantine was induced to order a council of Eastern bishops to meet at Cæsarea in Palestine.

No spot could be better chosen, for there Eusebius of Nicomedia possessed a second self in Eusebius the historian. It was largely attended by the bishops of that party. But Athanasius, in spite of the express and reiterated command of the emperor, refused to move from Alexandria.

The refusal of Athanasius to attend was represented to the emperor as an act of disobedience to his sovereign, as if at Alexandria there was a subject independent of the emperor.[1] He was thus induced to name a new council to meet at Tyre, and he sent letters with the severest menaces to Athanasius if he did not attend.

This Council of Tyre is a very notable event indeed in the history of the Church. It was held in the year 335, ten years after the Council of Nicea: as that had marked the twentieth so this marked the thirtieth year of the great emperor's reign. It was summoned by Constantine, who, in his own letter to the Council, says, "I have sent to those bishops whose presence you

[1] Hefele, C.-G., i. 443.

desired that they may share your counsels".[1] It was neither an assembly of all the Church, nor of all the provinces of the Eastern empire; it was neither a metropolitan nor a diocesan synod. Athanasius as primate of Egypt was not bound to attend it; but he had received peremptory orders from Constantine to attend it; that is, the emperor used his power as an absolute sovereign to compel, as an act of civil obedience, what the rule of the Church did not require. Immediately following those words of the emperor to the Council, that he had chosen those bishops whom they desired, there follow the words: " I have despatched Dionysius, a man of consular rank, who will both remind those prelates of their duty who are bound to attend the Council with you, and will himself be there to superintend the proceedings, but especially to maintain good order. Meantime should anyone, which I do not suppose, venture on this occasion again to violate my command and refuse his attendance, a messenger shall be despatched hence forthwith to banish that person, in virtue of an imperial edict, and to teach him that it does not become him to resist an emperor's decrees, when issued in defence of the truth."

The best comment upon these words of the emperor is that of the Council of Egyptian bishops held four years afterwards, in 339, whose narrative of these events is the most authentic history we possess of them.[2] "How can they have the boldness to call that a council, at which a single count presided, which an

[1] Eusebius, V. C., iv. 42.   [2] *Historical Tracts*, p. 25.

executioner attended, and where a chief jailor, instead of the deacons of the Church, introduced us into court, and where the count only spoke and all present held their peace, or rather obeyed his directions. The removal of those bishops who seemed to deserve it was prevented at his desire; and when he gave the order, we were dragged about by soldiers, or rather the Eusebians gave the order, and he was subservient to their will. In short, dearly beloved, what kind of council was that the object of which was banishment and murder at the pleasure of the emperor?" "If, as bishops, they claimed for themselves alone the judgment of the case, what need was there for the attendance of a count and soldiers? or how was it that they assembled under the sanction of royal letters?"

The contriver of such a council as this, in which not only the bishops were convened by the emperor's order, and such only as were thought desirable by the party who swayed the emperor, were summoned by him, in which a count from the emperor's side presided, with power to inflict banishment or death upon recalcitrant bishops, had the skill to persuade the emperor that he was all the while maintaining the decrees of the Nicene Council; that he was restoring peace to the Church, and was exercising for the glory of God that absolute power with which the Divine Providence invested him. His concluding words to the bishops are: "For the rest it will be for your sanctity, unbiassed either by enmity or favour, and in accordance with the ecclesiastical and apostolic rule, to devise a fitting remedy, whether for positive offences or unpremeditated faults, in order that you may at once free the Church from all reproach, relieve my anxiety, and, by restoring the blessings of peace to those who are now divided, procure the highest honour for yourselves. God keep you in His guard, beloved brethren."[1]

We are but ten years from the Council of Nicea, and the same Constantine, who then stood at the door with the sword of state to make its decrees as they issued from the sanctuary to be also laws of the empire, has now, by his officer, entered the sanctuary and uses the sword to choose the bishops who shall enter, to force them to enter whether they will or not, to order what shall be done, and to execute what has been so ordered.

Athanasius, the second bishop of the Church, who, by the "ecclesiastical and apostolic rule" which Constantine cited, could be judged only by the bishop of Rome,[2] thought it expedient not to refuse the emperor's command in the case of the council called at Tyre, as he had in the case of the council called at Cæsarea. He went attended by forty-nine bishops of his patriarchate. It is needless to say that instead of presiding over the council, as was his right, Flaccillus, the bishop of Antioch, intruded after the deposition of Eustathius upon that see, being second to him in rank, he was

---

[1] *Life of Constantine*, iv. 42, the translation a little altered.

[2] As Julius writes in his letter, A.D. 342,

Διὰ τὶ δὲ περὶ τῆς 'Αλεξανδρέων 'Εκκλησίας μάλιστα οὐκ ἐγράφετο ἡμῖν; ἢ ἀγνοεῖτε ὅτι τοῦτο ἔθος ἦν, πρότερον γράφεσθαι ἡμῖν, καὶ οὕτως ἔνθεν ὁρίζεσθαι τὰ δίκαια; εἰ μὲν οὖν τι τοιοῦτον ἦν ὑποπτευθὲν εἰς τὸν ἐπίσκοπον τὸν ἐκεῖ, ἔδει πρὸς τὴν ἐνταῦθα 'Εκκλησίαν γραφῆναι.

treated as a criminal, was deposed from his see, and represented to the emperor as engaged in traitorous plots against his authority. They ordered a packed commission of bishops to proceed to Egypt and to collect evidence against him; but before it started Athanasius left the council and presented himself suddenly before the emperor as he entered Constantinople. Seizing the bridle of his horse, he appealed to him for justice. Constantine listened unwillingly, but he listened. The result was that he summoned the council which he had ordered to proceed from Tyre to Jerusalem, in order to be present at the consecration of his church of the Resurrection, to attend upon him at Constantinople. A deputation only came, composed of the two Eusebii, Theognis, Patrophilus, Ursacius, and Valens, the chief leaders of the Arian party. It was no longer of heresy, but of an offence against the State—of preventing the transmission of grain to Constantinople —that they accused Athanasius. The result was that the emperor, a few months before his death, condemned Athanasius to banishment at Treves; but he refused to acknowledge his deposition from his see and the appointment of another bishop at Alexandria.

During the thirteen years of his sole rule Constantine wielded all the power of the Roman empire with as little restriction as is imposed on a general who conducts a campaign in the field. The empire in fact rested upon him for its existence, and the law of self-preservation allows all liberty of action to those who execute it. He named himself Victor Constantinus Maximus Augustus, and the first title was well earned. He was in truth as a commander always successful; he was a legislator of large views, an administrator of vigorous execution; in every civil aspect a dictator whose tenure of office might be illustrated by citing the famous charge of former times which invested even the consuls of free Rome with absolute authority, "See that the commonwealth suffer no harm". He towered by the head and shoulders above those around him, ruling single-handed, while his ceaseless energy pervaded the whole mass of that huge government—a very Saul in his imperial surroundings, and by many thought a very David in his conduct to the Church. In his own notion he was ever a faithful son to her; and when in his last year he was trying to compel Alexander, the first bishop of his new capital, to receive Arius to communion, he thought that he was maintaining the Nicene Creed.

Had he been indeed baptised by Pope Sylvester when he entered Rome in triumph after the defeat of Maxentius, and was received as the saviour of society; or, again, had he fallen into the hands of Athanasius, when he had moved the centre of the empire eastward, instead of taking for his counsellor Eusebius of Nicomedia, he would probably, in addition to the imperishable glory of being the first Christian emperor, have left a name in all respects corresponding to that title: the fame of his life, as an individual and a ruler, might have equalled his position. But he remained to the last not even a catechumen, with a soldier's ignorance of Christian doctrine, with an impetuous temper's disregard of Christian restraint in his dealings with men: and he thought he was doing the Church service when he was inflicting deadly injury on her doctrine and her discipline.

Eusebius of Nicomedia laid hold of the dictator by his weak point, and persuaded him that in calling the Council of Cæsarea first, and that of Tyre afterwards, he was repeating the great success of the Nicene Council, as indeed his special friend, the historian Eusebius, has left upon record a comparison of these councils with each other, setting Tyre upon the same level as Nicea.[1]

It is certain that in the seven last years of Constantine Eusebius of Nicomedia, beginning with the deposition of St. Eustathius of Antioch, had devised the weapon which, in imperial hands, was to push the Church nearer to the edge of dissolution than any heresy or schism has done in any other time of her history. And this weapon was an episcopal council, the members of which should be chosen and summoned by the emperor, and in its session be dragooned by an officer of the emperor present at its discussions; its course of proceeding indicated by him; its decrees be supported by the imperial omnipotence, inflicting banishment at pleasure upon the bishops of any see, even the highest. The perpetual recurrence of this is what we have to witness in the time of Constantine's immediate successors; but the first instance of this weapon's employment is the Council of Tyre, which being composed of about sixty bishops, besides those of Egypt, from various provinces, pronounced the deposition of Athanasius, in defiance of the

[1] *Vita Constantini,* iv. 47.

discipline which had existed from the beginning to the Nicene Council. Yet the first historian of the Church lauds Constantine for calling this council as the noblest and most devoted of the Church's defenders.[1]

The special point which made this invention of Eusebius so dangerous was this: a subtle mixture of the Church's original constitution with an innovation. On the one hand Constantine, in summoning the council at Cæsarea, and then that of Tyre, which he further directed to proceed to Jerusalem, fully recognised the exclusive right of bishops to judge in matters of faith and Church government. So far he did not meddle with the constitution which he found in unbroken possession of the Church at the Nicene Council, and which he respected both during its session, and in carrying out its decrees. But, on the other hand, the innovation consisted in his convoking provincial councils, wherein he selected not merely the provinces which should send bishops to them, but the members of the episcopate which should attend them. And more than this: the convocation itself arose not from the harmonious action of the two powers, civil and spiritual, together, as in the case of the Nicene Council, but from the civil power alone; and the power of the council so convened was extended beyond its right, had it been legitimately convened. When Constantine required Athanasius to attend

---

[1] *Vita Constantini*, iv. 41, 43, 47. Eusebius calls the council at Jerusalem, to which place the Council of Tyre was ordered to proceed by Constantine, "the greatest of which we have any knowledge next to the first which he had summoned at the famous Bithynian city".

a council of bishops at Tyre selected by himself from various provinces, he disturbed the hierarchical order of the Church. Athanasius owed no obedience, as bishop of the second see in the Church, to such a council: his only superior was at Rome, as his predecessor St. Dionysius had acknowledged in accepting the judgment of Pope Dionysius more than seventy years before. In this particular case Athanasius was made subject to his inferiors, and not only so, but to a selection of those inferiors made really at the instigation of his enemies under cover of the civil sovereign. But far more important than any individual injustice was the precedent established and the tribunal created. If we attempt to analyse the view of the Christian hierarchy entertained by Eusebius of Nicomedia, and no less it would seem by Eusebius the historian, there appears at the bottom of his mind an Eastern church dominated by the emperor from his seat of imperial power at Constantinople, and uncontrolled by Rome. I do not suppose that he disclosed this view to Constantine; but he flattered the emperor by making him the prime mover in all ecclesiastical matters, while he represented the Council of Tyre with its continuation at Jerusalem as the counterpart of the Council at Nicea.

The result was that when Constantine died in 337 his government, in the years during which he had fallen under the ecclesiastical direction of Eusebius, had afforded a foretaste of all the evils which State despotism inflicted on the Church first under his sons, and then under their Byzantine successors. The Nicene Council is the dividing line. Up to it and in it he is the Church's advocate: from the founding of Nova Roma he tends to become the Church's patron. Under the hands of Eusebius he dies, deeming Athanasius a firebrand in the Church or a plotter in the State, and banishing him from his see, yet not deposing him.

The special malignity of the Eusebian persecution consisted in that it was conducted, so far as the use of episcopal councils, "according to the outward forms of ecclesiastical law, charges of various kinds were preferred in council against the orthodox prelates of the principal sees, with a profession at least of regularity, whatever unfairness there might be in the details of the proceedings. By this means all the most powerful churches of Eastern Christendom, by the commencement of the reign of Constantius, had been brought under the influence of the Arians; Constantinople, Heraclea, Hadrianople, Ephesus, Ancyra, both Cæsareas, Antioch, Laodicea, and Alexandria."[1] The hand which brought these cities under Arian influence as to doctrine was dividing them by the same stroke from the See of Peter at Rome in government. The two movements kept pace with each other: and it is remarkable that the chief point of attack was the bishop of that see of St. Mark, which of all the Eastern sees was united by the closest ties to its parent See of St. Peter at Rome, as it was the second to it in rank. Through the whole Arian conflict Rome and Alexandria took side against Antioch and Constantinople. These sees had fallen under Eusebian bishops,

---

[1] Newman's *Arians*, 288.

who supplanted orthodox bishops, and were imposed by court influence.

Now we have to see how the scheme of government devised by Eusebius of Nicomedia prospered in the forty-two years which succeeded from the death of Constantine to the accession of Theodosius.

Constantine had reigned thirty years, with such a vigour of mind and body that every part of the mighty empire was pervaded by his presence. The three sons, Constantine, Constantius, and Constans, who divided his empire, were far indeed from inheriting his genius or his success. Constantine II. reigned but three years, Constans thirteen, and Constantius twenty-four years, during the last eleven of which he was sole emperor; and this period of twenty-four years forms one of the saddest times in the long history of the Church. It is true that the emperors Constantine II. and Constans protected the West during their life-time, but a large portion of the Eastern sees were in possession of the heretical party. First Constantine, and then Constans, were taken away. From that time the imperial omnipotence was used to the uttermost and with the most terrible effect against the doctrine established at the Nicene Council by the surviving son of the first Christian prince, whose chief glory it was to have called the Council together, to have given it free action, and to have made its decrees laws of the empire.

From the beginning of his reign Constantius fell under Arian influences, but was kept in check by his elder brother Constantine, who reigned in Gaul and

Spain, and by his younger brother Constans, who reigned in Italy, Illyricum, and Africa, while the East was his own portion. The three brothers agreed in 338, by a common decree, to recall the bishops whom their father had banished, and thus after two years and four months spent in exile at Treves, Athanasius returned to Alexandria, Nov. 23, 338. This was his first exile. About the same time Paulus, the orthodox bishop of Constantinople, was deposed, and Eusebius, having passed by court influence at a former time from the see of Berytus to that of Nicomedia, then the seat of the court, was now able, by the same influence, to violate the canon a second time, and get himself made bishop of Constantinople. Thus, in eight years after the feast of that city's dedication, the possession of that see was the great object of desire to Eusebius, the leader of the Arian party. There is a fitness that the model and most accomplished specimen of what was to be the worst pest of the Church through all succeeding generations, the Court-Bishop, should, in violation of the canons, mount the throne of that see which owed everything to the patronage of a court. And again there is a further fitness that this same man conceived and initiated the work of separating the East from the West, which one successor in that very see, Acacius, attempted with ill-success, but which another, Photius, in worse times accomplished.

Paul, who had been elected by the Catholic portion of Alexander's flock to succeed him, was banished by edict of Constantius, and Eusebius, enthroned at Constantinople, proceeded to attack Athanasius with all his wiles. The party led by Eusebius accused him to the three emperors, and sent a priest and two deacons to Pope Julius with charges against him. Athanasius then convoked a council of all the bishops of Egypt, nearly one hundred in number, who heard his cause, and acquitted him, and he sent their acquittal to the three emperors and to the Pope. The emperors of the West, Constantine II. and Constans, being faithful to the Nicene Creed, supported him. Pope Julius resolved to consider, in a fresh council, those accusations which the Eusebians had repeated against him, on the authority of their Council of Tyre. In the meantime the Eusebians, having the emperor Constantius on their side, sent from the court of Constantinople an intruder, Gregory of Cappadocia, to drive Athanasius from Alexandria, and to take possession of his see, which he accomplished by the aid of the prefect Philagrius, committing every sort of tyranny and violence upon the people. Four days before his arrival Athanasius fled to Rome, on the 19th March, 340. He arrived there after Easter. The Pope then summoned the Eusebians at Antioch to meet Athanasius in a council at Rome, but the Eusebians refused to come; and after Athanasius had waited at Rome eighteen months for his accusers to appear, Julius held a council at Rome of more than fifty bishops, at the end of 341, who considered the cause of Athanasius and other bishops expelled by the Arian party, acquitted them, and remained in communion with them, and restored them to their sees.

But the Eusebians, who refused to meet Athanasius before the Pope at Rome, had the art to persuade their emperor, Constantius, to call a great council at Antioch on the occasion of dedicating the great Church there. More than ninety bishops attended this council; they passed celebrated canons, one of which ran : " A bishop who has been deposed by a council may not resume his office, nor be restored by any subsequent council, if, after his deposition, he has dared to execute ecclesiastical functions ". Athanasius had been deposed at Tyre, rightly or wrongly ; after his return from banishment in 338 he had zealously resumed his work as bishop. This canon was pointed at him, just as the synod of Antioch repeated, under Constantius, all the faults which that of Tyre had incurred under Constantine, in transgressing the conciliar practice which the Church had followed from the beginning.

Pope Julius, as the result of the council he had held, issued the great letter which Athanasius has preserved, in which he points out the flagrant transgressions against the order of the Church which the Eusebian party had committed, reminds them that the bishop of Alexandria could only be judged at Rome, and reverses the violent depositions of bishops which they had committed.

Thus, in the year 341, we have the two sides marshalled against each other : at Rome, Pope Julius, who does justice to Athanasius when expelled from his see by an intruder despatched from the court of Constantinople, and introduced by force, and maintains at once the ancient order and the true belief of the Church; at Antioch, under Constantius, the court party, led by Eusebius, which is also the heretical party, introducing a new belief and a new government. As to the former, "four or five creeds, instead of the Nicene, were successively adopted by the assembled Fathers," and "all these creeds bear the same character. In all is seen the endeavour to come as near as possible to the Nicene faith, without using the term consubstantial."[1] As to the latter, instead of admitting the right of the Pope to judge the cause of the second see, they were declining to attend the council to which Pope Julius invited them, and by procuring from Constantius instead a council at Antioch, they were endeavouring to set up a State-Church under the headship of the Eastern emperor. The double innovation upon creed and discipline proceeded together. The Council of Antioch had received no mission to do what it did; and the Greek historian Socrates, in recording it, says pointedly: "Julius, bishop of old Rome, was not there, nor did he indeed send a representative, although the ecclesiastical canon expressly commands that the churches shall not make any ordinances without the sanction of the bishop of Rome".[2]

In the year 340 Constantine II. ended his short reign, and Constans succeeded him as emperor of the whole West; and in 342 Eusebius, who had begun at Berytus, and then moved to Nicomedia, and in 338 to Constantinople, ended his career in this last city. But his party survived him in full vigour. Pope Julius and bishop

---

[1] Newman's *Arians*, 456; Hefele, i. 508.   [2] Socrates, ii. 8.

Hosius urged Constans to move his brother Constantius that a council of the East and West might be summoned to put an end to all contentions respecting Athanasius, Marcellus of Anacyra, and Paul of Constantinople, and to terminate the dissension upon doctrine and the person of Christ. The two emperors agreed that a council should be called at Sardica, the present Sophia, which lay on the confines of their two dominions ; and thither about 200 bishops from 35 provinces of the East and West assembled in 343. At their head was Hosius of Corduba, with the Roman priests Archidamus and Philoxenus, who represented the absent Julius, and who presided at Sardica as he had at Nicea. There would appear to have been about 94 Western and 76 Eastern bishops ; and the first act of the latter was to refuse to sit in council with Athanasius, as having been condemned by two Eastern synods—that of Tyre in 335, and that of Antioch in 341. His acquittal at the Roman council of the same year they would not recognise. Their claim was absolute ; that an ecclesiastical decision once passed in a council, especially concerning the nomination or deposition of a bishop, should not be subject to revision.[1] As Hosius and the Western bishops entirely rejected this claim, the Eusebians retired secretly to Philippopolis, fifty miles distant, and held a counter-council there. The legitimate council proceeded with its work. They heard afresh the causes of Athanasius and the other inculpated bishops, and acquitted them, restoring the exiles to their sees. They deposed Gregory, who had been intruded at Alex-

---

[1] Hefele, i. 591.

andriá, and likewise the chief bishops of the Eusebian party—Theodore of Heraclea, Narcissus of Neronias, Acacius of Cæsarea, Stephen of Antioch, Ursacius and Valens, Menophantes of Ephesus, and George of Laodicea.

They passed also canons which became famous, censuring bishops for changing their sees, and recognising the Pope's right to act as supreme judge in the cause of bishops: a recognition which Hosius introduced with the words, "Let us honour the memory of the Apostle Peter".

The Sardican canons were specially pointed against the attempt of the Easterns, in the Councils of Cæsarea, Tyre, and Antioch, to set up an authority derived from the emperor against the ancient rule and custom of the Church, which recognised its highest authority in the successor of St. Peter. If a provincial council could be called by the emperor, create and depose bishops, and be subject to no revisal, there was an end of the Church's independence and of its unity together. The Roman empire was parting into two; this was the effect of the founding of Constantinople as New Rome, immediately upon its founder's death. The Eastern bishops of the Arian party maintained that it was beneath their dignity to allow questions decided by themselves to be reconsidered by Western bishops. This was the pretension openly put forward by those of the Arian party who retired to make a council of their own at Philippopolis. They not only persisted in the deposition of Athanasius and the other bishops whom they had banished, but they excommunicated Hosius and Pope Julius himself.

In the relative positions therefore assumed by the Western bishops at the Council of Sardica, and the Eusebian party who withdrew and held a counter-council, the complete question of the Church's unity and the Church's independence was raised.[1] Was there an universal Church governed by its own hierarchy, at the head of which was the bishop of Rome, "in honour of the Apostle Peter"? had this Church one faith, as it had one government? had its dogma and its discipline equally a centre, from which a common rule was perpetually maintained? or did authority in government and in dogma vary with the variations of temporal rule and the vicissitudes of nations? At the moment, it was only that a certain party in the East, under cover of the Eastern emperor's authority, claimed for its bishops independence of the West. Had it succceeded, when the empire was divided not into two parts, but into twenty different nations, each tribe of conquerors would have pretended, in virtue of the same principle, to organise in its own domain a church reputed national, but really dependent on the local sovereign.

Against this the Fathers of Sardica did not institute a new, but recognised the ancient honour paid to the memory of the Apostle Peter, upholding thereby the monarchic principle, the keystone of the arch which sustains the unity, the independence, and the doctrine of the Church together.

But the battle was not yet won. The Council of Sardica was ever esteemed by the Popes as a defence

---

[1] As noted by Broglie, iii. 75-6.

and a sort of completion of the Nicene Council, identical with it in doctrine, and in the ancient discipline of the Church which it maintained. The Eusebian bishops denounced it, and set their emperor against it. Their party in the East refused to accept it; the division became worse instead of better.[1] The orthodox on the one side, the Arians on the other, stood like two hostile camps over against each other. The heads of the Arian party were excommunicated by the West; the Western episcopate itself, with Julius, by the Easterns; and it added to the gravity of the case that the violence exercised for many years in the East had caused many more Eastern bishops to stand on the Eusebian or Arian side than on that of the Nicene and Sardican Council.[2] Before the Fathers even separated a bitter persecution of the latter began in the Eastern empire. Constantius issued a decree ordering that the gates of the cities in Egypt should be closed to those who returned from Sardica, and that if Athanasius and his priests attempted to enter Alexandria, they should be seized and beheaded. Athanasius, in narrating this, remarks: "Thus this new Jewish heresy not only denies the Lord, but has learned to kill ".[3] Constantius instantly punished with exile two bishops who had left the Eusebian party at Sardica, and joined Hosius. Adrianople, adhering to its bishop Lucius, refused communion to the Eusebians, for which ten laymen were punished with death, two priests and three deacons banished to Armenia. Constans defended Athanasius, and is said to have threatened his brother

[1] Niehues, p. 277.   [2] Hefele, i. 601.   [3] *Historia ad Monachos*, c. xix.

to bring him back to Alexandria with an army, but it was only after the death of Gregory in 345 that he was allowed to return in October, 346, having been absent from his see since March, 340. This was the end of his second exile. On his way back he had visited Constantius at Antioch, and met his request that the Arians should be allowed *one* church at Alexandria with the counter request that the Catholics should be allowed *one* in Antioch. For he found the great see of the East in the possession of the Arian Leontius, his predecessor Stephen having been deposed two years before for an infamous plot against the bishop of Cologne, who had been sent to announce the issue of the Council of Sardica to the emperor. Athanasius, when at Antioch, could only worship in a private house, with those who recognised the bishop Eustathius, who had been deposed fifteen years before. Upon the death of Eusebius at Constantinople in 342, Paulus, the legitimate bishop, had attempted to return, but he was banished by Constantius, and subsequently martyred. Macedonius was placed there, and the see of New Rome remained for forty years in Arian hands until St. Gregory of Nazianzum set up the Catholic worship again in a private house, which he called the church of the Resurrection. From the condition of Antioch and Constantinople we may judge of the condition of the Eastern empire in general.

But by the untimely death in 350 of the emperor Constans, who was the support of the Catholics in the West, another and a far worse state of things began. Constantius succeeded to the undivided empire, and when his victory over the usurper Magnentius had set his hands free, the Arian bishops persecuted the orthodox with the full force of the empire at their command. Constantius was alone in his omnipotence, and he confessed in the interview[1] with Pope Liberius that he longed for a victory over Athanasius more impatiently than he had ever desired to punish the usurper who had deprived his brother of throne and life.

Constantius, his father's favourite son, was the most like him, though with a most inferior likeness. Very small in body, short-legged and bandy-legged, he had the same skill as his father in military exercises, the same patience under fatigue, the same moderation in food, the same remarkable continence. With the same taste also for uncontrolled power, he put forward the same literary and theological pretensions, and loved to show off his eloquence and harangue his courtiers. But that solid foundation of talent and genius which set off in Constantine the brilliance of his outward gifts, and tempered defects only too real, was wholly wanting in Constantius. He had no grandeur of ideas, no firmness of resolution, no generosity of feeling, to justify his thirst of absolute power. Impatient of every rival authority, jealous even of the merit which distinguished itself under his own orders, he was at the bottom weak, irresolute, a prey to the secret domination of subordinate influences. Thus one who knew him described him in saying that he had great influence with his eunuch chamberlain Eusebius. A sort of consciousness of his

[1] Theodoret, *Hist.* ii. 16.

own incapacity was apparent even through his ridiculous conceit, and contemporary writers have more than once ridiculed the affected gravity with which he did not venture in public to move, or cough, or spit, or make any gesture, lest the natural movement should break in upon the assumed dignity.[1]

Constantius, just at the time when he succeeded to the sole rule, had married a most accomplished and beautiful lady, the empress Eusebia, who was a declared Arian, and during the whole of her life he was under her influence. When the battle of Mursa decided the fate of the usurper Magnentius,[2] Constantius was in a chapel distant from the field of battle praying for victory. The victory had been won, but while he was still in the agony of hope and fear, bishop Valens of Mursa, who, by messengers secretly posted, had learned the issue, came to him in the church and announced, as the message of an angel who had appeared, that he had conquered. Constantius kept the holy man, who enjoyed the visit of angels, always near him, and shewed him the highest regard. Valens had been a notorious Arian, but had conformed and recanted after the Council of Sardica; he went back again, and, with the empress, became the most dangerous enemy of the orthodox. From this time forth during the eight years to the end of the emperor's life was a time of trial for all the bishops who held the Nicene faith, the like of which does not occur in the history of the Church.

[1] I have drawn this character from Broglie, iii. 7, who refers to passages from Themistius, Ammianus Marcellinus, Aurelius Victor, Liberius, and Julian.
[2] Niehues, 280.

The great object was to destroy Athanasius, who was, in the eyes of the emperor, "a rival of his own sovereignty".[1] "Considering then that he was too great for a subject, Constantius, as if for the peace of his empire, desired his destruction at any rate." "He demanded of the Church to inflict a sort of ecclesiastical ostracism, for the very eminence of Athanasius rendered it unsafe, even for the emperor, to approach him in any other way. The patriarch of Alexandria could not be deposed except after a series of successes over less powerful Catholics, and with the forced acquiescence or countenance of the principal Christian communities. And thus the history of the first few years of the persecution presents to us the curious spectacle of a party warfare raging everywhere, except in the neighbourhood of the person who was the real object of it, and who was left for a time to continue the work of God at Alexandria, unmolested by the councils, conferences, and usurpations which perplexed the other capitals of Christendom."

The first attack was made at Arles in 353, it being at that time the residence of the court. There the emperor held a council, which was attended by legates of the new Pope Liberius, who had succeeded Julius the year before. The Eusebians had already addressed him, hoping to find him more tractable than his predecessor. The Pope, who had been decided in favour of Athanasius by the letter of an Egyptian council, besought the emperor for a general council at Aquileia. But, at this Council of Arles, his trusted legate, Vincent of Capua,

[1] *Arians*, 318, 319.

who had been a Roman legate at the Nicene Council, betrayed his confidence, and was so weak as to fail with the other Fathers who, worn out with sufferings, consented to depose and even excommunicate Athanasius. Paulinus of Treves was nearly the only one who stood up for the Nicene faith and for Athanasius. He was accordingly banished into Phrygia, where he died.

The Pope repudiated the act of his legates, and sent Lucifer of Cagliari to the court, to urge the summoning of a general council. Constantius agreed to call a council, though not a general one, at Milan, where he held his court in 355. More than 300 Western bishops met there. Constantius had just put to death his cousin, the Cæsar Galeus. It was remarked that for the first time after seventy years there was only one crowned head in the whole Roman world; his courtiers addressed him as "your Eternity". He had reached the height of human prosperity, and the time had come when he had promised the Pope Liberius to put an end to the differences which rent the Church. He was in truth entirely resolved to hold in the same hand the spiritual and the material world. For the moment all his power was directed to put down one man, who, at Alexandria, continued to pursue tranquilly his office of bishop, his life of prayer and charity, but who had committed the crime of never flattering his sovereign.

The Council of Milan was held at first in the chief church. The bishops were called upon to consent to the condemnation and deposition of Athanasius. Eusebius of Vercelli and Lucifer of Cagliari offered the strongest opposition. The emperor transferred the council to his palace. He had himself drawn out an edict against Athanasius in the choicest words. He had it presented by his bishops for signature, listening himself behind a curtain to what was passing. They urged his resolution to put an end to the divisions of the bishops, by the will of God, who had made him sole emperor. As this was received with murmurs, he came from behind the curtain, and broke in upon the discussion, exclaiming, "It is my doctrine which you resist; if it is false, as you say, how is it that God has prospered my arms and put the whole world under my law?" Then Lucifer of Cagliari, but just released from the prison in which the emperor had put him for the freedom which he had already shewn in the council, resisted him to the face. "Your doctrine," he said, "is that of Arius, neither more nor less; and those who support it are the precursors of Antichrist. Your power and your success prove nothing in your favour. Scripture is full of apostate kings who have disobeyed God, and whom He has not punished at once." The emperor recurred to the condemnation of Athanasius. When the bishops alleged his absence, he broke in, saying: "What need of so many forms. I am his accuser. Believe, on my word, all that is said against him." "No, emperor," said Eusebius and Lucifer together; "you cannot be the accuser of an absent man: if you were, his absence alone should prevent his being judged. It is not here a matter of government in which you might decide as sovereign: it concerns a bishop; and in the Church accuser and accused must stand on equal terms. Your kingdom," they added, "is not your own : God gave it you, and He can take it away. Do not mix together Rome and the Church, the imperial power and the canons." At this word canons the emperor cut them short. "Let my will be the canon," putting his hand on his sword; "for so the Syrian bishops accept it. Either obey or go into banishment."

Yet the threats prevailed. The mass of the bishops subscribed. But neither the Papal legates, nor Eusebius of Vercelli, nor Lucifer, nor Dionysius bishop of Milan. These were banished into distant provinces, and put under ward of Arianising bishops. Dionysius died in exile in Asia Minor, and Auxentius, an Arian, was put into his see.[1]

Of those who thus suffered, Athanasius, describing this scene, says: "The Saints, shaking off the dust from their feet and looking up to God, gave way neither to the emperor's threat nor his bared sword, but took banishment as the solemn discharge of their ministry; and in their passage from city to city, though in chains, they preached the gospel, proclaiming the true faith, while they anathematised the Arian madness, and gibbeted the turncoats Ursacius and Valens. And herein the purpose of the plotters was reversed. For the more distant the banishment, the more hatred against these was increased. The long pilgrimage of the banished was a proclamation of the others' impiety. Who that looked upon these on their way did not admire them as confessors, while he abominated the others as exe-

[1] Athanasius, *Hist. Arian.* 34-38, from whom this account is taken.

cutioners and homicides, and anything rather than Christians ".

The Council had been overawed, and the consent of a large majority extorted, but this time the Pope's legates had not failed, and still less had the Pope yielded; and the emperor, " though he knew," says the heathen historian, " that his will as to condemning Athanasius was accomplished, burnt with the desire that it should be ratified by that authority also with which the bishops of the eternal city are invested."[1]

But here Athanasius shall speak again.

" Nor had they from the beginning spared even Liberius, bishop of Rome, but extended their madness even thither. Nor did they reverence Rome either as an apostolic throne, or as the capital of Romandom; nor did they remember that they had formerly styled them in letters apostolic men. But, muddling everything, they forgot their own muddle, and were careful only for their impiety. For, seeing that he had the right faith, and hated the Arian heresy, and strove to turn everyone from it, they reasoned in their impiety, if we can persuade Liberius, we shall quickly prevail over all. And they represent him to the emperor as being in their favour. He immediately, hoping to draw all men to him by means of Liberius, sends the eunuch Eusebius with letters and presents, enticing him with the one, threatening him in the other. So the eunuch went to Rome, and began by inviting Liberius

---

[1] Licet sciret impletum, tamen auctoritate quoque, qua potiores æternæ urbis episcopi, firmari desiderio nitebatur ardenti.—Ammianus Marcellinus, xv. 7.

to add his signature to the condemnation of Athanasius, and to communicate with the Arians. This, he said, is the emperor's wish, and offering the presents, and taking his hands, Accept these, and oblige the emperor.

"The bishop, in reply, attempted to instruct him. How can this be done with Athanasius? Not one synod only, but a second,[1] drawn from all parts, has entirely acquitted him: the Roman church, too, has dismissed him in peace: how can we condemn him? Who will receive us if we reject, in his absence, one whom we loved and had in our communion when present? This is not the ecclesiastical rule; we never received such a tradition from the Fathers, who received theirs from the blessed and great Apostle Peter. But, if the emperor really cares for the peace of the Church, if he demands the abrogation of our judgment about Athanasius, let all that has been done on the other side against him and against all be abrogated too, and then a council of the Church be held, far from the palace, not in the presence of the emperor, neither attended by a count, nor threatened by a judge, but where the fear of God alone suffices, and the apostolic constitution. Thus, before every thing, the faith of the Church will be preserved, as our Fathers defined it in the Nicene Council, and those who are of Arius's mind will be cast out, and their heresy be anathematised. After that judgment can be taken upon the charges against Athanasius, or anyone else, and upon the charges against them; the guilty be

---

[1] The synod of Rome in 341, and that of Sardica in 343.

expelled, and the innocent be free. For the faulty in
their faith cannot sit in a council; nor may enquiry as
to a fact precede the examination of faith. All dis-
agreement as to the faith must be terminated, and then
other matters may be enquired into. For our Lord
Jesus Christ did not heal the sick before they had
declared their faith in Him. This is what we have
learnt from our Fathers: this report to the emperor,
which is at once for his service and the church's edifica-
tion. Do not say this to Ursacius and Valens; for
they formerly repented, and now are not faithful."

The eunuch, he says, forgetting that he was before a
bishop, with violent threats went off with his presents,
and committed a great impiety by offering them "at
the Martyrium of the Apostle Peter". When Liberius
learned this he was highly indignant with the guardian
who had not prevented the profanation, and he threw
them away as "an unhallowed sacrifice," which made
the eunuch still more indignant; and returning to the
emperor he moved the whole household of eunuchs: "for
there are nothing but eunuchs with Constantius: they
can do anything with him, and nothing can be done
without them". So the emperor writes to Rome, and
officers of the guard, and notaries, and counts are sent
there, and the prefect is instructed either to get Liberius
by trickery out of Rome and send him to the court, or
to bring him by force. Who can tell, he proceeds, the
terror and the plotting that filled the whole city: how
many were threatened; how many solicited; how many
bishops hid themselves; how many ladies retreated to

their country houses. How many snares were laid for those of strict life; how many sojourning there were obliged to leave; how often they set guards on the harbour and the gates to prevent the faithful having access to Liberius. Rome also had a taste of these enemies of Christ, and learnt what it had not believed before, how the churches in every city had been blockaded by them. Eunuchs were everywhere at the bottom of this. Who shall narrate these things to another generation?"

At last Liberius was taken by force to the court, and the people being warmly attached to him, he was removed with difficulty in the middle of the night.[1] When dragged before Constantius[2] he spoke with the utmost freedom, refusing to condemn a man whom he had not heard.[3] The Pope demanded the convocation of a general council, in which the Nicene faith should be reaffirmed. Then we can all meet at Alexandria, the accused and the accusers, when our brethren have been recalled from their banishment and restored to their several sees. Constantius expressed a personal hatred of Athanasius, as having set both his brothers against him. Liberius replied, O emperor, do not execute private enmity by means of bishops. The hands of bishops are made to bless. The emperor replied: One thing is required of you. My will is, when you have

---

[1] Ægre, populi metu, qui ejus amore flagrabat, cum magna difficultate noctis medio potuit asportari.—Amm. Marc. xv. 7.

[2] ἕλκεται Λιβέριος πρὸς βασιλέα.—Athan. 39.

[3] I have here epitomised the detailed account of the interview given by Theodoret, *Hist.* ii. 13.

embraced communion with the churches, to send you back to Rome. Take therefore the course of peace. Subscribe and return to Rome. "I have already said farewell to my brethren in Rome: for the laws of the Church are greater than residence in Rome." "Take then three days for reflection, whether you will subscribe and return to Rome, or name to what place you wish to be sent." "A delay of three days does not change the mind. Send me therefore whither you will." As Liberius after two days remained unchanged in his resolution, Constantius ordered him to be banished to Berœa in Thrace. As Liberius went out, the emperor sent him five hundred pieces of gold for support. Liberius said to the bearer, Give them back to the emperor who needs them for his soldiers. The empress also sent him the same. Liberius replied: Return them to the emperor, for he needs them for his soldiers: or if not, let him give them to Auxentius and Epictetus;[1] for they need such things. When he would not take them, Eusebius the eunuch offered him others: Liberius answered him: You have made desolate the churches of the world. Do you offer me alms as a convict? Go: first become a Christian. And after three days, having taken nothing, he was banished.

So Liberius departed, an admiration to all, says Athanasius: but the emperor, to heighten the punishment of the bishops he banished, sent each by himself, that they might not comfort and support each other, in

[1] Auxentius was the newly imposed Arian bishop of Milan: Epictetus, of Cività Vecchia, a court-bishop.

which his persecution surpassed that of Maximian. Of Liberius he says that "after a banishment of two years, his courage was broken and he subscribed, through fear of death, with which he was threatened. But this also shews their violence, and the hatred of the heresy which Liberius had, and his testimony to Athanasius, so long as he had freedom of action. For acts done under torture, contrary to the mind's original decision, are acts of the tormentors, not of their victims." [1]

On all this conduct of the Arian party Athanasius says: "The Saviour is meek and teaches 'If anyone wills to come after Me,' and 'he that wills to be My disciple'. He comes to each, but forces him not; rather He knocks and says, Open to Me, My sister, My spouse, and if they open, He comes in; if they hesitate and are not willing, He retires. For the truth is announced, not by swords and spears and soldiers, but by persuasion and counsel. How do persuasion and the dread of an emperor come together? How is there counsel when resistance has banishment and death in prospect? The emperor forces all by power, that it may be clear to all how their prudence is not divine but human, and that the party of Arius have in truth no king but Cæsar, for by him they do whatever they will." [2]

"One thing is asked of you," said Constantius to Pope Liberius, "to condemn Athanasius." Now Athanasius had returned to Alexandria with the express consent of Constantius in October, 346. Councils had

---

[1] *Hist. Arian.* 41.   [2] *Ibid.* 33.

been held at Arles in 353, at Milan in 355, to condemn him: all who would not do so—Paulinus of Treves, the metropolitan of the Gauls; Dionysius of Milan, the metropolitan of Italy; the Pope himself—were in banishment. Yet at the beginning of 356, Athanasius, after more than nine years' continuous occupation of his see, was still at Alexandria in the undisturbed practice of his great authority and saintly life. Then at last Constantius ventured to attack the man who was more hated by him than the usurper of the empire. He first sent Diogenes, a notary, who required Athanasius to leave Alexandria. "I am here," said Athanasius, "by the order of the emperor, sanctioning my return. Show me his order for my removal." There was none forthcoming, and Athanasius remained, until the duke Syrianus with the legions stationed in Egypt arrived, and made the same demand, and received the same answer: "Shew me the express order of the emperor for my removal. This is needful to justify a bishop in leaving his flock." Syrianus had none to shew, and consented publicly to do nothing until a deputation from the city could be sent to learn the emperor's pleasure.

Twenty-three days after this, the 9th February, 356, Syrianus broke his faith, and Athanasius[1] recounts the following scene: "It was night, and some of the people were keeping vigil all the night for the ensuing feast, when the duke Syrianus suddenly broke in with more than five thousand soldiers, fully armed, with drawn

---

[1] *Apologia pro fuga sua*, 24.

swords, bows, weapons, and clubs, and he surrounded the church, posting his troops so close together that none could leave the church and pass through them. Now, as I thought it monstrous ($ἄλογον$) to leave the people in such a confusion, and not rather to be the most exposed to risk, being seated on my throne, I bade the deacon read the psalm, and the people answer, 'His mercy endureth for ever,' and thus all to retire, and go to their home. But as the duke pressed forward and the soldiers surrounded the sanctuary to seize me, the clergy who were there and some of the laity cried out, urging me to withdraw. I said that I would not leave until all were safe. So then rising and enjoining prayer, I earnestly besought all to go before me, saying that it was better that I should be in danger than any of you be hurt. Now when the greater part had gone out and the remainder were following, the monks about me and some of the clergy came up and dragged me away. And so I call the truth to witness, while some of the soldiers encircled the sanctuary, and some surrounded the church, we passed through them, the Lord guiding and guarding us, and got away unperceived by them, glorifying greatly God that we had not betrayed the people, but, having sent them on before us, had been able to save ourselves and to escape the hands of those who sought us."

Athanasius, from his throne as bishop, had not been able to see all which passed. During the prayers conflicts had ensued, swords flashed and arrows flew, sacred virgins were killed. When the morning broke

dead bodies trampled out of recognition strewed the
pavement; women fainting and half stripped lay on the
steps; everything was covered with blood, and Alexandria
learnt that a great crime had been committed, the flock
had been slaughtered, and its bishop had disappeared
no man knew whither.

The people appealed to the justice of the emperor,
but in vain. After waiting many weeks they learnt
that Constantius justified all that had been done. The
Arian prelates at Antioch chose for the successor of
Athanasius a man of bad reputation—George of Cappadocia,—who by the end of Lent appeared under charge of
a high officer with an armed force, and was so installed.
Aided by the civil power, he proceeded to search every
spot for the proscribed traitor. Churches, houses,
gardens, convents, even tombs, were examined and
despoiled by a furious soldiery. The friends of
Athanasius were every moment exposed to persecuting
visits; the gates were guarded; the vessels entering or
leaving the harbour were searched. Athanasius could
nowhere be found.

This tyranny of Constantius which we have been
reviewing was drawn in its true colours at the time by
the two great confessors. Hosius dared to use in his
letter to the omnipotent despot words which afterwards
led to the loss of his life by cruel treatment: "Cease
these proceedings, I beseech you, and remember that
you are a mortal man. Be afraid of the day of judgment
and keep yourself pure thereunto. Intrude not yourself
into ecclesiastical matters, neither give commands to us

concerning them. God hath put into your hands the kingdom; to us He hath entrusted the affairs of His Church; and as he who should steal the empire from you would resist the ordinance of God, so likewise fear on your part lest by taking on yourself the government of the Church you become guilty of a great offence. It is written, 'Render unto Cæsar the things that are Cæsar's, and unto God the things that are God's'. Neither therefore is it permitted unto us to exercise an earthly rule, nor have you, sire, any authority to burn incense."

"Such were the sentiments, and such the letter," says Athanasius, "of the Abraham-like old man, Hosius, truly so-called." His own were similar: "When was such a thing heard of before from the beginning of the world? When did a judgment of the Church receive its validity from the emperor? or rather, when was his decree ever recognised by the Church? There have been many councils held heretofore, and many judgments passed by the Church; but the Fathers never sought the consent of the emperor thereto, nor did the emperor busy himself with the affairs of the Church".[1]

Constantius reigned for nearly six years after the outrage upon Athanasius which has just been described, and during all that time Athanasius was a fugitive in hiding from place to place, but ever guarded by the inviolable fidelity of those whom he trusted. He has not furnished us with a history in detail of his dangers.

---

[1] Athanasius, *History of the Arians*, 44 and 52, Oxford translation.

and escapes; but a considerable portion of his surviving writings was composed during this period. All the power of the emperor failed to track the bishop whom he prosecuted as an enemy of the public peace, and pursued with unrelenting hatred, though he was able to maintain the intruder George in the place of the true bishop at Alexandria. This was a man of whom the heathen historian [1] says, "He forgot that his profession obliged him to the exercise of justice and mercy". Constantius could not foresee that the intruder whom he had forced upon the second see of the Church would be torn in pieces by the vengeance of the people, and that Athanasius, after escaping the rage of a Christian emperor, would return with a triumphal acceptance to his diocese, in virtue of a decree issued by the cousin whom he had just made Cæsar, when that cousin had become sole emperor in his own place, after denying the Christian faith, so that an ardent worshipper of the heathen gods would undo the work of a son of Constantine, the patron of heresy.

This third banishment of Athanasius lasted from February, 356, to February, 362.

It is needless to dwell upon the councils held in the last five years of Constantius. In 357-9 the Arians[2] and Semiarians successively draw up fresh creeds at Sirmium. In 359 the great Councils of Seleucia and Ariminum, being one bipartite council, represent the East and West

---

[1] Ammianus, xxii. 11.

[2] See Newman's *Arians*, p. 457-9. Some alterations are made in the translations which follow.

respectively. At Seleucia there were 150 bishops, of which only the twelve or thirteen from Egypt were champions of the Nicene "Consubstantial". At Ariminum there were as many as 400 bishops who, worn out by the artifice of long delay on the part of the Arians, abandoned the "Consubstantial" and subscribed the ambiguous formula which the heretics had substituted for it. As to these times the words of those who lived in them have the greatest weight, and great scandals are best described by saints, and the shortcomings of bishops by bishops. Of the Council of Ariminum, St. Jerome's words make any other needless; when he says "the Catholics of the whole world were strangely surprised to find that the Council had made Arians of them"; and again, "nearly all the churches of the whole world, under the pretence of peace and of the emperor, are polluted with the communion of the Arians".

In the year 360, St. Hilary, a bishop, a great confessor and a doctor of the Church, sums up the period of thirty-five years just passed to Constantius himself: "Since the Nicene Council we know very well that we have done nothing but write the Creed. While we fight about words, inquire about novelties, take advantage of ambiguities, criticise authors, fight on party questions, have difficulties in agreeing, and prepare to anathematise each other, there is scarce a man who belongs to Christ. Uncertain winds of doctrine blow us about: if we teach, we throw into confusion; if we are taught, we fall into error. Take for instance last year's Creed: what alteration is there not in it already? First we have the Creed which bids us not use the 'Consubstantial'; then comes another which decrees and teaches it; next the third excuses the term 'substance' as adopted by the Fathers, in their simplicity; lastly, the fourth, which instead of excusing condemns. . . . We determine creeds by the year or by the month; we change our own determinations; we prohibit our changes; we anathematise our prohibitions. Thus we either condemn others in our own persons, or ourselves in the instance of others, and, while we bite and devour one another, are like to be consumed one of another."

And Gregory of Nazianzum, in his panegyric of that man's life who, of all others, was a contrast to any such weakness, says of this time: "Surely the pastors have done foolishly . . . for excepting a very few, who either on account of their insignificance were passed over, or by reason of their virtue resisted, and who were to be left as a seed and a root for the springing up again and revival of Israel by the influences of the Spirit, all temporised, only differing from each other in this, that some succumbed earlier and others later; some were foremost champions and leaders in the impiety, and others joined the second rank of the battle, being overcome by fear, or by interest, or by flattery, or, what was most excusable, by their own ignorance".

Such a general condition as that described in these passages of three contemporary saints can scarcely be found at any other time in the eighteen centuries of the Church's history. "The prospect was dark indeed when Julian, proclaimed emperor by his soldiers and refused recognition by his cousin, was advancing to meet him. Suddenly the Roman world was startled with the news that the last son of Constantine at the age of forty-four had been carried off by a fever, having just had time to receive baptism from Euzoius, the Arian bishop of Antioch. He too, like his father, had remained outside the Church to the last moments of his life, while he presumed, not being even a catechumen, to judge her most sacred doctrines, to banish her chief bishops, to fill her greatest sees with heretical intruders. His government, since he became sole monarch, had been in all his conduct towards the episcopate a miserable parody of his father's worst deeds, and he finished the counterfeit by receiving baptism on his deathbed from the Arian Euzoius, whom court favour had placed as bishop in Antioch, as Constantine had received it from Eusebius, whom court favour had placed in Nicomedia.

On the death of Constantius, St. Jerome exclaims: "The Lord awakes from sleep: the beast dies: tranquillity returns".

Constantius died November 3, 361. Julian reigned sole emperor until June 27, 363, somewhat short of twenty months, when the javelin of a Persian terminated his duel with "the Galilean". In this short time he had first recalled the banished bishops to their sees, in the hope that the intestine contests of the bishops might weaken the Church which he had deserted, the effect being that Athanasius returned in triumph to his patriarchal chair, after six years' outlawry, in virtue of an apostate's decree. Julian had thrown off the mask of equal dealing, and had compelled Athanasius before the end of the year 362 to a fourth banishment, being made furious by the great effect of a synod which Athanasius had summoned in 362, immediately upon his return, and by the wisdom and gentleness he had shewn in healing the wounds of the Church. After abundant persecutions of individuals, Julian had left for his Persian expedition, intending upon his triumphant return to set on foot a general persecution of the Christians. Instead of that he left his throne, at the age of thirty-two, to be inherited by a very loyal Christian officer, Jovian; and upon Jovian's sudden death, by another, Valentinian, both of whom Julian had in vain tried to seduce from their faith. Thus within a period of two years and four months[1] the Roman world saw four successive emperors on its throne—Constantius, Julian, Jovian, and Valentinian; and the last, on the very day of his election, March 1, 364, was required to name a second emperor; and in July, 364, he had given the East to his brother Valens, and himself taken the West. Thus thirty-four years after the founding of Constantinople, the New Rome, the definitive division of the great empire took place. Divided on Constantine's death in 337 under his children, it was united under Constantius in 350, yet he soon named his cousin Gallus Cæsar, and upon his execution another cousin Julian, who

[1] From Nov. 3, 361, to March 1, 364.

reigned for twenty months alone, and Jovian for eight months. When Valentinian was chosen, the strong influences, public and private, which divided the East from the West made themselves permanently felt: the Eastern jealousy of Rome had found a citadel for itself in the new capital: more than that, two different spirits were seated, one on the banks of the Tyber, where the old republic had left imperishable memories; the other in that peerless Eastern queen of cities, where the despotism which from time immemorial had ruled Egypt, Assyria, Persia, and the realms descended from their Macedonian conqueror had found a gorgeous dwelling in a far more propitious site than that enjoyed by Babylon, or Nineveh, or Memphis, or Thebes, or Persepolis, and strove henceforth to rule Europe after the fashion of Asia. But that Peter who sat at Rome had prepared another destiny for Europe and for the world.

The brothers, Valentinian and Valens, governed their dominions separately; whereas the tyranny of Constantius had been exercised over the bishops of the East and West at once. The change was great for the Church. Valentinian was a Catholic, jealous of his temporal rights, but not inclined to infringe spiritual liberties; indeed no emperor of the fourth and fifth centuries was so careful as he to keep the two powers apart. Perhaps the mischief wrought by the perpetual interference of Constantius dwelt upon his mind. It would appear, at least, that in May, 364, when he[1] was still in Thrace,

---

[1] Tillemont, *Empereurs*, v. 9.

some Eastern bishops having spoken to him of disputes respecting the faith, he replied that it was for bishops to treat these questions, and to meet when they chose for that purpose: for himself he was a layman, and it was not allowable for him to mix himself in this sort of difficulties;[1] and St. Ambrose quotes and praises his expression that it was not his office to be judge between bishops. He loved and favoured the Catholics, but without troubling the Arians or any other heretical sect. From the commencement of his reign he made express laws, giving liberty both to heretics and to heathens to follow what belief they pleased, assuming as it were a neutral position.

The persecution in the West had ceased; but in the East the emperor Valens had been baptised by Eudoxius, the Arian bishop of Constantinople, and had fallen under his influence. An Arian court-bishop and a narrow-minded despot fitted at once into each other, and from this time forth Eudoxius, during the three years which elapsed to his death, was the counsellor and guide of Valens in all his dealings with religion. This man had followed the example of his predecessor Eusebius, having been bishop first of Germanicia, then of Antioch, and lastly of Constantinople. Thus Valens in the year 367, as the first fruits of his Arian baptism, published an edict banishing from their sees the bishops who had been banished by Constantius and restored by Julian.

---

[1] Socr. 6, c. 7. ἐμοὶ μὲν ἔφη μετὰ λαοῦ τεταγμένῳ οὐ θέμις τοιαῦτα πολυπραγμονεῖν. οἱ δὲ ἱερεῖς, οἷς τούτου μέλει, καθ᾽ ἑαυτοὺς ὅπη βούλονται συνίτωσαν.

For the remaining years of his life, which were eleven, he attempted to repeat in the East the persecution which Constantius had exercised through the whole empire. Equal to him in malignity, he fell considerably beneath the power which a son of Constantine could wield.[1]

Athanasius, having returned from a great episcopal visitation, received from the prefect an order to leave his see at once. The people rose in his favour: the prefect as in the former case consented to refer to the emperor. But Athanasius was not deceived; as soon as the sedition was appeased, he retired on a dark night to a secret retreat, and the same night his dwelling was surrounded and rigidly searched. This was the fifth and last banishment of Athanasius, but Valens did not long persist in it, and then, until his death in 373, the great confessor remained undisturbed, regarded by the whole world with awe and admiration.

The words of St. Basil to him just before his death may fitly be inserted here, inasmuch they bear double witness to the greatness of Athanasius and to the condition of the Eastern church.[2]

"The more the sicknesses of the Church increase, so much the more earnestly do we all turn towards thy perfection, persuaded that for thee to lead us is our sole remaining comfort in our difficulties. By the power of thy prayers, by the wisdom of thy counsels, thou art able to carry us through this fearful storm, as all are sure who have heard or made trial of that

---

[1] Broglie, v. 78.
[2] S. Basil, Ep. lxxx.—Translation of Card. Newman, in the *Arians*, p. 381.

perfection ever so little. Wherefore cease not both to pray for our souls, and to stir us up by thy letters; didst thou know the profit of these to us, thou wouldst never let pass an opportunity of writing to us. For me, were it vouchsafed to me, by the co-operation of thy prayers, once to see thee and to profit by the gift lodged in thee, and to add to the history of my life a meeting with so great and apostolical a soul, surely I should conceive myself to have received from the loving mercy of God a compensation for all the ills with which my life has ever been afflicted."

During eleven years the Eastern episcopate in general groaned under that tyranny of Valens to which Basil here refers. One incident will be sufficient to mark the character of the man. · He had left Constantinople in 370, on his way to Antioch, when at Nicomedia he received information of the death of his counsellor Eudoxius. The Catholics of his capital sent him a deputation of eighty ecclesiastics, the most virtuous and distinguished whom they could find, to plead with him in favour of Evagrius, whom they wished to elect bishop. He received them haughtily, and in dismissing them gave a secret instruction to his prætorian prefect Modestus, who accompanied him, to put them to death. The prefect, fearing that he would excite a sedition if he attempted the public execution of so many, pretended to send them away in exile, and they were embarked as if for their several places · of banishment. But the sailors were commanded to set the vessel on fire as soon as they reached the mid sea. This took place in the

Astasian Gulph. The crew set fire to the ship, took refuge in a small barque which followed them and escaped. The burning ship was consumed with those shut up in it.[1]

There is no reason why we should dwell upon the cruelties which Valens practised, or upon the resistance offered to him by the great Basil and others. The final scene of his life was that in the year 378 he led a great and well-appointed army, commanded by his best generals, against the Goths, in the neighbourhood of Adrianople. The Romans were beaten that day as they had not been beaten since Cannæ. Two-thirds of their force were destroyed, and Valens, wounded by an arrow, could not fly, and took refuge in a peasant's cottage. The cottage was set on fire, and the emperor's retinue fled, leaving him in it. There he waited for the flames which consumed him; and no part of his body was found.

The consternation at Constantinople on the arrival of these tidings was extreme, as also that of Gratian when they met him upon his march eastward to the succour of his uncle Valens, by whose death he became, at the age of nineteen, sole emperor. Looking around him in perplexity for one whom he could summon to help him, he chose Theodosius, the son of the renowned general of the same name, who had been unjustly executed three years before; since which the son had lived in retreat upon his property in Spain. Theodosius obeyed the summons, met the present crisis by wise arrangements,

---

[1] Socrates, iv. 16; Tillemont, v. 97; Broglie, v. 93.

and on the 19th January, 379, was proclaimed by Gratian emperor, who gave to him the part of the empire which had been governed by Valens, while he added to it the province of Eastern Illyria, which he detached from the West, an act which afterwards led to the most important ecclesiastical consequences. Theodosius, being ill of a fever in the winter of 379-380, was led by the danger he was in to receive instruction and baptism from Ascholius, bishop of Thessalonica. During his convalescence he learnt from the bishop the religious condition of the empire which he had just been called to govern. Ascholius informed him that "so far as Macedonia the Nicene faith prevailed ; but that at Constantinople and throughout the East in general the Arian heresy and many other sects divided the people". Part of what Ascholius told the new emperor must have been how very much his immediate predecessor Valens had brought about this state of division. The most miserably torn city in all his dominions was the capital itself, then ruled by the Arian bishop Demophilus. He was the successor of Eudoxius, who "is said to have bound Valens by oath at the time of his baptism that he would establish Arianism as the State religion of the East ; and thus to have prolonged its ascendency for an additional sixteen years after the death of Constantius."[1] Theodosius may have thought that the evil which one emperor had wrought another might remove ; but he was in no doubt as to the terrible danger to the empire which these divisions caused, and by which the Eastern episcopate was utterly deranged ;

[1] *Arians*, 389.

and on the 28th February the following law was issued :

"The emperors Gratian, Valentinian, and Theodosius, to the people of the city of Constantinople : [1]

"It is our will that all the peoples who are governed by our clemency hold the religion which is proved to have been delivered to the Romans by the divine Apostle Peter, since it has been maintained there from his time to our own, and which it is notorious that the Pontiff Damasus follows, and Peter, bishop of Alexandria, a man of apostolic sanctity ; that is, that according to the discipline of the Apostles and the doctrine of the Gospel, we believe one Godhead of the Father, and the Son, and the Holy Ghost, of equal majesty, in the Holy Trinity. Those who follow this law we order to take the name of Catholic Christians ; the rest, whom we judge demented and furious, shall suffer the infamy of heresy; their meetings shall not take the name of churches : we reserve them, first to the divine vengeance, and next to that punishment which we shall be inspired to inflict." And another law, issued the same day, brands as the civil crime of sacrilege the wilful ignorance or neglectful violation of the law so enacted.

In this law two expressions are to be noted as joined

---

[1] Cunctos populos quos clementiæ nostræ regit temperamentum in tali volumus religione versari quam divinum Petrum Apostolum tradidisse Romanis religio usque nunc ab ipso insinuata declarat ; quamque Pontificem Damasum sequi claret, et Petrum Alexandriæ episcopum, virum Apostolicæ sanctitatis : Hoc est ut secundum Apostolicam disciplinam Evangelicamque doctrinam Patris et Filii, et Spiritus Sancti unam Deitatem sub parili Majestate et sub pia Trinitate credamus, &c.

together while distinguished from each other: the apostolic discipline, that is, the *polity* set up by the Apostle, the living Church ; and the evangelic doctrine, which is the teaching which it carries on from age to age. Both together make up the religion, the perpetual subsistence of which from the time of Peter to the time of the law's issue it declares to be evidence that Peter delivered it to the Romans. It would be difficult to devise a stronger historical testimony to the truth of Peter's teaching at Rome, and of the episcopal descent from him, than this record of the Roman State given by its rulers three hundred and thirteen years after the date of his martyrdom.

But it likewise exhibits the rulers of the Roman empire presenting to their subjects the church founded by St. Peter at Rome, and the bishop of that see, Damasus, as being to the whole Church the keystone of discipline and belief, the bearer of the whole apostolic tradition, to the whole Church, just as the bishop was the keystone of his particular diocese, as to government and as to doctrine.

CHAPTER VI.

FROM CONSTANTINE AT NICÆA TO THEODOSIUS AT CONSTANTINOPLE.

WHEN the remarkable law of 380, which stands at the head of the ecclesiastical legislation of Theodosius, was issued, the exercise of imperial omnipotence in the fifty years preceding it had well nigh disorganised and corrupted the Eastern episcopate. The great Constantine, from the time that he left Rome, and fell under the influence of Eusebius of Nicomedia, began the attack upon the constitution of the Church; it was repeated with deadly effect by his son Constantius, as soon as he became sole emperor; at his death the West was delivered from it, but it was continued through the East by Valens, until the sword of the Goths rescued the Church from the heretic, as the spear of the Persian had rescued her from the infidel.

In what did the attack consist? During the whole period of the pagan persecution, from Nero to the peace of Constantine, the Church had been governed by her episcopate, under the paternal influence of a sort of Triumvirate, which consisted in the three sees of Peter

—Rome, Alexandria, and Antioch. In the great Nicene Council, the first in which the episcopate had met as one body representing the whole Church, the three primatial sees were seen acting in strictest union. In the first place the 318 bishops met "directed from Rome,"[1] and secondly, they were presided over by her legates Hosius and two priests; there the bishop of Alexandria pleaded the cause against Arius, while the bishop of Antioch, Eustathius, was a fervent defender of the Nicene Creed. The council, convoked by Constantine's authority, was convoked also in full agreement with all the three sees. So things remained until Eusebius, having been first recalled from banishment, then by flattery and obsequiousness rose to be the guide and inspirer of Constantine in affairs of the Church. In 328 Athanasius had succeeded Alexander; so that the great champion of the "Consubstantial" sat on the second throne of the Church, at the head of the hundred bishops of Egypt; and Eustathius, equally zealous, was on the third throne of Antioch. What a position this was may be estimated from the fact that in the sixth century the patriarch of Antioch[2] stood at the head of 12 provinces, having 163 suffragan bishops. The provinces were Syria Prima, with Antioch, and 9 bishoprics; Phœnicia Prima, with Tyre, and 13 bishoprics; Phœnicia Secunda, with Damascus, and 14 bishoprics; Arabia, with Bostra, and 15 bishoprics; Cilicia Prima, with Tarsus, and 8 bishoprics; Cilicia Secunda, with Anazarbus, and 10 bishoprics; Syria Secunda, with Apamea,

---

[1] See above, p. 35, note.   [2] See Hergenröther's *Kirchen-lexicon*, i. 940.

and 8 bishoprics; Provincia Euphratensis, with Mabug or Hierapolis, and 14 bishoprics; Osrhoene, with Edessa, and 13 bishoprics; Mesopotamia, with Amida, and 14 bishoprics; Isauria, with Seleucia, and 30 bishoprics; Cyprus, with Constantia, and 13 bishoprics. According to the discipline recognised, but not created, by the Nicene Council, the metropolitans of these provinces were consecrated by the bishop of Antioch; that is, their election was confirmed, and their authority conferred by him. As many of these cities in which the metropolitans sat, and also many seats of their suffragans, were populous and cultivated, splendid monuments of that Hellenic civilisation which Alexander's conquest had spread over the East, there is good ground for supposing that at the time of the Nicene Council the patriarchate of Antioch was the most flourishing portion of the Church.[1] Its bishops far outnumbered those of Egypt, but likewise their individual greatness, from the importance of the cities which they ruled, still more exceeded that of the Egyptian bishops [2] "over whom the successor of St. Mark had a sovereign because a solitary greatness". Therefore, though the "bishop of Antioch was comparatively a little man, because he had so many rivals," the influence which a fervent supporter of the true doctrine in the great see of the East would exert, would be known by none better than the man who at Berytus had been a suffragan of one among his metropolitans, and was then the archbishop of Nico-

---

[1] See Newman's *Development*, p. 284, 2nd ed.
[2] See Newman's *Hist. Sketches*, iii. 339.

media, the seat of the court until it moved to the new capital, Constantinople.

The result of "the apostolic discipline and evangelical teaching" which the imperial law of 380 declares to have been instituted in Rome and delivered to the Romans by St. Peter, was that at the end of the great conflict of three centuries with Græco-Roman heathenism the bishop of Rome sat in the council of his brother-bishops, as it were on a dais of three steps, of which the lowest was occupied by the bishop of Antioch, the second by the bishop of Alexandria, the third by himself. These two great bishops were in no sense his rivals, nor animated by the spirit of jealousy towards him. On the contrary, the precedence which they enjoyed over so many of their brethren was grounded precisely on the same principle as his: a purely ecclesiastical and spiritual principle, their descent from Peter as the root of the whole hierarchy. It was a part of the divine Providence, in plain words, no doubt an express direction of our Lord, that Peter chose these three cities: and especially Rome as the capital of the empire, the mother city. Peter was the gardener; Rome the soil.[1] No other soil would have suited the gardener so well, but the blessing was given to the gardener; the divine power was in the commission "Be shepherd over my sheep," the pastures of which he was appointed to choose and allot.

Now let us see how Eusebius, who was of Berytus, and is of Nicomedia, and is to be of Constantinople,

[1] Niehues.

not holding the doctrine of Peter, set himself to overthrow his discipline.

His deposition of Eustathius, bishop of Antioch, has been already described. A word must be said upon its consequences,[1] which were to cause a schism in the church of Antioch, that was not fully healed for ninety years. There was an Arian and an orthodox succession of bishops. When Eustathius had been deposed on a false charge of sabellianism and adultery, an Arian bishop Euphronius was put in his place, with the result that the Catholic congregation met in another quarter of the city. At the council of Sardica Stephen was bishop. He was deposed by Constantius, in 344, for an infamous plot against the bishops sent to represent to the emperor that council's decrees. He was succeeded by another Arian, the eunuch Leontius. Upon his death, in 357, the see was fraudulently seized by Eudoxius, bishop of Germanicia, who was afterwards translated to Constantinople. In 361, Meletius, bishop of Sebaste, being supposed to be an Arian, was translated to Antioch; but turning out to be orthodox, was banished by his own party thirty days after he had entered Antioch. Euzoius, a friend of Arius himself, was put into the see. The church of Antioch was now divided into three parties: the Catholics who had always been faithful to Eustathius, who were in communion with the Pope and Athanasius; a middle party who held to Meletius; and the Arians under Euzoius. Paulinus became bishop of the first. Meletius had returned

---

[1] See Stephen's *Life of S. Chrysostome*, pp. 17-20.

from exile under Julian; he was banished again under Valens: he died when presiding over the council of Constantinople; and instead of Paulinus succeeding him, according to the covenant made by the two parties, and earnestly pressed upon them by St. Gregory of Nazianzum, Flavian was elected.

During this whole century, from the deposition of Eustathius in 330, this Christian community of Antioch, which Chrysostome calculated at 100,000 souls, was torn in pieces by rival successions and opposing creeds; but the prevailing party for thirty years, until Meletius, was Arian. The effect of this confusion at Antioch, not only upon its own people, but further upon the bishops and metropolitans of which it stood at the head, may be conceived.

At Constantinople it was still worse. Even in the lifetime of Alexander, in 335, the first council held in the city, dedicated five years before, and intended to be entirely Christian, was held by the Arian party.[1] At his death, in 337, the two parties, Catholic and Arian, stood over against each other armed for the conflict. The Catholics elected Paulus, whose whole life for fifteen years was a series of banishments and restorations. When first deposed he appealed to Pope Julius, and was restored by him: he was again deposed by Constantius, and finally martyred by the Arians at Cucusus in 352. Eusebius, not contented with Nicomedia, got himself removed to Constantinople about the end of 338, after which, for forty years, that city was mainly in Arian

[1] Photius, i. 9.

hands. Eusebius died in 342. Macedonius, after a second banishment of Paulus, was established by force, when the prefect of Constantius committed in the church itself a massacre. "His exploits," says Socrates,[1] "on behalf of Christianity, consisted of murders, battles, incarcerations, and civil wars." He was at length deposed by Constantius for moving without his leave the coffin of Constantine, and was succeeded by Eudoxius, in 360, who had himself moved by Constantius from Antioch. He became afterwards to Valens what Eusebius had been to Constantine. He died in 370,[2] when about to consecrate a bishop for Cyzicus; by which is seen that the bishop of Constantinople in these first forty years under Arian mastery had accustomed himself to interfere with the neighbouring dioceses. The confusion of the time favoured usurpation, and these early acts made precedents on which future ambition might lay hold. At the death of Eudoxius, the Catholics chose Evagrius, the Arians Demophilus, bishop of Beroea. Demophilus remained by the help of Valens in possession, and treated the Catholics with great severity.

The result of the first fifty years from the foundation of the city which Constantine meant to be purely Christian, was that the Catholics, when the death of Valens[3] at last set them free from the most cruel oppression, scattered and headless as they were, cast their eyes upon the most illustrious living champion of the Nicene faith, Gregory of Nazianzum. They invited

[1] Socrates, ii. 38.   [2] Photius, i. 16.   [3] Photius, i. 18.

him to take up his abode among them, and when he came, in 379, he preached his most famous discourses in the room of a private house. The churches were in the possession of Demophilus the Arian; and he contended with five different sects: Eunomians, Macedonians, Apollinarists, Photinians, and Novatians. He was often pelted with stones; and once his enemies forced their way into his chapel, which they sacked. His life was in continual danger from their plots.

From Antioch and Constantinople we turn to Alexandria; and here the glory won by the great Confessor, in his pontificate of forty-five years, from 328 to 373, is such that the mind rests upon his unbroken fortitude and faultless maintenance of the faith, rather than on the evils which the violence of his opponents, having ever the imperial omnipotence at their command, inflicted on his city and patriarchate. His own banishments were five. First he fled from the council of Tyre to plead his cause in person with Constantine. This was in 335. The result was that Constantine sent him in exile to Treves, though he did not confirm the deposition from his see which the council of Tyre attempted to inflict. After two years and four months at Treves, Athanasius, in consequence of a general edict by the three emperors, returned to Alexandria, November 23, 338. Then ensued an interval of fifteen months, during which Athanasius was exposed to many plots; and at the end of which the intruder, Gregory of Cappadocia, is sent from the court of Constantinople with an armed force to take possession of his see; and

Athanasius, four days before his arrival, flies to the Pope at Rome, in March, 340, where he arrives after Easter. He remains at Rome three years; and though restored by the Pope at his Council held in 341, and again at Sardica at the end of 343, orders were given by Constantius to behead him, and the priests with him, if he went back to his see. The forcible intrusion of Gregory was confirmed by the council of the Encænia at Antioch in 341, when he was appointed bishop of Alexandria, and there he continued in full possession until his death, June 26, 345. Athanasius did not find it safe to return until October 21, 346, having been absent more than six years and a half from his diocese, during which every sort of iniquity and violence had been practised on his people. After this he remains more than nine years in possession of his see, though the chief object which Constantius had, as soon as he became sole emperor in 350, was to expel him. Constantius had him condemned at the council of Arles, where he then held his court, in 353; again, as we have seen, at the council of Milan, where he held his court, in 355, and where, finding Pope Liberius resolute in defending Athanasius, he banished him to Thrace. At length, on the 9th February, 356, the Duke Syrianus, having in his train a second intruder, George of Cappadocia, burst upon the city, and found Athanasius on his throne in the church, when the scene ensued which we have given above in the words of Athanasius himself. From this time he was an outlaw in hiding for six years. The miscreant George, enthroned by violence in 356, committed every atrocity upon his people, until he was massacred by the pagans at the end of 361, when Julian had succeeded; and Athanasius, after an absence of six years in this third banishment, returned in triumph, in 362, in consequence of Julian's decree restoring all bishops to their sees who had been exiled by Constantius. The first act of Athanasius was to hold a great council, in which he showed so gentle a wisdom, and did so much to heal the wounds of the Church, inflicted by the eleven years of tyranny under Constantius, that Julian, in a fury, banished him at the end of that same year, 362, ordering that if he did not quit the city by the 1st December his life should be answerable for it. This fourth banishment lasted only about eight months, Julian being killed in June, 363, and succeeded by Jovian, who summoned Athanasius to Antioch, and received his advice as to the course which he should take in regard to the state of the Church. Then ensued three years of peace, until, in 367, Valens renewed the decree of banishment for those bishops who had been expelled by Constantius. Once again the prefect of Egypt was ordered to seize upon Athanasius; once again, warned in time, he disappeared, and is said to have lain hid four months in his father's tomb. After this he was brought back, and not again disturbed to the time of his death, May 2, 373.[1] But this was only a personal exemption; for after his death the Arians not only possessed themselves of the see of Alexandria, but were guilty of the most frightful crimes and cruelties

[1] Hefele, i. 715.

there. His legitimate successor, Peter, had to fly, poor as a beggar; his priests were driven into misery: whoever bewailed them, men and women, were scourged; and the Arian, Lucius, was put in his seat.

What this penalty of banishment was, we may see from a bare enumeration of the facts in this case of the most illustrious of all its victims. Not only was he practically deposed from his see, but twice he saw the see usurped during periods, each of more than five years, by intruders, bad in personal conduct, heretical in their belief, put in by force, maintained by force, persecuting his flock. The cruelties recorded by Athanasius himself are such as not to have been exceeded in any pagan persecution of the three centuries. And these violences extended over his patriarchate as well as his own diocese, where we read, in 356, of the banishment of sixteen bishops for refusing the new-made creed.

From the time of the Church's peace, inaugurated by Constantine, the position of bishops throughout the empire was, as we have seen, one of great dignity. In addition to all their rights of sacred character, which had been accepted by the State without derogation, and to the homage of Christians which attended on every bishop in his see, they had become imperial officers of high rank: their judgments had been made of legal force: the decrees of Nicæa had been made laws. Moreover, in all the greater sees, the generous piety of the Christian people had placed large temporal endowments in the hands of the bishops. A well-known story describes how one of the greatest Roman nobles, still a heathen, said jestingly to Pope Damasus—"Make me bishop of Rome, and I will become a Christian". Scarcely inferior was the position of the bishop of Alexandria; so that at the end of the fourth century we have Orestes, the prefect of Egypt, indignant at what he termed his "mastery,"[1] as overshadowing his own rank, and trenching even on imperial grandeur.

Now of all this the bishop might be, at the word of the emperor, at once despoiled. Such was the whip of scorpions which the first Christian emperor had used himself, and put into the hands of his successors to use, and which one of his sons used with no small success. The way of its application was that a synod was convoked by the emperor, not ecumenical, not provincial, but composed of some provinces, and of such bishops as, instructed by his courtier bishops, he chose.[2] The council so summoned passed canons, deposed bishops, and put others in their place. Thereupon, the emperor sent into banishment the man deposed. How this was done may be seen three times over in the case of Athanasius. Thus, Eustathius was banished from Antioch to Thrace, in virtue of an Eusebian council; so Paul from Constantinople, ending his days after several returns and banishments by Arian cruelty at Cucusus, an evil name afterwards in the history of his great successor, St. Chrysostome. Thus Dionysius of Milan was banished after the council of Milan in 355, refusing to

---

[1] δυναστεία, Soc. vii. 11.
[2] See this fact mentioned by Eusebius in his life (iv. 42), in the case of the council of Tyre, who evidently considers it as worthy of the highest praise.

sacrifice Athanasius, or to accept Arian doctrine, to Asia-Minor, where he died, and whence his relics were brought back in triumph by his successor, St. Ambrose, in doing which he was helped by the great Basil, who has written thereon one of his most touching letters. Thus St. Hilary, condemned by a Gallican council, was sent from Poitiers to Asia, whence he wrote, in 360 :[1] " I am not speaking of things foreign to my knowledge, I am not writing about what I am ignorant of; I have heard and I have seen the shortcoming of persons who are round about me, not of laymen, but of bishops. For excepting the bishop Eleusius and a few with him, for the most part the ten Asian provinces, within whose boundaries I am situate, are truly ignorant of God." By these are meant the east and south provinces of Asia-Minor, pretty nearly as cut off by a line passing from Cyzicus to Seleucia through Synnada. Happily St. Hilary, after years spent in exile, during which he was not silent nor inactive, was restored to his see.

But take one more instance. Constantine had bestowed on Pope Sylvester an imperial palace situated in the finest part of Rome, and within it he had built the church first in dignity among all the churches of the world, as the patriarchal church of the first bishop. There Sylvester, Mark, and Julius had lived in dignity, unrivalled even on its temporal side since the emperor himself had quitted Rome, and left there no imperial representative; for the prefect of Rome was a less man than its bishop: the power of the former ended with

[1] Quoted in *Arians*, p. 488.

the city; the word of the latter traversed sea and land over the whole empire. There, too, dwelt Liberius, in highest renown both for his orthodox belief and for the works of charity of which he was the centre. His legates had refused their assent to the conclusions which the emperor, with the most barefaced imposition of his will, as the living canon of the church, had forced upon the majority of the bishops at the council of Milan. Then the heathen historian remarks, that though he had gained his will with these to condemn Athanasius, he was not satisfied "unless he could add to it the authority which the bishops of the eternal city enjoy". So the all-powerful eunuch was sent with gifts and threatenings to bend the Pope, but both were vain. Then the prefect was instructed to seize his person, and send him under durance to the court. For this it was requisite, so much was he beloved, to smuggle him out of the city by night, and under false pretences. When brought before Constantius, the Pope, as we have seen, equally resisted his will, and met the threat of banishment with the words, "I have already taken leave of my brethren at Rome". Thereupon he was sent to Berœa in Thrace, severed from his counsellors, put in charge of an Arian bishop as jailor, deceived with false reports, beset with frauds, threatened finally with death, unless he yielded what, he was told, was already accomplished, and what his resistance would not prevent.[1] For two years he resisted the change from the Lateran Palace to the gaol

---

[1] The parallel with Napoleon's treatment of Pius VII. in captivity is to be noted.

in Thrace: from the headship over all bishops to thraldom under one, a heretic : from being the centre of all spiritual life in the greatest of cities to loneliness, deception, and every proceeding that could break the spirit deprived of counsel. Then, to use the words of St. Athanasius, he was "broken" for a moment. He returned to Rome, and from that time recovered his resolution : he refused his assent to the council of Rimini ; and when he died, eight years after, it was with the reputation of a saint, as he is treated by St. Ambrose and St. Basil.

The bitterest drop in the chalice of the exiled bishop was not the loss of dignity and liberty, not even the severance from the daily support of sacerdotal life, the counsel and friendship of similarly minded brethren, not poverty or any kind of privation, but the thought that he was dismissed to be supplanted by one of unsound belief, who would corrupt the people committed to him. The martyr Pope, the predecessor of Liberius a hundred years before, as he offered his neck to the executioner in the catacombs, when his mass was over, could feel that one like himself of the same faith would be seated presently in his place by the free choice of his brethren. But Paul at Constantinople, Eustathius at Antioch, Dionysius at Milan, Hilary at Poitiers, Athanasius at Alexandria, had to feel with the full intensity of anguish which the true shepherd who gives his life for his sheep has a right to feel, that he was moved to give place to a hireling who would sell the sheep for an emperor's favour; who would ruin the faith for the maintenance of which the bishop existed; and yet would carrry on the same worship in the same church with the same words, so that the counterfeit might be most complete and deadly.

Herein Arianism was a worse enemy than paganism, and this power of arbitrary banishment a more dangerous weapon in the hands of a so-called Christian emperor than the axe or sword in the hands of a heathen emperor; and it must be added that, in all the heathen persecution, no such havoc is recorded as that wrought in the Arian persecution among the chief pastors of the flock.

St. Basil, through the eight years of his episcopate, was struggling against the havoc thus wrought; and in the year when Athanasius died this is the cry which he uttered as one among thirty-two bishops addressing their brethren in Italy and Gaul:[1] "For the danger is not for one church, nor are they two or three that have fallen on this tempest, since this evil of heresy is eating its way almost from the borders of Illyricum to the Thebaid. Its evil seeds, indeed, were sown by the miserable Arius; but they have taken deep root in the soil by the labours of many in the interval who have cultivated the impiety, and now have sprung up into deadly fruit. Pious belief is overthrown, the laws of the Church thrown into confusion. The ambitions of those who fear not the Lord vault into high places: prelacy is openly offered as the reward of impiety: and so the utterer of the worse blasphemies is the favoured

[1] St. Basil, Ep. xcii. (Migne).

candidate for the episcopate. Sacerdotal gravity is perished; pastors who feed the Lord's flock with knowledge are wanting, while the ambitious turn aside the patrimony of the poor to their own enjoyment and the bestowing of gifts. Observance of the canons is slighted: licence to sin is great. They who have reached to rule by exercise of human art, reward the place so won by entirely gratifying those who have faultily helped them. Just judgment is gone. Every one walks after the liking of his own heart. Wickedness is unbounded, the populations uninstructed, their rulers voiceless. For they who through men have gained superiority for themselves are the servants of those who have obliged them. Indeed, some have devised a pretended defence of orthodoxy as a weapon of warfare against each other, and conceal their private enmity under the garb of zeal for piety. Others, again, to avoid conviction for basest faults, set populations at the uttermost variance to cover their own by public evils. Now, this is an unnatural war when those who have done evil dislike the general peace, as revealing their deeds of shame. In such a state of things unbelievers ridicule; those of little faith fluctuate; faith is ambiguous; ignorance steals over minds, because those who adulterate the word with craft counterfeit truth. The mouths of the pious are silent, while blasphemy is blatant. Holy things are profaned. The sounder people avoid the houses of prayer as schools of impiety, and raise in the desert their hands to the Lord in heaven, with groans and tears. For surely what happens in most of the cities is come to your knowledge: how the people, with women and children, and even old men, crowd themselves outside the walls and pray in the open air, enduring with all patience inclemencies of the weather, in hope of help from the Lord."

"What lamentation can express these calamities? what tears suffice for such a multitude of evils? While, then, there are some who seem still to be standing,[1] while a trace of the old constitution is still preserved, before the churches are utterly wrecked, press to us, press on, most loving brothers. Give your hand to those who are on their knees. Let your fraternal pity be touched for us. Shew us your sympathy. Do not permit half of the world to be swallowed up by error, nor endure that the faith be extinguished among those who were first enlightened by it." He continues that they were divided among themselves, and likens their condition to that of the Jews at the taking of Jerusalem, as having the evils of foreign and civil war at once upon them, "which has brought the churches to the extremity of weakness". "And in this we most need your help, that those who profess the apostolic faith should dissolve the divisions which they have invented, and be obedient to the authority of the Church, that the Body of Christ may be whole, returning to the use of all its members." "For indeed we consider as the greatest blessing the gift bestowed by the Lord on your piety of distinguishing the alloy from the pure and genuine metal,

---

[1] ἕως ἔτι ἴχνος τῆς παλαίας καταστάσεως διασώζεται. 3.

and of proclaiming the faith of our fathers whole and entire."

When at last the Eastern bishops met upon the summons of Theodosius at Constantinople in 381, under the presidency of Meletius, whose name stands first in the letter of Basil just quoted, the repeated words of his great friend Gregory, and still more the treatment which Gregory experienced, fully bear out the terrible picture of the state to which the Arianising of her bishops in the preceding fifty years, and councils called by emperors and overawed by them, had reduced the Eastern episcopate. It was after the issue of this council that he wrote the well-known words:

"If I must speak the truth, I feel disposed to shun every conference of bishops; for never saw I synod brought to a happy issue, and remedying, and not rather aggravating, existing evils. For rivalry and ambition are stronger than reason—do not think me extravagant for saying so — and a mediator is more likely to incur some imputation himself, than to clear up the imputations which others lie under."[1]

At this very council, when Meletius had died, Gregory used his utmost efforts to induce the bishops to terminate the schism at Antioch, existing for more than fifty years, since the deposition of Eustathius in 330, the fatal act which opened the Arian persecution, and began that attack upon the Church's constitution by which Basil described it as all but destroyed. The

---

[1] Quoted in *Arians*, p. 460. Ep. cxxx. to Procopius, whether secretary of Theodosius or prefect of Constantinople (aliter 55).

clergy of the two parties of Meletius and Paulinus had made the most solemn promise to take whichever of these should survive the other as sole bishop; notwithstanding which, Flavian, who had taken the engagement, accepted their election of himself to succeed Meletius; and Gregory appealed to his colleagues on behalf of peace and unity in vain. Himself, after the labour and danger of two years, in which he had in part restored New Rome from the forty years' domination of heresy which it had suffered, after being welcomed by the people and the emperor as a bishop who would adorn the see of the empire's new capital, they suffered to resign his charge in disgust at the utter worldliness which he encountered on every side. Basil's friend exceeds, if it be possible, Basil himself in portraiture of the times. "Will they take from me the first rank? What wise man ever was smitten with love of it? And now, as I think, it is the first mark of prudence to avoid it. This is the cyclone that whirls us all about. For this the ends of the world suspect each other, involved in a sort of mute and nameless war. For this we that are born of God peril to become mere men, and to lose the great new name. Would that there were no first place, no precedence, no prerogative, that we might be known only by our worth. But now the right hand, and the left hand, and the middle place, and the higher seat, and the lower seat, and the going first, and the going side by side, have wounded us sorely for nothing, driven many into the pit, and put among the goats not those only of low degree, but pastors, who, being teachers in Israel, knew not these things."[1]

And again looking back from his retirement on those whom he had left—" Take, then, thrones and lordships, you, since you prize them above all things. Rejoice, insult, assume patriarchal titles. Let the great world yield you place. Change sees for sees: cast these down, raise those up. This is your pleasure. Go: I will turn to my God, in whom I live and breathe, to whom alone I look."[2]

And the meek-minded man, who sat for a few weeks to please others in the chair for which Eusebius left Nicomedia, and Eudoxius Antioch, and then resigned it to gather up his soul in solitude with God, seems in these few words to have described the tyranny of fifty years, which swept over the Church from Constantine to Valens, and humbled her more than all the rage of the heathen in the struggle of three hundred years.

For down to the peace of the Church her episcopate had been united; and rarely had a bishop fallen after the manner of Paul in the Chair of Antioch. Christian authority[3] was represented to the eyes of the people in the person of the bishop. When in 381 the new emperor's first act, after entering his capital, was to invite the bishops of the Eastern empire to meet at Constantinople, it was for the double purpose of con-

[1] Orat. xxvi., p. 483, Migne.
[2] Poem on himself and the bishops, 797-804. πατριαρχίας κληροῦσθε: a comment on the Canon of 381, exalting the see of Constantinople.
[3] Broglie, ii. 345.

firming the Nicene faith, together with the doctrine of the Holy Spirit, attacked by the Macedonians, and of restoring order in the dioceses of Asia. The words of two such bishops as St. Basil and St. Gregory speak for themselves how episcopal authority had been shaken, because the fixedness and unity of the episcopal character had been lost. If Theodosius may be said to have saved the empire, when he came to the assistance of the young Gratian after the defeat of Valens, no less may he be said to have preserved the Eastern episcopate after the havoc wrought by the remorseless tyranny of Constantius and Valens. Arianising belief had dissolved its unity ; a worldly spirit had broken its strength. It was after witnessing the proceedings of the council, and upon being invited to attend another council at the same place next year, that Gregory uttered those scalding words upon the councils of his time in general. For had they not been the chosen means taken by Eusebius from the councils of Cæsarea, Tyre, and Antioch, onwards, by which the imperial despotism summoning the council, too often directing its acts by the presence of an imperial commissioner with an armed force, and then carrying out its decrees by banishment of bishops, and by fierce persecution inflicted on their clergy and people, had thrown into disorder that previous paternal constitution in which every province had enjoyed its proper rights, while the rights of all, the place of all, the doctrine of the whole Church, were guarded by the Roman See upon the traditions of St. Peter and St. Paul, and supported by the concurrence of the two great sees of the East, at the head of their respective metropolitans.

This was the tradition which the council of Sardica had endeavoured to maintain. Against it the Eusebian bishops in the encyclical which, after separating themselves from the council, they issued from Philippopolis, put forth plainly the pretension that an Eastern council should suffer no revision by a Western, under which words they included the Primacy of the Pope. They had judged Athanasius, the second bishop of the Church, at packed councils, the first summoned by Constantine at Tyre, the second summoned by Constantius at Antioch; Athanasius had appealed to Pope Julius, according to the old law of the Church, as Julius reminded them in his letter to them; had been acquitted by Julius at the head of his Roman council. The Eusebians refused to receive his acquittal. Another council had been called by the two emperors of the West and East, in conjunction with the Pope, at Sardica, in 343. It sanctioned the appeal of a bishop, when incriminated, to the Pope. The Eusebians first refused to sit in the council because Athanasius was there, in virtue of his acquittal by the Pope, when he had been condemned and deposed by themselves. And when their plea was rejected, they retired from Sardica to Philippopolis, held a council of their own, and openly declared that an Eastern council was independent of a Western. What they really trusted to was the Eastern jealousy of the West and the practical division of the two dominions under distinct sovereigns. What they practically substituted for the mild control of the Pope was the imperial power convoking councils, schooling them in their session, carrying out their decrees by force. In the eleven years during which Constantius reigned over East and West this proceeding, which had been checked by his brother Constans so long as he reigned in the West, was carried out through the whole empire. The many councils of his sole reign are but the dictates of imperial power, impressed upon bishops who risk their dignity, their liberty, their life itself if they resist. Never from the day of Pentecost to the present day has the episcopate been reduced to such a condition as it was in at the last year of Constantius. The Church was delivered from her bondage by the death of a tyrant at the age of forty-four, who was succeeded by an apostate emperor, and was delivered a second time from a general persecution by the death of the apostate himself, after a reign of scarcely twenty months, at the age of thirty-two. A double fresh succession ensued under the Catholic emperors Jovian and Valentinian: the West was allowed to return to its original constitution: the East was still further reduced by Valens, until we must leave the greatest of its bishops to describe its state after the death of Athanasius, in the words we have quoted.

It is important to observe the exact instrument which this thoroughly "secular faction"[1] of the Eusebians used in their attack upon the Church. They never denied that the bishop was the unit of authority in the Church: that bishops alone could meet in council with

[1] *Arians*, p. 264.

authority to judge of doctrine and discipline; what they did was to subject bishops to State control in the exercise of these functions; and the absolute form of civil government at the time enabled them to do this with great effect. According to their policy, the emperor was to set bishops in motion, control their movements, ratify their acts, and punish all opponents. By this policy they transferred the divinely instituted Primacy, which they denied, at least in practice, to the temporal sovereign, in cómpensation for which transference they always had the sovereign on their side. A great French writer says: "Arianism, when we consider it on its political side, is but a transformation of the old Roman despotism, which, when it despaired of crushing the Church, consents to an alliance with her, with the intention of making her its servant. Lictors attend on it: the pomp of courts it loves: it enunciates dogma in a form of law and an imperial edict, with the gesture and the tone of a Roman prætor. Arius is Porphyry become a priest to get entrance into the sanctuary. Constantius is Diocletian, willing to be baptised that he may remain sovereign Pontiff."[1]

These men, Eusebius and Eudoxius, who both became wrongfully, by court favour, bishops of Constantinople, they and their fellows shew themselves in their acts eunuchs of an Oriental despot rather than either bishops of the Church of Christ, or counsellors of Christian kings. When we come to consider their place in the long roll of history, we find them

[1] Broglie, iv. 500.

forerunners of Mahomet in doctrine, and of Photius in government.

But the accession of Theodosius, followed by the law of 380, together with the creed of the council consisting of the bishops from his own part of the empire, which he summoned to meet at Constantinople in 381, may be considered to mark the end of the Arian persecution so far as it was carried on within the empire by imperial support. The good which that council did was to add the sanction of the Eastern bishops to the emperor's law reaffirming the Nicene Creed, a sanction of the more importance because it was precisely the dissensions of Eastern bishops which, in the preceding fifty years, had perpetually betrayed that Creed. Arianism was an Eastern malady. They further censured the Macedonian heresy, an offset of the Arian, which its thirty-six bishops sitting in the council would not give up, and so were cast out, and they added to the Nicene Creed the affirmation of that doctrine concerning the Holy Ghost which the party of Macedonius had impugned. In their second canon they reaffirmed that arrangement of the Eastern dioceses under the greater metropolitans, which the Nicene canon had more briefly contained, and which the Arian violences in the East had set at naught. For the derangement of order as well as the derangement of belief was Eastern, and sprung from the same party. The privileges of the Egyptian patriarchate had been utterly violated at the council of Tyre, and at following councils of Antioch; and now, in 381, Egypt was endeavouring to impose Maximus as bishop on Constantinople. The second canon, therefore, was a restoration of the original order. Of the third canon we shall speak hereafter. Here it is sufficient to say that this council was not acknowledged as ecumenical at the time, or long after; only for the sake of its creed it was so acknowledged in the sixth century, by Pope Vigilius, and then by Pelagius and Gregory I., but only as to its creed. St. Leo expressly says that its canons had not even been sent to the Roman See; and St. Gregory I. declares that "the Roman church hitherto neither has nor receives the canons or the acts of that council, but has received it so far as its definition against Macedonius".[1]

Let us now turn to the very important point which remains for consideration in reviewing the history of the fifty-six years which elapse between the Nicene Council and the first council of Constantinople. This is the development of the Pope's dignity, firstly, in Rome; secondly, in the West; thirdly, in the whole Church; and further, the maintenance of his independence, which followed from the many bearings of the act of Constantine in founding a Nova Roma on the Bosphorus.

1. Constantine had quitted Rome[2] in September, 326: he never returned. The next imperial visit to the old capital was that of his son Constantius, when he was sole emperor, in 357; the third was that of

[1] Hefele, ii. 30; Leo I., Ep. cvi. ad Anatolium; Greg. I., Ep. vii. 34. See also Photius, i. 85.
[2] See Broglie, ii. 105.

Theodosius, after his victory over Maximus, in 389; and a fourth of the same emperor is believed to have taken place in the short interval between his final victory over Arbogastus and Eugenius in September, 394, and his death at Milan in January, 395. In all this time, when the most important changes in the political structure, and frequent successions in the rulers of the empire, were taking place, Rome had ceased to be the seat of rule. The Western emperors, when they were not in motion, held their court at Milan, or in Lyons, or in Treves, whence they watched over the movements of the northern tribes. The great city which Augustus boasted to have found of brick and to have left of marble, had been made by his successors the glory of the earth for its theatres, palaces, its innumerable multitude of statues, the finest works of Grecian art. Had they not poured into it with lavish hand the riches of the subject world during three centuries? When the unworthy son of Constantine went to Rome at the beginning of its twelfth century, he was accompanied by the Persian prince, Hormisdas. They visited the temples of the capitol, whose golden roofs and army of statues shining in mid-air were in all their splendour; they visited the baths, which bestowed on the poorest citizens all the luxuries which wealth and civilisation could draw together; they visited the theatres, market-places, and took up their abode in the palace of so many Cæsars, looking down on the Forum, the shrine of Roman liberty in the time of the Commonwealth, the centre of imperial grandeur in the empire which had succeeded it. Constantius was forced to confess that all his father's efforts to create a rival city had failed to reach the original. But one scene especially—the Forum of Trajan—is said to have overcome him. He admired the horse on which the statue of the emperor was placed, and turning to Hormisdas, he said—"That is a fine piece of sculpture; that at least I can have copied, and I will". "Take care, sir," said Hormisdas; "before bringing the horse, you must build the stable for him."[1] And when the prince was asked what he thought of Rome, he replied—"My only consolation is, that here also men die".

But the city, which had not ceased to be decorated by every emperor down to Constantine, had long before him ceased to be the constant residence of the emperors. Since the time of Septimius Severus their absences had been frequent and long; but their temporary courts at Antioch, Nicomedia, Sardica, Sirmium, Milan, Arles, Treves, had not touched the supremacy of the old capital. Athanasius has left written of this very Constantius, that in his treatment of the bishop of Rome, whom at the time of his visit he had sent into exile for the faith, he had not remembered that the city, of which he was bishop, was the head of Romandom (Romania). But in the fifty years succeeding the foundation of Constantinople Rome had begun to learn the bitter lesson that its political supremacy was usurped by a rival. That senate to which prostrate provinces had

[1] Broglie, iii. 377, from Ammianus, xvi.

looked so long, first as the living temple of Roman liberty and dignity, then as the bestower of empire or the ratifier of it when bestowed, was becoming a mere municipal institution. Her nobles were still the richest of the earth; and their estates, scattered over all the countries which border the Mediterranean, could support legions of slaves; but their palaces at Rome, rich in every luxury, no longer witnessed the occupation of their masters with the political thoughts and discussions which issue in rule.

It seems agreed that at the time Constantine left Rome a large majority of the senate and the richer classes were still heathen. The old Roman spirit, as manifested in Trajan and Decius, which bound up the greatness of the empire with the worship of its gods, had its stronghold there. Constantine is supposed to have found in the old capital stronger resistance than anywhere else to his intention of establishing the Christian religion in an alliance with the empire. One of the many motives which he had in founding a new capital is said to have been that he might make the seat of empire a Christian city from its very birth. His munificent endowments of the Roman bishop, his construction of a patriarchal church, and of the sanctuaries of her two patron Apostles, had not won the heart of the heathen city, nor converted its nobles; and so he went and left her bishop in possession of a royal palace in the best quarter of Rome, and withdrew that presence which alone could overshadow the successor of St. Peter in his Lateran home.

From that time forth we are told[1] the widowed empress of the world began, slightly at first, but with an ever-increasing impulse through the century, to feel that there was a greater domain even than the temporal empire sliding from her grasp, of which she was the basis and the centre. I speak now not of the feeling among Christians, but of that which radiated from them upon the heathen around, with whom they were in habits of daily intercourse. Constantine's conversion had made the empire not indeed Christian, but an ally of the Christian Church, which, instead of a proscribed rebel, had become a support; and, beside multitudes which became nominally Christian from temporal motives, multitudes were also drawn to examine the title-deeds of the Christian Church, with the result that some were enrolled among her members, while those who continued heathen regarded the Church with very different eyes from the persecutors of a former generation. Between Constantine and Theodosius, the heathen majority in the senate and higher classes had been largely reduced. And in all this time the greatest resident in Rome, the perpetual dispenser of large funds in beneficent acts of kindness to the suffering, was the successor of the Fisherman, placed by the emperor himself in the Lateran Palace. All through this century the Christian tide was rising, the heathen tide was falling. Again, the legislation of Constantine, of his sons, and their successors—the exaltation of bishops to be magistrates of the highest dignity, so that

[1] Gregorovius, in his first volume, draws this out.

their tribunals had legal jurisdiction, beside the highest temporal courts, even in secular matters—drew attention not only of Christians, but of heathens also, to the Christian hierarchy. Thus, Ammianus Marcellinus, officer and friend and praiser of Julian as he was, knew in part at least the internal discipline of the Christian hierarchy: he speaks with judgment and moderation of Christian things and persons, and in no ambiguous terms of the exclusive authority of the Roman bishop, which Constantius, at the height of his predominance, was anxious to secure on his side. Many, like this historian, who had not courage to break with heathenism, and take on them the yoke of Christian morals, came to see, even from outside, the grandeur of the Christian structure, and could even discern the immovable basis on which it rested. And in this they were helped by the imperial absence from Rome. At Milan, at Antioch, at Constantinople, the army of courtiers, the host of officers, the multitude of civil servants, could invest even the petty figures of Constantius or Valens with majesty. At Rome, the majesty of a higher order had opportunity to grow upon all thoughtful minds. The house of Æneas, continually changing its transitory occupants, seemed to cede from the unmoved rock of the capitol, only to show the Roman Father exercising sway over minds, and transforming the empire of force into that of charity.

A special historian [1] of Rome notes that from the time of Constantine a double process was going on. Life and

[1] Gregorovious, i. 76, 105.

death, bound together and struggling with each other in the same frame, produced a sort of double nature which has nowhere else been seen. The ancient city was decaying, and in and upon its decay a most vigorous life was making itself felt. From the very first, he remarks, the Church had taken possession of the city of Romulus for her own. Pope Clement, under the suspicious eyes of Domitian, had divided the fourteen regions among his seven notaries, charged to write the acts of the martyrs. Pope Evaristus gave presbyteral titles to the several districts of the city, while seven deacons specially attended on the bishop. This spontaneous and entirely spiritual formation was complete by the time of Constantine; and when he determined to rob Rome of her temporal crown, the spiritual crown, sparkling with the martryrdoms and enriched with the labours of ten generations, was ready to descend upon her brow. Romulus and Remus were succeeded by Peter and Paul: the brothers of whom one killed the other for temporal power by the brothers whose names stand together in undying union at the head of the Church's sovereign acts through all time. But the fourth century was the appointed time when what had been preparing for three hundred years came visibly to light. And it is helped on by an unconscious agent. Constantine, meaning to found a new empire, instinct with Christian life and unity, withdrew from Rome, and gave it a new capital. And then, just in proportion as old Rome decayed new Rome rose out of it, a second birth, the same historian remarks, unknown to any other city in the world— a gigantic marvellous transformation. The Arian conflict of fifty years, which began precisely with this desertion of the old capital, was linked with it, and inspired by it throughout. And these fifty years mark the first stage of this new birth. As the Church emerged from heathen persecution, her Primacy emerged from that latency which covers the whole daily life of Christians in the first period; for the secret teachings of the catacombs have left few outward traces,[1] and the first great age of Christian writers, preachers, and theologians begins at the same time. The early ages have no Athanasius, or Gregory, or Basil, or Ambrose, or Augustine, or Cyril; but the early ages, by doing and by suffering, prepared for these men to arise in the time of Providence. So the acts of the Popes preceding Constantine's peace are, in general, lost to us, and great, says Cardinal Newman, is that loss; but they laid a solid foundation for the structure which Constantine found, and which, as the heathen city decayed, from the fourth century onwards, rose out of its very ruins into a spiritual empire. And once more I must quote the same historian, who says, "That the Roman church was already an organisation which nothing could shake, when the ancient kingdom fell, is one of the greatest facts of history in general:[2] for the collective life of Europe was founded anew upon this firm foundation-stone of the Church".

2. When Constantine, seduced by the fawning homage of a courtier bishop in the last ten years of his life,

[1] Broglie, iii. 116. [2] Gregorovius, i. 18.

raised the Arians from the ignominy in which the Nicene Council had left them, what did they accomplish in that Eastern realm which Constantine by his new creation hoped to consolidate and unite? They made, as we have seen, the three great cities of Alexandria, Antioch, and Constantinople scenes of cruelty, lawlessness, and dissension for fifty years; and the same was the case in almost all the cities of the East in proportion to their importance. Even where they least succeeded, as at Alexandria, they banished Athanasius five times, and placed four intruders in his see: Pistus, Gregory, George, and after his death Lucius. They degraded Antioch from the deposition of Eustathius for a period of nearly 90 years, so that it could offer no resistance to the loss of its rank in the hierarchy. And Constantinople was yet more entirely in their hands, so that when St. Gregory in 379 accepted the earnest invitation made to him to go there, it required every effort of the most eloquent preacher and the most finished theologian of the Church to collect a few Catholics in a private house, which was truly, as he called it, a Resurrection. During all this time the Arian persecution, having the imperial power of Constantius and Valens at its command, inflicted cruelties which were certainly unsurpassed, if they were equalled, by any under the heathen emperors. Perhaps there is no one recorded act on the part of a heathen equal in atrocity to the burning alive of eighty ecclesiastics, Catholic deputies from Constantinople to Valens, whose sole crime was asking him to allow the election of a Catholic successor to Eudoxius.

The prefect who so carried out his master's order was that same Modestus who threatened St. Basil that he would tear out his liver, and received for reply, that if he did so, it would be a great service, since it had made him suffer all his life. Not only were the great sees in the possession of the Arians, but a large majority of Eastern bishops were infected with some shade or other of Arian misbelief, and their submission in councils to the dictation of the emperors, joined to their incessant wrangling with each other, as described by St. Gregory and St. Basil, were such as to destroy for the time all respect for the episcopal character in the East.

Let us turn to the West, and note the succession to St. Peter's See during the same time.

St. Sylvester sat up to the death of Constantine, holding the see for more than twenty years, undisturbed, and honoured by all. Marcus succeeded him for a few months in 337, and then Julius sat for fifteen years, the defender of Athanasius, who met the innovations and insolence of the Eusebians with the mild dignity of one conscious that his feet were planted on a rock. He moved the two emperors to agree to the convocation of a general council at Sardica; and in union with Hosius, his legate there, strove to maintain the old constitution of the Church. At his death in 352 his place was taken by Liberius, whose resistance to all the threats of Constantius, and acceptance of voluntary exile, would place him in the same rank with Athanasius, but that a charge of having yielded, after two years' endurance, to some unworthy concession, and of having returned to Rome in consequence of it, lies against his memory. What is certain is, that from the time of his return to Rome he maintained the Nicene faith, from which he had never swerved in conviction, and that St. Ambrose and St. Basil speak of him in terms of veneration. He died in 366, and was followed by Damasus, who sat till 384, and during the whole time vigorously maintained the faith. Thus, through the period of the fifty years during which the Arian storm was raging, the Roman See was the bulwark of orthodoxy, and the West in general stood firm under its guidance. It was sufficient for Theodosius, in his great law of 380, to refer his people as a standard to the faith of Damasus at Rome and of Peter at Alexandria—the legitimate successor, after the expulsion of Lucius, to that great confessor who had looked to Rome for support at the beginning of the troubles, and had found it in Julius, Liberius, and Damasus.

Taking the date of 380 as the point at which the imperial power returned from the aberration of Constantine to the position which he himself occupied at the Nicene Council, it must be observed that the conduct of the Popes during that time had vastly increased the reverence felt for St. Peter's See. Their steadfast and unswerving faith shone forth in the strongest contrast with the incessant fluctuations of the Eastern bishops. That one Eastern bishop whose light streamed to the whole world from the Pharos of Alexandria, an unfailing beacon, never for a moment dimmed, was the friend of Julius, Liberius, and Damasus from his consecration in 328 to his death in 373. In the schism of Antioch he was with Rome throughout. He met the first attack of the Arian innovators by taking refuge with Pope Julius: his successor, Peter, was joined with Damasus as the exponent of orthodoxy in the law of 380, the death-blow of official and imperial Arianism. In the whole conflict, which was an experience unlike anything felt in the great heathen conflict of three hundred years, and made a trial of the episcopate such as it had not yet gone through, the First and the Second sees stood together: St. Peter protected St. Mark, St. Mark stood at St. Peter's throne. But the words of St. Gregory Nazianzene must have expressed the thought of many hearts; and it must have become apparent that wherever the strength of the Church lay, it was not in episcopal councils summoned by emperors and dictated to by counts and prefects, or addressed by court-bishops while the emperor listened behind a curtain.

3. The Arian heresy in its revival, caused by Constantine's recall of Eusebius and Arius from banishment, and the founding of Constantinople were contemporaneous. The heresy itself and the policy which founded Constantinople appear throughout the conflict to have a close connection with each other. The subtle flattery of Eusebius caressed a special weakness of the great Constantine, the form which his self-confidence took in his later years. This was a notion that he was as successful in theology as in arms. Eusebius of Cæsarea joined his great friend and fellow-worker, and, it must

be added, fellow-believer, of Nicomedia in persuading
the emperor that the Synod of Tyre, with its sequel of
Jerusalem, was a repetition of the Nicene Council, and
that in both the emperor was the saviour of the Church's
doctrine. That power which Constantine then assumed
was the mainstay of the faction throughout. Its leaders
fostered Oriental despotism, and relied upon it, used it
without remorse: banished, tortured, massacred by means
of it. They were, moreover, for ever playing upon the
Eastern jealousy of the West, which the founding of an
Eastern capital, the seat of administrative power, had
not, indeed, created, but to which it had given a most
favourable opportunity of exhibition. The mind of the
East had perpetually chafed under the predominance of
the Western animal fibre, which seemed to the Greeks
of Alexander's empire and the kingdoms into which it
was parted like the servitude of soul to body. It welcomed the turning-back of the Roman eagle's flight
from West to East. Moreover, the overwhelming advantages of site of the new capital gave the Eastern
portion of the empire a unity which it had never before
possessed. It gravitated more and more to Constantinople. The Arian leaders used these secular feelings to
the utmost. They worked for an empire whose head
was Constantinople. They applied their political principles to the Church of Christ. They chose not the
Nicene hierarchy with the Roman Peter at its head,
which allowed and enjoyed a large autonomy, but an
Eastern despot moving his obedient bishops. And they
were nearest to success when such a despot, inheriting

the absolute spirit of a great father without a particle of his genius, entered Rome in triumph with the senate walking before his chariot, the long files of his barbarian guards making for him a safely-hedged path, banners floating above him — himself with steady gaze not changing a feature or answering a salute, but, as the Turkish sultan proceeds to the mosque, taking no notice of the homage paid to so sublime a majesty; his only motion being that when he passed a triumphal arch he bent his diminutive body, as if the lofty portal could not otherwise receive him. And to complete the picture of the Arian triumph on that day, the Pope was absent from his city, banished to a Thracian prison and the custody of a misbelieving bishop by the monarch who had said to his bishops assembled at Milan : " What is this? You talk to me of canons? My will is your canon. So my Syrian bishops tell me. Either obey me, or go into banishment."

His Syrian bishops would be those whom Constantius had found so obsequious at Antioch in condemning Athanasius and confirming the court-minion Gregory, sent from Constantinople in his place.

So Constantius interpreted Arianism; so the Arians chose their head ; and their art consisted in persuading the bishops who followed their lead that they were protecting episcopal independence in the East from infringement by the Primate of the West, much as servility to the king in France bore the name of the Gallican liberties.

The short reign of an emperor who had returned to

heathenism interrupted Arian predominance. At his death the Church recovered her freedom in the West. Liberius and Damasus set themselves to repair the ruin wrought. But in Valens the Arians of the East found another Constantius. Valens, when given by his brother Valentinian the Eastern empire, had been orthodox; but such knowledge of the Christian faith as he possessed he had learnt in his instruction for baptism under Eudoxius, the bishop of Constantinople, from whom the evil spirit went forth, which at once infused Arian doctrine and flattered despotism. Valens played Arian and despot with a vigour equal to his predecessor, but only in the Eastern half of the empire. And Eudoxius repeated most faithfully the work of Eusebius of Nicomedia. With the death of Valens the Arian heresy lost its head; with the accession of Theodosius, a Western spirit upon an Eastern throne, it received a ruler who was not seduced into its ranks by the spirit of despotism, but who did not rescue the empire from all its consequences.

4. Theodosius had indeed the greatest difficulty in restoring order, subduing party spirit, reconciling personal enmities and rivalries among his Eastern bishops. The very year in which he called together the council, which was the first after his accession, gives a striking proof of the difference in spirit between the bishops of the East and West. Thirty-two bishops met at Aquileia in September, 381, two months after that council had finished its difficult task. Its bishops, under the guidance of St. Ambrose, came to unanimous resolutions. Among his letters, we have one written in the council's

name to the three emperors, in which their interposition is requested to put down the troubles which Ursinus was endeavouring still to stir up at Rome against Damasus—a matter which, if disregarded, might, they say, "disturb the body of the Church throughout the whole world, and throw everything into confusion". Accordingly they entreat the emperors not to suffer "the Roman church, the head of the whole Roman world, and that sacrosanct faith of the Apostles to be disturbed, which is the source whence the laws which regulate our venerable communion go forth". The Western church, they testify, had gathered itself up under this authority: "through all its regions, and even the most retired country places, even to the ocean itself, all were joined together in one spotless faith".[1]

While the Western bishops were thus expressing the vast importance of the Roman See in their eyes, those of the Eastern bishops who met at Constantinople had passed a canon which was an innovation upon the whole order of the Church up to that time, carrying with it the gravest consequences. After the canon renewing the Nicene canon upon the relative rights of the Eastern metropolitans, they had added, "Let the bishop of Constantinople hold precedence next after the bishop of Rome, because that city is New Rome".

This canon gave precedence, but no jurisdiction; still at one stroke it deposed the bishop of Alexandria from the second rank and the bishop of Antioch from the third rank in the Church, which they had held from

[1] Ambrose, Ep. xi. 2, 4; xlii. 8.

apostolic times in virtue of their descent from the chief Apostle, and it gave this rank to the new bishop precisely upon a secular ground, because he was bishop of a city which, in the order of the empire, had been placed next to the old capital. It insinuated what it did not express, that the rank of the Roman bishop arose from his being bishop of the capital. Thus it attached the Christian hierarchy to the political sovereignty, whereas it had formed itself by a principle of innate growth during three centuries in which it had waged a struggle of martyrdom and confessorship with that very sovereignty. There was complete antagonism between the principle on which the hierarchy was built and the principle which gave precedence to the bishop of the new capital. The descent of spiritual power from the chief Apostle, which, by the original arrangement of the Apostolic College, had been carried out through the whole hierarchy, indicated the origin of that power as a delegation from Christ himself. The giving to the bishop of a new city the second rank in the whole Church because the city had been raised from one of no importance to be a capital, indicated a secular origin of hierarchical power. In the hierarchy, as seen at the Nicene Council, there was no rivalry, because all stood upon one ground; but by this canon rivalry was created at once between the bishops of Old Rome and New Rome, because they stood upon different grounds—the one being apostolic descent, the other secular rank.

In contrast therefore with the original and continuous authority of St. Peter's See at Rome, which the council of Aquileia so tersely stated as the source whence the laws of the Christian communion went forth to all, an element entirely unknown to the hierarchy at the Nicene Council was now brought into it—an element pregnant with mischief.

Looking back upon the fifty years which had passed since the act of Constantine, we see plainly that the founding a new permanent capital in the Eastern part of the empire carried with it the forming that portion into a distinct government. This began even at Constantine's death, when the whole East fell to the lot of Constantius. Jealous as he was of his power being shared, he had scarcely become sole emperor by the death of his brothers in 350, when he named to be Cæsar, first his cousin Gallus, and, after the execution of Gallus, then his cousin Julian. When a few years later Valentinian was elected emperor, he was obliged at once to consent to the division of the empire, and from 364 onwards the two parts formed separate administrations, and had each a spirit of its own. But upon this condition of secular affairs came the Arian division, which affected equally polity and doctrine. By their successive hold upon the imperial mind in Constantine, Constantius, and Valens, the Arians had let loose the utmost force of heresy and schism upon Alexandria, Antioch, Constantinople, Ephesus, and the other chief cities of the East; so that upon the accession of Theodosius the Eastern episcopate was in a state of utter dislocation. All the power and popularity of Theodosius were exerted in vain to heal the schism at

Antioch, after Flavian had been elected bishop at the Council of 381, in violation of the compact made shortly before between Meletius and Paulinus. And when in 383 Theodosius had for the third time invited the bishops of the East to meet at Constantinople, their dissensions rose to such a pitch that the emperor ordered each party to lay their confession of faith in writing before him. When the ablest of each side had prepared these documents, the bishops were summoned on a certain day to the imperial palace. Nectarius and Azelius, as the chief of the orthodox; Demophilus, who had been under the Arians bishop of Constantinople, as their representative; Eleusius of Cyzicus, for the Macedonians; Eunomius, for the Anomæans. The emperor received them kindly, took their confessions of belief, retired with these to an apartment, besought there enlightenment of God, read through all the documents delivered in to him, rejected and tore up all except the orthodox, inasmuch as they introduced division into the Holy Trinity. He then by decree suppressed the assemblies of the various sects, forbidding them to hold their worship or disseminate their doctrine, or ordain clergy, and threatened them with severe civil punishments. But upon the Antiochene schism not even the orthodox bishops could come to agreement, as the bishops of Egypt, Arabia, and Cyprus recognised Paulinus for the lawful bishop, and demanded the expulsion of Flavian, while those of Palestine, Phœnicia, and Syria were in favour of Flavian.[1]

[1] Hefele, ii. 39-40.

Thus the Arian misrule and violence, acting upon the practical division of the empire into two parts, and combining the Eastern jealousy of the West with unlimited concession to an Eastern emperor's despotic rule, had broken in the East that constitution which had subsisted from apostolic times. This third canon passed at Constantinople was a sign of what they had wrought. It intimated the political need of making the bishop of the new capital the centre also of the Eastern episcopate. Up to that time though the see of Constantinople had been sought by the two Arian leaders, Eusebius and Eudoxius, the one passing to it from Nicomedia in 338, the other from Antioch in 367, it had legally only the position of a suffragan under the metropolitan of Heraclea. Now after forty-four years, during which Arianism had so triumphed at Constantinople that St. Gregory, at his first coming, could hardly collect a congregation there, its bishop was raised, so far as his Eastern colleagues at that council could raise him, to the second rank in the whole Church.

The exaltation of Constantinople's bishop which thus began was favoured by every Byzantine sovereign, good or bad; for instance, by Theodosius now, and by Marcian at a further point seventy years later. It was clearly a political reason of constant force which led them to this. Though Alexandria and Antioch were chief cities of their empire, they had little control over bishops whose greatness consisted in their headship from the beginning of Christianity over great numbers of bishops, ranged in hierarchical order, which was not derived from the State; but the bishop of the new royal city had no apostolic descent, and nothing whatever to raise him from the condition of a suffragan except the temporal rank of his see. Moreover, he was member of the imperial court, and forever overshadowed by the imperial power: what was given to him was exercised under the inspection and control of the emperor. He may be said to have been in his single person a living image of the relation between Church and State which Arianism had tried to introduce, a relation which may also be said to have been the very life of Arianism in its political aspect. But this, which is plain enough in the retrospect, was probably not at all divined by Theodosius, whose work in maintaining the tottering empire was one almost surpassing human power, while the work of restoring order to an episcopate which imperial despotism had well-nigh ruined required every help.

The succeeding bishops of Alexandria, Timotheus, Theophilus, Cyril, and Dioscorus, resented to the utmost this degradation of their see, and shewed it not a little in the share which they took in the deposition of St. Chrysostome and St. Flavian, who suffered for the faith, as well as in that of Nestorius, who suffered for heresy. It was otherwise with the third see, for schism had reduced Antioch to impotence; so that it could not actively resist a loss of rank which it must have deeply felt. And the West never accepted the canon. It was silently acted upon by those who ruled and by those who sat at Constantinople, with results which will be seen later.

From this time, the Arian conflicts being over, and the emperor become the protector of the orthodox faith, and the separation of East and West in all matters of administration being an accomplished fact, the bishop of Constantinople was able to make use of the natural advantages which belonged to his residence at the seat of power. These were to be a mediator[1] between the court and the bishops, between East and West, to draw to his own cognisance ecclesiastical matters which were brought before the emperor, and so to extend his power over the other bishops of the empire. It was natural for the bishop of the first city in the Eastern empire to aim at making himself also the first bishop of the Eastern church, and, as New Rome was the rival of Old Rome, was, in St. Gregory's words, "the first city after the first," and inclined to contest even that preference, so also to put himself by the side of "the great leader of the West". And, in fact, from the appointment of Gregory's successor, Nectarius, this tendency comes into full action. The first step was that the relation of dependence on Heraclea was tacitly dropped. The bishop of the new capital became exarch of the Thracian province. That is, he started for his career of advancement on a par with the exarchs of Ephesus and Cæsarea in positive jurisdiction, while in a sort of precedence he was placed, as bishop of New Rome, next the bishop of Old Rome. Before tracing the further growth of power which he obtained in the following seventy years, it is worth dwelling upon the respective positions of the two

[1] Photius, i. 24.

great cities, as given by a contemporary, himself, during a few weeks, bishop in one of them. "Nature," he says, "though she has not made two suns, has made two Romes, luminaries of the whole world, the old and the new power, in this distinguished from each other, that the one spreads its light over the East, the other over the West. In beauty they are equal. As to their faith, the one was upright of old time, and now also is binding the whole West together in the word of salvation, as is meet for her who presides over all, and keeps inviolate the whole divine harmony. The other was first upright, but now no longer. I speak of her once mine, but mine no more, who lay in the depths of destruction, since Alexandria, the light-minded city, full of all evils, in senseless passion sent forth Arius, the abomination of desolation."[1]

In these words St. Gregory precisely agrees with St. Ambrose, when speaking in the name of the council of Aquileia; and no words could express more accurately the respective attitude of Rome and Constantinople towards the faith in the fifty years which we are considering.

5. They were no common years, for in them was worked out the first settlement of that new relation between Church and State, which their alliance, succeeding to their antagonism during the heathen persecution, could not fail to produce.

Constantine found the whole power of what had been the Roman commonwealth, and was the Roman empire,

[1] St. Greg. Naz. on his own life, v. 562-578.

as it were, personified in himself.[1] Part of that power, and a part indeed viewed as most precious, and guarded with the utmost jealousy, was the Supreme Pontificate. When he became a Christian emperor, holding the power of the Supreme Pontificate, which gave authority over all religions and sacrifices, he passed into the exalted duty of being the Church's protector. He would then by right join the empire of the world with the advocacy of the Church. And this is the conception of his office and of his duty which he originally formed. It is apparent in all his conduct down to the time that he became sole emperor, and to the convocation of the Nicene Council, in all which he acted in union with St. Sylvester, Hosius, and the episcopate. And in all his legislation he very markedly shewed his conception of the Christian ruler's duty to protect the Church, by the privileges which he granted to the clergy, and even more by the laws which carried out Christian principles, and made sins against Christian morality to be crimes against the State, by which many of the worst heathen enormities were made punishable.

Again, both he and his sons pressed upon the bishops many functions which, in an accurate partition of the domains belonging respectively to the Two Powers, would seem rather to belong to the civil than to the spiritual. Even " the first foundation of the temporal sovereignty is to be found in the fact that, from the fourth century the Pope, like other bishops in the Roman empire, and yet more than they, received,

[1] Phillips, *Kirchen-recht*, sec. 118.

though in subordination to the emperor, the administration of many civil attributions, which was for the good of the country ".[1]

Constantine in no way interfered with the free action of the bishops in the determination of doctrine at the great Council, and he loyally carried out their decrees, giving them the sanction of laws, in which he exercised in excellent degree his office as advocate of the Church. And the respectful way in which he is spoken of by such a man as Athanasius, whom he grievously maltreated, and left at his death a banished man, though not a deposed bishop, at Treves, seems to shew that he never swerved in intention from loyalty to the Church, and maintenance of what he supposed to be her doctrine.

But his great ignorance of that doctrine, as that of a man who had never received instruction in it with the humility of a disciple, his overweening self-confidence, his passionate desire to benefit his empire by enlisting in its service the unity of the Church, and the expectation which he had entertained of succeeding in this, led to a grievous change in his conduct from the time that he fell under the influence of Eusebius. His attitude to bishops, when he called the council of Tyre, was a strong contrast with his attitude to bishops at the Nicene Council, or with his words to St. Sylvester at the time of the council of Arles, and his conduct in regard to the Donatists, who threw themselves at his feet after the manner of Eusebius.

Thus, at his death, he had supplied his son Con-

[1] Phillips, sec. 119, p. 87.

stantius with precedents of the worst kind for his treatment of bishops who should resist his will. The council of Milan was held only thirty years after the Nicene Council; but in it the Roman emperor, the favourite son of Constantine, and for the moment lord of the whole empire, has taken his place in the sanctuary itself, and openly proclaims the reign of force. He tells the bishops, "My will is the rule of truth; obey it, or quit your sees". And he executes this upon the Pope himself, as well as upon Athanasius.

It is due even to Constantius, as well as to the other sons of Constantine, to say that their legislation, as over against heathenism, continued to be Christian. In this point they did not swerve from their position as advocates of the Church. Yet it is one striking mark of this astonishing time that Christians must have felt relief when the sceptre of Roman power passed from an heretical tyrant to a frank apostate. And his twenty months of power did not give him time to persecute effectively more than individuals.

The changes immediately ensuing on his death brought deliverance to the Church in the West, and enabled the Popes, Liberius and Damasus, to exert all the influence of their see in behalf of the Nicene doctrine. The tyranny of Valens, re-enacting in a smaller sphere that of Constantius, served to bring out more strongly the contrast between the East and West. An episcopate completely broken up by divisions as to doctrine justified the words of two great saints and doctors concerning it, while their own acts and writings were a seed in their day of better times, and testify now the profoundness of the wound which Arian discord and misbelief, with the utter worldliness and servility to power so engendered, had inflicted upon their portion of the flock. It may be noticed that St. Gregory, in the contrast which he draws between the faith of the two cities, Rome and Constantinople, in special regard to the Arian heresy, speaks of the faith of Rome as then and always upright. He seems quite unconscious even of a momentary lapse on the part of Liberius.[1]

6. Thus the first fifty years of the new relationship between the spiritual power and the temporal power, indicated by Constantine's conversion, were disturbed and saddened by the attempt of heresy to use the power of the emperor, then legitimately absolute in secular things, for its own purposes. The heretical party was willing to introduce the Supreme Pontificate of the old heathen empire into the Church of God,[2] that it might rule as eunuchs ruled under Constantius. In the West it did not succeed. In the East it gained long possession of the most important sees for its own adherents: the Eastern episcopate was utterly divided. St. Basil speaks of the last trace of the old constitution being on the point of effacement. The council of Tyre, engendered by the flattery of Eusebius upon the self-confidence of Constantine, is followed by a long series of councils in which the episcopal character is fearfully

---

[1] τούτων δὲ πίστις ἡμὲν ἦν ἐκ πλείονος
καὶ νῦν ἔτ᾽ ἔστιν εὔδρομος.

[2] Athanasius remarks that the court of Constantius was nothing but eunuchs.

lowered, the old order of the Church disregarded, and the faith itself becomes a target transfixed by the arrows of contending parties. The permanent result is that the distribution of hierarchical power in the East, as it had existed from the beginning, and through all the age of heathen persecution, is deranged. The most faithful of emperors himself favours the conferring of all but the highest rank in the Church on a new bishop, a secular creation of yesterday; and he does so because the prospect of reducing to unity and order a divided, wrangling, and worldly episcopate seems almost hopeless, and requires, as he thinks, a home bishop at his right hand to terminate the ecclesiastical causes brought perpetually before him as sovereign. The rise of the bishop of Constantinople is itself the proof that love of rank had eaten into the heart of the Eastern hierarchy. Arius could not destroy the Church's faith, but Arius did destroy episcopal autonomy in the East. He degraded Alexandria and Antioch, and in them the whole mass of metropolitans and bishops at whose head they stood, but he exalted Constantinople. And by the same stroke Rome came out, as the maintainer of the faith and the bulwark of independence,

What could be more opposed to the principles, the practice, and the desires of Sylvester, Julius, Liberius, and Damasus than the course of things which has been thus described? At the beginning, Julius protected Athanasius. He replaced him in his see, when he was unlawfully deposed, first at Tyre, then at Antioch. He appealed to the practice of the Church down to his time against the Arian innovators. He endeavoured to obtain an ecumenical council at Sardica for maintenance of the Nicene faith and order. For this Liberius suffered grievously; and as soon as he was back in his see resisted with all his influence the progress of heresy and demoralisation. Damasus held council after council for the same purpose. Theodosius was called suddenly to the throne by a helpless youth of nineteen, when the disaster of Adrianople shook the empire to its centre, and the first fruit of his baptismal instruction was to undo the evil work of Constantius and Valens. He found it sufficient to refer his subjects as a standard to the faith of Damasus, handed down to him from St. Peter, and that of the Alexandrine bishop, successor of Athanasius, whom Rome had supported.

Thus the whole Arian persecution, with its manifold catalogue of evils and oppressions, its furtherance of encroachments upon the liberty of the Church by imperial despotism, its temporary degradation of the episcopal character, its banishment of a Pope for two years from his see to a Thracian prison, ended in placing the See of Peter on a pinnacle. It supplemented by visible facts the right of bishops to sit in council as judges of doctrine, with the proviso that their canons, in order to be in accordance with the faith, must have the assent of the Roman bishop. This, which had been the rule from the beginning,[1] became evident in the course of the fourth century by the consequences of its

[1] As attested by the Greek historian Socrates (ii. 8), when he is noting its transgression at the council of Antioch in 341.

transgression. The Arian insurrection, by its alliance with Constantius and Valens, largely helped to make the Roman See the symbol to all, and the providential instrument of the Church's independence and liberty.

Constantinople was only beginning that course of instruction which it has supplied to the world for fifteen hundred years.

7. History is rife with acts carrying great consequences, which have not only been unforeseen by the doers of the acts, but contrary to their intentions. The founding of Constantinople by Constantine is a very signal instance of this kind. The great commander, in the height of his sovereignty, had a prescience of the dangers to which the enormous mass of disjointed territories forming his empire was exposed. He felt the weakness of Rome as a military station; its complete exposure to the north, where a storm was always ready to arise. After years of anxious thought, he selected the site for a new capital; and so felicitous was the selection, that there is no city yet known in the world which can compare with it for beauty, grandeur, and security, and for headship of a great realm. He intended it to be the foundation-stone of a new empire, which should consolidate and strengthen the empire, to the sole headship of which he had reached. The result was that, dying seven years after the foundation of his new capital, he found himself constrained to divide the empire, which began from that time to form itself into rival kingdoms—different in spirit, in tendencies, above all, in the character of its several peoples, and the

government which each assumed. He was probably well aware of this difference, but his act increased indefinitely its force and intensity. In Constantinople he gave the East a head, in which all its difference from the West found expression, and all its jealousy an effective instrument.

Again, Constantine had been displeased by the force of paganism in Old Rome, and the resistance offered by its senate and great families to his design in favour of the Christian Church. He purposed that his new capital, while it should have the fourteen regions of Old Rome, together with forums, palaces, public buildings of every sort to match it, should have a purely Christian population. Thither he transplanted Christian families, and he would have no heathenism. The result was that from the time he left Old Rome that city gradually became more and more Christian, until Theodosius was able, at the end of the century, to witness the conversion of the large majority of the senate and the chief families. The temples were closed as places of worship, and remained only as public monuments. But from the time of Constantine's death to the accession of Theodosius Constantinople fell into Arian hands. It was the scene of some of the worst deeds of persecution; and its bishops, Eusebius and Eudoxius, as specimens of everything which bishops ought not to be, made it infamous. The virtues and the eloquence of Gregory began to raise it from what he calls "the depth of perdition".[1] But in the fifty years now under revision

[1] ἐν βυθοῖς ἔκειτο τῆς ἀπωλείας.

it was the foster-mother of heresy; and these years are the fitting prologue to long centuries of a portentous history.

Once more, Constantine intended his new capital not only to be Christian itself, but to propagate the Christian faith, while maintaining it in the empire, to the North and to the East. What it did was to propagate the Arian heresy, by the acts of Valens, among the unsuspecting nation of the Goths, who embraced with the simplicity of heroic barbarians and the ardour of genuine natures what they supposed to be the true faith of Christians, and which their great missionary, Bishop Ulfilas, is said to have received as such. And the noblest of the northern races, which was destined to conquer Rome itself, remained for generations in the heresy which it had derived from the deceit of the meanest and one of the worst among Eastern tyrants. What Constantinople inherited from Rome was the full mass of heathen corruption existing there in defiance of the Christian leaven working on society. But instead of carrying from the great mother the faith of Peter, "imperial Byzantium," to use the words of a great historian, "suffered Christian civilisation to die out in Asia, while it threatened Europe with Asiatic despotism".[1]

I would not venture to say that what happened in Rome as a consequence of Constantine's permanent withdrawal of the imperial residence from the old capital, so far as regarded the free play which it secured to the exercise of the Church's great primacy

[1] Photius, i 4.

therein, ever presented itself to his mind. There is no appearance on his part of jealousy at the special prerogatives of the Roman See. It was the deeply-rooted heathenism of the people and the senate at which he took offence. His actions in regard to the Pope and the churches of Rome, in building and endowing them, were so munificent that they favoured the report, which was long believed, that he had been baptised by St. Sylvester in the Lateran Baptistery. But it is certain that no favour which he conferred on the Roman church was equal to the indirect and unintended one of relieving the Pope from being member of the court to a resident emperor. That deadly honour was reserved for the Bishop of Byzantium, and it made him what he became from the time of Nectarius. In Rome, the Apostolic Throne became more eminent as the Cæsarean Throne was fixed at a distance. But had it not been the Apostolic Throne from the beginning, no absence of the emperor could have made it what it became, just as no presence of the emperor could make Byzantium apostolic.

CHAPTER VII.

CHURCH AND STATE UNDER THE THEODOSIAN HOUSE.

THE whole internal progress of the Church in defining doctrine and maintaining discipline from age to age carries with it, as a necessary result, a more distinct recognition of the central power in the Church, and accordingly a strengthening of the force which it exerts. There is no end to this application of the words in which de Maistre so happily expressed the growth of St. Peter's See by the similitude which a Roman poet had given to the fame of a single Roman noble.

"Crescit occulto velut arbor ævo"

is at once history of the past, and prophecy of the future, and a picture of the kingdom of Christ seen from beginning to end in its vital power. It is not individual energy, or, as the enemy would call it, ambition in this or that pope, but the nature of things—that is to say, God's constitution of His Church as a kingdom—which produces this result.

There are, however, times which seem especially favourable to this growth, and they are usually times of difficulty and danger. Constantine's recognition of the Church in the convocation of her first General Council was coincident with the invasion of a most terrible heresy, which touched the most vital doctrine of the Church, and called forth all her life to meet it. The fifty years' struggle from 330 to 380, which ensued upon Constantine's patronage of Eusebius and the party espousing that heresy—a patronage continued by Constantius and Valens—was accompanied and followed by the most brilliant display of learning, eloquence, and reasoning which the patristic age can shew. This exuberant burst of life lasts from the monarchy of Constantine in 323 to the end of St. Leo's Pontificate in 461. A galaxy of renowned Fathers flourished in this interval, and they produced a vast variety of works, which attest the quickness of life and energy in the Church at that time. I would here note that the development of the Primacy in this same interval kept equal pace with the building up of doctrine.[1] As the Church emerged by the act of Constantine from the persecution of the pagan State into a world-power, her own government and her theology came into full light and exercise. The growth of the universal episcopate from the Person of the God-man, to which three centuries were given by the providence of God, was a divine structure of government as the faith which went forth from the mouth of the God-man was a divine word. As the faith was developed in the course of

---

[1] The analogous growth of Papal power in the Church and of the Church's doctrine are mentioned by Möhler, *Hist.* i. pp. 586-9, and by Riffel, pp. 505, 509, 519.

ages, was drawn out by resistance to the assault of heresies, was elaborated through the pondering of the faithful mind upon the tradition which had carried down both creed and polity, was quickened by the suffering of its defenders; so, in like manner, the Primacy bestowed on Peter, the pastorship of the universal flock, which had its sole root in the Person of Christ, its sole expression in the words of Christ, first promising and then performing, grew and matured amid the conflicts of doctrine, the jealousy of emperors, the rivalry of parties. Thus the period of five generations, beginning with the Nicene Council, as it was a period of incessant conflict, in which the due expression of doctrine was brought about, so it was a period of incessant growth in government. These two advances form my present subject, and I shall endeavour to draw out the intimate relation in which they stand to each other.

Let us take our stand with Theodosius in 381, when he called his council of purely Eastern bishops at Constantinople, and review in this light the fifty years which passed until his grandson, Theodosius II., called the Council of Ephesus in 431.

When the young Gratian summoned to his side the son of a famous general, unjustly executed through a court intrigue, by his own order, Theodosius had to pardon a father's death, and to take up the rule of an empire, the fate of which seemed to tremble in the balance. A tremendous defeat, in which Valens and his army were exterminated, had left Constantinople open to the sword of the Goths. Theodosius ruled for only fifteen years, and died at the age of forty-nine; and during those years the Roman empire may be said to have rested on his prudence, on his valour, and on his piety. Yet twice even in his time it was brought to the brink of destruction: he saw two sons of the emperor Valentinian, emperors themselves, and of the highest promise, murdered by insurgents. He was obliged to recognise the first of these, Maximus, as Roman emperor in Gaul, and after enduring him as a colleague for five years, with difficulty subdued him. He had a similar and even more hazardous conflict with another usurper, Eugenius, the creature of Arbogast, who had first served and then murdered the young Valentinian, legitimate colleague of Theodosius, and brother of his second wife, Galla, the beautiful daughter of the elder Valentinian. As soon as he came to the throne he found the episcopate of his own proper Eastern portion of the empire torn to pieces by the fifty years' domination of Arian princes, making and unmaking bishops, and using them for tools. This is the picture given us of the things seen and suffered by themselves in their own times by the noblest of Eastern bishops, Athanasius, Basil, Gregory of Nazianzum: a picture filled in by the touches of St. Hilary and St. Jerome. Three councils of Eastern bishops did Theodosius convoke at Constantinople in the years 381, 382, and 383, in the endeavour to bring back this disturbed and demoralised Eastern episcopate to harmony with itself and a common profession of the truth. But his first act of all was to issue, in conjunction with his

Western colleagues, the famous law of 380, in which he directed all his subjects to look to Damasus of Rome and Peter of Alexandria for the teaching which was the standard of true doctrine. I have already dwelt upon the immense importance of this law, and upon the unrivalled and incontrovertible witness which it offers— the witness of the empire speaking in its rulers—to the teaching of St. Peter at Rome, and to the whole mass of "the apostolic discipline and evangelic doctrine" stored up by descent from him in the See of Rome, and thence imparted to the whole Church. Theodosius terminated the whole Arian controversy by naming St. Peter at Rome and his disciple, St. Mark at Alexandria, both seen in their line of descent to Damasus and Peter, as the standard of doctrine respecting the key to the whole Christian profession, belief in the most blessed Trinity. Thus, in 380, the Roman church reaped the reward of its constancy, shewn by the succession of its bishops from Constantine, Sylvester, Mark, Julius, Liberius, and Damasus; while Alexandria, thrice invaded by Arian usurpers, stood in the glory of Athanasius, to whom Peter had succeeded, after first suffering expulsion from an Arian intruder immediately after the death of Athanasius.

It cannot be doubted that Theodosius, from the moment that he was instructed and baptised by Ascholius at Thessalonica, recognised at once, with the eye of a statesman and with the heart of a Christian, the necessity of the Church's co-operation for the maintenance of the empire. All thoughtful men of that day, whether secular or ecclesiastical, must have seen it. Heresy had torn the episcopate, but it had almost dissolved the empire. Theodosius especially embraced with all his heart the Christian Church: not this or that sect, still less a writhing tangle of warring sects, biting each other with poisoned fangs, but the one Bridal Chamber of Christ. With the greatest clearness of view, and with the resplendence of imperial testimony, he pitched upon Rome as its seat. He did more: he said that it had been there from the time of St. Peter; that St. Peter had founded it there; that Damasus now held it there; and he proclaimed that those should be Catholic who held what Damasus held in the most sacred of all Christian mysteries; and that those should be heretics who denied or confused what he held. And from this time forth to the end of his reign he strove to overcome the evil which his heretical predecessors, Constantius and Valens, who were no less tyrants of the worst kind, had introduced into the empire and into the Church. That Empire and Church should agree, that they should work together for the common good, this was his conception of the relation between the Two Powers. This was the conception of the whole Theodosian house. And I think it may be said that this conception was inherited by Marcian, Justinian, and the whole imperial line. For when any individual emperor fell into heresy, he conceived that heresy as if it were the one Christian faith, and used his power as emperor to make it so. No one of them embraced a sectarian indifference to truth as such; but the worst heretic among them strove to make what he chose to consider the truth to be the one Christian truth. In the principle of unity in religious belief an iconoclast emperor did not differ from a Catholic, nor Photius, the author of schism, from Pope Nicholas, the centre of unity, who condemned him.

From this point we may pass at once to the end of the fifty years now under review, and quote the act of the grandson as setting forth the mind and the conduct of the grandsire.

The emperors of the East and West, Theodosius II. and Valentinian III., after the heresy broached by Nestorius had been detected by St. Cyril of Alexandria, and brought before the notice of Pope Celestine, convoked a general council to meet at Ephesus. For this purpose they issued a letter of invitation, dated the 19th November, 430, which was addressed to St. Cyril, and the several metropolitans of the whole Church. The opening sentences of this letter express the relation between Church and State, as held by the imperial power itself, with such distinctness that they may be aptly quoted, while, as an imperial document, they form an unimpeachable historical testimony on the subject.

"The constitution of our commonwealth depends on the religion with which God is worshipped, and there is a close relationship and community of interest between these two. For they are bound up together, and each increases by the advancement of the other, so that true religion is shewn by upright conduct, and the commonwealth which consists in both flourishes in both together.

Since then God has placed in our hands the reins of empire, and it is His will that we should be the bond both of religion and temporal prosperity to our subjects, we preserve inviolate the union of these two things, as mediators therein between the Divine Providence and men. Thus, we are the ministers of Providence for the advancement of the commonwealth, while, inasmuch as we represent the whole body of our subjects, we protect them at once in a right belief and in a civil polity corresponding with it. Both these objects are our care, for it is impossible to watch over the one and neglect the other. We take special pains that the condition of the Church should continue befitting God and suitable to the wants of our time; that general concord may breed tranquillity, and civil security ensue from ecclesiastical peace. Moreover, that there may be not only purity of doctrine, but irreprehensible conduct, and the clergy, especially such as hold high rank in the priesthood, may be free from blame."

If Constantine himself had attempted to express his idea of that relation between the civil and the spiritual powers, which it was his purpose to introduce into the empire, he would probably have chosen such words as these. In the course of a century that relation tended to become more fixed and clear, and these words of the two grandsons of Theodosius, then holding the empire between them, and put forth to all the metropolitans of the Church on the occasion of summoning for the second time in the history of the Church an ecumenical council, have both in themselves, and for the occasion on which they were uttered, the greatest weight. The good which they represent to consist in the harmony of the Two Powers is no transient good, peculiar to a special concurrence of circumstances, but a good for all time. That every action of the great Theodosius was guided by this view there can be no doubt, or that this is the exact view which the Theodosian family held of their position as emperors in regard to the Christian religion. It is no less true that the Fathers who lived in their time, and bore an unshaken loyalty to them amid all the disasters which befell the empire after the death of the great Theodosius, and partly through the weakness of personal character in his sons and grandsons, entertained the same conception as to the intimate bond between religion and temporal rule which ought to subsist under Christian kings. There is a touching incident respecting this circular letter, since a copy of it was addressed to St. Augustine, inviting his presence at the council, though he was not a metropolitan. It arrived only after his death, and was laid upon his tomb by the Archbishop of Carthage, and then opened and read. There can be no doubt that it was in exact agreement with the doctrine of that great Father as to the duty of Christian sovereigns, as well as with the belief and practice of St. Athanasius, the two Gregories, St. Basil, St. Ambrose, who lived in the century following the time of Constantine. And if rulers, who still call themselves Christian, have come to repudiate this duty of maintaining the intimate relationship between spiritual and temporal things, as the chiefest obligation of their sovereignty, it is the more requisite, for the right understanding of the times in which this duty was fully acknowledged, though not always consistently practised, to bear in mind this conception of the sovereign's duty as head of the civil order. At least Constantine, Theodosius, and their successors had no doubt as to their position in this respect. Even those emperors who supported heresy, supported it not because they thought it indifferent to support truth or error, in their character of princes, but because they were mistaken as to what was truth. And so they were more respectable even in their error than those who, being materially right in their personal belief, are indifferent as to truth and error in their public acts.

It would be well therefore to distinguish between the fixed and permanent duty of all Roman emperors from the time of Constantine, as here delineated by the two rulers of the East and West, and the errors as to fact committed by some emperors in supporting heresy with the weight of the imperial power. For instance, no worse persecutors of the true faith can be found than Constantius and Valens. They attempted to establish one or other form of Arian misbelief, but they did not swerve from the conception itself of the emperor's duty, inasmuch as they elevated their own misbelief into the position which belonged to the Christian faith. And so with other Eastern emperors who followed them. As head of the human commonwealth, as representing and bearing in their single persons its full authority, they considered themselves the official defenders and propagators of the spiritual power. It was in virtue of this duty that emperors summoned general councils[1] with the agreement either expressed or understood of the chief bishops; most of all of the Pope. Nor did any council so summoned rank in the time succeeding it as general which did not, before it was esteemed to be general, receive the Papal confirmation.[2] But it was as friends, not as enemies, nor yet as rivals of the Church, that the emperors summoned these councils, while the enormous concentration of civil power in their hands rendered their summons indispensable according to the existing laws. For they could prohibit any bishop as a subject from attending them : and they could at their pleasure banish any bishop from his see ; nor could bishops of the West meet in the East, or those of the East in the West, without permission of the respective emperors. The civil act of the emperors convoking the council would not recite the previous consultations with Pope and Patriarchs which had led to it, but the consultation took place, as is seen in the cases of the Council of Ephesus in 431, of the second Council of Ephesus, the Latrocinium in 449, and the Council of Chalcedon in 451.

From the law of the three emperors in 380, directing their subjects to look upon Pope Damasus at Rome and Peter of Alexandria as the standards of doctrine, to the convocation of the Ephesine Council, the fifty years which passed were full of great political changes and convulsions. But the letter convoking the Council expresses, with extraordinary precision and force,[3] the

---
[1] Riffel, p. 859, on the convocation of the Council of Ephesus.   [2] *Id.* p. 283.
[3] Thus alleged by Leo XIII. in the Encyclical, *Immortale Dei.*

relation between the Two Powers, spiritual and temporal, which the Roman empire, if it could still be called one empire, accepted equally in its Eastern and Western administrations. It sums up the conduct of the great Theodosius himself; of his sons, Arcadius and Honorius; of his granddaughter, Pulcheria; and his daughter, Galla Placidia; of his grandsons, Theodosius II. and Valentinian III. It is necessary also for due intelligence of the whole structure of laws which they passed in regard to the Church.

First, the imperial power considered itself as the representative of human society. It claimed no less than this; and it may be said that its subjects generally admitted that claim. But further, it considered that society to rest collectively on the ordinance of God the Creator, and its own authority to be divine, because it was the minister of God in exercising it. "We have been appointed to reign by God," the emperors say. In this certainly they were quite faithful to the tradition of Constantine, who had ever this word in his mouth. But there was not a statesman or a churchman of the day who did not acknowledge this. It was a permanent, unchanging principle. They conceived as a divine delegation the natural order on which all government of the human society rested,[1] with which delegation they were clothed who were rightful emperors. And it was the strong perception of this by the subjects of the Roman empire which, amid constant changes of the

---

[1] See Leo XIII. in the above Encyclical, who declares that all power of man over man is only given by delegation from God.

imperial family and frequent abuses of power by individual rulers, invested the imperial authority with so vast a respect.

But parallel to this natural order, which the governors and the governed so strongly held, they looked upon the Catholic Church as the one representative of the supernatural order, which completed and exalted the natural, while it presupposed it and was built upon it. Of the many nations, races, or tribes which composed the empire, there was not one which was not accustomed to see the public religion joined with the public government. And when Constantine accepted the Church, as the result of her long conflict and proscription, instead of the heathen worship with which all the several nations then merged in the Roman empire, but the Roman city especially, had grown up in closest identification, he accepted her as the bearer of the one divine revelation. That this revelation was *one*, and that its bearer was Catholic, he even perceived with less difficulty than the substance of the revelation itself as to its special doctrines. Eusebius of Nicomedia could entangle him as to the doctrine of the Blessed Trinity, but not as to the claim of the Church to be one and to be Catholic in oneness. And now the inheritors of his power based their own sovereignty on one double foundation, terming themselves the mediators between the Divine Providence and men their subjects, as guardians of the union between the spiritual and the temporal power. They looked upon human life as one integral whole,[1]

---

[1] See Stimmen aus Maria-Laach, 7th Feb., 1886, p. 126.

made up of social order as concerns the present, and religion as bond of the present and hope of the future. They did not admit a dualism or inward opposition between these two. They did not leave in silence the divine rule,[1] as if either of three alternatives were possible: the first, that there was no God, or at least none who cared for human society; the second, that man, whether single or in society, owed no duty to God; the third, that any sovereignty could even be imagined which did not recognise God for its origin, its force, and its authority. And they drew from the fact that their sovereignty rested on this one double foundation the necessary conclusion that there must be a co-ordination between these two, the spiritual and the temporal power, which has often been compared to that of soul and body in the human compound. What runs through this letter convoking the second General Council is the sense that the first and chiefest duty of the ruler is to maintain unbroken the society of the Two Powers, and as part of it the one revelation of the will and knowledge of God entrusted to the Church. It followed that any heresy which attacked the doctrine, and any schism which attacked the unity, of the Church, was equally an enemy to the imperial power.

But as the various tenants of the imperial throne agreed in this as the double foundation of human society, so did the Christian hierarchy itself, as we have its convictions recorded in the preserved writings of its chief Fathers. Augustine, the most illustrious of them all, may

---

[1] See the Encyclical, *Immortale Dei*, 1st Nov., 1885.

be taken as their mouthpiece in this. And it is remarkable that his episcopate began in the year 395, in which Theodosius died, while it lasted through thirty-four years of the empire's agony which followed on the death of its last great emperor. Augustine, having been consecrated as successor to Valerius, bishop of Hippo, in his lifetime, succeeded him when he died in 396, and witnessed every great event which affected the empire, while he took an important part in every controversy which affected the Church, to his death in August, 430, at the moment when the Vandals were besieging Hippo. In this fearful time he saw the sons of the great Theodosius, one having the East and the other the West as his inheritance from the father who had saved both, turn, through the rivalry of the ministers, Stilicho and Rufinus, the forces of their respective portions of the one empire against each other. When the great emperor died, Alaric the Goth, as a general in the service of Rome, attended at his funeral. Stilicho, the husband of his favourite niece, was highest in his favour. Had he lived, Stilicho and Alaric would probably have been the right and left hands of a spirit greater than theirs in defence of Rome. But Stilicho, as father-in-law of an incapable prince, after saving his throne repeatedly by a series of victories almost unprecedented, was put to death by the son-in-law under a suspicion of treason, which still rests upon his name; and Alaric, when Stilicho was removed from his path, instead of being Rome's defender, was by her capture to scatter for ever the halo of empire which for so many hundred years had rested on her head. It is in his great work, *The City of God*, caused by this event, that Augustine has shewn his power, not only of theological and philosophical insight, but the grasp of the historian and the wisdom of the statesman. Augustine, holding no higher rank than the see of an inconsiderable African town, had become, by the joint force of his character and his writings, the greatest name in the Church before his death, while he was to become greater yet after his death by the effect which his writings were to have in the formation of Catholic theology. Among the many who came under the control of his genius were two great officers who at different times held high rank over Africa under the emperor. In the year 414, Macedonius, being vicarius of that province, addressed a letter to Augustine, in answering which Augustine[1] expresses his view of the temporal ruler's duty to be that, before all things, he is required by piety and by charity to regard the eternal welfare of those whom he governs, and consequently to promulgate and defend the Christian faith both by legislation and by administration in accordance with it. The keynote of his argument is that the present life, in all its virtues, trials, sufferings, is ordered with a view to the future life. Then, coming to the relation between Church and State, he says: "We know you to be a lover of the commonwealth. Now, observe how the inspired Psalmist says that the source of happiness to the city is the same as

[1] Ep. clv.

that to the individual. 'Rescue me,' he says, 'out of the hand of strange children, whose mouth has spoken vanity, and their right hand is the right hand of iniquity; whose sons are as new plants in their youth; whose daughters are decked out; whose storehouses are full, whose sheep are fruitful, and their oxen fat. Who have no crying out in their streets. They call the people happy which has these things; but happy is that people whose God is the Lord.'" "If," says Augustine, "all your effort is, in accordance with these strange children, to increase the temporal riches of the people; if all your prudence, your fortitude, your temperance, and your justice are limited to this material prosperity, and do not go beyond this to direct those under your charge to the worship of the true God, in which lies the whole fruit of the tranquillity here enjoyed, whatever pains you take will profit you nothing for real happiness. It is to the more perfect attainment of this personal piety, and perseverance in it, that I would invite you as well as myself; and, indeed, if you did not already possess this, if you did not consider that your temporal honours ought to be subservient to it, you would not have said in your edict to the heretical Donatists, in the endeavour to bring them back to the unity and peace of Christ, 'This is your cause which we are pursuing; it is for you we are labouring, whether we be priests of incorrupt faith, or the emperor himself on his throne, or we his judges, all is alike for you'. And much more which you have put in that same edict, so as to make it evident that the thought of the heavenly commonwealth counts not a little to you in the circle of the earthly judge's duties."

Augustine deals still more strongly with the duty of the ruler in his letter to another great personal friend, Boniface, at that time tribune, afterwards count of Africa, a man of mournful celebrity in history. Led by false statements of his rival Aetius, chief minister of the empress Galla Placidia, he was induced to call the Vandals into his province of Africa, and afterwards returning to loyalty, sacrificed his life in vain in defence of the empire. In a letter[1] to him, dated in the year 417, St. Augustine maintains that kings can lawfully use their power as kings to compel heretics and schismatics to give up their heresy and schism for the unity of the Body of Christ, and that it is part of their duty as princes to do this. He uses to this effect the testimony of Scripture in the Old Testament in estimating the conduct of the Jewish kings, as well as the conduct also of heathen kings. He uses further the act of our Lord in converting St. Paul, and His words to His servants in the parable, "*Compel* them to come in".

Speaking in particular of the imperial laws against the Donatists, he says: "In the Apostle's words, whilst we have time, let us work good to all men. Let all be called to salvation, let all be recalled from perdition— those who can by the sermons of preachers, those who can by the laws of Catholic princes, in part through obedience to divine admonitions, in part through obedi-

[1] Ep. clxxxv.

ence to imperial commands; because when emperors make bad laws in behalf of falsehood against the truth, those who have a right faith approve themselves, and, upon persevering, obtain their crown. But when they make good laws in behalf of the truth against falsehood, the furious are cowed, and the intelligent are corrected. Whoever then refuses obedience to the laws of emperors, which are passed against God's truth, acquires a great reward; but whoever refuses obedience to the laws of emperors, which are passed for God's truth, takes to himself a great punishment. For in the times of the prophets all the kings in the people of God who did not prohibit or overthrow whatever had been set up against the commands of God are blamed; while those who did prohibit and overthrow meet with choice praise. King Nabuchodonosor, when the servant of idols, proclaimed a sacrilegious law to adore an image; but those who refused obedience to an impious command shewed piety and faith. But the same king, when corrected by a divine miracle, made a pious and praiseworthy law for the truth, that whoever should blaspheme the true God of Sidrac, Misac, and Abdenago should utterly perish with his household. If any despised this law, and deservedly suffered the appointed penalty, they ought to have said what the Donatists say, that they are just because they suffered persecution by the king's law. They certainly would say this if they are filled with such madness as those who divide the members of Christ, and spit out the sacraments of Christ, and glory in persecution, because they are prohibited from doing such things by the laws of the emperor, which they have made for the unity of Christ; and they deceitfully boast of their innocence, and seek from men that glory of martyrdom which they cannot receive from the Lord."

Presently, after detailing the horrible deeds of the Donatists, he continues: "Whoever thinks, when the Church was thus afflicted, that any extremity of suffering was to be undergone, rather than ask for God's assistance by the hands of Christian emperors, does not consider that no good reason could be given for such neglect. For, as to the objection of those who will not have just laws passed against their own impiety, namely, that the Apostles did not ask this from the kings of the earth, they do not consider the difference of the time, and that all things have their times. For what emperor had then believed in Christ so that he might serve Him by making laws in favour of piety and in punishment of impiety when the prophecy was still in course of fulfilment? 'Why have the gentiles raged, and the people devised vain things? The kings of the earth stood up, and the princes met together against the Lord and against His Christ.' But what the same psalm said a little further on was not yet come into action: 'And now, O ye kings, understand: receive instruction, you that judge the earth. Serve ye the Lord with fear, and rejoice unto Him with trembling.' How then do kings serve the Lord with fear, save by prohibiting, with religious severity, and punishing things done against the commands of the Lord? For the king serves in one way as a man, in another as a king. As a man, he serves by a faithful life; as a king, he serves by enacting, with suitable vigour, laws which enjoin just action and prohibit the contrary. So Ezechias served by destroying the groves and idol temples and the high places set up against the commands of God. So Josias served with the like deeds. So the king of the Ninivites served by compelling the whole city to appease the Lord. So Darius served by giving the idol to Daniel to be broken up, and casting his enemies to the lions. So Nabuchodonosor served, as we have said, by prohibiting all his subjects, by a terrible law, from blaspheming God. Thus then do kings in that they are kings serve the Lord, when they do for His service what none but kings can do.

"Accordingly, when kings in the time of the Apostles did not yet serve the Lord, but devised vain things against the Lord and against His Christ, so that all the predictions of the prophets might be accomplished, certainly acts of impiety could not then be prohibited by laws but rather be exercised by them. For so was evolved the order of the times, that both Jews should slay the preachers of Christ, esteeming that they did God service, as Christ had foretold, and the gentiles should rage against Christians, and that the patience of the martyrs should conquer all. But when the Scripture began to be fulfilled, 'And all kings of the earth shall adore Him: all nations shall serve Him,' what sane man will say to kings, Take no care who in your kingdom supports or oppresses the Church of your Lord: Let it be no business of yours who in your kingdom chooses to be religious or sacrilegious, since it cannot be said to them: Let it be no business of yours who in your kingdom chooses to be chaste or unchaste. For, since free-will is the gift of God to man, why should adulteries be punishable by law, and sacrileges permitted? Is it a lighter thing that the soul should not keep its faith to God, than a woman to her husband? Or if faults are committed against religion, not through contempt but through ignorance, granting that they deserve less punishment, do they deserve none at all?"

Nor does Augustine stop with the judgment of Scripture upon the royal duties of Jewish or heathen kings—he passes on to our Lord Himself. "No one can doubt," he says, "that it is better for men to be led by teaching to the worship of God than by fear of punishment or by pain. The cry of the good is, 'My soul hath thirsted for the living God,' but there are bad servants and deserters who need to be brought back to their Lord by the lash. Who can ever love us more than Christ, who laid down His life for His sheep? Yet while He called Peter and the other Apostles by His word alone, He not only stopped by His word but prostrated by His power Paul, who once was Saul, that was to be a great builder of His Church, after horribly laying it waste. And him He struck with bodily blindness to bring him out of the darkness and savagery of unbelief to desire the light of the heart. If that was not a punishment he would not afterwards have been healed. And when, with open eyes, he saw nothing, had he seen, Scripture would not tell how scales, as it were, fell from them at the touch of the hand of Ananias, that vision might be restored. Where is the accustomed cry, 'It is free to believe or not to believe? When did Christ use force? Whom did He compel?' Here is the Apostle Paul: let them acknowledge in him Christ first compelling and then teaching; first striking and then comforting. But it is a marvel that he who entered into the gospel by the compulsion of bodily punishment, laboured in the gospel more than all those who were called by the word alone; and that perfect charity cast out fear in the man whom the force of fear compelled to charity."

"Thus we shew that Christ compelled Paul, and the Church imitates her Lord, inasmuch as she waited before compelling any, that the preaching which prophecy foretold might be fulfilled by the belief of kings and of nations. Here, again, our Lord Himself ordered the guests first to be invited to His supper, afterwards to be compelled. When His servants had answered, 'Lord, it is done as Thou hast commanded, and yet there is room'. 'Go out,' He said, 'into the highways and hedges and compel them to come in.' The first obedience then was completed in those who entered of their own accord: force is put upon disobedience in those who are compelled. What means, 'Compel them to come in,' after it had been said, 'Bring them in,' and answer had been made, 'It is done as Thou has commanded, and yet there is room'? Had He wished us to understand that they were compelled by the fear of miracles, numerous miracles were rather done to those who were first called, to the Jews specially, of whom it was said, The Jews seek signs. Such miracles also, in the times of the Apostles, recommended the gospel to the gentiles also; so that if by such things they were ordered to be compelled, it would be rather the first guests of whom the word would be used. If then, by virtue of that power which in its due time the Church received as a divine gift through the religion and belief of kings, those who are found in the high ways and hedges, that is, in heresies and schisms, are compelled to come in, let them not blame the compulsion, but give their mind to what they are compelled. The supper of the Lord is the unity of Christ's Body, not only in the sacrament of the altar, but in the bond of peace."

In the argument thus used St. Augustine speaks not merely with his own authority, but he represents the one voice of the Fathers on the subject. The notion that Christian rulers were, in their legislation and their government, to hold an even balance between heathenism and the Christian faith, or between heresy and schism and the one Catholic Church, is entirely unknown to the Fathers, and to the whole line of emperors. Indeed, it may be said to contradict the whole purpose of Constantine's act. For how should the Christian prince give less devotion or protection to the worship of the true God than the heathen prince had given to the worship of the false God? If the temple of Jupiter at Rome was the centre of Rome's religion, if the golden statues flashing on the roof encompassed Rome with a divine splendour which identified religion and government, if all worship through heathendom in general was consecrated by a respect descending unbroken from primeval times, should the prince, who came to believe in the Blessed Trinity instead of a Pantheon, and, instead of deified malefactors consecrating every crime by their practice, had learned that God had become man to save man from his fall, give less to the Creator who had redeemed him than to the false gods whom he had ceased to trust? Honour, worship, and obedience passed complete and entire from the false to the true. This was the victory which martyrdom had wrought, not to enfeeble or divide worship, but to unveil its true object. It is only to the children of Voltaire and Rousseau that indifference belongs. It is only to those who have no faith of their own that truth and error stand on equal ground. It is only to those who have no creed and no theology that heresy and schism become names without meaning, or pass from their condition of mortal sins, in which they hold the apostolic letters, to meritorious exercises of man's chief prerogative, freedom of will as shewn in freedom of thought.

From the calling of the Council of Nicea in 325 to the calling of the Council of Ephesus in 431 is a period of 105 years. In it a most wonderful transformation had taken place. A few years before the first Council met, a society which had been persecuted unto blood during three hundred years by the Roman emperors had received toleration from them: to use an expression applied by an historian to the conduct of the emperor

Alexander Severus, in its regard, "it was allowed to be". Presently, the same emperor Constantine, after giving it equal rights with the heathen worship which it was displacing, began a course of imperial legislation which tended to give it exclusive support.[1] But by the time the second Council was convoked, all who were rash enough to attack the internal or external unity of that same society, its foundations and institutions, were put both to civil and ecclesiastical ban. And this for no less a reason than that the foundation of this society was also recognised to be the foundation of the Roman commonwealth itself. That is to say, the natural order of human society and the supernatural order of the Christian and Catholic faith were seen to rest together on the one authority of God, decreeing, in the first instance, that man should live in society, in the second that he should enjoy in that society the knowledge of the one revealed will of God.

How the imperial power, which regarded the harmony of Church and State to be so precious as to deserve the first care of temporal government, would regard the intrinsic government of the Church as contained in its Primacy and Episcopate, remains to be seen.

To form a right judgment upon this, the aspect in which the Two Powers reciprocally regarded each other requires to be carefully borne in mind; that is, we have to consider in what light the Church looked upon the Empire, and in what light the Empire looked upon the Church, and what was the result of this mutual estimation.

[1] See Riffel, pp. 673-679.

As to the first, when the emperor was a heathen, the Church still looked upon the civil order, at the head of which he stood, as a divine ordinance, which it continued to be, whatever were the personal demerits of the ruler. So our Lord had treated in His own person Herod, the most cruel of despots, in flying from his cruelty, and had acknowledged the Roman lordship of Augustus by making an act of imperial policy the incident which led to His own fulfilment of prophecy in being born at Bethlehem. So at the time of His great confession He had spoken of the power of Tiberius, as given to him and to his procurator from above. So the two chief Apostles had spoken of Nero, the minister of God, for good, in his character of ruler. But when the emperor received baptism, he became a son of the Church: he added to his title of civil headship all the duties and all the privileges which belonged to every Christian. And what the emperor, as soon as he was a Christian, became, that the whole structure of civil society and the officers which supported it, so far as they were Christian, also became. Besides, therefore, that justice which Justin Martyr could ask of Marcus Aurelius, and Tertullian of Severus, St. Sylvester could ask of Constantine the affection and devotion of a son. The heathen Pontifex Maximus, entering into the Christian Church, would offer to the Christian worship, its priesthood, its hierarchy, not only the deference which he had shewn to the heathen worship, but one so much higher, as the Christian faith was higher than the fragmentary tradition of the original belief. When Theodosius came to make good the work of Constantine as originally intended, but afterwards defaced by Constantius and Valens, this was the position he assumed. We must, therefore, remember that, to every bishop of the Church, it was a first principle to count upon the friendship of the Christian emperor and of the vast government which he administered. And in this light must be estimated the influence in calling councils, and in a great number of other acts, which was accorded to him. To think of his action, as exerted against the Church, her doctrine, and her discipline, would appear to them monstrous, an incredible perversion, unknown to heathenism itself. For it was not a fault of heathenism to abuse civil power in order to injure the worship which it acknowledged, but rather to absorb that worship into the exercise of civil power.

Now passing to the light in which the emperors regarded the Church, we must beware of supposing that they looked upon the Church with jealousy as interfering with their own government. So far is this from the case, that the imperial legislation begun by Constantine, continued even under Constantius, carried out more and more by Theodosius, his sons and daughter and grandchildren, completed by Justinian, is nothing but a putting upon the bishops through all the provinces of the empire a mass of duties and privileges which go beyond the strict limits of the spiritual government such as had come down to them by the Church's own internal constitution. It was such a devolution of civil authority to them, that the bishop stood over against

the prefect of the city everywhere; and, parallel with
the civil range of officers, the powers derived from consecration were seen to enter into the whole condition of
temporal life. A prefect of Alexandria was grievously
vexed at St. Cyril's civil jurisdiction, and the most
eminent pagan nobleman at Rome mocked the pomp
which attended on St. Damasus. The judgments of
bishops as arbiters in temporal matters were given legal
force; so that there were two courts in each city for
civil business — the spiritual and the civil, — which
created not a little jealousy in the legists of that day.[1]

Constantine, it may be here repeated, was eager for
the convocation of the first General Council; acknowledged it as representing Christ Himself; scrupulously
forbore from interfering with its judgment; and then
gave to that judgment the force of law.

From all this, it will be seen how the emperors
accepted, without grudge, that disposition of spiritual
power in the Church's hierarchy itself which they found
subsisting when the empire, in its chiefs, became
Christian. The first of them acknowledged Sylvester
at Rome, Alexander at Alexandria, Eustathius at
Antioch, and every metropolitan in his empire with the
rank which had come down to them, and the bishops
as being sole judges of doctrine. As again at the
Council of Ephesus, Theodosius II. declared that no one

[1] The Duke de Broglie, looking at this state of things with the eyes of a French statesman nurtured in the principles prevailing in France since her great Revolution, is naturally scandalised. The one blot, as it seems to me, on a work of the most finished elegance, learning, and thought is the applying the principles of the French Revolution to the relation between Church and State.

who did not belong to the sacred catalogue of bishops could sit in the Council.[1]

What Constantine, Theodosius, and Marcian wanted from the Church was the application of her unity, in government and doctrine, to the support of an empire which threatened to fall to pieces; they wished to inoculate the civil life of their degenerate populations with the vigour, the self-sacrifice, the faith of the martyrs, to obtain civilians as faithful to themselves in the order of the State as the priests had been to the Church in the time of persecution.

This was the attitude of the empire to the Church in these hundred and fifty years; and nothing can be more unlike the jealousy of spiritual power which is now so widely actuating the world of modern civilisation.

The old Roman formula of friendship for the peoples who were accepted as allies, that they were to have common friends and common enemies with Rome, would perhaps clearly express the attitude of Church and Empire to each other from the time of Theodosius. At the moment of his accession, heresy had brought the Church in the East, and with it the empire, to the brink of destruction. One of the means by which he strove to save the empire was by guarding the unity of the Church—a guardianship which, at the same time, sprung in him from the most cordial affection to her doctrine. This, without regard to any political effect, he espoused with all the loyalty of a straightforward and generous nature.

[1] See Photius, p. 107, for many instances.

It is by always bearing in mind this reciprocal attitude, together with the close and perpetual action of civil and religious affairs on each other from the time of Constantine, that we shall be best able to follow out the different results produced upon the condition of the Church in the East and in the West by the different conditions of civil life respectively prevailing. It is from the termination of the Arian struggle by the authority of Theodosius that the divergence of this result becomes more and more apparent.

We will first illustrate the condition of that immense territory which was governed directly from Constantinople, by noting the progressive exaltation of the bishop of Constantinople, proceeding from a double cause of equal potency—the supposed interest of the emperor, and the ambition of the bishop who was enthroned at the seat of temporal power.

It was a first object with that bishop to raise himself to such a rank of honour and of jurisdiction as would give him by right a place among bishops corresponding to his position at the imperial court. The first step to this was taken at the council assembled by Theodosius in 381, which gave to the bishop of the capitol no greater jurisdiction indeed, but a precedence of honour next even to the bishop of Old Rome. When Nectarius, a layman, was selected to take the place of St. Gregory of Nazianzum, his episcopate lasting sixteen years, from 381 to 397, shewed a continuous advance in the influence of his see. Starting with the exarchate of Thrace, from which the bishop of Heraclea was tacitly deposed, he set himself to purge it from Arianism. His advance in power had gone so far, that in the year preceding the death of Theodosius he held a large synod of bishops, at which, though even the patriarchs Theophilus of Alexandria and Flavian of Antioch were present, yet Nectarius presided; and a question concerning the possession of the metropolitan's see of Bostra, in Arabia — that is, in the patriarchate of Antioch — was regulated. And during this episcopate of Nectarius, the "Resident Council" took a definite formation. The source of this was in the imperial power itself, to gain favour from which bishops from all parts of the East frequented the court. Had there been no resident emperor, there would have been no "Resident Council". Sometimes as many as sixty bishops were present at the capital. They were convened and naturally presided over by the bishop of the diocese. The council seems originally to have exercised arbitration, but came by custom and degrees to be a regular and ordinary tribunal for the affairs of the higher prelates. This standing council became a powerful vehicle for the successive enlargement of authority to the bishop of the capital, whose vote generally carried its judgment with it.

In 398, John of Antioch, the renowned Chrysostome, succeeded. He exercised jurisdiction not only over the Thracian, but the Asian, exarchate. Being called in as arbitrator at Ephesus, he deposed six bishops and made Heraclides archbishop. After his own unjust deposition this act of his was impugned, and Heraclides also was deposed. One of the accusations brought against Chrysostome was the interfering with dioceses beyond his range. Nevertheless, his ambitious successors found in his example a challenge to go on with the extension of their jurisdiction; and such facts serve ordinarily for a proof of the right claimed; and so afterwards it was maintained that the archbishop of Constantinople had, even before the council of Chalcedon, the right to claim supervision and jurisdiction over the three exarchates of Thrace, Asia, and Pontus.

As to the sentence of the council at the Oak, which deposed Chrysostome, both he and Theophilus of Alexandria appealed to Pope Innocent. Chrysostome did not accept the canon passed at Antioch by the Arian council in 341, which Theophilus had used against him. Nor did Pope Innocent admit it, but desired a council of Eastern and Western bishops to be held at Rome, to which he invited Theophilus. This council he could not bring about, but he throughout defended the cause of Chrysostome, and strove to interest the emperor Honorius against the arbitrary conduct of his brother Arcadius, under whom a great persecution ensued against the friends of the deposed Chrysostome. While he still lingered in banishment and ill-treatment, Arsacius, a brother of Nectarius, but far inferior to him, succeeded for a very short time; after whom, and still during the life of the rightful bishop, Atticus, a man of great ability, was put, at the beginning of 406, in the see of Constantinople. This he held for nearly twenty years, and he had skill to use this time to the best for the advance of his power. They were years of terrible distress in the West, in which Rome was taken by Alaric, and in which the kingdoms of the two brothers often stood against each other, and in separate alliance with barbarians, who were striving to plunder or to ruin both. During this reign of eunuchs and favourites in the East, the bishop of the capital advanced: he even succeeded in getting from the weakness of Theodosius II. a law by which from that time no bishop might be chosen in the three exarchates without the consent and authority of the Resident Council at Constantinople, by which an overwhelming influence was secured to its presiding bishop. And in 421 he further obtained a decree by which the greater causes in the prefecture of Eastern Illyricum— that is, the two provinces of Epirus, the two of Macedonia, and those of Thessaly and Achaia—should not be decided without the cognisance of the bishop of Constantinople. In this Atticus was carrying out his own principles, that the ecclesiastical should follow the political organisation, and that since Gratian had ceded the prefecture of Eastern Illyricum to Theodosius in 379, it ought not to remain under the supervision of the archbishop of Thessalonica as vicar of the Apostolic See. He therein passed beyond the limits of the Thracian exarchate, and it was, moreover, a direct attack on the patriarchal rights of the Pope. Pope Bonifacius defended his actual vicar, Rufus, with success. The edict was reversed by another edict of Theodosius II.; but, however, in the end the first edict got into the Theodosian code, whence it passed into that of Justinian, while the second edict was omitted. The right of the Holy See in all this was incontestible: it was maintained afterwards by St. Leo; but after a long time this perfect specimen of Eastern trickery was carried out and prevailed, so as to detach that prefecture from the patriarchal jurisdiction of the Pope.

Atticus died in the year 425 or 426, as he was about to appoint a bishop for Nicæa, in the exarchate of Ephesus. He was succeeded for a very short time by Sisinnius, a bishop beloved for his piety and beneficence. He consecrated Proclus to be bishop of Cyzicus, which city, however, refused to receive him, and when Sisinnius appealed to the decree of Theodosius II., alleged it to have been personal to Atticus. Thus, an opposition to the advance of the see of Constantinople did not altogether fail, but, being taken up intermittently, was sure to drop. The end of it was that the bishops of Thrace, Asia, and Pontus, being far less wealthy than the bishop of the capital, who was supported by the imperial dignity, could not in the long run resist him, and came to pay regular attendance on the Resident Council. Thus, in these three exarchates he could ordain bishops, regulate all relations, and out of every such-like abuse draw new consequences for the future. When the three exarchs were brought into this subordination, an attack upon the jurisdiction, as before there had been upon the rank, of the two original Eastern patriarchs was not far off. Antioch was not in a position to resist, but it was otherwise with Alexandria.

The See of St. Mark, in strictest union with that of Rome, had by no means accepted the canon of the 150 Fathers in 381. It is said to have been passed before the patriarch of Alexandria and his bishops arrived. It was drawn so as to depose him from his second rank in the Church. Whatever human passion the patriarch Theophilus, who sat from 385 to 412, shewed against the person of St. Chrysostome, he was by no means devoid of right in opposing that increase of power in the Byzantine See which the great qualities of the preacher and saint tended to promote. His nephew, St. Cyril, who sat after him from 412 to 444, found an unexpected occasion to mortify Byzantine pride when, by the emperor's choice, another priest from Antioch had been called to the bishopric of the capital. Nestorius came with a great reputation, and in the first instance was heartily welcomed both by Pope Celestine and the patriarch Cyril. But when he publicly preached a denial of the Blessed Virgin's title to be "Mother of God," and sought to substitute for it the title "Mother of Christ," St. Cyril felt himself obliged to write to Pope Celestine. In his letter he said:[1] "God requires of us watchfulness in these matters, and the ancient customs of the Church prescribe to communicate them to your Holiness". Thereupon the Pope called a council in Rome in August, 430, approved the conduct of Cyril, condemned Nestorius, giving him ten days to submit, and charged Cyril with the remaining conduct of the case. Cyril called a council at Alexandria and issued

[1] Mansi, iv. 1011; Photius, p. 50.

his twelve anathemas; Nestorius replied at a council with counter-anathemas. The emperor Theodosius found himself compelled to authorise the meeting of a general council. Pope Celestine wrote to the patriarch Cyril that he should restore Nestorius to communion if he retracted his errors; and he charged the three legates whom he sent to the Council—the Bishops Arcadius and Projectus and the priest Philippus—to be guided by the advice and direction of Cyril, who was acting in his name. And the instructions ran: "We charge you to see the authority of the Apostolic See maintained: if it comes to any contest, you are to judge as to their voices, not to enter into a contest with them".

The end of the Council was that though Nestorius trusted to court favour, though John, the patriarch of Antioch, with his bishops, formed a party on his side, though the emperor thought all was done through the personal hatred and jealousy of Cyril, whom, together with Memnon, archbishop of Ephesus, he had imprisoned, and could hardly be brought to listen to the Council, he was at length induced to accept its decision, to restore Cyril and the archbishop of Ephesus to liberty, and to give legal effect on the part of the empire to the deposition of Nestorius and the consecration of his successor, Maximian.

The Council of Ephesus, when it was held, ranked as the next General Council after Nicæa. In it[1] the Chair

---

[1] Photius, p. 53. See pp. 34-5 for proof that the Council of Ephesus was at the time it was summoned considered the next General Council after the Nicene, and that the council of 381 was acknowledged neither by Alexandria nor by

of Alexandria maintained its high rank and renown for orthodoxy, through the firmness of Cyril. The Primacy of the Roman bishop had shewn itself in the most marked manner to the Easterns. Not only had its legates, without contradiction, set forth its full power of jurisdiction as descending from Peter, but the Fathers themselves had, in their acclamations and official utterances, most strikingly exhibited their reverence for it. While the legate on the one hand said in council that St. Peter, as nobody doubted and all knew, being the head of the Apostles, the pillar of the faith, the foundation of the Catholic Church, was given by our Lord Jesus Christ the keys of the kingdom of heaven, and authority to bind and loose sins; and that up to the present time, and for all future time, he lives and judges in his successors:[1] the Council, on the other hand, said, in the very decree in which their judgment was expressed, "We have been compelled by the canons and by the letter of our most holy Father Celestine" to pass against Nestorius the sentence of deprivation. These words of the legate are only somewhat more explicit than those which the council of Arles, the greatest council of the Antenicene period, used spontaneously in their synodal letter to the absent Pope Sylvester, expressing their regret to him that he was unable to be with them, because he could, by no means, "leave that place in which the Apostles (*i.e.*, St. Peter and St. Paul)

Rome, except so far as its doctrinal decrees against Macedonius were confirmed by Pope Damasus.

[1] ὅστις ἕως τοῦ νῦν καὶ ἀεὶ ἐν τοῖς αὐτοῦ διαδόχοις καὶ ζῇ καὶ δικάζει.—Mansi, iv. 1296.

sit from day to day, and their blood, without intermission, bears witness to the glory of God". But now the way in which the Council of Ephesus acted upon the double statement of the Roman legate, by using the expression that they were compelled, not only by the canons, but by the letter of the most holy Father Celestine, to depose the bishop of Constantinople, shews that they entirely admitted the fact that, down to the time of the Council, that is, four hundred years after the day of Pentecost, not only was St. Peter universally known to be the head of the Apostles, the pillar of the faith, and the foundation of the Catholic Church, and the holder of the keys of the kingdom, and that he had been given all this by the personal act of the Redeemer Himself, which is one thing, but also that he lived and judged in his successor, the bishop of Rome, for the time being, had done so down to their time, and was always to do the same, which is another thing. Thus, the next General Council after the Nicene gave this most emphatic testimony to an historic fact, that the bishop of Rome was, in his episcopate, the successor of St. Peter: and gave it by dwelling on the authority which his sentence, in a matter of faith, carried with it. For how could he shew more signally that the authority of Peter dwelt in him than by deposing for dereliction of the faith the bishop of the capital, whom three emperors had nursed into the possession of vast influence, and whom the last of the three, the actual emperor, was supporting with all his power.

Nothing, I suppose, can exceed the force of this testimony as an utterance of the Church herself, but circumstances of another kind, relating to the centre of gravity with regard to political power at the moment, lend it an additional guarantee as a testimony of the temporal power also.

It has been already observed that long before the Nicene Council Rome had ceased to be the habitual residence of her emperor. But five years after it a new capital had taken her place, and given a centre, on the banks of the Bosphorus, to the vast territory which we call the East. And now, in 431, power had deserted the Tyber and went forth from the Bosphorus. Honorius had died eight years before; and, at his death, his nephew, Theodosius, after punishing an usurper, had assumed the right to make his cousin Valentinian, a child of four years old, nominal emperor, under the guardianship of his mother, Galla Placidia, at the same time proclaiming her empress, in return, it is said, for the Western Illyricum, which also she ceded to her nephew, as her uncle Gratian had formerly ceded the Eastern to her father. Rome, twenty years before, had been taken and plundered by Alaric. Gaul, Spain, and Africa were more or less occupied by various settlements of northern tribes. Galla Placidia, now sole remaining child of the great Theodosius, had twice been doomed to marry, as a scapegoat, first, the Goth Ataulph, successor of Alaric, and then the general Constantius. She was resting what remained of her son's empire upon a barbarian arm, that of the able, but unscrupulous, Actius, as her feeble halfbrother, Honorius, had before rested on Stilicho. She dared not live with Valentinian unshielded at Rome, but sought protection in the unassailable fortress of Ravenna. Then it was that a Roman legate, in an Ecumenical Council mainly composed of Eastern bishops, proclaimed the full power of the Pope as derived from St. Peter's Roman episcopate, which the Council accepted and the Eastern emperor acknowledged, while all his desire and effort were to absolve the bishop of his capital, whose influence his father and grandfather had fostered, and whom the Pope was condemning and deposing.

What must have been the force of overwhelming consciousness filling the mind of the Church at that time which caused such an acknowledgment of the Primacy, when what remained of the Western empire was in such a state of feebleness, and when the Eastern emperor was the superior lord, as from the death of Honorius in 423 he did not cease to be.[1] We must add to this that the Eastern bishops, during the time of the Arian struggle, and at the councils convened at Constantinople in 381, 382, and 383, and in the succeeding times, made almost every greater synod a scene of their ambitious rivalry. In this Council of 431 they were subjects of Theodosius, not of Valentinian; yet they accepted, without a word of dispute, the Primacy which the Roman legates laid down as universally known to proceed from the episcopate of St. Peter at Rome. St. Cyril, their greatest man, was himself presiding over the Council, in virtue of a mandate from the Pope. Their conduct otherwise had given already abundant

[1] See Reumont, i. 775.

proofs of that internal weakness[1] which, eighteen years afterwards, in the Robber Council held in this same city, and in the course of the monophysite struggle, yet more betrayed itself. The utter want of character in bishops dependent on a court, and using that court for their own ends, while they at the same time humoured all its desires, was coming more and more to light, and leading to the most shameless misuse of the Church's holiest institutions.[2] But here, Rome being politically powerless, her Primacy, declared without stint, was received without reclamation; that is to say little, was confessed and dwelt upon, and carried out by the successor of St. Athanasius, as at once second bishop of the Church, and presiding over the Council in the Pope's name.

While at this council Rome and Alexandria stood together, the patriarch of Antioch and his bishops, influenced by the doctrine of Theodore of Mopsuestia, whose pupil Nestorius was, and perhaps by jealousy of St. Cyril, fell into great discredit by the support given to Nestorius. They lingered on their road to the council; they tried to form a council apart; they sided, in fact, with the court party, and the plainly expressed wishes of the emperor, and the arbitrary conduct of the count whom he had sent to maintain order. For the moment, the see of Constantinople received a great humiliation in the fall of its bishop, in which the clergy also shared, though its bishop was a stranger called from Antioch by the emperor, when he would not take

---

[1] Photius, p. 55, translated.   [2] Photius, p. 58.

any of his own clergy, not even the highly-gifted Proclus, whom the people had desired.

Nevertheless, the upward course of the bishop of Constantinople was scarcely checked by the fall of Nestorius. The election of Maximianus, highly approved by Pope Celestine and the patriarch Cyril, followed; and when he died in 434, his place was taken, through the choice of Theodosius, by Proclus. He was a renowned preacher; he had thrice been asked for as bishop by the people. His prudence, mildness, and eloquence did great service to the Church. He induced the emperor to bring back the relics of his own revered master, St. Chrysostome, and inter them with solemn procession in the church of the Apostles. In a great episcopate of twelve years, Proclus extended the influence of his see.

When Flavian, distinguished alike for purity of belief and virtuous life, succeeded him in 446, these qualities only added to the great position which had been attained by his see. Thus, Ibas, bishop of Edessa, was charged with heresy before his superior, the patriarch of Antioch, and afterwards accused to the emperor. Upon this Theodosius deputed the hearing of the case to the bishop of his capital, who delegated thereto the bishops of Tyre, Berytus, and Himeria, together with his own deacon Eulogius. The decision, afterwards read and approved in the council of Chalcedon, expressly mentioned the judgment of archbishop Flavian, and the order of the most religious emperor. Thus the bishop of Constantinople seemed to extend his authority even over the patriarchate of Antioch, from which he had delegated bishops, with a deacon of his own, to hear an episcopal cause.

To such a point in the hierarchy of the Church had risen the bishop of a see entirely unnoticed at the Nicene Council—if, indeed, there was any present. It had taken him scarcely more than two generations, in virtue of a canon of a local council, held in 381, never received at Rome, and repudiated at Alexandria, to pass from the position of a suffragan bishop of Heraclea, in Thrace, to the position of a patriarch, not only over Thrace, but over the exarchate of the great St. Basil; and over that of Ephesus, founded by St. Paul and St. John; and to meddle, besides, with one of the three Petrine sees. All this was brought about simply because Constantinople was New Rome, and the Eastern emperor thought it to be his permanent interest to rule the bishops of his whole empire by the hand of one who had no other title than that he was the bishop of the capital. His value in the sight of the emperor was that he was *not* apostolic.

Theodosius had left the throne of the East to Arcadius, a youth of eighteen; and the throne of the West to Honorius, a boy of eleven. That youth of eighteen was only seen in the midst of his guards,[1] who were clothed in brilliant armour and uniform, with gilded spears and shields. He sat in a coach drawn by white mules, plated with gold and adorned with precious stones. His dress from head to foot was studded with jewels. He had a

[1] Reumont, i. 718.

diadem sparkling with diamonds, costly earrings, and bracelets. The splendour of the palace answered to the brilliance of its lord: its halls were filled with the costliest mosaic work and silken tapestries, and men trod upon gold dust sprinkled even over its courts and stairs. In times when the safety of the vast domain which supported this luxury required the energy of a Constantine and the justice of a Theodosius to preserve it, the ministers who practically ruled it were favourites, chiefly eunuchs, engaged in perpetual rivalry—corrupt and malignant as only eunuchs could be. After thirteen years of such a reign, Arcadius died at the age of thirty-one, and left his throne to a child of seven, Theodosius II. The vain empress who had persecuted St. Chrysostome was cut off in all the glory of her youthful beauty before her aged victim; and her husband, who had permitted him to be banished, and in the banishment to be martyred by ill-usage, only just survived him. As Theodosius II. grew up, he was directed by the noblest and most capable mind which the family of the saviour of the empire ever produced—his own scarcely elder sister Pulcheria, to whom was due whatever good the Eastern empire enjoyed in his reign of nearly forty years.

Now that we have mentioned the succession of the see of Constantinople from Nectarius to Flavian, and the prodigious rise which it accomplished in those sixty-four years, let us glance at the position of the bishop in that great pleasure-loving, turbulent, and luxurious capital, as shewn in his internal administration of his diocese.

The diocese of Constantinople, like the city, seemed to have no infancy. Seven years after its birth the courtier Eusebius had left Nicomedia for the new residence of the emperor, and the see, of which he was the rightful occupant, cost the virtuous Paul a life of persecutions crowned by a martyr's death. Eudoxius, another bishop, was the baptiser, chief minister, and corrupter of Valens. The city let the great Nazianzene depart in disgust at the evil return which it made for his deliverance of it from the Arian heresy. With Nectarius another time began. There grew up around the bishop a household second only to that of the emperor, and his rank, with the outward reverence shewn to it, yielded only to the imperial state. This is borne witness to already by the Goldenmouth himself, all whose saintliness it required to maintain an ascetic life in the midst of the pomp with which he was surrounded, and to shew his love of poverty in the distribution of vast revenues. The bishop of the capital took precedence of all temporal dignitaries. The emperor usually listened to his requests; his intercession and his counsel carried great weight. He was enjoined to use a litter in the great processions, though the emperor went on foot. His officers, such as the treasurer, the archdeacon, the archpriest, the chief-sacristan, the notaries, of whom the archdeacon was the chief, the law-officers, called Defenders, the wardens, all in holy orders of priest or deacon, became great functionaries. The syncellus, who began by being a sort of private companion, the witness of the bishop's life and conversation, from which was taken his name, signifying the sharer of a cell, developed into the chancellor of future times, who is even yet supposed to direct a sovereign's conscience. That vital power of organisation, which dwelt in the bishop's person, and appeared in every diocese from the time of Constantine, nowhere shewed a more luxurious growth than in the capital of the Eastern empire. About the middle of the fifth century, the number of clergy in the cathedral exceeded four hundred. The good patriarchs ever enjoyed a vast influence and respect. But their ever increasing power and wealth could not fail to engender increased dependence on the court. We are told that Flavian was the last who disdained to yield to court influence.

Concerning this period of which we are now treating, the hundred and fifty years following the peace of the Church, we have a weighty judgment given, that in the line of emperors from Constantine I. to Leo I., and even later, not one dared directly to maintain that the supreme power of government and judgment in the Church belonged to the sovereign, or that the Church, in her domain, was not independent and free, but subject to the temporal ruler. On the contrary, the emperors maintained in theory the autonomy of the religious and ecclesiastical sphere, even if in practice they often transgressed it.

But in later times this practice, contradictory to theory, became more and more the rule, and after Flavian, who would not sue for court favour, and who was beaten to death at the Robber Council, bishops became ever rarer who, at the call of duty, ventured to represent the freedom and independence of the Church against the self-will of the autocrat. Thus, only the more courageous monks of the capital and the provinces on one hand, and the Popes of Rome on the other, repulsed the encroachments of the emperors on the Church's domain. In the Byzantine, more than in any other, Church, the pulse of ecclesiastical self-government ceased to beat. The Church of the Eastern capital became more and more closely swathed in the bonds of the civil power.[1]

Such was the atmosphere which the policy of the empire, the devotion of the people, and the alliance between the Two Powers spread around one who had become the chief bishop of the East during the seventy years in which the Theodosian house reigned at Constantinople. Between the council there held in 381 and the great council of Chalcedon, held in 451, a State-made patriarch had been created. The process of creation was after this manner. In 330 there was a simple suffragan of the exarch of Heraclea, who leapt into prominence by the act of Constantine in founding a new capital. He thus became from the bishop of Byzantium —an almost unknown see—bishop of the second city in the whole Roman empire. After fifty years, during which the bishop of this see had mostly been the favourite and minister and corrupter of the two Arianis-

---

[1] Photius, i. 109. Pages 96-110 contain a learned account of the internal state and government of the church of Constantinople, from which the above is drawn.

ing emperors, Constantius and Valens, when Theodosius began a new era, he was given, so far as the votes of 150 Eastern bishops could give it him, the rank of second bishop after the bishop of Rome. Theodosius began this exaltation, and his son and grandson carried it on with such effect that, at the death of Theodosius II., the bishop of the new capital had not only subjected the exarchates of Thrace, Ephesus, and Cæsarea, so as to form, by their absorption, a greater patriarchate for himself than the patriarchates of Alexandria and Antioch, but he was encroaching upon them also, and becoming the interpreter of imperial wishes to the whole Eastern episcopate.

CHAPTER VIII.

CHURCH AND STATE AND THE PRIMACY FROM 380 TO 440.

Now let us turn to the history of the Church in the West, from Damasus to Sixtus III., in these same sixty years. In the year 380, the law of Theodosius, promulgated especially to the bishops of the Eastern empire, who were still seething in the Arian turmoil, had pointed to Damasus as the heir of St. Peter's See and doctrine, and had attested the continuous teaching of that doctrine during the three centuries which had passed from St. Peter's martyrdom. As a counterpart to the State-made patriarch of Constantinople, whose action begins from the same Theodosius, let us trace the action of Damasus and his successors, which is entirely based upon this succession from St. Peter.

Pope Damasus died in 384, after a pontificate of eighteen years; and was succeeded by Siricius, who sat fourteen years, from 384 to 398. Respecting Pope Damasus, St. Jerome says that he had at one time assisted him as secretary in answering the questions which were directed to him from all parts of the world in the East and West. Such questions had been directed to the Popes from the earliest times; and it is remarkable that we possess the Papal answer to one of the first, written at the time when the Apostle St. John was still living. This is the letter of Pope Clement I. to the church of Corinth. These questions and the answers to them were carefully kept in the archives of the Apostolic See. But they are supposed to have been destroyed in the last great persecution, as well as the genuine acts of the martyrs in the city of Rome, which the notaries of the Holy See were ordered to make up. A very few fragments of these letters survive in the period which extends from the letter of St. Clement, about A.D. 96, to the great letter which Pope Julius in 342 sent to the Arianising bishops at Antioch, and which has been preserved to us in the writings of St. Athanasius. Pope Julius sat from 337 to 352; his successor, Liberius, from 352 to 366; Damasus from 366 to 384. Had the complete acts of the Holy See in these fifty years been preserved, they would have supplied us with more and surer information respecting that most troubled period than all the other writings which we possess, especially as to what concerns the government of the Church. But there are only a few letters and fragments of these three Popes which have been preserved. One letter of Damasus, however, Theodoret has given us, addressed, he says, "to the bishops governing the East". They had requested from him the condemnation of Apollinaris and his disciple Timotheus. The Pope wrote to them that he had already condemned them, and this is his letter:—

"That your charity, most honoured sons, assigns to the Apostolic See the fitting reverence, tells most for yourselves. For if we hold the chief place in the holy Church, wherein the holy Apostle, by sitting,[1] instructed us how it behoved us to steer the rudder which we received from him, still we confess ourselves to be inferior to this honour; but for this we labour to the utmost of our power, if by any means we may be able to reach the glory of his blessedness.

"Know, then, that long since we condemned the profane Timotheus, disciple of the heretic Apollinaris, together with his impious doctrine, and trust assuredly that the remains of it are of no account. But if that old serpent, once and again struck down, raises his head again for his own punishment, and, being outside the Church, does not cease trying with his poison-fangs certain men without faith, avoid him as a pestilence. Remember, at the same time, the apostolic faith, that especially which was set forth in writing by the Fathers at Nicæa; and resting on this as a sure basis, do not permit henceforth your clergy and laity to listen to vain words and worn-out questions. For we have already given the proper form,[2] so that he who confesses himself a Christian may keep what has been handed down from the Apostles, as St. Paul says—'If any preach to you beside what you have received, let him be anathema'. For Christ our Lord the Son of God

---

[1] Theodoret, *Hist. Lib.* x. c. 5. The term *sitting*, καθεζόμενος, is the technical expression for a bishop sitting in his see.

[2] The term *proper* form, τύπος, is a doctrinal exposition imposed by authority.

brought a most full salvation to the human race by His own passion, that He might set free from all sin the whole man, who was involved in sins. If anyone, filled by the spirit of the devil, should say that He has an imperfect Godhead or Manhood, he shows himself the son of hell. Why, then, do you ask of me again the condemnation of Timotheus, who, together with his disciple Apollinaris, in the presence also of Peter, bishop of the city of Alexandria, has been deposed here by sentence of the Apostolic See, together with his disciple Apollinaris, and in the day of judgment will suffer the fitting condemnation and torment? But if, after by his own confession changing his true hope in Christ, he persuade any light-minded men, as if he had a true hope, whoever chooses to resist the rule of the Church, will perish equally with him. God preserve you in health, most honoured sons."

This is a sample of Pope Damasus. But with his successor, Siricius, a continuous though not a complete series of these letters has been preserved. The first of these, bearing the date of February, 385, is written to Himerius, metropolitan of the Spanish province then called Tarragona, in answer to questions addressed by him to Pope Damasus, which did not reach Rome till after his death, and so came into the hands of his successor. Only the reading of this letter throughout will give an adequate notion of the authority with which it is written. This authority ranges over the whole sacerdotal life, giving specific instruction as to the rite of baptism, as to the dealing with apostates, as to marriage, as to the laws respecting penitence, as to the monastic life, as to the continence which ought to be observed by priests and deacons, as to the age and life and rule of those who receive holy orders. The authority which dictates this letter shews itself to be supreme, tranquil, settled in full and undisputed possession of itself, both in the belief of the writer and of those whom he addresses.

But upon what is this authority based? The answer to this question is very important, because not only in this letter, but in every other in the long series of Decretal Letters, of which this is the first, one only source is alleged. It is not the rank of Rome as the capital city, nor is it the decree of an emperor, nor is it the ordering of a council. It is best to give the source alleged in the very words of the letter, which begins— " The report of your fraternity, directed to our predecessor, Damasus of holy memory, found me, by the will of God, already placed in his see. And since it was necessary for us to succeed to the labours and cares of him to whose dignity, by the grace of God, we have succeeded, after informing you, as was fitting, of our promotion, we do not refuse a sufficient answer to the several points of your consultation, as the Lord has deigned to advise us; because, upon consideration of our office, we are not free either to conceal or to be silent, inasmuch as a greater zeal for the Christian religion is incumbent upon us than upon all others. We bear the burdens of all who are laden; or rather the blessed Apostle Peter bears them in our person, who, as we trust, protects and defends us as the heirs in all things of his government."[1]

In giving the rule about baptism Siricius writes: "All bishops must observe this, unless they be willing to be torn from the solid mass of the apostolic rock, upon which Christ has built his universal Church".

As to priests and deacons, who, on pretence that priests in the old law were married, do not observe chastity, he says: "They must know that they are deposed from all ecclesiastical rank, which they have unworthily used, by authority of the Apostolic See".

"We think," concludes the Pope, "that we have made sufficient answers to all the causes which you have referred to the Roman church, as the head of your body,[2] and request you to make them known to the bishops of all the surrounding provinces, of Carthagena, Lusitania, Bœtica, and Gallicia."

Was this specific claim of the Pope to sit in the See of Peter, and to be charged, as his heir, with the government of Peter, acknowledged by the bishops to whom he wrote? In the year 389 he addressed an encyclical to the bishops of various provinces, condemning, as heretical, to exclusion from the Church Jovinian and others. In his answer to this encyclical St. Ambrose,[3] with other bishops, says: "We have recognised in the letter of your Holiness the watchfulness of the Good Shepherd, in that you diligently guard the door entrusted

---

[1] Siricius, Ep. i.; Coustant, pp. 624-638.
[2] De quibus—ad Romanam ecclesiam, utpote ad caput tui corporis, retulisti.
[3] Ep. xlii. 2-965.

to you, and, with pious solicitude, protect the fold of Christ, as one worthy for the Lord's sheep to hear and to follow. And inasmuch as you knew the lambs of Christ, it is easy for you to catch the wolves, and you meet their attack as a provident pastor." Thus, one of the greatest saints and doctors of the fourth century has no more doubt about the origin, the character, and the extent of the Pope's power than the Pope himself. He assigns to him, by this simple allusion, the palmary passages in the gospels of St. Matthew and St. John.

It is in this character, as the heir of St. Peter's government, that Pope Siricius and his immediate successors issue canonical letters to the bishops of Gaul, of Africa, of Illyricum, similar in character to that quoted above, which was addressed to the Spanish metropolitan. We have but a single letter from Pope Anástasius, who sat three years, from 398 to 402, in which he writes to John, bishop of Jerusalem, that he will guard the discipline of the Roman church all over the world, by rejecting profane doctrine. "Certainly, I will never be wanting in the guardianship of the Gospel's faith among my peoples, and will communicate by letter with the parts of my body, scattered through various regions of the earth, that no profane interpretation may creep in among them to darken their minds."[1]

The next Pope, Innocent I., sat for nearly fifteen years, from 402 to 417, and we have thirty-six of his

---

[1] Coustant, p. 728. Mihi certe cura non deerit evangelii fidem circa meos custodire populos, partesque corporis mei per spatia diversa terrarum, quantum possum, literis convenire.

letters testifying his universal action in the affairs of
the Church. His pontificate covers the capture of Rome
by Alaric in 410, and a most disturbed period, in which
the governments of the two brothers, Arcadius and
Honorius, appear, through the intrigues of their ministers, to become not only separate but almost hostile
kingdoms, and in which, moreover, large parts of the
Western empire are occupied by the Northern tribes.
In the midst of this confusion his authority, as Pope, is
exercised in all directions, as well in matters of administration as in matters of doctrine. In a letter answering
the difficulties of Victricius, bishop of Rouen, he goes
over the same range of subjects as Siricius in his letter
to Himerius of Tarragona, and again in another letter
to the bishops of Spain. St. John Chrysostome appeals
to him under the persecution of the emperor Arcadius
and the patriarch Theophilus. The great preacher gives
a most graphic picture of the sufferings which he himself and his people were undergoing. The Pope defended the cause of the sufferer. When he was already
banished by the emperor Arcadius, the Pope wrote "to
the priests, deacons, all the clergy and laity of the
church of Constantinople under the bishop John," in
which he spoke of the Nicene Canons, as alone received
by the Church, to exclude, it would seem, the canons
passed at Antioch in 341, under cover of which St.
Chrysostome had then been deposed, as St. Athanasius
before had been. The Pope said that nothing but an
ecumenical synod would still this storm. He afterwards
moved the emperor Honorius at Ravenna, in 406, and

caused him to send five bishops, two priests, and a deacon, as a deputation to his brother Arcadius, asking for a council to be held at Thessalonica. They were very ill received, and the end was that Pope Innocent withdrew his communion from Atticus, who had been intruded as bishop of Constantinople by the emperor, during the life-time of St. Chrysostome, from Theophilus of Alexandria, and from Porphyrius of Antioch. They were only restored to communion some ten years afterwards, when the name of St. Chrysostome had been replaced in the diptychs in each of the three great Eastern sees, a condition which the Pope exacted.

The action of Pope Innocent upon the African bishops is seen specially in the reference of the two local councils of Carthage and Milevi, and in his confirmation of their decision upon the doctrine of grace.[1] On this occasion the famous words of St. Augustine were uttered: "Upon this cause two councils have already been sent to the Apostolic See; and answers from it have been received. The cause is ended. Would that the error may be ended also."[2] To estimate the force of these words, it is requisite to consider the language which these two councils used to express the Pope's authority, as well as the language in which the Pope answered them: and from both these to infer what was that "Principate of the Apostolic See,"[3] of which St. Augustine attests the existence from the beginning.

Here a question of faith was concerned, while the

---

[1] See the letters, 26-31, Constant, p. 867-904.
[2] Sermo, cxxxi. cap. 10.
[3] Ep. xliii., Tom. ii. 91.

mode of dealing with it throws light upon the existing discipline, particularly upon the bond which united the African church with the Apostolic See.

In the year 416 the African episcopate met in two great provincial councils held at Carthage and at Milevi to consider the attack made upon the doctrine of grace by Pelagius and Cœlestius. The result was that both councils condemned them, and then transmitted their judgment to Pope Innocent for his confirmation. Sixty-nine bishops of the council held at Carthage under the Primate Aurelius addressed a synodical letter to the Pope in which they say: "We have considered that what we have done should be made known to your holy charity, lord and brother, that the authority of the Apostolic See may be added to the statutes of our mediocrity, to protect the salvation of many, and to correct also the perversity of some".

At the same time sixty-one bishops at the council of Milevi, of whom St. Augustine was one, write another synodical letter to the Pope, which they begin in these words: "Since the Lord by the signal gift of His grace has placed you in the Apostolic See, with a special fitness for the needs of our times, so that we should be rather charged with negligence, if we failed to bring before your veneration what concerns the Church's interest, than that you would either decline or neglect our information, we beseech you to apply your pastoral diligence to the great dangers of the weak members of Christ. For a new and most pernicious heresy is attempting to raise its head." " But it is our

judgment that, by the mercy of our Lord God, who
deigns both to direct your consultations and to hear
your prayers, the authors of these perverse and pernicious opinions will more easily yield to the authority
of your Holiness, which is derived from the authority
of the holy Scriptures.[1]

In these last words the Fathers of the council state
that the authority of the Pope, to which they refer, is
derived from the grants made to St. Peter in the Gospel,
and inherited by him as Peter's successor.

In a third and longer letter, not synodical, but as it
were private, from five bishops, Aurelius of Carthage,
Augustine, Alypius, and two others, which is in fact a
short treatise upon the true doctrine of grace, and is
placed among the works of Augustine, the Pope is
informed at greater length upon the subject in question.
This letter begins: "We have sent to your Holiness
letters subscribed by no small number of bishops from
the councils of two provinces, Carthage and Numidia,
against the enemies of the grace of Christ, who trust in
their own virtue, and say to our Creator, Thou hast
made us men, but we have made ourselves just". And
it ends with these words: "The great kindness of your
heart will surely pardon us for sending to your Holiness
a longer letter than you would wish. In this we are
not pouring back our rivulet to increase your own
ample fountainhead. But the time is full of trial from
which we beseech Him to whom we say, Lead us not

---

[1] Note of Constant, p. 876. Hic declarant Milevitani Concilii Patres Romani Pontificis auctoritatem ipsa Scripturarum auctoritate fulciri.

into temptation, to deliver us. And our purpose is to have it proved by you that our rivulet springs from the same head of streams as your abounding river, and to be consoled by your rescript in the consciousness of participating one grace."

We have separate answers of Pope Innocent to both the synodical letters and to the private letter of the five bishops dated Jan. 27, 417, a few weeks before the death of the Pope. In the same year, after his death, St. Augustine[1] wrote to Paulinus, bishop of Nola, a letter in which he says: "Pope Innocent of blessed memory answered all that we said as it was right and as it became the prelate of the Apostolic See".

The words of the Pope on which St. Augustine spoke this emphatic commendation run as follows, first to the Fathers of the council of Carthage:—

"In examining the things of God, which require to be treated with the utmost care by bishops, and especially by a true, just, and Catholic council, observing the precedents of ancient tradition, and mindful of ecclesiastical discipline, you shewed the strength of your religion not less now in consulting us, than by sound reason before you pronounced sentence, inasmuch as you approved of reference being made to our judgment, knowing what is due to the Apostolic See, since all we who are placed in this post desire to follow the Apostle himself, from whom the very episcopate and all the authority of this title sprung. Following him, we know as well how to condemn the evil as to approve

[1] Ep. clxxxvi. 1.

the good. An instance of this is that, in accordance with the duty of bishops, you maintain the institutions of the Fathers, and will not suffer to be trodden under foot what they decreed by no sentence of their own as men, but by that of God. This is that, whatever was being done even in distant and remote provinces, they would not consider as determined until it was brought to the knowledge of this see; by the full authority of which the just sentence should be confirmed, and that thence all other churches might derive what they should order; whom they should absolve; whom as being bemired by ineffaceable pollution the stream which is worthy only of pure bodies should avoid. So that as from their parent source all waters should flow, and through the different regions of the whole world the pure streams of the fountainhead well forth uncorrupted."

In these words the Pope seems to take up and apply the metaphor of the fountain used by the five bishops in their letter to him. They term the decrees passed by the 130 bishops in two councils, and the doctrine of grace defended in their decrees, a rivulet, of which the Pope is the fountainhead. He accepts this expression of their humility, and exhibits the whole Church under the image of a stream welling forth from one head, the See of Peter, and carrying everywhere unity of belief and purity of doctrine.

The Pope's answer to the letter of the Numidian Council dwells upon the same thought. He says that among the other cares of the Roman church, and the occupations of the Apostolic See in answering consultations brought to it from different quarters, the decrees of the synods had been brought to him. "It is with diligence and fitness that you consult the secrets of the apostolic honour; that honour, I mean, on which, besides those things which are without, the care of all the churches attends, as to what judgment is to be passed on doubtful matters. In this you follow the prescription of the ancient rule, which you know, as well as I, has ever been observed in the whole world. But this I pass by, for I am sure your prudence is aware of it. For how could you, by your action, have confirmed this save as knowing that, throughout all provinces, answers are ever emanating from the apostolic fountain to inquirers. Especially, so often as a matter of faith is under inquiry, I judge that all our brethren and fellow-bishops ought not to refer save to Peter, that is, the source of their own name and honour, as now your affection has referred for what may benefit all churches in common throughout the whole world. For the inventors of evils must necessarily become more cautious when they see themselves, at the reference of a double synod, severed from ecclesiastical communion by our sentence."

On the same day the Pope returned an answer to the letter of the five bishops, with great praise of the faith and religion shewn in it.

In one of his letters St. Augustine speaks of the Principate which has always existed in the Apostolic See. And, as we have seen in another letter to St. Paulinus, he speaks of the answers made by Pope Innocent on this occasion as being in all things just and right, and such as became the Apostolic See. Putting these two facts together, we obtain the following particulars as belonging, in the mind of St. Augustine, to this Principate. First, it was an authority beyond and including the authority of local councils, which, when they had done their best, referred to it for approval and ratification of what they had done. No part of the Church was more autonomous than the African; yet, when 130 bishops had met under the Primates of Carthage and Numidia, and were as sure as to the truth of the doctrinal statements which they opposed to error as bishops could be, St. Augustine himself being one of them, they did not think their labours concluded until they had sent their decrees to be ratified at Rome. St. Augustine described their authority as being a rivulet when compared with the fountainhead.

Secondly, it was an authority based upon Scripture, so that they hoped Pelagius, if he did not yield to them, would yield to it. But there is no other way of explaining how the authority of the Pope was based upon Scripture in a manner in which their own authority was not based upon it, except in virtue of the divine promises made to Peter, that is, as the Church's foundation and doorkeeper, the bearer of the keys, the confirmer of his brethren, the universal pastor, coupled with the inheritance of these powers by the Pope. It was not the truth of doctrine to which reference was here made by the council of Milevi, for that they possessed, as well as the Pope: it was not this to which the fautors of heresy "would yield more easily," but a divine promise known and acknowledged by all from the beginning, as made to one person.

Thirdly, in his answer to both of the councils, the Pope speaks of "the episcopate itself, and all its authority springing from the person of Peter," in whom our Lord had placed it originally, as if the bishops themselves knew Peter to be "the author of their own name and honour": nor was this language peculiar to Pope Innocent, for Siricius had used it before, speaking of Peter, "from whom the beginning both of the apostolate and the episcopate sprung," in 386; and Pope Zosimus,[1] who followed Innocent, used it also to these same African bishops, speaking "of the ecclesiastical discipline following its own laws, and paying reverence to the name of Peter, from whom itself descended," which is repeated by his next successor, Boniface, who says that the "whole rule of the Church took its beginning from Peter, and is summed up and consists in him". St. Augustine does not start away from this doctrine, but covers it with his approval, as expressed in the two rescripts of Pope Innocent. It occurs, indeed, in his own exposition of Scripture, as where he says:[2] "Peter himself, to whom He entrusted His sheep as to another self, He willed to make one with Himself; that so He might entrust His sheep to him". "Among the Apostles Peter alone, almost everywhere, was thought worthy to repre-

---

[1] Zosimus, Ep. xii., Constant, 974; Boniface i., Constant, 1037.
[2] Tom. v. 240; v. 1194; v. 415.

sent the whole Church. On account of that very representing of the Church, which he alone bore, he was thought worthy to hear, I will give to thee the keys of the kingdom of heaven. For these keys not one man but the unity of the Church received." " One for many he gave the answer, being the oneness in the many." But, in accepting this doctrine, when solemnly enunciated by the Pope of the day in his answer to councils, he identifies the Pope's authority with that of Peter, which is a different thing from attributing certain qualities to the Apostle Peter. And this identification with Peter, and descent from Peter, run through the whole rescripts of the Pope which St. Augustine receives.

Fourthly, this authority of the Principate, which leads the bishops, after doing their best in council in defence of the faith, not to stop with their own decrees, but to carry them to the Pope, is described by the Pope in his answer as "following the examples of ancient tradition," as "carrying out the Church's discipline". It is then no new thing, but existed from the beginning; for indeed, as it sprung from the promise of Christ alone, it could not be an innovation, not the tightening of a doubtful bond by an advancing power, but the original constitution, " that in which its sum consists," to use the words of Pope Boniface. This also is comprehended in the approbation of St. Augustine.

Fifthly, the Pope also in his rescripts refers to this authority as notorious. The bishops themselves know that answers are ever emanating from the Apostolic See to all provinces. This is a permanent, ever-acting power.

The bishops, in observing it, "guard the institutions of the Fathers as part of their episcopal office; for they established it, not by human, but by divine decree," which words mean, not by the canons of a council, which would make it of *ecclesiastical* institution, but by the words of Christ, prior to all councils, and beyond their reach. This also St. Augustine spontaneously accepted. "I think," he says,[1] addressing Julian in one of his last works, "you might have been satisfied with that part of the world in which it was the will of the Lord to crown the first of His apostles with a most glorious martyrdom. Had you been willing to listen to the blessed Innocent then ruling that church, you would have escaped the Pelagian snare even in your perilous youth. For what could that holy man answer to the African councils save what the Apostolic See, from ancient times, and the Roman church, together with the rest of the churches, holds without a break."

But all the preceding points are joined in one by this fact, that the Principate, in St. Augustine's conception of it, as herein expressed, justified its name. He gave it the name which belonged to the Roman emperor. All the power of Trajan, that is, of the empire at its culminating point, was summed up in the word Principate. By this word, St. Augustine delineated the authority of the Apostolic See. This conception runs through the two rescripts of Pope Innocent. His authority being given by Christ was supreme, and was final. It was "of the Fathers," but not given by them;

[1] Lib. i. 4; Tom. x. 503.

it was not of "human but divine sentence". Most of all, in matters of faith, this supremacy, this finality, are essential. And here St. Augustine's language—the last touch which he gives to the Principate is the clearest—where he said, "Causa finita est".

This was in a matter of faith, in which, as being one and universal, the action of the Primacy is more easily recognised than in matters of discipline. In all this proceeding, the spontaneous action of the two councils, the rescripts of the Pope, the repeated comment upon the whole afforded by St. Augustine, are most clear. Nothing in all that the Pope said was strange to him, nor does he hint any exaggeration on the part of the Pope as to the privileges of his see. On the contrary, his metaphor of the fountain had even invited the strongest expressions used by the Pope. It is also to be noted that these rescripts were quoted about two hundred years later by three African councils of the Numidian, Byzacene, and Mauritanian provinces to Pope Theodore, who succeeded two years after the death of Pope Honorius. These bishops express their assent to them in the strongest language.[1]

Among the more remarkable exercises of authority by Pope Innocent is certainly to be noted a letter to Rufus,[2] bishop of Thesalonica, dated in June, 412, that is, less than two years after the taking of Rome by Alaric. The Pope begins by noting how Moses, to whom God had committed the entire charge of delivering and ruling

[1] Manzi, x. 919.   [2] Ep. xiii., Constant, 815.

Israel, had, by the advice of Jethro, delegated certain judges to judge the lesser matters and refer any great matter to himself. And again he notes the rule followed by the Apostles, who, being themselves appointed rulers of the Gospel, committed the minor charges to their disciples, as Paul had committed to Titus the affairs of Crete, and to Timotheus those of the Asiatic province. The examples here alleged sufficiently shew the basis of supreme power thus tacitly assumed. The Pope was acting after the example of Moses and "the form of the Apostles," language which would be very unfitting except in the mouth of St. Peter's successor. Thereupon the Pope, following, he says, the examples of his predecessors, Damasus and Siricius, commits to the bishop of Thessalonica a vicariate representing the Holy See over the metropolitans of the ten provinces, then constituting the government of Eastern Illyricum, that is, Achaia, Thessaly, Old and New Epirus, the two Dacias, Mœsia, Dardania, and Prœvalis. "Take, therefore, dear brother, the charge, as our vicar, over the above-named churches, preserving the rights of primates (that is, metropolitans); and being yourself the first of the primates, let them leave to your decision what should be transmitted to us. Thus we order either that the matter shall be terminated by your experience, or, if you think good, be carried up to us." And he gives the bishop power to associate with himself such bishops of these provinces as he may judge fit for the determination of any particular matter.

Concerning the immense power thus delegated to

Rufus, Tillemont[1] remarks that the Pope takes pains to remind him that it is given to him by the Roman church, and not derived from the dignity of the see of Thessalonica, which in the civil order was metropolis of Eastern Illyricum. Moreover, this power dropped with each Pope who gave it, and with each bishop to whom it was given. It was renewed therefore at the succession of a new Pope, as well as at the vacation of the see, as Pope Innocent at his own accession had renewed the grant of it to Anysius, the predecessor of Rufus.[2]

The first recorded instance of this power is the bestowal of it by Pope Damasus on Ascholius, the bishop of Thessalonica, in 381. This would seem to suggest that it was instituted when the government of Eastern Illyricum was detached from the Western, and given to the Eastern portion of the empire by Gratian on the accession of Theodosius.

It is to be noted that the authority thus created of subjecting the bishops and metropolitans of a number of provinces to one of themselves in the character of Vicar of the Apostolic See was not part of the original disposition of the Church as seen at the Nicene Council. It is a distinct unfolding of the power inherent in the Primacy. In making it the Pope leaves the rights of metropolitans in their several spheres untouched, but he creates a superior over them, for certain purposes representing himself.

A somewhat similar power was given to the bishop of

[1] x. 644.   [2] Ep. i.

Arles over the metropolitans of southern France, and to the bishop of Seville over the Spanish metropolitans, and to the bishop of Syracuse over Sicily. Atticus, bishop of Constantinople, endeavoured to use the despotic power of the Eastern emperor to draw away the bishops of Illyricum from the old tie which bound them to the Roman See, and to obtain himself the authority thus given to Thessalonica, not as vicar of the Pope, but as bishop of the capital. The law procured by him from Theodosius in 422 was withdrawn, but at a much later time the bishops of these provinces followed the civil jurisdiction of the Eastern empire. But Atticus based his encroachment simply upon the temporal authority. The Pope exerted a purely spiritual power, in the name of his inheritance from Peter, when the city of Rome lay powerless before her enemies.

It is important to trace facts as they appear in original and contemporaneous documents. Here, in these first preserved decretal letters of the Popes, we are enabled to see a double process going on. Not only do the Popes, in answer to questions addressed to them by metropolitans from Spain, Gaul, Africa, Illyricum, issue letters which unfold the discipline of Christian life then observed at Rome, but they create the institution of vicariates in the several provinces, which links the episcopate closer to them. These vicariates represent in the spiritual structure of the Church the flying buttresses in a Gothic cathedral. While they support the central fabric, they bear witness likewise to its unity. The unity of the faith is, in fact, the centralising power, as appears so manifestly in the letters of the African councils, and the rescripts made to them, and the emphatic approval of both by St. Augustine. In the very first of these letters, that of Siricius to Himerius of Tarragona, the Pope points out the one basis upon which all these answers and acts rest in the words: "We bear the burdens of all who are laden, or, rather, the blessed Apostle Peter bears them in our person, who, as we trust, protects and defends in all things the heirs of his own administration". Whether the Pope issues answers on discipline, or decrees on doctrine, or creates vicars specially representing himself, all these acts have a common source in his mind. They are part "of the administration of Peter". The exact identity of language on this point of the eight Popes, from Damasus to Sixtus, who precede St. Leo, can only be duly estimated by reading their own words. In these letters a living norma of faith and discipline, handed down by tradition from St. Peter, is continually referred to as existing in Rome. This tradition itself is viewed as a sacred thing. Thus, in the rule about ordination, Siricius speaks of those who inconsiderately ordain a priest or deacon, "as if they were better than Apostles, whose precepts they dare to change". He goes on: "I warn you that this be not done. I proclaim that, as we have one faith, we are bound to agree in what is handed down, to be peaceable in Christ, and to have charity in observing apostolic rules. In the presence, therefore, of the Father and His only-begotten

Son, and the Holy Spirit, and the Trinity of one Godhead, I charge you that the Catholic faith and our discipline in these things remain untouched. Nor let anyone think that ordinations are earthly things, for the priesthood is heavenly. So the glory of the same dignity shall remain to the faithful, and the accuser have nothing to cite before the tribunal of Christ."[1]

The combination of faith and discipline as the constituent parts of one divine polity continually appears in these papal letters, and it is remarkable that the first of them all, the letter of St. Clement, issued nearly three hundred years before that of Siricius, in delivering judgment respecting an episcopal ordination, makes in like manner an express appeal to the Blessed Trinity—the first in time, it would appear, extant after the New Testament. We have given the words of the later Pope; let us put beside them the words of the earlier: "Receive our counsel, and you shall have no occasion of regret. For as God liveth, and the Lord Jesus Christ liveth, and the Holy Spirit, who are the faith and the hope of the elect, so surely shall he who, with lowliness of mind and instant in gentleness, hath without regretfulness performed the ordinances and commandments that are given by God, be enrolled and have a name among the number of them that are saved through Jesus Christ, through whom is the glory to Him for ever and ever, amen."[2]

In the same way Pope Innocent writes to the bishop of Rouen: "Though all points of the Church's rule of

---

[1] Siricius, *Ad diversos episcopos*, Ep. vi. [2] St. Clement, Ep. i, s. 58.

life and teaching are familiar to you, yet, as you have earnestly desired the norm and authority of the Roman church, I have annexed to my letter a digest of life and approved conduct, by which the peoples of the churches in your country may perceive, each in his own profession, the rules of Christian life, and the discipline which is preserved in the churches of the city of Rome ".

In these two things, the answers on all points of Christian life and usage, and the creation of vicariates, the " compages" of the Church is strengthened, the whole process falling under that " administration of Peter," which the Pope claims as his heir. While the civil dissolution of the empire, stemmed with difficulty by the vigour of Theodosius, was in full process during the forty-five years between his death and the time of St. Leo, the Popes, in all this interval, went on consolidating the great fabric of the episcopate, in the name of him in whose person the authority itself began. And it must not be omitted that the whole of this action tended to define, and so establish, the authority of the individual bishop by the common standard of faith and conduct which it always propagated. The last glimpse of temporal prosperity which made the presence of the sovereign acceptable at Rome, when Honorius triumphed upon the victories of Stilicho, was in the year 404, the same year in which the Pope wrote to Spanish bishops: " Every good bishop should struggle that those who are scattered should be collected on the basis of doctrine to the unity of the Catholic faith, and that one body should form an impregnable whole. If this be severed into parts, it will be torn to pieces everywhere, and suffer from an inward pestilence if the structure itself be in conflict." Powerful words, surely, when the Vandal was presently to be in Africa, and the Goth in Spain, and the heir of Alaric to wed an unwilling bride in the daughter of Theodosius, and pay her dowry with the spoils of Rome. Had there then been no Pope, where would have been the Church ?

Six letters of Pope Innocent, the 19th to the 24th, refer to the end of the Antiochene schism, about the year 415, eighty-five years after its commencement in the year 330, by the Arian deposition of the legitimate bishop Eustathius. As a condition of receiving the bishop Alexander to his communion, the Pope required the name of St. John Chrysostome to be placed in the diptychs, which involved an acknowledgment that he had been unjustly deposed. In his twenty-fifth letter, addressed to the bishop of Antioch, he refers to the rule of the Nicene Council as having acknowledged the see of Antioch to be set not merely over a single province, but over all the provinces constituting the "diocese" of the East. This, he says, was not so much on account of the city's greatness, as because it was known to have been the first see of the first Apostle, which would not yield to the see of the city of Rome, except that Peter had passed from Antioch, whereas he had been kept by Rome to the end. "And so, dear brother, our judgment is, that as you ordain the metropolitans yourself, so you should not allow the other bishops to be made without your consent; with respect to those at a distance, you can, by letter, empower those to ordain them who do it now on their own authority only; those who are near, you can, if you think proper, require to come for the imposition of your own hands. As the care of these things belongs to you, they ought to await your judgment."

On this rule Tillemont remarks[1] that it was to give a great authority to the patriarchs, and greatly to diminish that of the metropolitans; but it would seem, as the Pope gives this counsel, that it was what the Popes practised themselves in the provinces more immediately depending on them.

"As to your inquiry whether, when the emperor divides a province, there should be two metropolitans, we think that the Church of God should not follow the changes of human things; and, therefore, that the metropolitans should remain as before."

He ends by requesting the bishop of Antioch to make known his answers to the bishops either by a synod, if that can be done, or by transmission of his letter; "in order that what you have so necessarily inquired, and we have so distinctly answered, may be kept by common consent and zeal of all".

This letter, therefore, sets forth the relation of the Pope to the third see of Peter in the year 415—the Pope being the subject of the emperor Honorius, and the patriarch of the emperor Theodosius II.

About the same time, St. Cyril of Alexandria terminated the suspension of communion, which had arisen

[1] Tillemont, x. 644.

from his uncle's persecution of St. Chrysostome, by replacing the name of that saint on the diptychs; and the like was done by Atticus at Constantinople, who had been the most obstinate in his enmity to the saint, into whose see he had been intruded during his lifetime. The Pope, in all the three cases, had obtained the condition which he had laid down.

Pope Innocent died in March, 417, after a pontificate of nearly fifteen years, and was succeeded by Zosimus, who sat only about twenty months, but has left letters setting forth his authority even in stronger terms, if it be possible, than those used by Pope Innocent, as in his twelfth letter to the council of Carthage. After him, Boniface I. occupied the Apostolic See during four years, from 418 to 422; Celestine, ten years, from 422 to 432; Sixtus III., eight years, from 432 to 440. The letters of these Popes are of exactly the same tenour as those of St. Innocent. In order to avoid repetition, it will be best to consider in one mass at the end the authority disclosed in the series of these letters from Damasus to the accession of Leo. In the meantime, I turn to the condition of the empire and the civil government.

Theodosius had been nominated by Gratian, in January, 379, his colleague, and had received from him the administration of the East, together with the province of the Eastern Illyricum, then first detached from the West. He died in January, 395, at forty-nine years of age; and during these sixteen years he may be said, by his wisdom and courage, to have suspended the fall of the empire. Yet he was doomed to witness and to suffer terrible things. The emperor Gratian was murdered at Lyons in 383, by Maximus, and Theodosius was obliged to acknowledge the successful insurgent as Roman emperor in Gaul, Spain, and Britain, while he was just able to maintain Valentinian in Italy and Africa. This state of things lasted five years, when Maximus advanced into Italy itself; Valentinian fled from Milan before him; and Theodosius was reduced to fight for his own throne and that of Valentinian, whose beautiful sister Galla he had taken for his second wife. Under the walls of Aquileia, in 388, he conquered Maximus, and restored the whole West to Valentinian. Yet, a few years later, as Gratian had been murdered by Maximus, so Valentinian was murdered by Arbogast, whom Theodosius himself had made commander of his army; and Theodosius had once more to contend for his throne and life with Eugenius, the creature of Arbogast. A final victory near Aquileia in 394 delivered him from these, and for the last time the whole Roman empire was in his hands. But four months later this noble life was ended. St. Ambrose had uttered words of deepest lament over the two young emperors—first Gratian, then Valentinian, taken away in all their bloom and promise; and now Theodosius, the saviour of the empire, followed them at the highest point of his maturity; and once more the great bishop and statesman uttered the voice of prayer and consolation over a Roman emperor, this time the noblest of all who had been invested with that terrible power, and whose fatal death left the Eastern throne to his eldest son, Arcadius, a youth of eighteen; and the Western to his second son, Honorius, a child of eleven. The sixteen years of Theodosius had been years of incessant action, requiring at once heroic vigour and superhuman skill. He had put an end to official Arianism in the East, though he could not undo the evil which Valens had done by fostering its propagation among the Goths; but it was beyond his power to heal the schism of Antioch. He had the art to use the valour of the Goths for the defence of the empire, and Alaric was a general in his service at his death; while Stilicho, the Vandal, was his chief minister, and had received in marriage his niece, Serena, dear to him as a daughter. He was the last Roman emperor who, while he ruled in the spirit of Augustus and of Trajan rather than of Diocletian, worthily supported the imperial name, and the idea of sovereignty in human government which it had embodied. Of him the Gothic king, Athanarich, said—"The emperor is God upon earth; whoever raises the hand against him atones for it with his blood".[1]

Yet from the time of Constantine, the empire had only subsisted by enrolling in the ranks of its armies the bravest of the northern races, who were surging onwards to destroy it; and even by promoting to high rank, both civil and military, the most distinguished men of these races, Frank, or Vandal, or Goth.[2] Thus the German element was ever pressing in upon the

[1] Quoted by Reumont, i. 698. [2] Reumont, i. 699.

Roman; it invaded not the army only, but government, the ranks of official life, the whole order of society. With Gratian and Theodosius there is a rapidly increasing number of these figures who bear Roman titles while they are of northern race. In the Western empire they were chiefly Franks. Under Gratian one, Merobaudes, stood at the head of the admistration; another, Vallis, had the command of the army. Arbogast and Bauto were great at the court and army of the younger Valentinian; Mellobaudes, of royal descent, commanded the guards of Gratian. Richomer stood high in the Western court, and was an esteemed and fortunate commander under Theodosius. In the East, the Goths were conspicuous; in the army most, but also in the administration.

These were forces which Theodosius could rule; but when his hand was withdrawn woe ensued to the divided empire. But let us consider the condition of Rome itself.

Theodosius, having re-established his young brother-in-law Valentinian on the throne in 388, spent the winter in Milan, and on the 13th June, 389, made his triumphal entry into Rome. Thirty-two years had passed since in 357 Constantius had entered it with the pomp of an Eastern despot. In all that time Rome had not seen an emperor, but five emperors had passed from the stage of life. Constantius had given way to Julian; Julian to Jovian; Jovian to the first Valentinian; Valentinian to Gratian; Gratian to Theodosius, who now was celebrating the tenth year of his accession in the ancient capital. Five years before this event Augustine had been at Rome, and received from Symmachus, as prefect of the city, nomination to a chair of rhetoric at Milan, which brought him under the influence of St. Ambrose, and was followed by his conversion. Three years before it, after the death of Pope Damasus, St. Jerome left Rome to practise the ascetic life in Palestine. Both these great men saw Rome in undiminished grandeur, so far as the buildings were concerned, with which four hundred years of imperial sway had decorated it; undiminished likewise in population; a nobility enormously wealthy, idle, and corrupt; a populace such as it had always been, greedy, wayward, restless, given up to shows and spectacles. Two societies were struggling against each other, the heathen and the Christian; and if the latter was gradually gaining predominance, its victory was by no means complete. It had to struggle with heathenism in its utmost corruption; and the alloy shewed itself too often in the Christian character, of which the complaints of St. Jerome and other Fathers give but too painful truth.

But political power had long departed from Rome. Milan had become the residence of the emperors in Italy, Lyons or Treves in Gaul.[1] The authority in spiritual things, which, according to the ancient constitution, had belonged to the emperor, and which had passed from the heathen over to the Christian emperors, was actually exercised in Rome by its bishop, which from Constantine, who left Rome in 327, to Theodosius,

[1] Reumont, i. 675.

who visited it in 389, only saw Constantius for a few
weeks in 357. This combination of secular and local
circumstances, together with the tradition of the Pontificate of the chief Apostle, which had remained constant
among the Christians, the remembrances and memorials
of martyrs running back to the first times, the reverence
which the name of Rome awakened in the general mass,
gave a place to the Roman bishop among the heathen
as well as the Christian population, which no other
possessed. From the moment that the Christian Church
was recognised by the empire, this place could not but
become more and more influential, more and more
evident, even in its outward surroundings. The law of
Theodosius in 380 only acknowledged in Damasus a
prominence which every heathen as well as every Christian in Rome had heard from childhood to be attributed
to its bishop. He was the ruler of the polity which
Peter had set up: that double fabric of doctrine and
discipline, of sacraments instinct with belief, which
made up together the daily Christian life. Constantine
built and endowed Rome's cathedral in the Lateran
Palace, which he had bestowed on her bishop, as well
as the Basilicas of the two Apostles, whom he found the
patrons of Rome.[1] Where is the voice of the nineteenth
century which would impugn the contemporaneous testimony of the two great Christian emperors, and affect
to deny what Constantine expressed in his actions and
Theodosius attested in his law?

But it is from this Rome that the series of papal

---

[1] See Gregorovius, L 97-8.

letters to bishops throughout the world, which we have been quoting, went forth: a Rome whose political power had passed, while its religious authority was daily increasing. At the very time when the presence of the emperor at Constantinople was making its bishop into a patriarch, the absence of the emperor from Rome left its bishop room to unfold the Papacy; for the root of the patriarch was the emperor, the root of the Pope was St. Peter.

Let us watch this effect of political changes upon spiritual authority in its increased action, from the death of Theodosius.

With this death the long agony of the Western empire began. In the course of his episcopate, from 395 to 430, St. Augustine beheld not only the capture and plunder of Rome during these days by Alaric, but the permanent settlement of the Gothic people in the south of France and in Spain; and he died as the Vandals were besieging Hippo, when the occupation of Africa by Genseric and his Vandals was even more fatal to Italy, and to Rome in particular, than the loss of Spain and France. Honorius began his reign as a child of eleven, in 395, and ended it at the age of thirty-nine, in 423. Theodosius had valued and trusted Stilicho, and not only bestowed upon him his niece Serena, beloved by him as a daughter, in marriage, but left him as guardian and prime minister to his son; and during thirteen years the utter incapacity of Honorius was supported and veiled by the vigour of the man who, in all but his Vandal lineage on the father's side, was a

Roman after the pattern of Julius Cæsar. His brilliant genius both as a commander and a statesman repeatedly saved the Western empire. Whether in the end he conspired against the weakling to whom he had successively married his two daughters; whether also he was secretly hostile to the Christian establishment of the empire, which he had rescued from destruction, remains one of history's unsolved problems. But he was slain by order of his son-in-law, in 408, who, in a reign of twenty-eight years, never struck a blow for a falling empire; with the result that in 410 the Alaric, who had been a general of his father, captured Rome: that Alaric's successor, Ataulph, espoused in 414 the proud daughter of Theodosius, who had disdained her cousin Eucherius as a Vandal, but yielded to the Goth whose bridal gifts were the spoils of her brother's capital, and the condition of her marriage the dismemberment of his empire. I dwell here only on the result of that fatal division ensuing on the death of Theodosius, which not only made the East and West two dominions, but reduced the former to a government of eunuchs under Arcadius, and the latter to a heap of ruins, when Honorius, having deprived himself of Stilicho, took refuge behind the marshes of Ravenna. These were the scenes which St. Innocent witnessed in that pontificate of fifteen years. He was himself at Ravenna pleading with the feeble folly of Honorius in behalf of his people. If we read the letters of this Pope to the bishops of the East and West, it would seem as if he spoke amid a world governed in perfect tranquillity, while in every year of the fifteen the Romans were quaking behind their walls at the rumour of some impending barbarian incursion. In fact, the actually existing walls of Rome were repaired by command of Stilicho in the utmost hurry under such an alarm.

Indeed, this first capture of Rome in 410, short as it was, filled the world with fugitives suddenly reduced to ruin, so that the noblest matrons and maidens were in danger of being sold as slaves in Syria by a recreant African governor. But it also remains as a landmark in history to point out the time when the majesty of heathen Rome, having been once violated, was lost for ever. Temporal sovereignty never sat again upon the eternal city; but at the same moment a spiritual sovereignty, carried thither more than three centuries before by the Galilean Fisherman, and planted in his tomb, came forth in full power, manifested as it were by the fall of the temporal city. From that time forth not Christian Rome only but heathen Rome also became fully conscious that it was the head of a dominion more than Cæsarean. It is no Christian but a rationalist historian[1] who writes: "Alone of all the cities of the world was Rome adorned with the divine title of 'Eternal'; and the poet's prophecy passed into fact— 'Imperium sine fine dedi'. The Roman empire, enthralled and worn out by the long imperial despotism, foundered in the mighty German deluge of nations. They redeemed the Western world from that immoral tyranny, renewed it, or created it afresh, when they had

[1] Gregorovius, i. 11.

taken Christianhood into themselves. The majestic city of the Cæsars collapsed when the Roman State and the ancient worship died out. It was in reality the Christian religion which destroyed Rome, but likewise caused its resurrection. It broke in pieces the city of the old Romans, but raised up a new Rome from the catacombs as a subterranean arsenal."

It was this new Rome which speaks still in those letters of the Popes: speaks from the beginning and at all times; for there is no *time* in them. Clement spoke under Domitian; Julius under Constantius; Innocent in the face of Alaric. But Clement, Julius, and Innocent speak with an authority which is in truth rooted in a catacomb, the grave of Peter, and expresses a succession independent of time, because spoken in the words of Him who said, "Before Abraham was made, I am"; and who said also, "Thou art Peter, and upon this rock I will build My Church: and the gates of hell shall not prevail against it".

This foundation came now to light. So long as the bishops sat over against civil prefects and governors throughout the empire, as Origen already described them, as the laws of Constantine recognised them, and gave them civil jurisdiction, many a heathen might consider them a sort of second civil magistracy; but when the Northern deluge swept away the civil magistracy, and the Christian episcopate remained standing among the empire's ruins, and the Pope addressed these bishops as if the peace of the Roman world dwelt all around undisturbed, the commission of

Christ to Peter became visible to heathen and Christian alike, and the divine kingdom rose out of the ruins of the temporal. In was in St. Augustine's time that all this took place. This City of God it was which the sacking of Rome, the banishment of her noblest who came in the pilgrimage of poverty to his doors, enabled him to see himself and to delineate for aftertimes more clearly than any had done before him, so that the taking of Rome unfolded the City which could not be taken, and the head of Charlemagne pillowed itself upon Augustine's book when four hundred years after Alaric the voice of a Pope made him "great and pacific emperor of the Romans".

This lesson was taught to the world amid terrible sufferings; probably history does not contain eighty years in which greater calamities were undergone than those which fell upon the countries comprised especially in the Western Roman empire from the death of Theodosius in 395 to the disappearance of the last shadow of Augustus in 476.

Within the ten years which followed the capture of Rome the kingdom of the Visigoths was founded under Ataulph, who wedded Galla Placidia in Roman dress as the friend of her brother Honorius. After his premature death her hand became the prize of Constantius, the brave commander who supported her brother's throne being named joint-emperor, and he too died in 421. He was followed by Honorius in 423, who was buried in pomp in St. Peter's church at Rome, and whose only epitaph was that his incapacity ruined the Western empire. At his death we are told his nephew Theodosius II. deliberated whether he should not reunite the West to the East. But the rise of an usurper diverted him from this purpose; and he resolved to acknowledge Galla Placidia as empress and regent for her infant son by Constantius, Valentinian III. A few months before Honorius died, Pope Boniface terminated his pontificate of nearly four years, and in that year 422, he had addressed to the bishops of the province of Thessaly, forming part of the great prefecture of Eastern Illyricum, the civil government of which had been taken from the West and given to the East in 379, a letter[1] in which he charged them to obey Rufus, the bishop of Thessalonica, in his character of Apostolic Vicar. The beginning of this letter runs in these words: "The institution of the whole Church from the beginning was derived from the rank given to St. Peter, in whom its government and whole sum consists. For as the culture of religion increased, the fountain of ecclesiastical discipline which he established diffused itself through all churches. The precepts of the Nicene Council bear witness to this, so that it did not venture to make any appointment over him, seeing that nothing could be conferred above his merit. In fact it was aware that everything was given to him by the word of the Lord. It is certain therefore that this Church is to the churches diffused through the whole world what the head is to its members: from which whosoever cuts himself off, becomes an alien to the Chris-

---

[1] Boniface I., Ep. xiv.; Coustant, 1037. See also Ep. xv.

tian religion, by ceasing to belong to the structure" (compages).

I cite this passage because nothing in the writings of any subsequent Pope, as, for instance, St. Leo, can exceed its distinct and peremptory assertion of supreme authority given by our Lord to St. Peter, so that the whole structure of the living Church is said to rest upon it, and to be continued on by St. Peter's successors. I note that it was issued to bishops, subjects of the Eastern emperor, a few years after the fall of Rome, when the Western emperor was afraid to live within its walls, when his empire was already in part surrendered to the Goths; and I note that there is not the slightest trace that the bishops to whom such language was addressed disputed its truth. It is in accordance with the language of the Pope's immediate predecessors, Zosimus and Innocent, to the African bishops, which those bishops, St. Augustine being one among them, received with deference; in accordance, also, with the language addressed nine years later by Pope Celestine to the Council of Ephesus, and which, as we have seen, and shall see later on, the Council accepted.

The capture of Rome had made its chief nobility a spectacle of humiliation and misery to the whole world. It had not in the least diminished the authority of its bishop, but had rather disclosed the foundation on which it rested. From the death of Honorius in 423 the Eastern emperor claimed to be and acted as the superior lord of the whole empire; but this did not interrupt the claim of the Pope to be the head of the whole Church.

As Spain, and Gaul, and Britain, and Africa were being detached from the feeble son and grandson of Theodosius, while the Roman bishop was holding the bishops of these countries together by the strong grasp of his Primacy, the lot both of the Church and of the State was different in the portion of the empire ruled, in name, at least, by another son and another grandson of the great Theodosius. Arcadius, indeed, and Theodosius II. were personally almost as feeble rulers as Honorius; but the empire over which they reigned is thus described by Gibbon:—

"The successors of Constantine established their perpetual residence in the royal city, which he had erected on the verge of Europe and Asia. Inaccessible to the menaces of their enemies, and perhaps to the complaints of their people, they received, with each wind, the tributary productions of every climate, while the impregnable strength of their capital continued for ages to defy the hostile attempts of the barbarians. Their dominions were bounded by the Adriatic and the Tigris; and the whole interval of twenty-five days' navigation, which separated the extreme cold of Scythia from the torrid zone of Ethiopia, was comprehended within the limits of the empire of the East. The populous countries of that empire were the seat of art and learning, of luxury and wealth; and the inhabitants, who assumed the language and manners of Greeks, styled themselves, with some appearance of truth, the most enlightened and civilised portion of the human species. The form of government was a pure and simple monarchy; the name of the Roman Republic, which so long preserved a faint tradition of freedom, was confined to the Latin provinces, and the princes of Constantinople measured their greatness by the servile obedience of their people."

Such a domain was the second Theodosius allotted to rule. For his education, when he succeeded his father as a child of eight years old, all that was possible had been done by the guardianship of the virtuous Anthemius, and afterwards by the great ability and still more admirable example of his sister Pulcheria. He was reigning at the age of twenty-four, when he condescended to invest his aunt Galla Placidia with what remained of the Western empire as guardian of her son, Valentinian. She with difficulty maintained a precarious rule, supported by the great ability in war and statemanship of her generals, Boniface and Aetius, whose union might have preserved the sinking West, "while their discord was the fatal and immediate cause of the loss of Africa".

In such a political state of things, while the bishops of the West looked to the Pope as the defender, champion, and exponent of the Church's rights, as the standard and maintainer of orthodoxy, the bishops of the East beheld a great preacher, called at the emperor's bidding from Antioch, as St. John Crysostome had been called thirty years before by his father to sit in the great see of Constantinople. The new bishop, as soon as he came, filled the capital with confusion by attacking the Blessed Virgin's title, "Mother of God". The two cousin-emperors, one in possession of the vast Eastern empire, with its impregnable capital, the other a child of eleven, for whom his mother could find no safe residence save the marsh-defended fastness of Ravenna, convened the Council of Ephesus to terminate the controversy.

Its assembly affords us a fitting standpoint at which to review, as a whole, the Church's government indicated in these letters of the Popes at the precise time when the Eastern and Western portions of the great empire were permanently settling into separate kingdoms, and particularly when the crown of secular greatness had for ever departed from Rome to rest for long ages upon Constantinople.

I will trace in as few words as possible the common character which belongs to these letters.

First, as to their own authority and position with regard to the other bishops of the Church, not only in the West, but in the East, the seven Popes, that is, Siricius, Anastasius, Innocent, Zosimus, Boniface, Celestine, and Sixtus, who sat from 385 to 440, and were the immediate predecessors of St. Leo, speak with one voice, and in the most precise language. What they say is simply this, that Simon Peter was invested by our Lord with the government of His Church, the kingdom of God on earth, by the three great words which our Lord addressed to him, as priest, as prophet, and as king; that he came to Rome, and deposited in that See, as its bishop, this special and unique power of government with which he was himself invested, and which descended to his successors such as he received it, unaltered. Each one of these Popes considers himself as invested with this power; speaks and acts to individual bishops, to large synods, as, for instance, those of Africa; to Eastern patriarchs, as to the bishop of Antioch; to the predominant bishop of the new capital, in the tone and with the authority which such a power would justify, and no less a power would justify.[1] And it is to be borne in mind that all the letters in question, though bearing the name of the Pope alone, were in the discipline of that age always agreed upon at a synod over which the Pope presided. This power is invariably ascribed to the personal gift of our Lord: is said not to be given by any council, to be above the gift of a council, to be not depending on the individual merit or sanctity of the person holding it. It is simply "administratio Petri,"[2] which each Pope took up from his predecessor when he became Pope, and left to his successor when he departed, alike without increase and without diminution. Such a power set forth to bishops in conciliar documents, framed with legal accuracy and peremptory distinctness, could only meet one of two things, acceptance or rejection.

I have quoted the words of the two most eminent bishops during this period, St. Ambrose and St. Augustine, as expressly recognising, in reference to these

[1] See, for instance, the 24th letter of Innocent I. to Alexander, bishop of Antioch, and the 6th letter of Sixtus III. to John, bishop of Antioch, and the letter of Celestine to Nestorius, as bishop of Constantinople.

[2] Siricius, Ep. i. Petrus, qui nos in omnibus, ut confidimus, administrationis suae protegit et tuetur heredes.

letters, the authority claimed in them to be "scriptural," that is, given by our Lord in the way stated: the one herein speaking as the metropolitan of northern Italy, the other as a member of the Council of Numidia.

On the other hand, nowhere can a bishop, or a patriarch, or a synod, in the fifty-five years herein comprised, be found who replied to the Pope that the authority thus claimed by him, as given by our Lord to Peter, was not given to Peter; or, again, that though given to the Apostle as a personal privilege, did *not* descend to the Pope as successor of St. Peter.

And, once more, I will quote the words of the Benedictine editor[1] of these letters, who says—"Of so many Pontiffs, renowned for learning and sanctity, no one can be found who did not believe that this prerogative was bestowed upon himself or his church, to be the head of the whole Church, while, among all the churches of the world erected by the Apostles and their successors, no one can be found whose bishop ventured to affirm himself to be the head of the whole Church. And it may be noted that, however zealous the bishops of Constantinople were in defending their rights, they were contented, down to Photius, with the second place of rank after Rome."

When John, bishop of Antioch, gave up the support which, together with the bishops of his patriarchate, he had for some time given to Nestorius; when Nestorius had been deposed, and a successor appointed, Pope Sixtus III. wrote to the bishop these words: "You

[1] Constant, Preface, p. iii.

have experienced, in the issue of this present matter, what it is to be of one mind with us. The blessed Apostle Peter has handed down, in his successors, that which he himself received. Who would consent to be separated from the teaching of him whom, together with the Apostles, the Master Himself first fully instructed. He was not instructed by hearing from another, nor by a written discourse. He was taught with the rest by the mouth of the Teacher. He had not to suffer questioning as to the meaning of Scripture or of writings. He received an absolute and simple faith, which admitted no controversy. It is this on which we are bound continually to meditate, and in it to abide; so that, following Apostles in the uncorrupted sense, we may be accounted apostolical. It is no small burden, no small toil, which lies upon us, that no spot or wrinkle may touch the Church of God."[1]

The vividness of the Roman tradition, and the force of oral teaching from the mouth of Christ Himself, could not be better expressed than in these words, in which point they are an epitome of all these letters, for in all of them there is reference to the storehouse of apostolical teaching deposited at Rome.

Now, the fact that Peter took for his see the capital of the Roman empire; again, the position of the Roman bishop after the transference of the imperial residence to Constantinople; again, the fact that the Pope was sole patriarch in the West: these circumstances exercised, no doubt, a certain influence upon the rank accorded to

[1] Ep. vi.; Constant, 1260.

him. They are, as it were, outward environments, which worked together for the exaltation of his see above all other bishops and patriarchs. But they could not provide that living consciousness of the Primacy, seated in the heart of the Church, to which the Popes throughout these letters constantly appeal. That could only rest upon a recognition from the beginning of a divine investiture of St. Peter with the guidance of the Church by our Lord, as part and parcel of the apostolic teaching.[1] The reception given to these letters proved that it was so recognised.

This is the first contrast between the Papal Primacy and the State-patriarchate which, in these fifty years, began to be set up at Constantinople. The former rested on the gift of Christ at the beginning; the latter upon a canon of a particular council of Eastern bishops held in 381. The canon itself gave no jurisdiction, but only rank; but even so it was rejected by Rome, rejected by Alexandria, while, on the other hand, it was fostered by the Eastern emperors.

The following contrasts are, as it were, corollaries of the first :—

2. The Primacy set forth by the Popes is throughout claimed as of divine institution. Being the gift of Christ alone, it is antecedent to all councils. It is, in fact, the generating power of the Church, which created gradation of ranks in an episcopate otherwise equal, and so bound it into one government, whereas the origin of the patriarchate on the Bosphorus was simply political.

[1] This is noted by Reumont, ii. 21.

It was instituted to make the emperor's bishop the first bishop of the emperor's kingdom, and grounded expressly on the fact that Constantinople was Nova Roma.

3. The Primacy, being divine, is independent of political authority. It is, indeed, true that St. Peter in the beginning, by divine guidance, chose the temporal capital for its seat, a choice which runs up for its authorship to Christ himself, who would shew His power by placing His vicar in the capital of His enemy. There is just this amount of truth in the canon of 381, which implied that Rome held the first rank in the Church because it was capital in the State. And the Primacy subsisted there through ages of persecution, latent so far as the Church was latent. When the Church was recognised it came forth also. In proportion as the emperors retired, the Primacy advanced. From Septimius Severus to Constantine the emperors were absent usually from Rome defending the frontiers, and the Primacy came more and more into view, so that, in the middle of that period, the emperor Decius, standing on the old Roman lines, recognised it as a mortal foe. Constantine went to the Bosphorus, and left the Primacy behind him, as well as a city heathen in the vast majority of its population, and specially in its senate and great families. At the end of the century Rome had become from a heathen city Christian. The worship of the false gods[1] dropped from its shoulders like a worm-eaten mantle of state, and Theodosius had laid the first steps on which his

[1] Gregorovius, i. 73, first edition.

patriarch's throne should be built; the tenant of which should as completely lean on the emperor as the Pope descended from St. Peter; for was he not to rank as second in the Church, simply because Constantinople was New Rome?

4. In these letters the Popes uniformly speak as maintaining the authority of the Nicene Council and the whole order of things antecedent to itself to which that Council bore witness, whether they be matters of doctrine or of government. The Nicene Council represents to them not only the faith of the Church respecting the Person of her Founder, but the whole anterior history of the Church. But the chief thing of all to the Popes is the living tradition stored up at Rome: "the Statutes of St. Peter and St. Paul," as Pope Liberius speaks of them; and Pope Julius in his letter of 342: "Not such are the dispositions of Paul; not so have the Fathers handed down: this is another form, a new custom. What we have received from the blessed Apostle Peter, this I signify to you; and I should not have written, believing it to be known to all, except that what has been done has disturbed us." Each Pope speaks as heir of the three preceding centuries, as carrying on a settled unchanging order.

Herein lies a strong contrast to the growing power of the see of Constantinople, which carried with it an innovation, upon the rank of others. The resident council of bishops sojourning at the new capital was the medium of this innovation. It issued in the degradation of Alexandria, so fiercely resisted by Theophilus,

Cyril, and Dioscorus ; and in that of Antioch, so tamely yielded to by successive bishops, through the weakness resulting from its divided condition since 330.

5. These letters are the same in tone throughout as they are in the beginning; the tone of those who are sure of their fact, never go beyond it, and never recede from it. It is a tone supreme, conservative, moderate, unaggressive, the very reverse of intrusive and meddling. Each bishop, each metropolitan, each patriarch, is maintained in the existing sphere of his duties. Where no wrong is committed, there is no interference. Disturbance of discipline, and, above all, violation of the faith, cause intervention. The Pelagian heresy is a great instance in point. The application of the African synods to St. Innocent in that matter, and his answer and the comment upon it by St. Augustine, bring out the strongest and clearest witness to the authority of the Roman See's Principate, as likewise does the heresy of Nestorius. For one faith absolutely demands one power to maintain it ; and a hierarchy, wherein that power seems distributed among its members in time of peace, is sharpened into the action of its head by conflict.

It was quite different with the rising power of the bishop in the new capital, which increased with each tenant by the aid of imperial support. This going beyond the limit of the bishop began with Nectarius ; increased by the virtues and ability of St. Chrysostome ; advanced still further under Atticus, and again under Proclus. In all these steps the temporal authority of the Eastern emperor was mixed up with the advance of the bishop of his residence.

6. It is somewhat more than what is said in the two preceding paragraphs that the Pope throughout these letters speaks as with the Church at his back. All that he does being based on one fact, the investiture of St. Peter, lodged in the deepest consciousness of the Church, he speaks as a lawful sovereign in his inherited monarchy; moreover, as a sovereign who, with his predecessors, has *made* his monarchy. For all that vast array of bishops, metropolitans, primates, and patriarchs is the outcome of the Apostolic Twelve, with Peter at their head. That the Twelve had a head is the reason why the whole episcopate, which the Pope beholds before him, has a graduated distribution of spiritual power. The distance of three hundred years had not obscured this origin. Therefore the honour of each bishop is, in the words of St. Gregory the Great, his own honour. And the relationship between them makes him their born defender. His authority includes theirs, and therefore protects it.

But if the bishop of Constantinople was greater when the second Theodosius died than when the first set himself to restore the broken ranks of the Eastern episcopate, what other reason for this was there than that the Eastern emperor exercised part of his political omnipotence through the bishop of his capital?

7. And here we come to one of the most remarkable incidents in the history of this power conferred on St. Peter's successors.

Up to the end of the reign of the great Theodosius, the empire both in the East and West still stood erect. In the thirty-five succeeding years, which so exactly coincide with the episcopate of St. Augustine, not only was Rome taken and sacked by the Gothic king, but the empire lost permanently its hold upon Southern France, Spain, Britain, and lastly upon Africa, the granary of Italy. The Popes beheld a vast rending of the civil structure which had grown together during almost twelve centuries. They mourned over terrible ruins; the rich became poor in a day; and patrician families at Rome who had owned vast estates lost, with their riches, their personal liberty. At that moment of destruction the hierarchy of the Church alone stood,[1] and that it was not broken up into as many pieces as the Franks, Burgundians, Visigoths, Vandals, Ostrogoths, conquered territories, was owing solely to the Pope's Primacy. It was a first effect of Constantine's alliance to invest the bishops throughout his empire with a great civil jurisdiction, as we have seen. It was a second effect of the barbarian inundation, which, on the fall of the Western empire, made the Church the sole school of learning, the sole preserver, so far as it was preserved, of a sinking civilisation. And the Popes, in the midst of a city trembling at every rumour of a fresh incursion, received from the vigilance, energy, and charity exercised under the woes which they vainly deplored, and did their utmost to mitigate, an influence greater even than they had enjoyed when the mind and the sword of Constan-

[1] See Matthieu, *Plouvoir Temporel des Papes*, pp. 48-51.

tine and Theodosius maintained their capital in security and the cities under their rule in peace. Here again, while the bishops of Constantinople were established in a splendid servitude to propagate the emperor's will in the Eastern episcopate, the Popes between the two violations of their city by Alaric and Genseric led the Western bishops in their struggle against war, famine, and heresy. The break-up of the empire may be said to have finally established their Primacy on a spiritual basis, by destroying the temporal rank of their city.

8. For the political prostration of the Roman city under these seven Popes is as remarkable as the preservation of the Eastern empire through the impregnable position of its capital. It was owing to this choice of Constantine that the monarchy which he founded, with Roman title but after Oriental fashion, over peoples so long accustomed to be ruled by absolute power, lasted in some sort for more than a thousand years. But absolute power was killed out in Rome by the barbarian sword, and its walls afforded no defence against the assault of hunger when it was once deprived of its African granary. Thus the time of desolation fully unveils its spiritual greatness. Had there been any truth in what was inscribed on the foundation-stone of the Byzantine patriarch's greatness, that the Fathers had given the Primacy to Rome because it was the capital of the empire, that Primacy would have passed to the city of Constantine when temporal supremacy rested on it. But the exact contrary of this happens.

All power had passed from Rome when the second Theodosius gave a weak woman and her infant son the name of empress and emperor, and it was then that his own bishops, assembled in general council, accepted the full statement of the Roman Primacy, which the legates of St. Celestine presented to them, who bore a commission from the Pope couched in the words: "If it come to a discussion with the bishops, you are to pass a judgment upon their sentence, not to enter into a conflict with them". Scarcely ninety years had passed since the Eusebian bishops at Antioch had sought to deny to Pope Julius the rights of his see. In these three generations Rome had perpetually waned, and Constantinople as constantly grown; now it was all-powerful. The reigning emperor sympathised with Nestorius; the bishop of his capital was deposed by the sentence of the Pope, and his full authority recognised in a council where the Pope's legates were almost the only Western bishops present.

9. As the temporal city at Rome decays, the spiritual power of the Pope increases, and this double action is drawn out by a special historian, who by no means acknowledges the truth of the Christian faith, as a phenomenon unknown to any other city of the world. There is not in the whole of human history another instance in which the same city becomes head of a whole empire by the might of arms, and, when that empire perishes, becomes head of a second world-empire by the might of faith. Herein the contrast with Constantinople is perfect. The Pope comes out when Rome

ceases to be capital; the bishop begins when his city begins to be capital. His power is always in proportion to the temporal greatness of his city; but the Christian faith came into Rome as into the seat prepared for it, and out of the ruins of the political monarchy drew forth the giant form of the spiritual monarchy, the Church. That this was an immovable structure at the very time the old empire fell is one of the greatest facts of history, for the whole life of Europe was built afresh upon the Church's firm foundation-stone; and that foundation-stone itself was the Primacy given by our Lord to Peter.[1]

I do not know how history could offer a stronger confirmation to the belief of the Church that such a Primacy had been given to St. Peter, and had descended from him to the Popes, than its acceptance by the bishops as it was set forth in the letters of the Popes addressed to them out of a discrowned and captured Rome, and again, and further, as it was acknowledged by the Eastern bishops who were submissive subjects of the Eastern throne seated in Constantine's rival city, when the bishop of that city was himself impugned for misbelief and deposed.

A notice of this council, the circumstances under which it was held, and its decisive recognition of the Roman Primacy has been already given. We may add to what has been there said the great importance of this council as affording an estimate of the internal and

---

[1] Gregorovius, i. 6-13; see also 97-8, on St. Peter and St. Paul as patron saints of Rome.

essential development of the Church made in the first century after Constantine's alliance of the empire with the Church. There had been no council like it since the Nicene, because the council of Sardica, intended to be general, was frustrated of that distinction by the enmity of the Eastern emperor Constantius and the heretical spirit of his bishops. Again, the council of 150 Eastern bishops at Constantinople in 381, which was afterwards considered general because its decrees completing the doctrine concerning the Blessed Trinity by the condemnation of the Macedonian heresy respecting the Holy Spirit were confirmed by Pope Damasus, though its canons were never confirmed, was at the Council of Ephesus passed over in silence. It was then held to be only an Eastern council, and the precedence which it had voted to the bishop of the new capital was rejected both by Pope Celestine and by St. Cyril of Alexandria, who presided over the council in the Pope's name.

Accordingly, the Ephesine Council in 431 was the first meeting of the Church in plenary council since the great event of Nicæa, 106 years before. And from its acts it is apparent that a double new relation had been formed in the interval. The first was between the Papacy on the one hand, and the episcopate, the patriarchs, and general councils on the other. The second was between the Papacy and the imperial power.

It could not but be that both these relations were *new*, because the circumstances under which they were formed were new. As to the first, "Ecumenical councils were at that time a novelty in the Church".[1] Accordingly, until they took place the action of the Universal Primate with regard to them could not be adequately foreseen. The whole life of the Church before it was called together, while it was actively opposed, discouraged, or vehemently persecuted by the civil power, was different in its conditions from those which ensued when these circumstances were altered. The convening of the Nicene Council was the beginning of the alteration. As to the second relation, the whole action of the imperial power *within* the Church was new. It was an immense force introduced into the Church's constitution. The interaction, then, of Pope, patriarchs, bishops, and councils in reference to it, occasioned or affected by it, was new also. In both cases, the further action of immense political changes must be allowed for. It needs but to mention Rome under Constantine in 330, when the barbarian world of heaving force beyond the Rhine and the Danube was silent before him, and the great rival Eastern kingdom beyond the Euphrates counted his alliance an honour; and Rome in 430, under Theodosius II. and Valentinian III., when the walls of Constantinople sheltered one Roman emperor, the marshes of Ravenna the other, and the cities of the world trembled before the inundations of Huns upon Teutons, and of Teutons driven westward by Huns to flock as birds of prey upon the empire.

St. Augustine himself began his career as bishop under the great Theodosius, and ended it with Genseric

[1] Newman, *Causes of the Rise and Success of Arianism*, p. 101.

before the walls of Hippo; that Genseric who from that day to his death in 477 harried sea and land with the ferocity of a Barberine corsair.

In the Ephesine Council the Pope deputed St. Cyril, as bishop of Alexandria, to preside in his place over it. St. Cyril did not decline the office, nor the Council for a moment demur to being led by the Pope. The Pope did not wait for the Council to censure the doctrine of Nestorius, nor to depose him from his see if he did not correct it. The way in which the Council greeted the exposition of his Primacy by his legates, and especially the descent from St. Peter as first bishop of Rome, amounts to the acceptance by the second Council of precisely that authority in the whole Church which the letters of the Popes above quoted maintain.

This, therefore, is the result of the hundred years and five between the first Council at Nicæa and the second at Ephesus. Heresy has done its worst from 330 to 380; absolute power has created a nest for itself on the Bosphorus; the barbarians who served the empire under Constantine, Valentinian I., and Theodosius have now led their tribes into partial possession of it; the West is trampled on and devoured; Rome, for eight hundred years the queen of the earth, has had her royalty sullied by the Gothic leaders; Constantinople apes the former grandeur of Rome, and has taken what remained of her power; but while Eastern bishops are in the way to lose their independence under a despotic master, the Pope, from a defenceless Rome, shines a beacon of hope to the world, marshals the bishops of the West to the defence of the one faith, and is acknowledged by the East to act in the name of Peter, "who is the pillar of the faith and the foundation of the Catholic Church," "and up to this time and for all time to come lives and judges in his successors".[1]

[1] Council of Ephesus, see above.

CHAPTER IX.

THE FLOWERING OF PATRISTIC LITERATURE.

THE divine kingdom on earth, viewed as a sphere, may be said to revolve on the two poles of government and doctrine, for Christ never ceases to act in it as Prophet and as King, and the line of His Priesthood, passing through the centre of this sphere, gives one motion to the whole, and binds the poles together. A kingdom has its own life of thought and action, and cannot cease to grow so long as it lives. By the law of its being it must develop; and this, which is true of every kingdom, is in the highest degree true of the greatest, that is, the divine kingdom. Accordingly, in the hundred and five years between the Councils of Nicæa and Ephesus, government and doctrine have not only grown, but have kept even pace, not forestalling each other, as the revolution of a sphere on its axis is even and its motion one.

It has been my effort in the preceding chapters to draw out continually the parallel advance of government and doctrine from the Nicene Council. To carry this further on, I put together several points of view on which that Council is to be taken as a great epoque.

It must be repeated here, as a prelude to what follows, that its convocation is contemporaneous with the sole monarchy of Constantine, when, after defeating all his rivals and enemies, he united the empire in his single person, and proclaimed himself a Christian in his own personal belief and in the maxims of his government, though he neither sought for baptism nor received the regular instruction of a catechumen. Had he been instructed and baptised, he would probably have escaped the great errors which occurred in the last years of his reign, not to speak of the terrible tragedy which sullied his private life and made him the slayer both of wife and son.

The great event of his conversion seems to serve as a sort of common root to many consequences.

First, it was the beginning of union in Christian history between the Two Powers, which represent respectively the natural society of man, as constituted by God the Creator for the good of His creatures; and the supernatural society instituted by a personal advent of God the Redeemer—that is, the Church, the Family, and Kingdom of Christ.

Secondly, it was the beginning of freedom to the Church to meet by representation in her whole episcopate; for Constantine, by summoning the council, not without previous consultation with the great sees of Rome, Alexandria, and Antioch, gave the first recognition of the Roman empire to this representation. The

Church, indeed, had ever been ready in her hierarchy, drawn out of her bosom by the action of the Holy Spirit from the day of Pentecost, so to meet; but was never allowed, by the absolute power of heathen emperors, to exercise that inherent capacity. The act of Constantine, therefore, summoned into existence a force not hitherto exercised, for such was the collective action of the great Christian senate.

Thirdly, it was the beginning of deliverance to the Papacy from the pressure of the enormous superincumbent weight laid upon Christian society by hostile paganism. It was thus enabled to exercise its original and inherent, but hitherto latent, authority, and to work upon the whole Church. And as the difference between bishops spread over the whole world in their several provinces and local autonomy, and those bishops assembled in council and acting by impact on each other could not be discerned beforehand, so neither could the difference between the paternal presidence of the Pope over brethren in the episcopate, pressed like himself by heathen persecution, and the presiding over those brethren when free to meet and act in council, be anticipated before it came into effect.

Fourthly, the Nicene Council marked the beginning of freedom to all to proclaim the Christian doctrine, by word and writing, without hindrance from without, through the whole Roman empire. The time of apologetic defence was over; and henceforth the Christian spirit could set forth the Christian religion, not as an advocate defends a culprit who lies under suspicion, but as the messenger of a sovereign sets forth a positive system of doctrine and conduct, as much more potent in practice than Stoic virtue as it was more exalted in matter than Platonic discourses. This was a change, in the intellectual standpoint, no less great than the two preceding changes in external position.

Once more as great a development as the preceding is betokened in the introduction at this same time of the monastic life.[1] The pagan persecution ceased on the one hand; but on the other, Christians, by the simple fact that they were no longer persecuted, were thrown, especially in all the great cities, into a contact, which their former isolation had restricted, with the worst excesses of moral corruption. At the same time, it cannot be doubted that the number of converts from interested motives, which from Constantine's time pressed into the Church, lowered perceptibly the standard of Christian practice in the mass. Against all this, a life which aimed at perfection, by not merely performing the commands of Christ, but by carrying out His counsels in daily practice, shewed itself in the Christian people. It had existed from the time of the Apostles scatteredly and in secret; now it came forth from the privacy of the family to public gaze. The unbridled sensuality of heathen society, and the worldly conduct of converts for gain, received a rebuke and a correction in the Christian doctrine of virginity, and the celibate life was set forth with the utmost praise by the writers of this period. The enormous luxury which revelled in the great cities,

[1] Noted by Fessler, i. 337.

and the passion for theatrical exhibitions which corrupted their population, as well by immoral prostitution as by cruel sacrifice of the human body, were confronted by the self-chosen poverty and self-denial of those who lived upon God alone in the deserts of Egypt and Syria. Athanasius, taking refuge in Rome to defend the faith at its centre, under the protection of the Apostolic See, introduced there the history of St. Anthony. It bore fruit at once, while later in the century the noblest men and women in Rome deserted their sumptuous palaces for a life of prayer and poverty in Bethlehem. The Nicene Council may be said to mark when the religious life becomes a public institute, a fountain of holiness, moral strength, and also intellectual life and vigour, never to be dried up in the Church.

Again, simultaneously with the civil freedom granted to the Church, and the ending of the apologetic period wherein her writers defended her against the assaults of the Hellenic spirit outside her, there rose up in the very bosom of the Church the deadliest of heresies, denying the Godhead of her founder, and the most destructive of schisms, denying the unity of His kingdom; so that from this time the whole intellect of the Church was directed to the maintenance of these two assaulted truths. And in this way the Arian heresy and the Donatist schism, which arise together about the year 318, work together during more than a hundred years to elucidate doctrine and consolidate unity.

Now, bearing these several circumstances in our mind, let us consider the interval of a hundred and fifty years between the end of the pagan persecution and the overthrow of the Western empire by the Northern tribes, as being a period of wonderful intellectual vigour, shewn in the writers of the Church.

It has often been remarked that after the failure of the Persian attempt to enthral Greece, a great outburst of genius took place at Athens, which became the centre, drawing to itself the greater minds of the larger Hellas. The period begins with the dramas of Æschylus, and may be said to end with the death of Aristotle. Thus it lasted from the time that the independence of Greece was saved from destruction by the Persian invader, until a Grecian conqueror, in subjecting Persia, destroyed also his country's freedom.

There was no time like that before it in Grecian history, and no time after it, for the varied productions of genius. With the two great exceptions of Homer and Pindar, every poet and almost every historian and philosopher who have made Greece illustrious were born and flourished in this time.

Similar in duration, similar in exuberance of intellectual life, is that space of the Church's history which begins with Athanasius, the peerless confessor, and ends with Leo, the peerless ruler, both great writers, but men in whom the greatness of character surpasses the lustre of mind; and if an apostate, won by so much nobility to a transitory admiration, summed up the history of five banishments in the words, "The world against Athanasius, and Athanasius against the world," those who have studied the letters and sermons of Leo with a profound sense of the sanctity which utters itself in majesty, will yet more wonder at the greatness of the man, who sat unshaken upon the throne of Peter while the city of Romulus, having completed the augury of twelve centuries, was falling with its empire in ruins around him, yet betrayed not a single word of fear, a single consciousness of danger.

Almost the whole wealth of patristic literature lies between these two. The greatest of those who preceded them, as, for instance, Clement and Origen in the East, Tertullian and Cyprian in the West, are but preludes and foretastes of the vast work in subduing heresy, convincing judaism, exposing heathenism, commenting on Scripture, expounding doctrine, eloquence in the chair of teaching, thoroughness in catechising, and manifold illustration of the world around them in their letters, afforded by those who lived in this time. And after Leo many hundred years intervene before a similar period can be shewn. As soon as paganism had been conquered in the conversion of Constantine, and before the northern barbarism broke up the civilisation of the West, and the Byzantine despotism quenched the genius of the East, this short time was given by the Providence of God in which a Chrysostome should use the language of Plato in its old age with greater effect than Demosthenes in its prime: and in which a Rhetorician of Thagaste should take the worn-out language of Cicero, and deposit in it treasures of thought far beyond the range of "Rome's least mortal mind," and mark out almost single-handed the groundwork for the structure of theology and philosophy in the Church, so that his successors for fifteen centuries have drawn upon his treasure, and sought to complete what he had begun.

In this interval between heathenism and the Western desolation with the Eastern enslavement, the Church creates a greater intellectual Hellas and a greater intellectual Rome than were the heathen originals. By the powerful bond of her unity, or rather by the one Spirit who creates that unity, she subsidises a wider range of cities than Athens could touch in her proudest time. She selects champions from a number of races such as Athens never imagined, or despised, so far as she knew them, under the common name of barbarians. First and foremost in this great roll she calls Athanasius from Alexandria, and his brother confessor Eustathius from Antioch; later she sent Chrysostome, the greatest preacher of Antioch, to win the same place in Constantinople. From Edessa she calls Ephrem, hardly less powerful, as the chief Syrian teacher; Basil the Great from the Cappadocian Cæsarea, and his scarcely less eminent brother Gregory from Nyssa, his equal Gregory from Nazianzum; Cyril from Jerusalem, Epiphanius from the Cyprian Salamis; and presently another Cyril, greater than the former from Alexandria, together with Didymus, teacher of the chief school of Egypt, and the monk Makarius, great in its deserts. Synesius she calls from Ptolemais in Cyrenian Africa; Asterius from Amasea, Amphilochius from Iconium, Nemesius from Emesa in Phœnicia, Theodoret from Cyrus. This vast range of cities in Asia, Africa, and Europe is the greater

Hellas, survival of Alexander's empire, from which she evokes her warriors in the field of theology.

But she has likewise a greater Rome at her disposal. She finds in her Ambrose, son of a prefect of Gaul, himself governor of Milan, one on whom she lays her hand suddenly and makes him the model of a bishop, a Roman who converts Augustine, and informs with mildness the spirit of an emperor, teaching an irresistible conqueror to do penance for his hasty disregard of human life. She calls from Poitiers Hilary, a noble Gaul, to confession in Asia for long years in word and deed. She endows the Dalmatian Jerome with the language of Rome and the learning of Varro, to use them in behalf of Scripture interpretation, to set forth Christian counsels and form the ascetic life in the female sex. She rescues a burgher of a small town in Africa, after a servitude of fifteen years, from the phantoms of Manichæism and the turpitude of immorality, and makes him the wonder of his time and of all succeeding times for that vast stream of doctrine, that energy of thought penetrating every fold of the spiritual life, by which he lays the basis of theological structure, and utters the principles of true philosophy to be taken up by the Church after him, to be fostered through ages of trial and struggle, and built up eight hundred years later into the great mediæval temple of St. Thomas. Further, she calls Zeno from Verona, Philastrius from Brescia, Eusebius from Vercelli, Prosper from Aquitaine, Peter Chrysologus from Aquileia, Maximus from Turin, Pacian from Barcelona, Juvencus, Prudentius, Orosius, from

Spain, Optatus from the African Milevi. But likewise during the whole time in the line of her Roman bishops from Sylvester to Leo she shews an unmatched series of rulers, differing in national descent but instinct with the same faith, whose letters, directed to all parts of her domain, commence a series of historic documents which have no equal in human history. They draw out from age to age a Christian legislation descending to our own time, and promising for the future more even than they have done in the past.

The literature of the age of Pericles, the literature of the age of Augustus, the general literature of the present day, except so far as it is Christian, has no one spirit guiding it, no key therefore to its development or its interpretation. How different it was with the literature on which I am now engaged, I shall endeavour to shew. If I mistake not, it will be seen more and more clearly, as we contemplate it in a mass, to be the offspring of faith in the mystery of God incarnate and suffering, and to draw its whole life and inspiration from the working in the human heart and mind of that stupendous act of love, which these writers realised the more thoroughly because it was betrayed by many who were bound to proclaim it. This one fact it is of which they are one and all the defenders, whatever the particular mode of their defence, controversy, teaching, comment on Scripture, preaching. These, the intellectual champions of the great truth on which all Christian life and hope depend, even when they do not suffer the death of the body, are the martyrs of thought :

> "And they stand in glittering ring
> Round their warrior God and King,
> Who before and for them bled,
> With their robes of ruby red,
> And their swords of cherub flame."

The time then when Christian doctrine opened from the bud to the flower began with Constantine, as the great dogmatic struggles began with him. In the East they were occasioned by the Arian, Semiarian, and Macedonian heresies, and by some smaller sects ; in the West, by the schism of Donatus, involving heresy in its train, and by the heresy of Pelagius. Arius, a presbyter of Alexandria, denied the divine nature and eternal existence of the Redeemer, declared Him to be a creature of the Father, whom He had not begotten of His substance, but created out of nothing. Macedonius, bishop of Constantinople, maintained concerning the Holy Ghost what Arius asserted of the Son, making Him a creature of the Son[1] as Arius made the Son a creature of the Father. Nestorius, also bishop of Constantinople, set aside the true incarnation of the Son of God by maintaining that the Logos dwelt in the man Jesus only as in a temple, without really making the human nature His own, and uniting it in true indivisible union with the divine Nature in the one divine Person. His antagonist, Eutyches, an abbot in Constantinople, absorbed the human nature of Christ in the divine, and thus assumed there to be in Him not only one Person, but one Nature only. Apollinaris, bishop of Laodicæa,

---

[1] *Confer* Pope Damasus, Confession of Faith sent to Paulinus of Antioch IV. Anathematizamus Macedonianos, qui de Arii stirpe venientes non perfidiam mutavere sed nomen. (Migne, xiii. 359.)

denied a human soul to Christ. The Donatists in Africa, at first only denying the validity of the sacraments as conferred by a certain line of bishops, soon came to reject the whole Church except themselves. The Briton Pelagius and his companion Cœlestius maintained that there was no original sin, that man could attain blessedness by his own strength: that he needed neither actual or sanctifying grace. And in maintaining this, he denied the need, indispensable so far as the will of God is made known to us, of the Lord's incarnation and of His work in redeeming.

These errors therefore imperilled the whole Christian faith. It added to their danger that the authors of three of them, Arius, Nestorius, and Eutyches, were aided by the imperial authority at Constantinople, which sought to oppress and root out orthodox doctrine.[1]

Any one of these heresies, had it been accepted by the Church, would have destroyed the Christian faith, and the Church was incessantly occupied in resisting some or all of them, from the promulgation of false doctrine by Arius, to the great letter of St. Leo, which set forth the true faith concerning the two Natures and one Person of our Lord; and the council of Chalcedon which addressed the same St. Leo as their "Father," "the very person entrusted by the Saviour with the guardianship of the vine," "a Head presiding over them as members".

The literature intervening between these two events I look upon as called forth by the efforts of the several

[1] From Nirschl, vol. i. p. 2.

writers to defend what they most prized, the inheritance of the faith. They none of them wrote for gain or for vainglory. But heresy broke out in the midst of the Church: that heretical spirit began forthwith to set the Eastern bishops, who had fallen into its toils, against the original Primacy of the Roman See. At the same time, a vehement schism, in which bishops stood against bishops, divided the African church, and endeavoured to submit matters of doctrine to imperial judgment. This the Donatists did to Constantine, as the Arians afterwards to Constantius, of whom Athanasius said, "They have no king but Cæsar".

By this terrible danger to the faith and the unity of the Church, the intellectual efforts of its defenders are called forth. In this they were only continuing the course which Christian literature had taken from the beginning. "Christianity appeared in human history not as a result of scientific inquiry, but as the announcement of a divine revelation. Miracles contained the proof of the doctrine they taught: nay, the doctrines themselves, which language served only to expound. In consequence, Christianity demanded faith, the immediate basis of which was its own contents: proof and the thing to be proved coincided. The Apostles recounted their Lord's history, and the whole contents of Christianity were given with the history itself. Thus whoever had a mind receptive of higher things, whoever had an open spiritual sense, accepted the message without any notional development, and without any demonstration, which indeed could not have been given him. And so literary activity was almost needless; but every effort must have been spent on its exercise, had Christianity endeavoured to make good its footing as a result of human thought."[1]

The first age after the Apostles was meagre in writers; the second century on the contrary shews a great richness of them in all possible forms. The reason is that the Christian Church was assaulted from within and without. From without heathens and Jews presented the strangest distortions of it. The civil power used every effort to kindle popular hatred against it. Within, its doctrine was misunderstood. The false Gnosis caused it endless battles. "Throughout this century the direct refutation of heathens and heretics continued to be the main literary occupation of Church writers. It was a task which led them into a great range of thought, and introduced the most difficult problems."

"The result of the first two centuries is that Christian literature, from a meagre beginning, had developed itself to such an extent as to cause admiration when we consider the range of its productions, the variety of their subjects, their successful treatment, together with the shortness of the time and the external position of the Christian Church. The apologists, on whom the light of faith had only just fallen, failed not to give suitable answers to the challenges of Hellenic wisdom, and to meet with all their power the destructive inroads which it made into the guarded territory of Christian revelation. Much was done when this first assault of

[1] Möhler, *Patrologie*, 49, 178, 185.

heathenism and heresy upon conduct and doctrine was received so firmly and repulsed so definitely. That, however, was the main thing done. A proper and independent exhibition of Christian science could not yet present itself. That required a time of increased consolidation within, and of external peace." [1]

This situation continued during the third century. The hostile position of heathenism and the empire did not essentially alter. Persecutions even increased in intensity. The more the Christian faith spread among all ranks, and the deeper its influence on the hearts of men, the more apparent its effects upon society, in preparing a total change in what had hitherto been the relations of men to each other, the more did the State, with whose growth heathendom was intertwined, defend what seemed to it a part of itself. But within the Church every heresy and every schism had the sure result of leading the Catholic Church more deeply to comprehend its own being, to enunciate and maintain its unity and exclusiveness with more decision. In the first instance the teaching delivered by the Apostles to the Church had only been historically handed down. To grasp this heirloom of faith as an idea, to arrange it scientifically, was a progressive work, occasioned in the main by the Church's necessary defence of herself against heresy and schism. The false Gnosis led to the beginning of a Christian philosophy, of which a part was to work out the relation between faith and knowledge.

The Arian heresy was a most deadly attack; the

[1] Möhler, *Patrologie*, pp. 416, 420, 424.

movement of theological formation which ensued upon it was proportionally great. It was not the will of God that the outward peace given to the Church should find her at peace within; but the recompense bestowed on the Church for the terrible trial into which she was cast by the defection of her bishops, joined with the imperial authority as exercised against her by Constantius and Valens, in the fifty years from 330 to 380, was accomplished by turning what had been in the main the childlike reception of the faith by her children as an inherited tradition into the scientific exposition of that faith by acute intellects invested also with lawful authority. As the first of these I take Athanasius, as the last Leo. In that glorious battlefield he who sat in the see of St. Mark, which was also the second see of St. Peter, led the fight; he who sat in the supreme See of Peter terminated the fray, and in the act was acknowledged by the whole Church in plenary Council as her Father and Teacher, in whose person truth and unity were crowned together.

The martyrs who by their blood saved and propagated the faith of the Church in the first three centuries, the writers, often also martyrs, who from St. Clement the Pope and St. Ignatius, wrote in behalf of it, such as Hermas, Polycarp, Papias, Melito, Justin, Minutius, Athenagoras, Theophilus, Irenæus, Hegesippus, Pantænus, Clemens, Tertullian, Origen, Cyprian, Dionysius of Alexandria, Gregory Thaumaturgus, Methodius: these and others, individual ministers to the Church's unfailing Magisterium, carried her victorious through the great persecutions, through the perpetual assaults made by judaising sects, through the constantly-repeated efforts of the Gnostic sects to give their assumed and pretended knowledge supremacy over faith, which is the principle of heresy. In the second half of this period the great catechetical school of Alexandria had done immense service through the ability of the men who had imbibed all the wisdom of heathen antiquity, making use of its forms and modes of expression to draw the more cultivated heathen into the sanctuary of the Church. Yet if we could plant ourselves in the position of Athanasius, when about the year 318, being not more than twenty-five years of age, and before the promulgation of the Arian error, he wrote his two beautiful treatises—the one against the Gentiles, the other on the Incarnation of the Word, I suppose we might express the attitude of the Church over against those who were not in her bosom somewhat after this manner. She stood out in the face of all the false religions cultivated in the hundred provinces of the empire as a complete whole which had rejected in her doctrine all intermixture of human wisdom. She adored the Blessed Trinity in unity as the only God through the Word made Man for the salvation of men.[1]

The connection of her several doctrines with each other, their mutual relations, how they acted and reacted, their inward essence, and the indivisible

---

[1] For proof of this see the encyclical put forth by Alexander of Alexandria, at the rise of Arius (Nirschl, ii. 29), as well as the two just mentioned treatises of St. Athanasius.

life which ran through them all as a structural body,—all this existed, and was felt unconsciously by every martyr who suffered, by every writer who thought, by " Clement in his varied page," by " Dionysius, ruler sage in days of doubt and pain," by " Origen with eagle eye ". But to give these things their due expression, as, for instance, taking the highest, to state the eternal Sonship of the Logos, and the Person of the Holy Ghost the Sanctifier, in union with the Godhead of the Father, in appropriate terms, which would defy cavil, express the whole truth, and expel insidious heresy masking itself in double language,—this was the task of a later time. I suppose it commenced immediately upon the proclamation of peace to the Church by the empire. This sifting and separation, this advancing of the deepest mysteries into day, was accomplished with the greater struggle because it was the assault of error which the Providence of God was using more perfectly to delineate the truth.[1]

In the period from Athanasius to Leo that work of the human intellect upon the principles of faith, of which the Apostles' creed is, as it were, the exemplar, while a full catechetical arrangement of all Christian doctrine would be the complete structure, wherein the writings of doctors and the schools of the Church are laboratories which take part in that divine chemistry, of which the Councils of her Fathers and the Decrees of her Pontiffs state the result, which in one word we call Theology, ran its first stadium. Its effect is to bring

[1] In the above I have used and partly quoted Riffel, 277-9.

out in open day, and so to imprint by the use of unfailing standards on the popular mind, the truths which from the beginning have been the life of Christians, to guard them from the perversions to which human language so readily lends itself, and so to collect the vast inheritance of past ages for the benefit of all. What the labours of successive generations accomplish for a particular human science, theology does in forming the one divine science.

The great dogmatic struggle, which occupied four full generations from St. Athanasius to St. Leo, and received its definitive solution from the latter in the council of Chalcedon, while it raised a dense cloud of words, and cost its champions infinite pains to select the right form of words in order to safeguard celestial truths, was at the bottom very simple. On the side of error it was an assault upon the facts enshrined by St. John in the beginning of his Gospel, "the Word was God"; "and the Word was made flesh and dwelt among us"; and by St. Matthew in the baptismal formula, which made the whole Christian people: "the Name of the Father, and of the Son, and of the Holy Ghost". On the side of truth it was to maintain the Incarnation and the Blessed Trinity, on which two things the whole Christian revelation rested, and on which the whole Christian life had been supported from the day of Pentecost. The two cohere inseparably together. Arius, Apollinaris, Macedonius, Nestorius, Eutyches, attacked one or both. It is difficult in any way to misstate the doctrine that the Son of God became Man, without further misstating "the Name," that is, the Being, "of the Father, Son, and Holy Ghost". We find that almost all the writers of this period wrote against the impugners of these two doctrines. Against Arius and Macedonius, all the energy of faith and learning, all the force of prayer and science, were spent by Athanasius, Basil, Gregory of Nazianzum, and Gregory of Nyssa, Ephraem, Didymus, Amphilochius, Chrysostome, Cyril of Alexandria, Hilary, Ambrose, Marius Victorinus, Augustine, Prudentius, Lucifer of Cagliari, Eusebius of Vercelli, Zeno of Verona. Against Apollinaris Athanasius and Basil carried on the conflict; against Nestorius and Eutyches, Cyril of Alexandria, Proclus, Theodoret; against Eutyches, Leo and Cassian. Further, the error of Pelagius rendered the Incarnation unnecessary; for if man could be saved by the strength of nature, without grace, it was not necessary that the Author of nature should assume the creature, to restore it. In that case, certainly

"Mestier non era partorir Maria".

Against this most destructive heresy, which is said to have been the offspring of the Nestorian error, though preceding it in time,[1] Optatus of Milevi, Jerome, Prosper, but especially Augustine, contended; and the same against the Donatist schism, which tended to destroy the work of Christ in the unity of His spiritual body, as the Pelagian destroyed the need of His coming in the body

---

[1] According to the couplet—
Nestoriana lues successit Pelagianæ,
Quæ tamen est utero progenerata suo.

at all. Augustine further spent much time in exposing the Manichæan perversion of the Being of God, in which he had himself been so long involved. Jerome censured certain impugners of the Blessed Virgin's honour, Jovian, Helvidius, and Vigilantius.

It is apparent now, when we look back upon these heresies and schisms[1] as a whole, that they have a very close connection with each other. And for the historian it is most noteworthy that the great victory of the Church betokened by the conversion of Constantine, which seemed to mark the end of a pagan persecution, carried on by the mightiest empire that has yet arisen in the world's history, was simultaneous with the outbreak of a contest so deadly in the very bosom of the Church as to threaten her dissolution. It may be doubted whether any prospect can be found in all her annals more terrible than that which seemed to lie before her in the last year,[2] A.D. 361, of the reign of Constantius, when he was taken away by a fever at the age of forty-four. The force of heresy has never since risen higher: the episcopate has never since been so near failing. There is no one of the divine promises to the Church on which the mind has more need to dwell, or to which her nineteen centuries of life bear so

---

[1] I say schisms, because the position taken up by the Eastern bishops at the conciliabulum of Philippopolis against the council of Sardica threatened the unity of the Church as much as the Donatists.

[2] See for proof the opening of St. Hilary's libellus, A.D. 360, "Tempus est loquendi: quia jam præteriit tempus tacendi, Christus expectatur, quia obtinuit antichristus. Clament pastores, quia mercenarii fugerunt. Ponamus animas pro ovibus, quia fures introierunt, et leo sæviens circuit. Sustineatur tribulatio, qualis non fuit a constitutione mundi."

constant a witness, as that contained in the words, "the gates of hell shall not prevail". Between Athanasius and Constantius the forces seemed unequally divided; but the former endured five banishments and closed his episcopate of forty-five years in peace upon his patriarchal throne: the latter died in middle life, his work unaccomplished, his throne taken by the infidel cousin whom he feared and hated, and whose enmity as an apostate from the Church worked for her deliverance.

The mind also of Athanasius and his fellow-workers, united with their sufferings, prevailed. The knot of heresies generated by Arius, together with the schism which they animated, is extinct and exploded. The most that can be said for him is, that having infected the young faith of the noblest Teuton tribes, the Goths and Vandals, he was at length cast out of them, and they became members of the one Catholic family. The heresy expelled turned into an open foe, and finally Arius passed into Mahomet.

Now it is a fact that the rise of the Arian heresy was followed by a great outburst of scriptural study. What is the connection between these two facts? I conceive it to be that the defenders of the Church saw in the Scriptures the great arsenal of defence for what they had hitherto received by unquestioning inheritance in the order of the Church. St. Athanasius says in one place concerning the word being from eternity with the Father, of one substance with Him: "See, we are proving that this view has been transmitted from

Fathers to Fathers. But you, O modern Jews and disciples of Caiaphas, whom can you assign as Fathers to your phrases?" What he here says of this one great doctrine, he held likewise concerning the whole government and doctrine of the Church. They were all comprehended in "the rule of faith"; and this rule was the basis of his own teaching. "He assumes," says Cardinal Newman, "that there is a tradition, substantive, independent, and authoritative, such as to supply for us the true sense of Scripture in doctrinal matters—a tradition carried on from generation to generation by the practice of catechising and by the other ministrations of Holy Church. He does not care to contend that no other meaning of certain passages of Scripture besides this traditional Catholic sense is possible or is plausible, whether true or not, but simply that any sense inconsistent with the Catholic is untrue, untrue because the traditional sense is apostolic and decisive. What he was instructed in at school and in church, the voice of the Christian people, the analogy of faith, the ecclesiastical φρόνημα, the writings of saints; these are enough for him. He is in no sense an enquirer, nor a mere disputant; he has received, and he transmits." Again, "the fundamental idea with which he starts in the controversy is a deep sense of the authority of tradition, which he considers to have a definite jurisdiction even in the interpretation of Scripture, though at the same time he seems to consider that Scripture thus interpretated, is a document of final appeal in enquiry and in disputation. Hence, in his view of religion, is the magnitude of the evil which he is combating, and which exists prior to that extreme aggravation of it (about which no Catholic can doubt) involved in the characteristic tenet of Arianism itself. According to him, opposition to the witness of the Church, separation from its communion, private judgment overbearing the authorised catechetical teaching, the fact of a denomination, as men now speak, this is a self-condemnation; and the heretical tenet, whatever it may happen to be, which is its formal life, is a spiritual poison, and nothing else, the sowing of the evil one upon the good seed, in whatever age and place it is found; and he applies to all separatists the Apostle's words, *They went out from us, for they were not of us.*"

Thus he laid the utmost stress upon catechising, as in fact supplying the evidence of tradition as to the doctrine which Arius blasphemed. "Let them tell us by what teacher or by what tradition they have derived these notions concerning the Saviour."

"For who was ever yet a hearer of such a doctrine? or whence or from whom did the abettors and hirelings of the heresy gain it? Who thus expounded to them when they were at school? Who told them 'Abandon the worship of the creation, and then draw near and worship a creature and a work'? But if they themselves own that they have heard it now for the first time, how can they deny that this heresy is foreign and not from our Fathers? But what is not from our Fathers, but has come to light in this day, how can it be but that of which the blessed Paul has foretold, that *in the latter times some shall depart from the sound faith?"*

"Who is there, who, when he heard in his first catechisings, that God had a Son, and had made all things in His proper Word, did not so understand it in that sense which we now intend? Who, when the Arian heresy began, but at once, on hearing its teachers, was startled, as if they taught strange things?"

Cardinal Newman supports these statements by a great number of passages from many authors, and then adds: "From these it would appear that the two main sources of Revelation are Scripture and Tradition; that these constitute one Rule of Faith, and that, sometimes as a composite rule, sometimes as a double and co-ordinate, sometimes as an alternative, under the *magisterium*, of course, of the Church, and without an appeal to the private judgment of individuals". Indeed "the great and essential difference between Catholics and non-Catholics was, that Catholics interpreted Scripture by Tradition, and non-Catholics by their own private judgment".

I believe that in the words above quoted,[1] Cardinal Newman has given an accurate view of the position and principles held, not only by Athanasius, but by the whole body of writers in the period stretching from

---

[1] *Notes on Athanasius*, pp. 311, 250, 51, 63, 312, 264. The articles upon Definitions, Catechising, Heresies, Heretics, Private Judgment, the Rule of Faith, Authority of Scripture, Tradition, if read together, will be found to contain a view of the Antenicene Church, supported by vast erudition, and throwing much light upon that unknown sea. I have quoted some of these passages in Vol. IV. in a somewhat different connection.

Athanasius to St. Leo, and of the Church herself at the Nicene Council, and the succeeding period.

When, therefore, her very foundation was assailed, when the tradition on which her teaching, her sacraments, her daily rule of life, and her government alike rested, was in danger, her children, resting on that tradition itself, turned with hitherto unexampled ardour to the Holy Scriptures for support and corroboration. For instance, the very mystery in and by which her worship began, which her Fathers called "the tremendous and unbloody sacrifice," the priesthood, according to the order of Melchisedek, and the rite in which it was celebrated day after day from the beginning, all this expressed the Godhead of her Lord, being as an institution before, and independent of, its record, in the written gospels and the epistle of St. Paul. The negation invented by Arius evacuated this mystery of all its efficacy.[1] This, then, is one instance in which the Fathers sought by the testimony of Scripture to confirm what tradition had handed down to them.

Thus each assault of heresy threw the faithful upon a more earnest and complete study of Scripture. Of St. Ephraem, St. Gregory[2] of Nyssa says, that he was incessantly engaged in the study of scripture, and wrote commentaries on the whole Old and New Testament. Rufinus[3] writes of St. Basil and St. Gregory, that they

---

[1] Does not Athanasius allude to this when, as above quoted, he says, "Abandon the worship of creation, and then draw near and worship a creature, and a work"? *i.e.*, the Lord's Body in the Eucharist, which, as St. Augustine says, "we should sin if we did not adore," but which Arius made "a creature and a work".

[2] In his panegyric.   [3] Rufinus, *Hist.* ii. 9.

are said, putting aside all Greek literature,. to have passed thirteen years together studying the Scriptures alone, in doing which they followed out the sense, not from their private opinion, but by the writings and authority of the Fathers.

Theology itself may be termed the scientific exposition [1] and proving of the Church's traditional belief, and of this Athanasius has been called the father.

The movement, therefore, which drew all the great writers of this period to study, as a whole, the Scriptures of the Old and New Testament, and as a result of their study to make commentaries, and, further, to deliver homilies upon them, may be considered, not only a natural expansion of devotion, but also an effort to corroborate the existing order, discipline, sacraments, belief, and usages of the Church by the testimony of God Himself, whether delivered in prophecy to the writers of the Old Testament, or uttering the deep aspirations of the heart in psalms, or recorded as history by evangelists, or enforced as exhortation by Apostles, or seen in vision by the one who lay on the Lord's breast. The subject of unbounded interest to them in doing this was the illustration of faith and the enforcing of a holy morality. Into questions raised by modern criticism, and which not unfrequently serve to imperil faith and pervert morals, they did not enter. But the key which they used for unlocking Scripture was that so dwelt upon by Athanasius, the ecclesiastical sense.

[1] Nirschl, ii. 47.

But while those whom we now call "the Fathers" used the ecclesiastical sense as the key of knowledge in the interpretation of Scripture, Arius was remarkable for *not* using this key. Thus, instead of the rule of faith on the subject of the Divine Trinity and Filiation, he used a private key of his own reasoning: such as, How could a Father have a Son if He was not before Him, and how could a Son have a Father without being after Him? And how could the nature which is ingenerate be the same nature as that which is generated? As if "how could" entered into the being of the Almighty and Eternal One.

The result was, that Arius and those who followed him in this method of disregarding the ecclesiastical sense for the interpretation of Scripture, used these Scriptures not to corroborate the existing faith and order of the Church, as historically handed down from the beginning, but to substitute another belief, and to change the order.

I will mention here fifteen chief champions of the Church, in this period, grouping them partly from the time in which they lived, and partly from their work, in five triads.

The first triad shall be of the three writers and confessors, the chief glory respectively of Egypt, of Gaul, and of Syria: Athanasius, Hilary, and Ephraem. Athanasius was born, and Ephraem also, in the last decade of the third century; Hilary some twenty-five years later, but he died about 369, Athanasius in 373; Ephraem in or near 379. Thus they are exactly contemporaries, especially in the period of their intellectual work.

The world has been full of the glory of Athanasius for fifteen centuries since he went to his reward. I will let one who has lived upon him speak of him. Cardinal Newman says: "This renowned Father is, in ecclesiastical history, the special doctor of the sacred truth which Arius denied; bringing it out into shape and system so fully and luminously that he may be said to have exhausted his subject, as far as it lies open to the human intellect". He "accompanies his exposition of doctrine with manifestations of character which are of great interest and value". Himself nurtured by the tradition of the Church, he is fierce only against the denial of it; of a "prudent, temperate spirit and practical good sense"; "self-distrustful and subdued in his comments on Scripture and his controversial answers; he, the foremost doctor of the Divine Sonship, being the most modest as well as the most authoritative of teachers". And he quotes the judgment of Photius upon him, thus: "In his writings Athanasius is ever perspicuous, never wordy, never involved. He is keen, deep, nervous in his mode of arguing, and marvellously fertile. His argumentation has nothing poor or puerile in it, as happens in the case of the young or half-educated, but is philosophical and magnificent, full of thought and with broad views, fortified by testimonies of Scripture and weighty proofs. Especially such is he in his treatises 'Against the Greeks' and 'On the Incarnation,' and in his Pentabiblus against Arius, which is a triumphant defeat of every heresy, and eminently of Arianism. And if we were to say that Gregory Theologus and the divine Basil, as if drawing from a well, derived from this treatise their beautiful and luminous arguments against the heresy, I consider we should not be far from the mark." The Cardinal's own measure of him, as to style, is given in the words: "Erasmus seems to prefer him as a writer to all the Fathers, and certainly, in my own judgment, no one comes near him but Chrysostome and Jerome".[1]

Of his whole character St. Gregory begins his funeral oration with the words: "When I praise Athanasius I shall praise virtue. For to name him is to praise virtue, since he *had* in himself collected all virtue, or, to speak more truly, he *has*. For all who have lived according to God, though they depart hence, live to God. Whence He is said to be the God of Abraham, of Isaac, and of Jacob, who is the God not of the dead, but of the living."

And Basil,[2] in his utmost distress, wrote to him: "When we look at the state of things and consider the difficulties under which every exertion for good seems to be hampered as by a chain, we fall into quite a despair of ourselves; but when we turn to the weight which your character carries with it, and reflect how the Lord has provided you to heal the weaknesses of the churches, we recover our thoughts, and rouse ourselves from individual despair to the hope of better things."

A great number of his writings, dogmatic, historic,

---
[1] St. Athanasius, vol. ii. 51-9, vol. i. 152.   [2] Quoted by Migne, xxv. 275.

commentaries and letters, have been preserved; and fifteen of the Pascal Letters which he wrote in the forty-five years of his episcopate, a special function of the Alexandrine bishop exercised at the Epiphany of each year, have been lately recovered. Had all been preserved they would have given us much-needed information respecting that unrivalled confessorship, and the general history of the years during which it lasted, which is wanting.

What Athanasius[1] in the conflict with Arianism was for the East, his contemporary Hilary was for Gaul and Italy. As he resembled him in learning and in spirit, in piety, eloquence, and confessorship, he has been called the Athanasius of the West. He was born at Poitiers between 320 and 330, of a distinguished family; devoted himself to the study of the Latin and Greek languages and to Philosophy. From Philosophy he went on to the study of Holy Scripture. To use his own words[2]: "My mind was eager not only to fulfil these duties which it would be most criminal and miserable not to fulfil; but to know God, the author of so great a gift as life, to whom it owed itself entirely; in service to whom it placed its own nobility; whom it recognised as the source of every hope which it could form; in whose goodness it will rest as in a safe and familiar harbour amid the storm of pressing troubles. The keenest desire was kindled in me to understand or to become acquainted with this God."

The issue of his enquiry was that he became a Chris-

[1] See Nirschl, ii. 75, &c.   [2] *De Trinitate*, i. 8.

tian, and about the year 350 was baptised with his wife
and their only child, a daughter. Then he shewed
himself the model of a Christian. It would seem that
from his baptism he lived in continence. Soon after,
at least before 358, the unanimous voice of clergy and
people called him to the see of his native city.

He devoted himself entirely to a charge which he
deemed divine. The renown of his gifts and virtues
went beyond Aquitaine; but he was not permitted long
to wield his pastoral staff in tranquillity. The Arian
Constantius, though only a catechumen, had assembled
more than three hundred Western bishops at Milan in
355, and persecuted them into condemning Athanasius.
Those who would not yield were banished; as Eusebius,
bishop of Vercelli, Lucifer of Cagliari, Dionysius of
Milan; Paul of Treves was already an exile in Phrygia.
Presently the same lot fell upon Pope Liberius and
Hosius of Cordova. The Arian Auxentius took the see
of Milan; and Saturninus, metropolitan of Arles, promoted Arianism in Gaul. So the triumph of the heresy
in the West seemed complete.

Then Hilary appeared at the head of the Gallic bishops
against his own metropolitan Saturninus. They signed
a decree, which was probably drawn up by him, exclud-
ing Saturninus and the two Arian bishops, Ursacius and
Valens, the special instigators of Constantius, from their
communion. Saturninus, to punish Hilary, traduced
him to the emperor. He defended himself with brilliant
power; but the emperor caused the Cæsar Julian, who
then ruled for him in Gaul, to call a synod at Biterræ,

the present Beziers, which deposed him, and banished him to Phrygia, where he bravely bore witness to the truth. The Gallic bishops remained in communion with him, and his see was not filled up.

Hilary was active in his Phrygian banishment, writing a work on the Blessed Trinity, which continues in renown to the present day, by the side of St. Augustine's work. He strove to inform the Eastern bishops as to the importance of the great struggle, and the position of the Western bishops in regard to it. He was present at the great council of Seleucia, the Eastern counterpart of the council of Rimini, where he was received with much goodwill, and bore witness to the Nicene belief of the West, though he took no part in the public proceedings. He witnessed the denial of the Godhead of Christ, and saw the semi-Arian bishops, after the council, deprived of their sees, and replaced by partisans of Ursacius and Valens. Well aware that their support was in the emperor, he betook himself to Constantinople, and asked an audience of Constantius, in the intention of informing him. He composed a petition to him, asking to be allowed a public disputation with his metropolitan Saturninus. The party was afraid to grant this, and prevailed on the emperor to terminate his sojourn in Constantinople by sending him back to Gaul.

Thus, after four years' banishment, he returned in triumph to Poitiers. He was received with joy. St. Martin, who then lived in solitude in Pannonia, came to meet and salute the confessor, and afterwards, with the help of Hilary, built, in order to be near him, the first monastery of Gaul, Ligugé, close to Poitiers. Hilary worked with all zeal to exterminate Arianism in Gaul. Many synods were held for this. They all rejected the decrees of Rimini, and accepted the Nicene Creed. Saturninus and the other chiefs of the heresy were deposed and banished at a great council held at Paris; and, again, one at Biterræ, presided over by Hilary. The chief merit of restoring the faith in France belonged to Hilary.

When the emperor Valentinian had succeeded, in 364, Hilary also went to Milan, and attempted to convict Auxentius of the heresy. A public disputation was granted him, at which ten bishops were present. Auxentius was so hard pushed that he was reduced to confess the consubstantiality of the Son. But he had the art to persuade Valentinian both of his own orthodoxy, by a creed which he framed, and that his opponent was a disturber of the peace, who thereupon was ordered to return to his diocese. Auxentius from that time was at least obliged to conceal his heresy, and the victory was complete when, afterwards, St. Ambrose succeeded him.

This was the public life of Hilary, who is supposed to have died in 369, when he was not yet fifty years of age. His chief work is that on the Trinity, distinguished for its force of speculative thought, the completeness of its scriptural arguments, its logical order, the full refutation of opponents, and a most carefully finished style. It was the first Western work on the doctrine of the Logos, and a masterpiece.

Hilary also was the first Western to write commentaries on Scripture, which were upon St. Matthew and the Psalms: again, the first hymnnologist—and he has left a number of polemical writings. The letter against Constantius, when he was refused a public hearing, is of extraordinary force and freedom.

St. Jerome says of him: "I cannot blame so great a man, the most eloquent of his time, who is proclaimed, wherever the Roman name is known, for the merit of his confession, the industry of his life, and his brilliant eloquence". St. Augustine calls him no mean authority on the treatment of Scripture and maintenance of the faith. He was the first properly dogmatic Latin writer.

The most illustrious of the Syrian Fathers is Ephraem,[1] who has been called "Prophet of the Syrians," "Harp of the Holy Ghost," "Pillar of the Church," "Teacher of the world". He was born of poor Christian parents at Nisibis, in Mesopotamia, at the end of the third or beginning of the fourth century. He received a pious education, chose the life of solitude, and sought for his teacher James, bishop of Nisibis, who had such affection for him as to take him to the Nicene Council in 325, and, on his return, made him master of his school at Nisibis. Here Ephraem worked with great success until the city was ceded by Jovian to the Persians in 364, and they broke up the school.

Thereupon, Ephraem betook himself to Edessa, especially to venerate the relics of the Apostle Thomas. He

---

[1] Nirschl, ii. 255, &c.

remained for some time with the solitaries near the city, inhabiting a cavern.

Finally he took the city for his residence, was called by its name, and the school which he opened there became a centre of the faith. Ephraem drew all eyes upon him as a distinguished teacher, but also as a preacher of great power and unction, a most prolific writer of hymns, and a great opponent of the numerous heretics; moreover, as a pattern of penitence, humility, and poverty. And he communicated to his hearers what he felt himself, so that he was called "the Preacher of Penance". He became a deacon, and also, as is judged from passages in his writings, a priest. He had the greatest sympathy for the poor, and possessed an irresistible charm for all: his look, his word, his tone, would soften the hardest hearts into compassion. Thus he is said, during an epidemic, to have provided three hundred beds in Edessa for poor sufferers. He is also said to have spent some time in Egypt, visiting the monks and hermits there; and, quite in his last years, he paid a visit to St. Basil at Cæsarea, whom he had seen in a vision as a pillar of fire. The last recorded act of his life is a funeral oration over St. Basil, shortly after whose death he died himself, about the year 379.

He left a vast number of commentaries on the Scriptures both of the Old and New Testament, of homilies, and of metrical hymns on the chief mysteries of our Lord. They were written in Syriac, many afterwards translated into Greek, and, besides, moral and ascetical writings. His hymns and homilies formed part of the ritual of the Syrian church from his own days to the present time; and, as he preceded the Nestorian and Eutychean heresies in his own country, they also kept and valued his writings. Like St. Athanasius, he is a witness of the Antenicene church's faith.

His writings have been marvellously preserved in the Syrian monastery of the Wadi-al-Natrum in Egypt, whence they have been procured at the beginning of the eighteenth century for the great Roman edition, and in our own time by further manuscripts brought to the libraries of Paris and London. Among the latter are eight remarkable homilies for the services of the Holy Week. The fourth of these narrates the institution of the Eucharist and the whole doctrine of the Church respecting this sacrament and the sacrifice of the Mass. Before it are words which contain the most ancient testimony of the Syrian church to the Primacy of Peter and his prerogative of infallible teaching. They are thus translated from the original Syriac:—

"After Simon had obeyed the Lord and allowed his feet to be washed, the Lord resumed his dress, and, while the supper continued, took again his place. As they were all reclining, Jesus said, Know you why I have done this. If I do not explain My mysteries, who will understand them? If I do not fulfil the types, who will know My will? I must do all which the prophets have said concerning Me; it behoves Me to become the teacher of wisdom to you. Simon, My disciple, I have made thee the foundation of Holy Church. I have already called thee the Rock,[1] because thou shalt sustain My whole building. Thou art the bishop[2] of those who build Me a church on earth. If they would build anything reprobate, do thou, the foundation, repress them. Thou art the source of the fountain whence My doctrine is derived. Thou art the head of My disciples. Through thee will I give all nations to drink. Thine is that life-giving sweetness which I bestow. Thee have I chosen to be in My institution as the first-born, and to become the heir of My treasures. I have given to thee the keys of My kingdom. I have appointed thee the chief over all My treasures."

As a witness, St. Ephraem speaks for the whole Syrian church. During his life, say from 300 to 380, it was, I suppose, the most flourishing part of the whole Church, full of great cities, in which there was a large Christian population. Besides this testimony to the Primacy, and that which follows concerning the Eucharist (wherein he says: "What I have now given to you think not to be bread; receive, eat it, nor break it into crumbs; what I have called My Body is so indeed; its smallest crumb can sanctify millions, and is sufficient to give life to all who eat it"), there are in his extant works testimonies to the Godhead of Christ, the mystery of the Trinity, the number of the sacraments, the freedom of the will, the genuineness of the deutero-canonical scriptures, the veneration of the saints. He speaks for Syria as Hilary

---

[1] That is, Cephas, signifying in Syriac, the language in which our Lord spoke, at once Petra and Petrus.

[2] This word, says Dr. Lamy, signifies the same as the Greek ἐπισκύοπος.— Vol. i., p. 412.

for Gaul, and Athanasius for Egypt. It is to be remarked that he died sixty years before St. Leo's accession to the throne of St. Peter, and that he precedes all those letters of the Popes from Siricius forwards, which I have quoted above, and which rest on that foundation of authority which he has described in terms at least as absolute as theirs.

We come now to the Cappadocian triad, Basil and the two Gregories, as it were three passion-flowers of equal beauty, growing on the same stem. Basil was born at Cæsarea in 329, of a family distinguished for rank, but yet more for its piety, which has given seven saints to the Church: his grandmother Macrina, his father Basil, his mother Emmelia, his sister Macrina, his two brothers, Peter of Sebaste and Gregory of Nyssa. He studied at the most celebrated schools of the time: Cæsarea, Constantinople, and Athens. After five years' stay at the last, he returned to Cæsarea at the age of twenty-six, renounced the profession of rhetor, was baptised, became a *lector*, travelled into Palestine and Egypt, to learn the life of the hermits, and then withdrew into a solitude in Pontus, where his mother and sister had already established a convent. Here he spent a long time in prayer and contemplation, in labour and study, with his friend Gregory. In 364, when thirty-five years of age, he was made priest by his bishop Eusebius, and after some years' work in Cæsarea, during which at a time of famine he gave all his goods to support the poor and sick, he was elected to succeed Eusebius in the great see, which was at the head of fifty bishops. Here, for nearly nine years, he resisted the Arianism which the emperor Valens was trying to impose on the Eastern church, whose prætorian prefect Modestus, the same who caused eighty ecclesiastics of Constantinople to be turned adrift in a burning ship, assaulted him in vain with threats of banishment, confiscation, and death. The first three years of Basil's episcopate were the last years of Athanasius: he consulted and honoured him in life, and became at his death the chief pillar of the Eastern church, soliciting repeatedly the help of Pope Damasus in its troubles and confusion, of which his letters give the most terrible account. His severe life, together with the calamities which he strove to avert, wore out his strength prematurely, and he died in his forty-ninth year.

The extraordinary greatness of this doctor of the Church is manifest in the writings which he left: his dogmatic works in defence of the blessed Trinity and the Incarnation, his commentaries on Scripture, his homilies, his works on the religious life, and more than three hundred letters, masterly in style and contents.

Great in the practice of the religious life; great as bishop; great as preacher, as commentator, as a founder of orders, it is his least distinction that he was an accomplished gentleman in word and deed, through all the relations of life. He stands out, like his contemporary St. Ambrose, as the bishop who feared not emperors. The villany of Valens shrunk before him, whose ignominious death he just outlived; while Ambrose also lived long enough to embalm the memory of the conqueror, who had bowed to his reproof in the height of his power. In them the East and the West produced respectively two bishops of equal courage, vigour, and ability.

His friend Gregory, born in 326, shared Basil's life of study at Athens, and of ascetic retirement in Pontus, after being baptised at the age of thirty. At the age of thirty-five he was forcibly ordained priest by his father; and Basil, having become archbishop of Cæsarea, made him a bishop against his will in 372. He was pursuing a contemplative life in Isauria, when the death of Basil strengthened him in the resolve to leave the world. But in spite of himself he was drawn back into its troubles, being summoned by the emperor Gratian in 379 to Constantinople, in order that he might restore the condition of Catholics in the new capital, from whom the tyranny of Valens had taken their churches. Here, in a private dwelling, which he had made into the small church of the Resurrection, he reawakened, by the power of his eloquence, the dormant Catholic spirit. For a moment he sat upon the bishop's throne; but being as anxious to abdicate it as ambitious men around him to take possession of it, he speedily bade them farewell, and offered himself, as Jonas, to still the storm of conflicting interest, which arose upon the death of Meletius. The last years of his life he spent in retirement, dying in 389, at the age of sixty-three. He left behind him sermons, letters, and poems. The forty-five sermons take a rank unsurpassed by anything in patristic literature, and have won him the special title of "the Theologian". More than two hundred letters bear witness to his learning and kindliness. His poems, which perhaps should rather be called verses, are most valuable for the dogmatic and historical matter which they contain.

The third of this brotherhood, Gregory of Nyssa, is supposed to have been born in 330, a year after Basil, who, together with his sister Makrina, gave him the first instruction. He became a teacher of eloquence, not at first following the example of his brother and friend. But the earnest words of the latter moved him to renounce the world. He led for some time a solitary life; afterwards the bishops of his brother's province chose him for bishop of Nyssa, in 372, which he took against his will, and met with persecution and banishment until the death of Valens. Sorrow succeeded in the loss of his brother Basil, over whom he held a funeral discourse, going thence to the death-bed of his sister Makrina. Theodosius called him to the Council of 381, where he was among the most esteemed, preaching when his friend St. Gregory was installed in the chair of Constantinople, and at the funeral of Meletius of Antioch, president of the council. Again he preached there at the death of the empress Flacilla. He appears to have died about 394.

He has left a mass of writings which rank no way below those of his two friends. His refutation of Eunomius, defending the previous work of his brother Basil, is deemed by Photius, in elegance of treatment, fullness of thought, strength of argument, the best which has been written against the Arian leader. His great catechism is of the highest value. His work against Apollinaris is equally good. Like his brother, he has written on the work of the six days.

He is remarkable among the Eastern Fathers for the range of his knowledge. A systematic thinker of high order, endeavouring to grasp and establish doctrines in their organic connection, yet recognising faith as in a sphere as much above knowledge as revelation is above reason.[1] He grounds his proofs always upon Scripture, which he esteems the rule and fountain of truth. As a speaker he takes as high a rank as any in his own time and all antiquity. Photius calls his style brilliant and delightful.

What was the joint effect upon the progress of Theology produced by these three Fathers, so closely allied in family and intimate friendship? All the three were equally champions of the Blessed Trinity and the Incarnation. All the three were men who possessed all the knowledge of the time, with great natural abilities, suffering persecution for justice' sake. They are men in whose life and character, learning and ability, no flaw could be found. Masters of thought in the most beautiful of languages, which had lost none of its variety, elegance, or accuracy, whether issuing as the living word from their mouths, or fixed as the written word on their pages, they brought to the cause of truth, in respect of the two great doctrines which underlie the Christian faith, all which natural power could produce when

[1] Nirschl, ii. 212.

wrought into supernatural sanctity; and in this Basil and the two Gregories stand beside Hilary, Ephraem, and Athanasius himself.

Somewhat elder in birth than either of these three, but covering with his episcopate of thirty-five years almost the whole time in which they wrought and acted, was St. Cyril of Jerusalem. Born there in 315, and brought up in pious studies and exercises, he was made a deacon about twenty years of age, and seems to have led a strict ascetic life. At thirty the bishop Maximus made him a priest, and committed to him the office of preaching and of instructing the highest class of catechumens. To this we owe one of the most valuable works which have come down to us, the catechetical lectures which he delivered, eighteen in the Lent of the year 347, to those who were to be "enlightened," and five in the following Easter week, to those who "had received the illumination" of baptism. This occasion led him to expound the belief and practice of the Church at Jerusalem. The eighteen lectures preceding baptism illustrate the Creed; the five following illustrate the mysteries usually veiled at that time under the disciplina arcani. Thus in the fourth of their second series the Eucharist is set forth as a sacrament, in the fifth as a sacrifice. In the former the newly-baptised are enjoined "to be fully persuaded that what seems bread is not bread, though bread by taste, but the Body of Christ, and that what seems wine is not wine, though the taste will have it so, but the Blood of Christ". In the latter, St. Cyril goes through the actual Eucharistic

Liturgy, mentioning the washing of hands, the kiss of peace, the sursum corda, the preface and tris-agion, the conversion, the commemoration of the living and the dead, the Lord's Prayer, the communion, the mode of receiving, and the thanksgiving.

His words upon the eucharistic sacrifice itself are these :

"Then, having hallowed ourselves by these spiritual hymns, we invoke God, the lover of man, to send down the Holy Spirit upon what is lying before us, that He may make the bread the Body of Christ, and the wine the Blood of Christ. For assuredly whatever the Holy Spirit touches, that is sanctified and changed. Then, after having completed the spiritual sacrifice, the unbloody worship, upon that sacrifice of propitiation we invoke God for the common peace of the churches ; for the well-being of the world ; for kings, for soldiers, and allies ; for the sick ; for the suffering ; and, in a word, we all beseech for all who need help, and we offer this sacrifice. Then we make mention of those who have entered into their rest, first patriarchs, prophets, apostles, martyrs, that God by their prayers and intercessions may receive our request. Then also in behalf of those at rest before us, holy fathers and bishops, and in general all of those at rest before us, believing that the greatest help will be to the souls for whom prayer is offered, from the holy and tremendous Sacrifice lying before us."

St. Cyril received the crown of confessorship, since during his episcopate, which lasted from 351 to 386, he was banished during sixteen years ; first, five years under Constantine, and eleven years under Valens, from 367 to 378.

St. Epiphanius, the other great witness of Palestine, was born in 310, before St. Cyril, and died after him in 403, having been for thirty-six years, from 367, metropolitan of Cyprus. Thus his life stretched almost through that agitated fourth century, and he beheld the rise, the tyrannical domination, and the fall of its great heresy. Inferior in style to those hitherto mentioned, he was greatly esteemed for learning and revered for his uniform ascetic piety, and his steadfast witness to the truth. One of his works contains a positive statement of the right doctrine in the midst of the confusion caused by the Arian and semi-Arian conflicts; another describes eighty heresies which down to his time had sprung up: in his own words, "a medicine chest for those who had been bitten by serpents". St. Jerome sums up his praise in the words that he was "the father of almost all the bishops, and a remnant of ancient holiness".

Antioch, from the time its noble bishop and confessor Eustathius had been deposed in 330 by the faction of the Nicomedian Eusebius, was suffering from a disputed succession which entailed a schism, divided the population, and paralysed the legitimate influence of the great see of the East. It had been beyond the power of Athanasius, of Gregory of Nazianzum, of Pope Damasus, to heal this schism: it had defied and outlived Theodosius. But Antioch produced in the latter half of the century the great confessor and renowned preacher, for whose name of John subsequent ages in their admiration have substituted that of the Golden Mouth. Who shall deny greatness to Charlemagne, or eloquence to Chrysostome? He was born at Antioch, probably in 345, the only son of a distinguished officer, and a mother left a widow at twenty, who dedicated her life to the education of her son, and was only not a Monica, because he listened to her teaching and her example from the beginning. He received baptism from Meletius in 369, was made a deacon in 380, and a priest by Flavian in 386. He had devoted his youth to study, severe discipline, and for some years to a solitary life. When at the full age of forty he was appointed preacher in the cathedral church of Antioch, that luxurious capital listened for twelve years to a stream of eloquence which never failed in sounding all the depths of the Christian life.

At the end of these twelve years that unequalled renown led him to be called against his wishes to the most dangerous see of the Church, the arena of endless factions, in a people given up as a prey to courtiers, eunuchs, and barbarian soldiers of fortune. There during six years the preacher, who was unrivalled, shewed himself likewise an admirable bishop, living the strict ascetic life of a saint in the very centre of worldly pomp. Then, banished by the jealousy of rival bishops, and the pride of an offended empress, acting on a feeble mind in possession of absolute power, he passed the last three years of his life an exile in a wild Armenian village among the mountains, proclaiming almost with his last breath the truth which his example was shewing, that "no one can be hurt except by himself". Thus the greatest genius of his day was deposed from what was practically the second place in the Church, became a spectacle to men and angels, like the Apostle to whom he was devoted, and when at length he felt his strength ebbing, and was unable to follow further his enforced journey, he put on the white robe of the newly-baptised, and lay down to rest in the church of a martyr who had warned him in vision of his end, being himself one whose confessorship outshines the glory of many martyrs. And so he was the greatest of all men in word, but greater than himself in deed.

We possess large writings of St. Chrysostome, as a commentator on Scripture, both of the Old and New Testament: upon Genesis, Isaiah, St. Matthew, St. John, the Acts of the Apostles; 246 homilies on the Pauline Apostles; 486 on the whole New Testament. A word of St. Thomas Aquinas is recorded, that he would rather possess his commentary upon St. Matthew than the city of Paris. Of his language Suidas writes that it rushes down in a stronger stream than the stream of the Nile at the cataracts, and that never since the world began has anyone possessed such a fulness of language; while St. Isidore calls him "a wise discloser of the secret things of God". His discourses are likewise dogmatic and polemical, against heretics, Jews, and heathens, and his exile has provided us with 237 letters, a picture of his magnanimous, loving, and pious spirit. There is no more faithful or more manifold witness of Christian truth in the patristic age; no one who has given so vivid a picture of society, heathen and Christian, in his time.

The whole weight of St. Chrysostome's character, his living eloquence, and his writings were given against the Arian heresy, and its offshoots, the Apollinarian and Macedonian. As he was a great corrector of life both by word and conduct, so he was a great builder of doctrine by positive exposition in the language of which he was a master. Cyril, Epiphanius, and Chrysostome may be called the Trio of Jerusalem and Antioch.

CHAPTER X.

THE FLOWERING OF PATRISTIC LITERATURE.

WE now pass to the three great doctors of the West who belong to this period.

Ambrose was born, probably, in the year 340, at Treves, where his father ruled as prætorian prefect of the Gauls. His father's early death in 354 caused him to remove, with his mother and his brother Satyrus, to Rome, where his elder sister Marcellina was already an inmate of a convent. He received a learned education, and, together with his brother, distinguished himself greatly as a lawyer for his gift of speaking. His reputation, combined with his high birth, led Annicius Probus, prætorian prefect of Italy, whose friendship he enjoyed, to recommend him to the emperor Valentinian for governor of the Ligurian and Æmilian provinces. "Go," said Probus to him, " and govern, not as a judge, but as a bishop." So he came to Milan in 373. In the next year the Arian bishop, Auxentius, died, and a successor had to be chosen. The population, partly Arian and partly orthodox, was in a state of excitement.

Ambrose was answerable for the public order, and addressed a great crowd in the church upon the blessing of peace and union. They were listening with delight to his eloquence, when a child exclaimed, "Ambrose for bishop". The word flashed like lightning on the crowd, and was met with universal acclaim. In vain the governor, who was not yet baptised, but only a catechumen, utterly surprised and confounded, excused himself with entreaties and refusals, took to flight, and even attempted, by discrediting himself, to escape. The people would have Ambrose, and none but Ambrose; and the emperor, when appealed to as a last resource, failed him, and was only too happy to have governors whom the people would choose for bishops. Ambrose had to yield; he received baptism, then holy orders in a week's time, and was consecrated bishop the 7th December, 374.

Up to this time the life of Ambrose had been pure and blameless. Then a remarkable change took place. He recognised the will of God to make him a bishop, by an extraordinary choice of the people. He gave himself up to that will with the most perfect obedience. He began a severe life; bestowed most of his goods on the poor and the churches; studied the Holy Scriptures, and the works of the Fathers: Clement of Alexandria, Origen, Didymus, and especially the writings of St. Basil, who had become Archbishop of Cæsarea four years before. This he did under the guidance of the priest Simplician, to give himself the requisite theological training for the office of preacher. In this office he was unwearied, though, as he said himself, being taken from the eloquence of the bar, he had to learn while he was teaching.

I know not whether history offers any fairer vision than the episcopate so strangely begun. When, ten years later, Augustine, a teacher of eloquence, and still in the mazes of error, saw him in the midst of his work, he described him thus : "To Milan I came, to Ambrose the bishop, known to the whole world as among the best of men, Thy devout servant, whose eloquent discourse did at that time strenuously dispense unto Thy people the flower of Thy wheat, the gladness of Thy oil, and the sober intoxication of Thy wine. To him was I unknowingly led by Thee, that by him I might knowingly be led to Thee. That man of God received me like a father, and looked with a benevolent and episcopal kindliness on my change of abode. And I began to love him, not, at first, indeed as a teacher of the truth— which I entirely despaired of in Thy Church—but as a man friendly to myself. And I studiously harkened to him preaching to the people, not with the motive I should, but as it were trying to discover whether his eloquence came up to the fame thereof, or flowed fuller or lower than was asserted ; and I hung on his words intently, but of the matter I was but as a careless and contemptuous spectator. And I was delighted with the pleasantness of his speech, more erudite, yet less cheerful and soothing in manner than that of Faustus."

Again, a little later: "I could not request of him what I wished as I wished, in that I was debarred from hearing and speaking to him by crowds of busy people to whose infirmities he devoted himself. With whom, when he was not engaged (which was but a little time), he either was refreshing his body with necessary sustenance or his mind with reading. But while reading, his eyes glanced over the pages and his heart searched out the sense, but his voice and tongue were silent. Ofttimes, when we had come (for no one was forbidden to enter, nor was it his custom that the arrival of those who came should be announced to him), we saw him thus reading to himself, and never otherwise; and having long sat in silence (for who durst interrupt one so intent?), we were fain to depart, inferring that, in the little time he secured for the recruiting of his mind, free from the clamour of other men's business, he was unwilling to be taken off."[1]

Such was the ordinary day's life in his episcopate of twenty-two years. But Ambrose had also extraordinary work to do. About this very time he had to defend his Church from seizure by the Arian empress Justina; he risked his life, and he saved his Church. Then again, he had to go as ambassador to defend the throne of that same empress's son, Valentinian II., to the court of the usurper Maximus, who had murdered Gratian, and was reigning over Gaul, Spain, and Britain, acknowledged by Theodosius. In truth, his whole episcopate was cast in a terrible time. He witnessed the murder of the two young emperors, first Gratian, then Valentinian, in the bloom of their youth and promise; he was the adviser of the living and the praiser of the dead; he prefigured

---

[1] *Confessions*, lib. v. 13 and vi. 3, Edinburgh translation.

those mediæval bishops who were to be the personal friends and most trusted councillors of sovereigns, who were themselves set as stones in the all-encircling crown of St. Peter's See. And Theodosius, who had large experience of Eastern prelates, when he contrasted the subservience of a Nectarius, which admitted him to the inmost shrine at Constantinople, with the firmness which stopped him, red with the blood of a massacre, at the door in Milan, exclaimed, "In Ambrose alone have I found the bishop". Twice, also, had Ambrose beheld Theodosius narrowly saving his own life and the empire ; and, sorrow of sorrows, he had to weep over his body at last, with the thrice repeated words, "I have loved this man," and to feel that the sun of Rome set with him.

But he who was made a bishop from a neophyte, whose daily life was an unvaried round of doing and suffering, at the mercy of every enquirer, since he might be approached unannounced, who was no less ambassador, minister, councillor of Roman emperors, found time in that episcopate of little more than twenty-two years to leave such works behind him as made him the earliest of the Church's four Western doctors, and one of her chiefest witnesses. He formed into treatises a multitude of commentaries on Scripture which he had delivered as homilies. They have thus come down to us. He has given a work on the duties of the Church's ministers, which answers in Christian literature to Cicero's heathen work. Like all the Fathers of the period, he has dwelt with special zest on the virginal life. Hymns of his are enshrined in the services of the Church. Ninety-one letters written to emperors, bishops, governors, his brother Satyrus, his sister Marcellina, and others, are dogmatic, or moral, or scriptural, or confidential. All of them are valuable for history; all present the perfect Christian in the Roman noble, the Ambrose of his time; his activity for the empire and the Church; his zeal and also his learning; his cultivation and his piety, together with his prudence, kindness, and humility. He was to the West what Basil was to the East: a pair of bishops whose memory is a fragrance to all aftertime.

St. Jerome was born at Stridon, on the borders of Dalmatia; no less than a period of fifteen years is disputed as to the time of his birth, which is placed as early as 331, and as late as 346. I will follow the last date. From the age of seventeen[1] he was educated at Rome, in the school of Donatus, perhaps also by Marius Victorinus, and was baptised there before the death of Pope Liberius in 366. He had to lament passages of his life before he was baptised, but appears from that time to have been full of zeal. In a visit to the court of Treves in 369, he resolved to renounce the world, and formed part of a fervent company of young men at Aquileia during three years from 370 to 373. He then went to the East, and lived in the Syrian desert of Chalcis during five years until 379. At Constantinople

---

[1] Of a letter written in 373 to Heliodorus he says, in his letter to Nepotian: "Dum essem *adolescens, imo pœne puer, et primos impetus lascivientis ætatis cremi duritia refrenarem*". A greater age than twenty-seven can surely not be assigned to such expressions, which would put his birth in 346.

in 380 and 381 he enjoyed the friendship and instruction of St. Gregory Nazianzene. In 382 he was invited to Rome by Pope Damasus, and his residence there until August 385 was an important portion of his life. His reputation for learning and the ascetic life drew round him some of the highest nobility, men and women, such as Pammachius and Oceanus, Domnion, Marcellus, and Rogatian, Paula, her unmarried daughter Eustochium, her widowed daughter Blæsilla, Albina, and her daughters Marcella and Asella, Principia, Lea, Felicitas, and Fabiola. Thus St. Jerome was the means of transplanting the life of the Fathers of the desert into the patrician families of Rome, when the general corruption of Roman society was at one of its worst times.

In 385, Pope Damasus having been succeeded by Siricius, St. Jerome resolved to leave Rome for good with a small company, of which Paula and Eustochium formed part. After visiting Antioch, Jerusalem, Alexandria, and the monasteries of the Nitrian desert in Egypt, they settled at Bethlehem at the end of 386. Here St. Paula founded two monasteries, one for herself and her daughter and companions, one for St. Jerome, his brother, and other friends. In forming and watching over the inmates of these houses St. Jerome spent the remaining years of his life, thirty-four in number, being also engaged in incessant literary work, translation of the Scriptures, comment upon them; devoted to the maintenance of the religious life in himself and all around him, watching with all the keenness of one who loved the purity of the Catholic faith as others love wealth, pleasure, fame, that no error should arise undetected and unpunished; especially no error as to the Person of our Lord, or the honour of His Mother, or the rank of the virginal life, or the necessity of grace, or the magisterium of St. Peter's successor.

The greatest result of St. Jerome's fifty years of intellectual work, from 370 to 420, was that he gave to the Church a translation of the Scriptures which she has mainly used ever since. He was also one of the first masters of the spiritual life. We have 116 letters, the most charming and most original of his writings. They throw light upon the theological questions and struggles, and the ecclesiastical relations of his day, as well as depict his personal character. They are written in a style of which no less a judge than Erasmus has not feared to say: "He has an art of speech which not only leaves behind it all Christian writers, but seems to me to rival even Cicero. At least, unless my love to that holy man deceives me, when I compare a passage of Jerome with one of Cicero, it strikes me as if I missed something, I know not what, even in that prince of eloquence, so great in our Jerome is the variety, the weight of the sentences, the liveliness and many-sidedness of thought."[1] In his own day a man thought himself to be honoured by a single letter from him; but every heretic hated him bitterly. Among his letters may be mentioned that to Oceanus, on the virtues of a bishop; that to Nepotian on the life of the clergy; that to Paulinus on the ascetic life; that to Heliodorus on his

---

[1] Erasmus, *Life of Jerome*, quoted by Nirschl, ii. 423.

life in the desert; that to Lucian on contempt of the world; that to Magnus on reading heathen books. Most perfect in matter as in style are his letters to his chief friends Paula, Fabiola, Marcella, on Christian perfection; Demetrius, Eustochium, on the glory of the Virginal Life; Læta, on the education of her daughter, the younger Paula; Furia, Salvina, on widowhood.

Four of his own age said of him: Augustine, "a most learned man, possessing all the three languages"; Sulpicius, "always reading, absorbed in his books: he gives himself no rest, night or day"; Orosius, "I was retired at Bethlehem, sent by my father, Augustine, to learn the fear of the Lord, seated at the feet of Jerome"; and Prosper,

> "Hebræo, simul et Graio, Latioque venustus
> Eloquio, morum exemplum, mundique magister".

Twelve years after St. Ambrose had been called suddenly, and to his own great astonishment, from the seat of secular government to the chair of bishop in one of the greatest cities of the empire, an event as surprising took place, in which he was an agent, and the consequences of which surpassed even those of his own life and labours. There was then residing in Milan among the imperial professors a young man renowned for his eloquence, passionately devoted to literature, eager for distinction, but leading a heathen life, and tormented with doubt, even as to the Being of God and the certainty of truth. The example, the words, the very look of Ambrose, had an effect upon this young man; but he required a stroke of divine grace, like that which prostrated St. Paul, to convert him; and the Tolle, lege, of the child, directing him to the words of the Apostle, was empowered to work a change as great as in the Apostle himself, when the aspirant after secular fame rose from the baptismal water to become the greatest of the Church's doctors. Augustine was converted at the age of thirty-two years, during nine of which he had been a Manichæan; then he had fallen into doubt, so that he despaired of finding truth in the Church; during fifteen years he had been living in open sin. On Easter Eve, April 25, 387, he received baptism by the hands of St. Ambrose. From that day to the day of his death, forty-three years after, as bishop of Hippo Royal, he had but one thought, the glory of God; but one occupation, to bring all whom he met under the rule of that grace which he had received himself. The mother, whose prayers had done so much for him, was taken away when her work was accomplished; the son, whose precocious beauty of mind and character filled him almost with fear, was taken likewise. Then, after a year spent in Rome, during which he saw the great capital in the untouched splendour which imperial magnificence from the time of Augustus had thrown round it, he returned to his native Thagaste, and set up close to it a company of friends, who led with him the ascetic life. Three years afterwards, in 391, called by an act of charity to Hippo, he was seized upon by the people, against his wishes, for the priesthood. In this act the aged bishop Valerius discerned an answer to his own prayers, who had asked for one to help him in the work of preaching, for which, as a Greek, he was not well qualified, from defective use of the Latin language. In a few years he obtained his wish to make of the priest, whom he had found through the grateful violence of his people, a coadjutor. In 395 Augustine was consecrated bishop, and speedily succeeded to the see. From that time during thirty-five years his life shews a power of intellectual energy almost unequalled, directed by as great a fervour of piety. He appears to have had the faculties of imagination and reasoning both in extraordinary degree, so that they balanced each other and produced a judgment, which never failed in acumen or in moderation; while an inexhaustible treasure of ideas shewed itself on every subject to which he gave his thought. The producing and the criticising mind, so seldom united, were equal in him — both intellect and practice being guided by a glow of piety and charity.

When he became a Christian, he was already acquainted with Greek and Roman philosophy and history. We have still eight philosophical treatises composed in the interval between his baptism and his priesthood. In the forty years which ensued he was engaged in writing against the Manichees between the years 390 and 405; against the Donatists, from 400 to 412; against the Pelagians, from 410 to 430; against the Semipelagians, in 427; against the Arians, in 428. Commentaries upon the Old and New Testament stretch over the whole time: on the Psalms alone an immense volume; on the Gospel of St. John, 124 treatises; on his epistles, 10. On the greatest of his works, the *City of God*, he spent thirteen years, from 413 to 426. And Alaric's transitory seizure of the capital of the world became the occasion of delineating the empire of Him, "Cujus regni non erit finis": a philosophy of history the first and, as yet, the greatest; for human wit, learning, and genius have not yet equalled the doctor of the Church, and he has given to his best imitators what was most worth in them. His positive dogmatic writings likewise stretch over the whole forty years—one alone of these, that on the Blessed Trinity, running from 400 to 416. But the great speaker was an indefatigable preacher: more than four hundred sermons still survive; and 218 letters, some of them deep treatises, give us, like those of St. Jerome, the most manifold instruction as to his times. They would be a monument of him by themselves.

In opposing the heretics above-named, he had to deal with the deepest, the most interesting, and the most intricate questions of all which belong to man in his passage through time to eternity.

Thus, in dealing with the Manichees, he had to touch the Being of God, the origin of evil, the conflict between good and evil in single man and in society. The Donatist schism, already become a heresy, required him to grasp the nature of the Church's unity, the work of her sacraments, the promises made to her. The error of Pelagius was a sort of Western succession to the Eastern heresies on the Person of Christ, attacking the whole Christian life in the individual, inasmuch as it denied the power itself which it was the work of the Incarnate Saviour to produce in man; so that while Nestorius dissolved His Person, the Briton monk made his coming in that Person needless. The *City of God* dealt with the noblest and largest views of history: opened new ranges which had been entirely closed to the greatest writers of Greece and Rome. It answered at once the Gentile and the Jew. What is Tacitus, in his knowledge of human things, to the writer of the letter to Volusianus on the sequence of the ages?

The episcopal life of Augustine begins with the death of Theodosius, and witnessed through all its thirty-five years the ever-increasing and irretrievable decline of the empire. Nor for this did he falter in loyalty to the two hapless sons of the empire's former Saviour. It is among the advantages of his writings that they supply us with full information upon the respective positions of the spiritual and the civil power; of the mode with which heresy was treated by the actual legislation; of the respective value belonging to civil liberty and spiritual truth.

I shrink with dismay from the attempt to express the moral and intellectual work achieved by the life and the writings of St. Augustine. Down to his time the Greek mind had certainly had a large preponderance in exhibiting the theological construction of doctrine. St. Augustine's single weight made the balance even. He was more, indeed, to the line of bishops and peoples rising after him in the West than all the writers of the East together to those who came after them; but this is because the succeeding ages in the East were ages of defeat or of extermination: those in the West of growth and expansion, after trials and revolutions. The Pope made a new world out of Charlemagne; but schism, death, and corruption followed in the track of Mahomet. Instead of a Pope, enfeebled nations had Photius; instead of Rome, Byzantium. It is an unique fact in history that the writings of a bishop, whose see was a country town in Africa during thirty years at the beginning of the fifth century, should have been studied through thousands of monasteries for hundreds of years. The false Prophet had silenced in the churches of Africa, from Egypt to the Atlantic, the voice of prayer and praise to the Triune God: in him Arius and Pelagius had a joint triumph. But St. Augustine, when his country died, lived in his writings. From them the teachers of nations yet to be born drew light and consolation. The great African formed the spirit of Europe. And when, after full seven hundred years, the power of original thought reappeared in Northern tribes who had become Christian peoples, at length, by study of his works, doctors who can be named in the same breath with him matured and completed his doctrine, under the magisterium of the Church. St. Athanasius, St. John Chrysostome, St. Cyril, and St. John of Damascus were not so fortunate. The birthplace of Christian ascetic life is still the very home and centre of false doctrine and sensual life; and nowhere is Christ more vehemently scorned and denied than where His greatest teachers proclaimed His Godhead and Manhood, in the cities of Alexandria, Antioch, and Constantinople.

The see of Alexandria was at the height of its strength and influence when it was held, during thirty-two years, by one of the greatest Eastern doctors who completed the defence of the Blessed Trinity, effected by his predecessor Athanasius. The date of St. Cyril's birth is not known : he must have been at least forty years of age when he succeeded his uncle Theophilus, in 412. He died in 444, and during this whole period, from the firmness of his character, and his great ability while he stood at the head of the whole Egyptian church, would seem to have been a most powerful personage in the Eastern empire. He was contemporary with St. Augustine during sixty years, and took rank as one of the greatest defenders of the Church's belief in his day. When the erroneous teaching of Diodore of Tarsus and Theodore of Mopsuestia found an exponent in the disciple who had been exalted to the see of Constantinople, Cyril met his attack at every point, and set forth the doctrine of the Incarnation with a force equal to that of Athanasius, Augustine, or Leo. He shewed the same acuteness, clearness, and precision ; and he had the great honour to preside over a General Council, with the rank and commission of Pope Celestine superadded to his own dignity. In that council, and by his advocacy, the Blessed Virgin appeared manifestly in her character as destroyer of heresy ; inasmuch as the Church, confirming her title of Mother of God, defended thereby the Godhead of her Son, together with His

Manhood. A great mass of St. Cyril's writings is extant, though by no means all which he composed. Besides those numerous works in which he refuted Nestorius, he answered the emperor Julian's attack on the Christian faith, an answer which has the same sort of value as Origen's reply to Celsus. He has left a work of great power on the Blessed Trinity, so that he closed the controversy in the East on that subject, and was called by them "the Seal of the Fathers," as no one after him arose so great. Especially, he was devoted to commenting on the Scriptures, on every part of which he is said to have written. He was, likewise, a preacher of great renown, so that the Eastern bishops recommended his homilies to be learnt by heart. Seventy of his letters also remain. In all things of which he speaks, he speaks with clear unfaltering voice, incapable of double meaning, never sheltering opposite doctrines "with the stammering lips of ambiguous formularies". Particularly, his witness as to the belief of the Church in his day, respecting the Blessed Eucharist, is decisive. Of many passages, one may be cited :

"Pointing to them, He said, This is My Body, and this is My Blood, that you may not think what meets the eye is a figure, but that the oblations are really changed into the Body and Blood of Christ by some inscrutable secret of the Almighty God, by partaking of which we receive the life-giving and sanctifying power of Christ".

Theodoret, the learned bishop of Cyrus, was born to his parents after a long childless marriage, between the years 386-393. He received a most pious education in a monastery near to Antioch, his birthplace. He entered into the clergy early, and gave, on the death of his parents, his whole substance to the poor. On account of his extraordinary learning and ability he was made bishop of Cyrus, against his-will, when somewhat more than thirty years of age, and his diocese contained eight hundred churches. He laboured long to convince the various heretics who divided his diocese, and was often stoned for his pains. He was a pupil of Theodore of Mopsuestia, and among his comrades were Nestorius and John the Patriarch of Antioch ; and, when the heresy broke out, he was led to take the wrong side for a time, though, afterwards, he was reconciled with St. Cyril, and in the end condemned Nestorius.

Hardly any Greek writer has more distinguished himself than Theodoret. As expositor of Scripture, he bears a high rank, both in his interpretation of the Psalms and the Song of Songs, his commentary on the prophets, and the Pauline epistles. He has given, in twelve books, a defence of the Christian faith—the last, and by some thought the best, of those written by the old apologists. Similar in style and ability are his ten discourses on Providence, the best of their kind. He has left also a large number of letters, remarkable both in style and matter. There is a blot upon his writings, in that those which he wrote in the first instance against St. Cyril, lie under the censure of the fifth Council. He was deposed at the Robber Council of Ephesus, but appealed to St. Leo, in a letter which fully maintains the supreme authority of St. Peter's See. St. Leo restored him, and he sat accordingly in the council of Chalcedon. He then lived in peace to the end of his life, in 458. In the time both of his birth and death he was almost the exact contemporary of St. Leo. He closes the magnificent roll of Greek writers in this period, as St. Leo that of the Latin.

But the writings left by St. Leo, that is, his sermons and letters, are too intimately bound up with his government of the Church in his twenty-one years' pontificate to be dealt with separately. I will rather here touch upon some points which arise from considering the collective mass of this patristic theology, whose chief representatives have passed before us ; while narrowness of space has made it necessary to omit a far greater number.

It is difficult to convey an adequate notion of the vastness, as a whole, of the intellectual work on which the fifteen Fathers already named, and so many others who belong equally to this period, spent their lives. We may term it the mind of the Church working from the basis of Tradition upon Scripture. The product is a precision and enlargement of the language in which doctrine is stated, a result obtained by the theological sense thus called forth and matured. The period of time in which this happened forms the first stadium of theology. The Tradition which I here mean is that inherited Christian faith in which each man grew up in his own place : for instance, the Roman at Rome, the Alexandrian at Alexandria, the Antiochene at Antioch. Again, the inherited temper and principles of interpretation in the great schools, especially of Alexandria and Antioch, from which the bishops of churches connected with them would be often drawn. When the 318 Fathers, who were all Easterns but five, came together at Nicæa, this Tradition as held by each was the basis of their judgment upon the matters submitted to them. The decrees of the council expressed the result, upon which, when Pope Sylvester had set his seal, the Church rested evermore.

But as upon a basis never to be shaken for the further structure, I take the intellectual history of the next hundred and thirty years in the minds of all these Fathers to be a carrying out of the doctrinal conclusions then reached. The mind and heart of each had been formed by the daily life which he had passed in his own place. Thus St. Isidore of Pelusium, friend and contemporary of the patriarch St. Cyril, addresses a short letter to a monk who had fallen into the heresy of Macedonius : " If our God and Saviour, when He took manhood,[1] handed down that the most holy Spirit was the complement of the Divine Trinity, and is numbered with the Father and the Son in the invocation of holy baptism as delivering from sins, and makes common bread upon the mystical table the proper Body in which He became incarnate, how, madman, do you teach that the Holy Ghost is something created, or made, or of servile nature, not kin and consubstantial with the imperial, world-creating, royal Substance. For if He be

---

[1] Παρέδωκε. This word expresses the fact which I am noting. St. Isidore, Ep. i. 109.

servile, number Him not with the Lord ; if a creature, place Him not with the Creator. But He is so united, and so named together : for we must believe Christ, the accurate dogmatist of such things, who safely teaches what concerns His own Substance, even if your opinion be not so, who boast to be wiser, and to know the things of heaven better than God, or rather wag your tongue boldly against Him."

Now I conceive that such an argument as this was valid against the Arian, Semiarian, Nestorian, or Macedonian heresies, and every modification of them which individual phantasy might raise ; while it was drawn from what had come down by direct historic descent from Christ in the Church, and the existence of which in the Church was quite independent of the Scriptures, which also recorded it.

The baptismal and the eucharistic rite here referred to are only specimens of the vast body of truth which was enshrined in the service of the Church, known to every Christian in many parts, to the Church's own ministers in all, but a sealed book to the outside world. The Fathers who wrote in this period were in full possession of this treasure. And their possession of it must be borne in mind when we consider the fervour with which they threw themselves one and all upon the study of the Scriptures, both of the Old and New Testaments. To suppose that the Tradition here marked out was something uncertain, while the text of Scripture was certain, would be entirely to misrepresent the patristic position. The home of their dearest thoughts and habits was one vast Tradition, which comprehended the visible fabrics of the churches everywhere erected, the faith taught in them, and the worship in which it was embodied, as well as the Scriptures which were in the guardianship of the church, and to deliver which to the heathen was termed "treason". All this constituted a condition of things hard to be understood by those whose notion of a religion amounts to the lucubration of a single mind upon a book, lying helplessly subject to every reader.

The danger of the emergent heresy was that which in the first instance moved to the defence Athanasius and all who followed him. A very large mass of writings, all those which not only set forth the truth positively, but refute the opposite error, spring directly from the attack of Arius. But the natural ardour of the Christian spirit to unfold and communicate itself must be taken into account in all these writings.

I would now dwell specially on the devotion shewn to the study of Scripture.

Christian schools of great renown for learning flourished before the Nicene Council, at Alexandria, Cæsarea in Palestine, and Antioch, afterwards at Nisibis, Edessa, Rhinokorura. Alexandria and Antioch especially were centres and lights of Christian knowledge during the whole of this period. Ornaments of the former are to be named: Athanasius, Didymus the blind, Cyril. Representatives of the latter are Eusebius, bishop of Emesa, who died in 360; Diodorus, bishop of Tarsus, who died in 390; Theodore, bishop of Mopsuestia, who died in 428; and his brother Polychronius, bishop of Apamea.

Of the several principles of interpretation which distinguished these schools, it is only needful to say a word, which I will take from Cardinal Newman. First, of the literal:

"The immediate source of that fertility in heresy which is the unhappy distinction of the Syrian church was its celebrated Exegetical School. The history of that school is summed up in the broad characteristic fact, on the one hand, that it devoted itself to the literal and critical interpretation of Scripture; and on the other, that it gave rise first to the Arian and then to the Nestorian heresy."[1]

Of the mystical, he continues: "In all ages of the Church her teachers have shewn a disinclination to confine themselves to the mere literal interpretation of Scripture. Her most subtle and powerful method of proof, whether in ancient or modern times, is the mystical sense which is so frequently used in doctrinal controversy as on many occasions to supersede any other. In the early centuries we find this method of interpretation to be the very ground for receiving as revealed the doctrine of the Holy Trinity. Whether we betake ourselves to the Antenicene writers or the Nicene, certain texts will meet us which do not obviously refer to that doctrine, yet are put forward as palmary proofs of it. On the other hand, if evidence be wanted of the connection of heterodoxy and biblical criticism in that

[1] *Arians*, Appendix, p. 414.

age, it is found in the fact that not long after their contemporaneous appearance in Syria, they are found combined in the person of Theodore of Heraclea, so called from the place both of his birth and his bishopric, an able commentator and an active enemy of St. Athanasius, though a Thracian, unconnected except by sympathy with the patriarchate of Antioch. The case had been the same in a still earlier age : the Jews clung to the literal sense of the Old Testament and rejected the Gospel; the Christian Apologists proved its divinity by means of the allegorical. The formal connection of this mode of interpretation with Christian theology is noticed by Porphyry, who speaks of Origen and others as borrowing it from heathen philosophy both in explanation of the Old Testament and in defence of their own doctrine. It may almost be laid down as an historical fact that the mystical interpretation and orthodoxy will stand or fall together."

We may safely say that the devotion to the study of Scripture was common in this period to all who were zealous and learned in both schools. But take the lives of three men as an illustration of Cardinal Newman's division and analysis of spiritual affinities.

About the year 370, when Basil became archbishop of Cæsarea, two young men were studying together at Antioch. They were intimate friends and fellow-pupils together of a man who had received a learned education at Athens, and had gained high repute through his strict life as monk and priest at Antioch, and his strenuous defence of Christian truth against the heathen under the emperor Julian, and against heretics under the emperor Valens. Julian mocked his emaciated frame as a punishment of the gods. The great Meletius promoted him in 378 to be metropolitan of Tarsus; as such he was present at the council of Constantinople in 381, and he consecrated Nectarius to that see on the cession of it by St. Gregory. This was Diodorus, who wrote many books, commenting on almost all the Scriptures, among them on St. Paul's epistles. He turned away from the allegoric interpretation, seeking to expound only the literal historical sense.

Of his pupils, one was Theodore, who devoted himself with the keenest zeal and ascetic severity to the cloistral life and study. He suffered, however, a relaxation of this at one time, and was recalled to it by the earnest exhortation of his co-pupil John, afterwards St. Chrysostome. Theodore is described as a man of extraordinary eloquence, learning, and literary activity. But the boldness of his spirit led him in interpreting Scripture and dealing with mysteries to follow his own track. Thus a very early work on the Psalms gave offence. Cardinal Newman thus analyses his treatment:[1] "Bent on ascertaining the literal sense, Theodore was naturally led to the Hebrew text instead of the Septuagint, and thence to Jewish commentators. Jewish commentators naturally suggested events and objects short of evangelical as the fulfilment of the prophetical announcements, and when it was possible an ethical sense instead of a prophetical. The eighth chapter of Proverbs ceased

[1] *Arians*, Appendix, 418.

to bear a Christian meaning, because, as Theodore maintained, the writer of the book had received the gift not of prophecy but of wisdom. The Canticles must be interpreted literally; and then it was but an easy, or rather a necessary, step to exclude the book from the canon. The book of Job, too, professed to be historical, yet what was it really but a Gentile drama? He also gave up the books of Chronicles and Ezra, and strange to say, the Epistle of St. James, though it was contained in the Peschito version of his church. He denied that Psalms xxii. and lxix. applied to our Lord; rather he limited the Messianic passages of the whole book to four, of which the eighth Psalm was one and the forty-fifth another. The rest he explained of Hezekiah and Zerubbabel, without denying that they might be accommodated to an evangelical sense. He explained St. Thomas's words, 'My Lord and my God,' as a joyful exclamation, and our Lord's, 'Receive ye the Holy Ghost,' as an anticipation of the day of Pentecost. As might be expected, he denied the verbal inspiration of Scripture. Also, he held that the deluge did not cover the earth; and, as others before him, he was heterodox on the doctrine of original sin, and denied the eternity of punishment."

"Maintaining that the real sense of Scripture was not the scope of a Divine Intelligence, but the intention of the mere human organ of inspiration, Theodore was led to hold not only that that sense was but one in each text, but that it was continuous and single in a context, that what was the subject of the composition in one verse must be the subject in the next, and that if a Psalm was historical or prophetical in its commencement, it was the one or the other to its termination. Even that fulness of meaning, refinement of thought, subtle versatility of feeling, and delicate reserve or reverent suggestiveness, which poets exemplify, seem to have been excluded from his idea of a sacred composition."

The fellow-student and friend, whose powerful word drew back the young Theodore to the ascetic life, was St. Chrysostome, who became, as we know, the most renowned commentator on Scripture of the Antiochene school. But while he was the clearest exponent of the literal sense, he was free from the negative spirit of the school, being full of the love of God and man. His writings have made him a doctor of the Church; his sufferings have placed him in the role of her confessors with the halo of a martyr.

The history of Theodore is that, in 392, he became bishop of Mopsuestia, a city of Cilicia, and sat for thirty-six years, until his death in 428. He took the keenest interest in all Church matters. He is said to have written ten thousand tracts; his comments on Scripture filled forty-one volumes; he was the master of Nestorius, and the real author of his heresy, just before the promulgation of which he died. His writings were introduced to the knowledge of the Christians of Mesopotamia, Adiabene, Babylonia, and the neighbouring countries. He was called by those churches absolutely "the Interpreter," and it eventually became the very profession of the

Nestorian communion to follow him as such. "The doctrine of all our Eastern churches," says the council under the Patriarch Marabas, "is founded on the creed of Nicæa; but in the exposition of the Scriptures we follow St. Theodore." "We must, by all means, remain firm to the commentaries of the great Commentator," says the council under Sabarjesus; "whoso shall in any manner oppose them, or think otherwise, be he anathema." "No one since the beginning of Christianity," adds Cardinal Newman,[1] "except Origen and St. Augustine, has had such great influence on his brethren as Theodore."

Theodore and St. Chrysostome belonged originally to the same school, and had the same teacher. Their lives ran out to different issues. Perhaps, however, another parallel which the life of Theodore offers to that of St. Augustine is even more instructive : Theodore was born about 350, he became bishop in 392, he lived to 428 ; St. Augustine was born in 354, became bishop in 395, lived to 430. The writings which were to form the theology of the Western church, and the writings which were to form the mind and temper of the heretical communion which, "in the time of the Caliphs, was at the head of as many as twenty-five archbishops, extended from China to Jerusalem, and whose numbers, with those of the Monophysites, are said to have surpassed those of the Greek and Latin churches together," came forth from Hippo and from Mopsuestia exactly at the same time ; were drawn by fervent minds from the

---

[1] Quoting Lengerke de Ephraem Syro, *Arians*, p. 417.

same Scriptures: the one guided by the ecclesiastical sense, the other by the literal sense, according to his private judgment. A striking example of the different treatment of the same passage by the two commentators may be given here. Theodore, writing on the words, "He delivered us from the power of darkness, and translated us into the kingdom of the Son of His love," says, "He said not, His Son, but the Son of His love. For we do not become partakers of the kingdom of God the Word, but of the man assumed, in whose honour we participate because of the likeness of nature between us, when we shew a disposition towards Him by our works, whence, too, He called Him the Son of His love, as not being by nature the Son of the Father, but by love made worthy of adoption." St. Augustine says, "the Son of His love is no other than He who was begotten of His Substance". He[1] who gave this interpretation is at present the greatest doctor of the universal Church, while a few thousands in the Kurd mountains still profess the Nestorian belief, of which Theodore was parent; but likewise he can claim to be the father of modern rationalism, and his latest posterity bear striking marks of their descent.

Almost all the writers of this period are commentators upon Scripture; many, likewise, delivered as homilies their comments. Among the former are Eusebius of Cæsarea, Athanasius, Didymus, Ephraem, Basil, Gregory

---

[1] Theodore of Mopsuestia's *Commentary on St. Paul*, edited by Mr. Swete, vol. i. p. 260, to whom I am indebted for the quotation from *St. Augustine De Trinitate*, xv. 19.

of Nyssa, Cyril of Alexandria, Theodoret, Hilary, Ambrose, Augustine, and especially Jerome; among the latter are Ephraem, Basil, Gregory of Nyssa, but especially Chrysostome, Hilary, Ambrose, and Augustine. Closely allied to these is a third class—the Preachers. Of these, the most distinguished are, in the East, Eusebius of Cæsarea, Athanasius, the three Cappadocians, Basil and the two Gregories, Ephraem, Cyril of Alexandria, Asterius of Amasea. In the West, Ambrose, Augustine, Leo I., Peter Chrysologus, Maximus of Turin. They preached on passages of Scripture, on points of belief and morals, on festivals, on martyrs and saints, funeral discourses; and if the matter of these discourses belongs to a higher range of knowledge and feeling than anything which has come down to us from heathen Greece or Rome, so in many cases the mode of saying it equals that of those who used the two great languages with the greatest force at the time of their greatest purity.

This period produces many treatises which give a compendious statement of Christian doctrine. Such are Gregory of Nyssa's greater catechesis; Augustine's Handbook to Laurentius; Ambrose on the offices of ministers; Rufinus on the Apostles' Creed; Augustine's treatises on marriage; on the Church maintaining its unity against the Donatists; Chrysostome on the Priesthood; and Gregory of Nazianzum on the same subject in the verses concerning his flight; Pacian upon Penance.

Similar to these are all the works intended for the

instruction of catechumens by Chrysostome, Ambrose, and Augustine.

But amidst the immense inward movement caused by heresy, and the efforts to refute it, the defence of the Christian faith against the two permanent enemies outside, Judaism and heathenism, could not fail to be invigorated. Against Judaism valuable works were written by Eusebius of Cæsarea, Ephraem, and in eight homilies by Chrysostome. The twenty months' reign of the emperor Julian, and his efforts to depress the Christian cause, drew, perhaps, special attention to his writings. They called forth answers from Gregory of Nazianzum, Ephraem, and especially a work of great importance from Cyril of Alexandria.

The exposure of heathenism in general was conducted in the East by Athanasius in the two beautiful treatises, not the least interest of which lies in that they mark his mind before the Arian controversy arose—a mind of great ability, looking out in its virginal Christian ardour upon the heathen world, with its deceptions, impurities, and idolatries; while Theodoret, a hundred and thirty years later, closes the lists with the most elaborate and complete refutation of Gentile maladies by the practised controversialist. Cyril of Alexandria here also distinguished himself. In the West, Firmicus Maternus, Commodianus, Orosius. Again, Ambrose and Prudentius, in their works against Symmachus, as the champion of Cicero's "Immortal Gods," the defenders of the Capitol and Patrons of Rome, in which point of appreciation the city prefect of the fourth century agreed with the old Roman orator; while Augustine, in his great work, called in faith, learning, and truth in equal force to demolish the false worship whose only remaining root was the patriotic association with it of a lost temporal dominion.

The Fathers of this period were remarkable for the unanimous impulse with which they threw themselves on the exposition of Scripture. I think they were scarcely less unanimous in the burst of praise and admiration with which they met the public manifestation of the cloistral life, and that upon which it rested— the choice and maintenance of virginity. It has already been said how Athanasius, taking refuge in Rome from the persecution of the Arianising bishops, who had got possession of Constantine, introduced into the West the knowledge of St. Anthony's life in the desert. At a later period, after Anthony's death, he drew out a most attractive picture of his former teacher, which, as soon as it appeared in the year 365, was highly valued, and kindled among all ranks in East and West a fervent admiration for the ascetic life of the monks.

St. Anthony himself was born in Upper Egypt in 251, renounced the world at the age of twenty, and lived from that time in the desert, where he died at the age of 105. The renown of his sanctity, his wisdom, and his wonder-working power went through the whole empire, so that even Constantine and his sons besought, by letter, his intercession.

Pachomius, born of heathen parents in the Thebais forty years later than Anthony, was the first to build a monastery in the Nile island of Tabenna, while the monks of St. Anthony lived apart in cells. He thus founded the cenobitic life. In the first female convent which he founded his sister also entered. He made a rule for his monks, according to which, at his death in 348, three thousand monks were living in various houses, under the supervision of one superior abbot. A hundred years later the monks of the monasteries which followed his rule numbered fifty thousand.

It is not to be supposed that the life which now shewed itself, as the choice of so many, was a new thing in the Christian Church. On the contrary, four daughters of one of the first deacons, Philip, are said to have practised it in their father's house, whilst St. Petronilla and St. Thecla pursued it under the guidance of St. Peter and St. Paul. All through the time of persecution this life was cultivated in the secret of the domestic home, while it came occasionally to light in the splendid deeds of the martyrs; and Agnes, the Roman maiden of thirteen, who died to maintain it, in which act she was by no means solitary, invested it with a halo of glory.

But now the Church had won, in the conversion of the emperor and its consequences, what, looked at on one side, seemed to be, and was, a prodigious victory over the world; while, looked at on the other side, it led to an inroad of the world upon the Church. For the first time in Christian history, godliness might seem to have become gain, and the profession of faith in the Crucified One to lead to temporal honour and riches.

Undoubtedly the chief danger which beset the Church through all that fourth century was the crowding of worldly men and women into its ranks, in whom the profession of the Christian faith was not accompanied by the practice of a Christian life. The most terrible of heresies itself had, no doubt, its own own secret spiritual root,[1] but the extreme peril into which it brought the Church was caused by the attempt of court-bishops to use the converted imperial power for the purposes of their own ambition. They were seen at Sardica content to rend the Church in two, provided they might govern under the name of Constantius.

Now, to all this the life, which arose in the deserts of Egypt, under the auspices of St. Anthony, was presently collected and ordered under the rule of St. Pachomius, and was thence spread through the world in ever-increasing numbers of male and female communities, offered the strongest opposition. It was most fitting that the first monastery should be founded at Tabenna in the year when the first council exercised the intrinsic freedom of the Church to deliberate, so that the inherent force of grace, in its completest mastery over the springs of nature, should shew its capacity to meet and overcome all the difficulties which the freedom from heathen persecution might bring with it. If the cross could not exalt the human heart so as to fix it upon God alone, the victory over a Roman emperor was only the passage through worldliness to decay and even dissolution.

---

[1] A wonderful disclosure of this root may be seen in Cardinal Newman's treatise, *Causes of the Rise and Success of Arianism*.

We may therefore feel that it was a fidelity to Christian instinct which led Athanasius, and Basil, and Gregory of Nazianzum, and Ambrose, and Jerome, and Chrysostome, and Ephraem, and Augustine, to pour themselves out in the praises of the virginal life. But the greatest of all praise is *practice*—and in them too the deed preceded the word, either in their first choice or, if they had failed in that, in the surrender of the whole man which they were able to offer from the time of their conversion. And in this respect I know not whether the choice of St. Augustine, when converted at thirty-two, is not as striking as that of St. Anthony when at twenty he gave up the world, and the devotion of the bishop instituting the cenobitic life in his household and his clergy as remarkable as that of the ascetic in the wilderness. The type of St. Nilus, who in middle age left his palace as prefect of Constantinople, under the counsel of St. Chrysostome, carrying with him his son to become a monk on Mount Sinai, and leading his wife to a similar choice, is as strong as that of St. Ambrose, called from the uprightness of natural justice to the episcopal throne on which he exercised all supernatural virtues, and commended the mother of his Lord as the ensample and mistress of virginity. Certainly, to find a Father who does not act and write in favour of the virginal life is about as easy as to find a saint who is not devoted to our Blessed Lady.

St. Basil became the legislator of the cenobitic life for numberless monasteries which followed his rule in the Eastern empire. An important order of regular clergy took its origin from the very household of St. Augustine, and runs through the subsequent ages of the Church to the present day. The Christian ministry itself was from the beginning carried out according to the instructions of St. Paul : " Do thou then suffer hardship as a good soldier of Jesus Christ. No soldier involves himself in secular business, that he may please his Commander." But of all secular business there was none that so involved the whole life as the condition of marriage, which was a necessary and a perpetual servitude to the world. The only restriction which at first could be imposed in a society where marriage was universal, would be that bishops and deacons should be chosen from those who had only married once. But as soon as a generation had grown up which had the example of our Lord and His mother before them, the custom had become universal for the ministers of the Church to live either the continent or the virginal life. But now in this fourth century a vast accession of persons outside the ministry were being drawn powerfully to this life ; and what I would note is that the Fathers, by their example first and by their writings afterwards, offered them the most cordial welcome. St. Basil, St. Gregory of Nazianzum, St. Chrysostome, St. Ambrose, St. Jerome, St. Augustine, vie with each other in drawing all who come within their individual influence in either sex to this life. Regard for it forms the very inmost texture of their minds. A Christianity which ignored it would certainly not be their Christianity ; but a Christianity which reprobated it would be in their judgment an obscene apostasy which proclaimed that man was incapable of living a higher than the mere animal life.

The entrance of the religious orders from the fourth century onwards, as a fresh factor into the everlasting conflict between the Church and the world, is an event of the greatest moment. These Fathers loved the religious life because they saw in it the most perfect surrender of the whole human being to God. They did not know, when they first welcomed it, that the great work of Roman civilisation was about to be overthrown in the Western empire: that France, and Spain, and Britain, and Illyria, even Africa, and last of all Italy, were about to become the prey of ruthless and savage conquerors; that every misery would have to be endured by the inhabitants of populous cities; that wide lands would be reduced to desolation; that the only power left standing would be the Christian ministry in virtue of its organisation, linked together in one mass by its Primacy. Finally, that during hundreds of years the religious Orders springing up from the time of Constantine, and having their cradle in the deserts of Egypt, would be planted like so many fortresses of Christian life in all these desolated lands, and gradually create a race of Christian men and women, whose law should be the law of the Gospel, whose ensamples should be our Lord and His Mother for the two sexes, out of furious and hostile tribes, rude, violent, and without cohesion.

But the preference of the Fathers for the virginal over the married life was purely a religious preference. It had no political calculation in it. It had no anticipation of coming events. It may be said to be all gathered up in one word of the Teacher of the nations: "I would wish you to be without care. The unmarried cares for the things of the Lord, how he shall please the Lord; the married cares for the things of the world, how he shall please his wife. And he is divided. The unmarried woman and the virgin cares for the things of the Lord that she may be holy in body and in spirit; the married cares for the things of the world, how she shall please her husband."

To which we may add as a comment words of the first desert-father himself:[1] "We have heard St. Paul, when he came to speak of the honours of virginity, say, I have no command of God. He had no command, because not all can bear that heavy yoke. Therefore it was left to the choice of those who can bear it. Virginity is an unbroken seal: a perfect similitude which changes not: a spiritual and holy sacrifice: a watch-tower, affording an outlook upon the way leading to perfection: a diadem forming a wreath of excellencies: the sweet dew which gives freshness to all creatures. It is the gospel of life which reveals secrets hidden from all ages and generations. Truly the greatest inheritance and possession. He who despises it insults God and the angels."

And finally a few words of the writer[2] of St. Anthony's life give the source of this wonder: "'He hath regarded the low estate of His handmaiden: for behold from henceforth all generations shall call me blessed'. What

---

[1] St. Antonii, *Serm.* sect. xvii. (Migne, vol. xl. p. 974).
[2] St. Athanasius on Luke i. 26.

a thing is virginity! For as to all other virtues he who will exercise them is schooled by the law, but virginity, surpassing the law, and directing to a higher end the purpose of life, is a token of the life to come, and an image of angelic purity. Much might be said on it; but not to spend time on what is plain, I will by one single remark shew the greatness of this virtue. For God, the Word, the Lord of all, when it was the will of the Father to raise up and make all things new, chose that none other than a Virgin should become the Mother of the Body He was about to bear. And so it was done. And thus the Lord sojourned among us as Man; that as all things were made by Him, so also virginity should be made from Him, and through Him this grace further be given to men, and increase and abide among them. Now, what a glory this is to virgins, what a proof of the godhead in Him, we may know by this. If the parents of the holy martyrs are conspicuous for the fortitude of their children, and Sarah rejoices in the birth of Isaac, and they are blessed who have a seed in Sion and a household in Jerusalem (Isaiah xxxv. 10), as the prophet says, What would be the glory of the holy virgin and divine Mary,[1] in that she became and is called the Mother of the Word according to the generation of the flesh? For an army of angels hymned this divine offspring, and the woman who raised up her voice cried, 'Blessed is the womb that bare Thee, and the breasts which Thou has sucked'. And Mary, too, herself the Mother of the Lord and the Ever-virgin, knowing what

[1] Τῆς ἁγίας Παρθένου καὶ θεοειδοῦς Μαρίας.

had taken place in her, said, 'From henceforth all generations shall call me blessed'. But what was done in Mary is a glory to all virgins. For from that stem they hang as virginal branches."

The eremitic and cloistral life was illustrated by rules and precepts given for it by the great masters of it themselves, such as Anthony, Pachomius, Orsiesius, Isaias, Evagrius, Basil, the two Makarius, Cassian, whose work became of universal use in the ages following him in the West ; and again, by lives of its founders, given by Athanasius, Palladius, Theodoret, Jerome, and Rufinus.

In close connection with this stands the mystical life, of which Makarius the Great gives the first germs and principles ; while the full expansion is seen in the work of the accomplished theologian whose name is concealed under that of Dionysius, and who has given an introduction to the better understanding of the symbolic acts and ceremonies of the Church, for the use of the clergy.[1]

With regard to history in this period, the work carried down to the peace of the Church by Eusebius of Cæsarea was continued by Socrates, Sozomen, and Theodoret in the East; by Rufinus in the West. But I must candidly confess that if the records of the first three centuries, which are all that the learning and diligence of Eusebius could draw from the library of Cæsarea, are scanty, and leave untold a multitude of things necessary to form anything like a connected history, much more

[1] Nirschl, ii. 140.

do the fragmentary and desultory statements of his successors disappoint. A real history of the period, from the time at which Eusebius ends to the death of St. Leo would be of incalculable value and interest. If we had but a Christian Ammianus to describe reigns of such importance, and events so striking as the Eastern and Western empire discarding heathenism and assuming the Christian faith, it would be some consolation. The ancient writers whom I have named seem to me, in these particular works, quite unworthy of the grandeur of the theme which was to be recorded.

But the history of heresies, made by the same Theodoret, by Epiphanius, by Philastrius, and by Augustine, stands on quite a different footing, and that commencement of a literary history made by St. Jerome in his catalogue of illustrious men. Wherever Christian belief comes into question, there strength and accuracy appear. The failure seems to be in the historic mind, when considering the causes and connection of things, and the action and counteraction of the two great societies, the natural and the supernatural, in human affairs. This power is shewn in great force in the *City of God*, and I doubt not that the writer of that work could have given a history of the hundred years preceding his own death which would have satisfied the need of future times. If we only possessed a picture of Rome, such as presented itself to Augustine in the year after his conversion and his mother's death, which he spent there before he returned to Africa, and of the empire which in that very year Theodosius was delivering from the gripe of the usurper Maximus, and celebrating the conversion of the senate to the Christian faith, such a work would have an interest not surpassed by any which the great African has left. But neither from him nor from any other have we anything approaching to a continuous history of a time so enthralling in the revolutions which it witnessed, so terrible in the reverses of fortune, so magnificent in the saints which it produced.

There is, however, an immense treasure left by the Fathers, in the large number of letters which remain of so many. Among these we may name Athanasius, Ambrose, Basil, Gregory of Nazianzum, Chrysostome, Paulinus of Nola, Jerome, Augustine, Nilus, who has left more than a thousand; Isidore, who has left more than two thousand. So far as I know, this is a mine of knowledge which has been very imperfectly worked. There is nothing in Greek and Roman literature like these letters, except those of Cicero. And as these shed no dubious light upon the character of the great Roman and the circumstances of his time, so, I doubt not that if the letters of these saints were studied as those of Cicero have been, a similar result as to their individual characters, and a great enlargement of knowledge on scientific as well as ecclesiastical questions of their most important century, would ensue. Whether it would be in the power of anyone who had mastered their whole contents to construct a satisfactory history of the period, I can form no opinion. They rank, at any rate, among the choicest remains of ancient writings which we possess, and to live for a time, as it were, in the bodily presence of Athanasius, or Basil, or Augustine, or Chrysostome, to catch the turn of their thoughts and the wishes of their heart, to see, as it were, the face of men to whom the Christian faith was the dearest of all things, is a delight which no other literature affords. For on their brow the light of genius and of sanctity is blended, and the man-loving spirit of their Lord reflected.

The decay of language is far more sensible in verse than in prose, as anyone may judge who will compare the forty-five sermons which have given to St. Gregory of Nazianzum the title of Theologian, with the several thousand verses in which he has described incidents of his life. As history, these verses are touching and instructive. It is only to be lamented that, by the fault of the age, the form is not equal to the matter. It is painful to have the admiration awakened by a fine thought chilled by a defect of metre, such as would not be suffered in the task of a school-boy now. Yet he who composed the sermons on God shews a power of language which the best writers of the classical standard would acknowledge.

Something similar may be said of one with far greater poetic gift. Some may think that if the language spoken in the time of Prudentius had been that of Horace or Virgil, he might have reached the elegance of the one in his odes, or the dignity of the other in his epic. The sculptor must have pentelic marble as well as inborn genius to produce the work of Phidias. It is fair, however, to add that Claudian, whose birth was in Egypt, wrought with the same materials as Prudentius, and in the praises of Stilicho came nearer to Virgil's

> "Coursers of celestial race,
> Their necks with thunder cloth'd, and far resounding pace,"

than the noble Spaniard, twice entrusted with the government of a province by Theodosius. Yet he speaks often with poetic vigour, always with the true faith of a Christian, and the thought of a statesman. No encomium on Roman virtue, as shewn upon the phantoms which the flatterer of Augustus caused to pass before the eyes of his hero, surpasses that which Prudentius offered to the memory of his imperial patron when the last sun of temporal splendour was shining upon Rome ; at the end of the fourth century, Rome was at last, in its senate and nobility, accepting the yoke of Christ. Prudentius clearly discerned that what kept such minds as that of his adversary Symmachus in the old worship was not true belief or devotion to a worn-out imposture. What it was he says in lines which I attempt to render, since they give the view which a noble Roman held of Rome's position, and the future which he augured for it, in the interval between the death of Theodosius, and the entry of Honorius in triumph, with Stilicho by his side, in the year 403.[1]

> "The valour of the days of old, the world
> By sea and land subdued : these hold thee bound.
> Thy memory flies back to prosperous times,
> The thousand triumphs with their long processions,

---

[1] Lib. ii. *Contra Symmachum*, 577-637.

The forum crowded with the spoils of kings.
But hear from me, O Roman, the true cause
Which made thy labours fruitful; made the earth,
Which throve upon thy victories, draw thy car,
God saw the nations in their tongues discordant,
And severed in their worship; and He willed
To join them in one empire, and so teach
Civil obedience, gentle rule of peace;
Then add religion's bond, that so one mind
Might draw earth's various tribes to serve one Christ.
Union of hearts is the sole way to God;
And brethren's love due worship of a Father.
And in that peace earth finds tranquillity,
Which wild sedition or fierce arms had scared,
And feeds her children with the breasts of peace.
Through all the lands which Western ocean laves,
Or Eastern crimson dawn illuminates,
A furious strife devoured the human race,
And armed each savage hand to mutual wounds.
To quell this rage God moved the nations round
To bow the head beneath one yoke of laws.
All should be Romans whom the Rhine and Danube,
Tagus with golden sands, and mighty Ebro,
The Hesperian stream with horned front uprising,
Ganges, or heated banks of seven-mouthed Nile,
Owned for their children. All have common rights,
One name, one country, and one brotherhood.
In all these regions men should live as though
One city held them, and one fatherland,
And they themselves were brethren by one hearth.
Nor only distant regions, shores divided
By long sea-ranges, one tribunal find;
But arts and commerce further union make,
And blood alliance blend them in one race,
For mingled parents bear a common brood.
Those victories and those triumphs had this end:
Such was the road Christ levelled for Himself.
When Rome made friends her friendship led to Christ,
And the great Roman Peace served for His herald.
What place could God have in a world of arms,
Breasts torn with discord and competing laws,
Each striving for the mastery, in old days?
In senses torn by passion, in the wild

Resentments of conflicting minds, no pure
Wisdom could entrance find, nor God be there.

"But when the mind is under highest rule,
Subduing all the body's sensual force,
And reason tames the conquered animal,
Life takes a settled course and certain aim,
The heart drinks in its God, and serves one Lord.

"Almighty, Thou art here. So breathe Thy peace
Upon the realm that owns Thee. Lo! the world
Takes Thee for head, O Christ; for peace and Rome
Together hold Thee. Thou hast made them head,
And placed dominion here. Thou wilt have Rome
With peace: Rome's dowry gives to peace its charm."

He has expressed the same thought with a felicity so exquisite in his hymn to the great Roman martyr, St. Laurence, that I give it in the original:

"O Christe, Numen unicum,
  O Splendor, O virtus Patris,
  O Factor orbis et poli,
Atque Auctor horum mœnium,
Qui sceptra Romæ in vertice
  Rerum locasti, sanciens
  Mundum Quirinali togæ
Servire, et armis cedere;
Ut discrepantum gentium
  Mores et observantiam,
  Linguasque et ingenia et sacra
Unis domares legibus.
En omne sub regnum Remi
  Mortale concessit genus.
  Idem loquuntur dissoni
Ritus, id ipsum sentiunt.
Hoc destinatum quo magis
  Jus Christiani nominis
  Quodcunque terrarum jacet
Uno illigaret vinculo.
Da, Christe, Romanis tuis
  Sit Christiana ut civitas,
  Per quam dedisti ut cœteris

> Meus una sacrorum foret.
> Confederentur omnia
>   Hinc inde membra in symbolum :
>   Mansuescat orbis subditus ;
>   Mansuescat et summum caput,
>   Advertat abjunctas plagas
>   Coire in unam gratiam :
>   Fiat fidelis Romulus ;
>   Et ipse jam credat Numa."

Besides his merit as a poet, Prudentius is of the greatest value as an historian and recorder of Christian facts ; as an historian who was not thinking of history, but described the life of Christians as it passed before him. In one of his hymns he mentions that he was fifty-seven years of age. This was in 405. Thus he was born in 348, six years before St. Augustine, and exactly contemporary with St. Ambrose, like whom he was a Roman nobleman and high official. In this beautiful poem he reviews his life, his boyhood under the master's rod; how at sixteen the toga assumed brought with it disregard of truth ; then followed a youth, wherein he laments the stains left by dissipation, and this succeeded by a stormy period at the bar. Then he was twice given the government of great cities, which he administered righteously. Lastly, the emperor placed him in the highest rank next to himself, words which would seem to indicate a prætorian prefecture. Thus occupied, age had stolen on him unawares. "What (he concludes) will all this profit when once the body is dead ? Thy mind will have lost the world which it worshipped. These things were not of God, but thou wilt be God's. At least at the end, O sinning soul, cast off thy folly. Praise Him with the tongue, if thou canst not with deeds. Give each day to hymns; nor let the night be silent in God's praise. Fight against heresy; set forth the Catholic faith; tread under foot the heathen rites. Destroy Rome's idols. Crown the martyrs with song; praise the Apostles. So while I write or speak, let me spring up free from the bonds of the body, and utter my last note."

This is the Prudentius whom we now possess: he gives the same sort of historical testimony to the Rome of the fourth century as Horace to the Rome of Augustus, or Juvenal to the Rome of Domitian. Thus, in his hymn to St. Peter and St. Paul, he bears witness that it was the great feast of the year at Rome, kept on the same day, the multitude flocking to the two basilicas, one on each side of the river. In his best style he paints the baptistery of St. Peter, constructed by Pope Damasus on the Vatican hill, how the water flows through rich marbles, and is received into a large basin, where the splendid ceiling is reflected in its waves. "There the shepherd himself nourishes with the cooling fountain his sheep, whom he sees to be thirsting for the streams of Christ:"[1] words which a late commentator explains by saying that Damasus had inscribed over the baptistery the words:

"Una Petri sedes: unum verumque lavacrum";

and that probably the famous chair of the Apostle was placed here, sitting on which the Pope gave confirmation

---

[1] See two excellent articles in the *Questions historiques* of April and July, 1884, by Allard, to whom I am indebted.

to the newly baptised. As great admiration Prudentius exhibits for the Basilica of St. Paul: "On another side the Ostian way marks the name of Paul, where the river flows against the left bank. It is a place of royal grandeur: a good sovereign[1] raised this fabric. The roof he covered with golden plates, so that it flashes like the dawn; and under it he drew four ranges of marble pillars, with carved arches. Behold the two dowries of the faith which the Supreme Father bestowed, giving them to the worship of the city of peace. Through both the thoroughfares flock the people of Romulus: a single day is busy with the double festival. Let us speed to both and enjoy the hymns of each. Hasten we first over the river by the bridge of Hadrian, then seek we the left bank. Watching for early dawn, the priest performs the first rite beyond the Tiber; then comes hither and duplicates his vows. This is enough for Rome to have shewn thee: go home, and remember to keep the double festival."

Here Prudentius describes the Feast of St. Peter and St. Paul, as he saw it at Rome, say, in the year 400. The double dowry which Rome worshipped at the two Basilicas I suppose to be the Keys of St. Peter and the Sword of St. Paul, the Teacher of the Nations, as he says (v. 7):

> "Scit Tiberina palus qua flumine labitur propinquo
> Binis dicatum cespitem tropæis
> Et crucis et gladii testis".

It would require a volume to illustrate Prudentius.

---

[1] Theodosius is supposed to be intended, who in the year 386 gave orders for the construction of the building thus admired.

I will end with his parting words to St. Eulalia:[1] "Let us venerate her relics and the altar which is placed over them. She, put beneath the feet of God, looks on what we do, is pleased with the homage of our verse, and cherishes her people." The sacrifice being offered on the stone, under which St. Eulalia was buried, he says that she is "seated under the feet of God".

St. Paulinus of Nola had said with equal felicity:

"Casta tuum digne velant Altaria corpus;
Ut templum Christi contegat ara Dei".

As the human body had become the temple of Christ, so the martyr beneath the eucharistic slab was "seated under the feet of God". The two miracles which brought down God and raised up man are seen in contact; and the heathen mind, with regard to the dead body, has undergone a complete revolution. The Incarnation and the Eucharistic Presence belong to one faith; and are here attested together by Paulinus and Prudentius.

In his hymn to St. Hippolitus he notes that he had read a great number of inscriptions on tombs; but once he had found sixty martyrs deposited in one monument: "their names are only known to Christ, who has honoured them with His friendship".[2] This reminds of

[1] " Sic venerarier ossa libet
Ossibus altar et impositum.
Illa Dei sita sub pedibus
Prospicit haec, populosque suos
Carmine propitiata fovet."
Peristephanon, iii. 211.

[2] " Quorum solus habet comperta vocabula Christus,
Utpote quos propriæ junxit amicitiæ."
Peristephanon, xi.

the still visible inscription placed by Pope Pascal over the bodies of 2300 martyrs, which he had translated to the Church of St. Praxedes, " whose names are known to the Almighty ".

It may well be supposed that Prudentius, in his prayers and praises for the city of Rome, as the head of the empire, becoming a Christian city, which event is assigned to the last fifteen years of the fourth century, looked forward to a period of great glory both for the empire and the Christian faith. Two heathens, about the same time—Claudian in describing the great deeds of Stilicho, and, what is more remarkable, Rutilius, twelve years later, and five years after Alaric's capture—speak with a sort of rapture concerning Rome, as the maker of the Roman peace. Spain utters her voice in Prudentius ; Gaul in Rutilius ; Egypt, it is said, in Claudian. Together they express that profound sense of the greatness of Romandom which all the provinces composing it had at this time, and long afterwards. "It was," says Reumont, "as if, with the calamity which was bursting over empire and city, the sense of their importance for the world was even increased. The Christian Church, which was destined to succeed to the spiritual inheritance of Rome, in that she continued the work of civilisation amid the ruins of the political power, strengthened and perpetuated this sense. She recognised in the laws of Rome the voice of God in the mouth of her rulers. She proclaimed that Christ had put the sceptre in the hand of Rome, and subjected the world to the toga of the Quirinal. The

Roman realm remained, to human eyes, the ideal type of the commonwealth, the seat of legitimate authority, the bearer of civilisation. Whatever was not subject to the laws of this kingdom was barbarism. Barbarism had many shapes; but the empire was unity. The peace of the world was the Roman peace. Whom Rome bound it made brethren. This view was not merely a specifically Roman view. For centuries the foreign populations, which had struggled against and for Rome, had uttered it by the voice of their princes in their relations with the emperors. They thought themselves bigger by connection with Rome. Conquest seemed to them to convey no title so long as it remained unconfirmed by the Roman emperor."

Now to speak of this vast movement of mind, this scintillation of intellect, which appears in the Church between her first and her fourth Councils, what is the nature of it? In the first Council, which the newly converted Roman emperor was the instrument of calling, but which he called in perfect union with Pope Sylvester, and Alexander of Alexandria, and Eustathius of Antioch, the Church appeared in her imperial power. Attack had been made on the faith by which she had subsisted through the long conflict with the heathen State. The attack was repelled. Then a time of fiercest trial ensued. The doubtful language of many bishops— we must even add their doubtful mind—was aggravated by the conduct of certain emperors, who had a most fixed intention to subjugate the Church. The whole doctrine of the Trinity and the Incarnation was passed under strictest review. The doctrine, also, of grace : the doctrine of the Church's unity. Heresy and schism were cast out and condemned, but, ere they departed, they tore and rent their victim, whom the arm of Christ raised up and restored. In this long process the language of the Church became more definite, while her doctrine was unchanged. Tertullian and Cyprian, had they lived in St. Augustine's time, would have exulted in his doctrine. Clement and Origen would have been by the side of Athanasius. As a general result, whereever there was imperfect expression or incomplete idea in the Antenicene writers, it was amended, and the whole idea precisely articulated. Cardinal Newman dwells on " the wonderful identity of type which characterises the Catholic Church from first to last ". " It is confessed on all hands, by Middleton, Gibbon, &c., that, from the time of Constantine to their own, the system and the phenomena of worship in Christendom, from Moscow to Spain, and from Ireland to Chili, are one and the same." But, further, "as to the system of Catholic worship, the idea of the Blessed Virgin was, as it were, magnified in the Church of Rome as time went on, but so were all the Christian ideas, as that of the Blessed Eucharist ".

In this last sentence I find a fact stated which occurs so constantly in the period under review, that it seems to me to be its most salient characteristic. In the period between Nicæa and Chalcedon all doctrines tend to increase and come out more and more. Discussion enucleates them. Immense is the advance in distinctness with which the doctrine of the Blessed Trinity comes to be held in consequence of the attacks made upon it. In this way Arius and Macedonius have elucidated the Second and Third Persons. Nestorius and Eutyches have led St. Leo to define, in imperishable language, with uncontroverted authority, the doctrine of our Lord's divine Personality and two Natures: Nestorius has further fixed for ever the title of Mother of God, which he strove to take from our Blessed Lady, and the Divine Maternity shines through the Godhead of the Son, revealing an infinite greatness bestowed upon the creature. Pelagius has done a similar benefit to the doctrine of grace, to our knowledge of the fall of man and its results. The Eusebians and the Donatists brought out into clearest light the unity of the Church: the former set a brand upon Greek schism five hundred years before Photius was able to accomplish it; the latter, in all their course, most of all in the destruction which they wrought, condemned the attempt to found national churches. The reward of Donatus was Genseric. The Primacy, both at Ephesus and at Chalcedon, received the full confession of two councils, almost all whose members were Eastern bishops, who thus branded also the schismatic council at Philippopolis, which frustrated for the moment the work intended to be done at Sardica. The authority which Pope Julius mentions so gently in his letter to the bishops forming the heretical party at Antioch is expressed in no ambiguous language by Pope Celestine, ninety years later, in the instructions given to his legates for the Council of Ephesus; and the Council, with St. Cyril at its head, receives them with the greatest deference; while Cyril terms the Roman Pontiff, dwelling in a Rome almost under the feet of barbarians, "archbishop of the whole world". The whole process of defining doctrine brings out the authority of the Primacy, as is seen in the great letter of St. Leo; and every danger of the Church has the same result. Thus, the extreme peril with which the Church was threatened, of consenting to heresy in a general council legitimately called, as was the Ephesine Council of 449, was dissipated by St. Leo's peremptory act, annulling its decrees. The act which saved the Church exhibited the supreme authority of her pastor. In these hundred and thirty years especially the Church learnt to fix her eyes upon her centre of unity, to learn by experience where her strength lay, and to declare that she was built upon the Rock of Peter.

"All Christian ideas," to use Cardinal Newman's words, "are magnified in the Church." The Fathers of this period, further, give us the strongest witness as to their cultus of the saints, and as to their belief in the Blessed Eucharist. Ideas in the Church are magnified, I suppose, because the Church is a kingdom. But it is to be noted that in all heresies and schisms exactly the opposite effect is to be seen. Such communities in process of time lose their grasp of the very truths which they once held. It is not only that they lose what they themselves, by the nature of their heresy or schism, discard, but they lose also what they most prized, or at least seemed to prize, when their heresy or schism began. Thus, the very documents which initiate their separated existence may express the doctrines of the Trinity and the Incarnation, and, after the lapse of a few generations, if they survive so long, those who use them will be honeycombed with disbelief, both in the Trinity and the Incarnation. Minds nurtured in heresy and schism have become unfitting and unequal to such grandeur. So again a community, which begins with denying purgatory as a human invention, will end in flying back to an invented purgatory as a consolation from the thought of eternal justice in the punishment of sin. This it will repudiate, as unfitting such a character of God, as its feebleness is able to reach. Heresy and schism begin their course by imposing new opinions of their own as if they had been sanctioned by divine authority, but end by representing heresy and schism themselves to be legitimate exercises of private judgment. In a society where they dominate the wildest of errors will be lauded as the prerogatives of free thought. All which, I suppose, is only an illustration of the fact that, while the Church is a kingdom which grows through the ages, heresy and schism are to perform their office towards the world in one country after another by the ever-repeated process of self-destruction. The ultimate result is that they recommend the infallibility of the Church by their confusion, and her unity by their division. The Church remains the kingdom, and points back to their carcases in the past centuries of her enduring life, lying outside her in their putrefaction.

Vincent of Lerius, an author who lived in this period, and was noted for his learning and sanctity, and for renouncing high secular rank in order to enter the religious life, has left, in the single work which hands down his name, a passage which, for the purpose of distinguishing true from false development, is without its like in the whole patristic literature. Written in 434, it exhibits the formation of the Rule of Faith, in terms which might serve for an exact history of the work done from the council of Nicæa to that of Chalcedon. In this point of view I quote it.

" 'O Timotheus,' the Apostle says, 'keep the deposit, avoiding profane novelties of words.' Who is now this Timotheus? Either in general the whole Church, or specially the whole body of prelates who are bound to possess themselves, or infuse into others, the entire science of divine worship. What means 'Keep the deposit'? Keep it against thieves, against enemies, who, while men sleep, oversow tares upon that good seed which the Son of Man sowed in His field. 'Keep the deposit.' What is the deposit? That which was entrusted to you, not what you found out. What you received, not your own brain-work. Produce, not of genius, but of learning; not of private interpretation, but of public tradition; not what you produced, but what came down to you. In which you are to be not author, but custodian; not beginner, but follower; not leader, but led. 'Keep,' he says, 'the deposit.' Preserve, inviolate and untouched, the talent of the Catholic faith. What was put in your trust, keep in possession and hand it down. Gold you received, render back gold. I will have no alteration, neither the impudent substitution of lead, nor the fraudulent substitution of gilding. I will have not what looks like gold, but what is gold. O Timotheus, be thou bishop, writer, or doctor, if a divine gift has made thee capable, by genius, by exercise, by learning, be the artist of the spiritual tabernacle. Finish off the precious gems of the heavenly doctrine. Put them together faithfully, set them skilfully, so adding to them brightness, grace, and elegance. Let the clearness of your exposition bring out what faith believed while it was obscure. Let those who come after be thankful to you for comprehending what those who came before respected without comprehending. Yet teach the same which you learnt, so that, if the expression be new, the meaning be old.

"But some one may say, Shall there then be no progress of religion in the Church of Christ? Certainly there is, and a very great one. For where is he, so envious of man, so hateful to God, who would attempt to prevent it? But then it must be a true progress, not a change of faith. For it belongs to progress that a thing's own nature supply the material of its growth: to change, that it be altered into something else. Therefore, let there be growth, and great and powerful progress in the individual and in the mass; in every man and in the whole Church, as generations and centuries succeed. Progress in intelligence, in knowledge, in wisdom, but ever homogeneous; that is, progress in the same dogma, the same sense, the same intention. Let the soul in religion imitate the body in growth. The body, in the course of years, unfolds its proportions, which still remain the same. Great is the difference between the flower of youth and the maturity of age. Nevertheless, those who were youths become old men. There is a change in the man's condition, but his nature and his person remain one and the same. The nursing baby's limbs are small, the grown man's great. But they are the same. The infant has so many joints as the man. If anything be produced by maturing age, it was seminally there already. Thus in the old man nothing is exhibited which was not latent in the child. No doubt then we have here a right and legitimate rule of progress, a settled and beautiful order of growth, if advancing age unfold in larger size the parts and forms which creative wisdom had first placed in miniature. But if the human form be changed into something not of its own kind, or at least some member be added or taken away, the whole body will either perish or become monstrous, or at least debilitated. In the same way dogma in the Christian religion should follow these conditions of advance. Let years consolidate it. Let it broaden out with time. It will be bigger as it ages. But it must remain unchanged and untouched. It must be full and perfect in all its proportions, limbs, and several senses. It must admit no alteration, no loss of property, no variety of circumscription. For instance, our ancestors sowed of old in this field of the Church wheaten seed of faith. It would be iniquitous and incongruous that we their posterity should reap error for truth, tares for genuine wheat. A due and proper sequence would require that first and last should not disagree; that from good wheat sown we should gather the full ear of wheaten dogma. So when in process of time the seed gives increase, shews a fair harvest and ripening, there shall be no change in the quality produced. A clearly defined shape and beauty may come out, but each kind must remain the same. God forbid that the rosebuds of Catholic plantation be turned into thorns and thistles; that the spiritual paradise of cinnamon and balsam be filled with shoots of darnel and aconite. Thus, whatever the faith of our fathers sowed in this culture of God's Church, let the industry of their children ripen and guard. May it flower and mature, progress and be perfected. For it is right that in process of time the original dogmas of that divine philosophy receive cultivation, finish, and smoothness; it is wrong that they be changed, cut short, or mutilated. In evidence, in clearness, in distinctness, they may advance, but let them keep their fulness, integrity, and proper character. For if once this licence of impious deceit be allowed, I shrink from uttering what danger of destroying religion will ensue. For if any part of Catholic dogma be given up, others and others again, and further others, will follow from that allowance. If one part after another be rejected, total repudiation in the end must ensue. Again, if once new be mixed with old, foreign with our own, profane with sacred, that custom will become universal. The sanctity, purity, integrity, spotlessness of the Church will all be lost. The shrine of holy truth will be turned into a den of debauchery for impiety and error to revel in. May the divine piety save His own from this and leave it to the rage of enemies. But the Church of Christ as a careful and cautious guardian of the dogmas entrusted to her never changes aught in these. Nothing does she take away, nothing add; she does not cut off what is needful, nor put on what is superfluous. Her own she does not lose, nor take that of others. All her industry is directed to this one thing, to deal faithfully and wisely with her inheritance. If anything has come down to her unformed or embryonic, she works it into shape. What has already form and expansion, she presses together and strengthens. She preserves what is already strong and definite. In fine, what did she ever strive for in the decrees of councils but to form a simple into a more accurate belief; to rouse a keener interest in what may have been slackly taught; to cultivate with more anxious care what had been held before in security. This, I repeat, and nothing more, has the Catholic Church, roused into action by the innovations of heretics, effected by the decrees of her councils. What she had received from those before her on tradition alone, she set her seal upon for posterity by the handwriting of Scripture also; and therein she comprehended a vast matter in a few words, and generally marked out a sense to be believed which was not new by using a new expression which cast upon it a revealing light." [1]

[1] Part of the above passage is quoted, as a description of true progress, in the Vatican Council.

CHAPTER XI.

ST. LEO THE GREAT.

"In the Robber Council of Ephesus, when all the bishops and even the patriarchs were failing, if the great Leo, imitating Him of whom it is written, 'The Lion of the tribe of Judah has conquered,' had not been divinely stirred up to open his mouth, and to rouse the whole world and the emperors themselves, and to move them to pious action, the Christian religion would have perished."
—*Pope Nicolas I. to the Emperor Michael*, A.D. 847.

No such intellectual outburst of vigour as we have been trying to describe in the period from Athanasius to Leo is to be found in the Church after this age until eight hundred years had expired. Then in certain great minds of the 13th century, especially the three chief schoolmen, St. Thomas, St. Bonaventure, and Scotus, a work was effected which may be compared in certain respects with the result of the hundred and fifty years succeeding the Nicene Council. The gigantic intellect of St. Thomas rose, as it were, upon the shoulders of St. Augustine,[1] and laid out in orderly disposition the fabric which his genius had prepared.

But now, in the year 440, there was placed at the head of the intellectual work achieved, and of the vast

---
[1] A similitude suggested to me by the windows of Chartres, where the evangelists are seen raised upon the four great prophets in the Sanctuary Virginis parituræ.

society out of which it had sprung, a man, from the strength of his character one of the greatest rulers to be found in any age, and from the quality [of his mind as fit to be judge in works of intellect as to direct in practical government. St. Leo the Great bore at once the Keys of Peter and the Sword of Paul. And he bore them one-and-twenty years without haste, without passion, without fear, with the serene dignity of one whose eyes were ever fixed upon the Lord whom he represented, in the days of Attila and Genseric, when the race of Theodosius ended in uttermost shame and ignominy at Rome, ended also at Constantinople in the noblest of his descendants, the empress and virgin Saint Pulcheria.

At the moment of Leo's accession, what remained of the Western empire had been governed since 425 by the empress Galla Placidia, the only surviving child of the great Theodosius, as guardian for Valentinian, her son by Constantius, who had obtained her unwilling hand as the most valiant Roman general of the time, and the mainstay of her brother's throne. France was occupied by German races, Burgundians, Franks, Alemans, Alans : the Visigoth kingdom, whose seat was at Toulouse, while recognised by Rome, had scarcely more than nominal connection with it. The Vandals and the Sueves were in Spain; but, worse yet, Genseric had invaded Africa in 429, and after a warfare of ten years had obtained full possession of it. Carthage was his. Britain had already been lost to the empire when Stilicho had been reduced to withdraw the Roman forces for the defence of Italy. Western Illyricum had been ceded to Theodosius II., when after the death of his uncle Honorius he had overthrown an usurper and placed his aunt, Galla Placidia, with her infant son, on the throne. From that time forth the emperor at Constantinople acted as a sort of superior Lord[1] over the Western empire. But by Leo's time it was well-nigh restricted to Italy, which itself, by the loss of Africa, Rome's chief granary, was reduced to a state of constant alarm lest the means of subsistence should fail. What Prudentius could say in 403 was no longer true :

>   Respice num Libyci desistat ruris arator
>   Frumentis onerare rates, et ad ostia Tibris
>   Mittere triticeos in pastum plebis acervos.—*2 Con. Sym.* 936.

Leo was elected when absent from Rome, having been sent by Valentinian III. into Gaul to reconcile, if possible, the two imperial generals, Aetius and Albinus. In fact, what empire remained depended upon the great ability of Galla's minister, Aetius, who repeated in a singular manner the story of the triumphs, the suspected loyalty, and the unseemly death of Stilicho in the previous reign. On two men, Stilicho and Aetius, in lineage half barbarians, but far surpassing any native of Rome or Italy in warlike genius, political ability, and the power to sustain a falling empire, that empire rested for such political life as it continued to have from the death of Theodosius until his unworthy grandson slew

---

[1] Reumont, i. 775-780. When Anthemius was made emperor, 467, in den Versen des Galliers (Sidonius Apollinaris) klingt nur zu sehr durch was schon die Geschichte von Anthemius' Erhebung verkündete, dass das neue Rom an der Greuze zwischen Europa und Asien das Scepter führte.

Aetius, as Honorius had slain Stilicho; and as Stilicho was avenged by Alaric, so was Aetius by Genseric. On both these great men rests a suspicion that they had failed in perfect fidelity to the sovereigns whom they served—a suspicion which those who have most warmly sympathised with their great actions have not been able to dissipate; but it is certain that from the death of Stilicho the reign of Honorius was an unvaried series of disasters, while the assassin's stroke, which Valentinian had dealt upon Aetius, destroyed himself at once, and after a few years, in which successive emperors were murdered, put an end to the empire itself; or rather, strictly speaking, left to the ruler at Constantinople the sole title to what was still called the Roman empire.

The state of the Eastern empire at Leo's accession was different. Theodosius II. had succeeded Arcadius in 408, at the age of seven, had been wisely and carefully educated by his minister the regent Anthemius, and then by his sister Pulcheria, who was made empress at sixteen. The two together had done all for him that loyalty and affection could do. But he had inherited no spark of genius from the grandfather whose illustrious name he bore; no particle even, it would seem, of his mother's spirit, the beautiful and wilful daughter of Bauto, the Frankish general. As soon as he came forth from the hands of Anthemius and Pulcheria, the only function of which he seemed capable was to be clothed in the imperial robes, stiff with jewels, to wear the purple buskins, to ride in the golden carriage, and be waited on and advised by obsequious courtiers and eunuchs, and those who were worse than both—time-serving bishops looking for promotion. Thus he had reigned for thirty-two years, at first by his regent and his sister, then himself, a man of personal piety, but who had the ill-luck to be ever on the wrong side in ecclesiastical affairs—a result due no doubt to the parties prevailing in a court directed by the three sorts of councillors above described. He had, however, just brought back with honour the relics of the great saint whom his unhappy parents, Arcadius and Eudoxia, had so ignobly persecuted to death, and had placed them with the honours due to confessorship in the Church of the Apostles, sepulchre of the bishops, and of Constantine's line.

The empire of which he stood at the head had passed under his father and himself through times of great peril. It had, however, contrived to turn the greed of Alaric away from itself upon the realm of Honorius. It had looked upon the dissolution of the Western empire almost with feelings of jealous satisfaction, in so far, at least, as first Goth and then Hun seemed to be diverted from its own shoulders. On the death of his uncle Honorius, the nephew, a young man of twenty-two, had thought of taking the West under his immediate control. But his courage or his strength failed, and he was content to invest an aunt and a child-cousin with the imperial title, and to place them over a diminished domain. But though East and West had been under separate administrations since the death of Theodosius, the Roman empire, in the mind of its rulers, was one and indivisible. This was a fixed principle through all the changes of dynasty which succeeded at Constantinople, even down to the time when Leo III. set the imperial crown on the great hero, so far more powerful that the Eastern Cæsar. But now, while Galla Placidia and her son Valentinian, ruled by the arm of Aetius only, the emperor at Constantinople was at the head of a still mighty realm, containing the richest provinces and the fairest countries in the world. Theodosius possessed Asia Minor, from the Egean-Sea to Lake Van, and beyond, with the wealth and civilisation of seven hundred years from the time of Alexander; with its store of Grecian cities, one of which alone, Pergamos, reconstructed by the touch of an architect to its ideal beauty, is enough to astonish the mind. Theodosius, dwelling in the impregnable city of the Bosphorus, the bride so often wooed by every imperial lover, from his day to our own, was undisputed lord over a multitude of cities such as Pergamos. Egypt was his, Syria was his, and the great Balkan peninsula, from Dyrrachium and Sirmium to the Euxine Sea and the Malean promontory. As the West fell to pieces, the East formed itself more and more into an empire under its new capital. The grandson of Theodosius needed only to be a ruler such as his grandsire was, to secure the prosperity of the wonderful domain which he inherited.

Such was the political condition of the East and West; but what were the circumstances of the Church in July, 440, and particularly the position of the Roman pontiff?

In regard to this, the acts of the Council of Ephesus in 431 seem to me of supreme importance, as being, when it was held, the first Council since the Nicene in which the East and West had met together. It must be remembered that the council of Sardica, called in 343, by common consent of the emperors Constantius and Constans, at the wish of Pope Julius, was intended to be an ecumenical council, like the Nicene, and to terminate those controversies which had arisen in the eighteen years passed since that Council. But this intention was frustrated by the intrigues of the Eusebian bishops, who had at their command the tyrannical power of the Eastern emperor, Constantius. Again, the council at Rimini was intended by its contrivers to be an ecumenical council, but instead bipartite councils were held, one at Rimini, the other at Seleucia. The council of 150 bishops, called by Theodosius at Constantinople, in 381, was never intended to be ecumenical, no Western bishops were invited to it, and it was composed of Eastern bishops alone. At Ephesus this council was passed over in silence. Nothing could be more obnoxious to St. Cyril than a canon which it made, elevating the upstart see of Constantinople above his own see, the second in the Church from the time of the Apostles, and above Antioch, which was the third, equally from St. Peter's time. Accordingly, when the Council of Ephesus was held in 431, no one thought of the council of 381 as ecumenical.[1] Thus the actions of

---

[1] Observe that Eutyches, in appealing to Pope Leo in 448 (Ep. xxi.), while pointedly referring to the Councils of Nicæa and Ephesus, entirely passes over

the Council of Ephesus exhibit the Church as meeting for the first time in plenary synod since that of Nicæa, which was held a hundred and six years before. In that century there had been great contentions. The most violent of heresies had shaken the Church to its foundation, not by its intrinsic force, but because the despotic power of emperors had been placed at its disposal. Especially this power had been invited by Eastern bishops to act against the Roman Primacy; and an emperor had sent a Pope into banishment. When the Church met at length in 431, the city of Rome had descended very low from the political position which it occupied down to the foundation of Constantine's Nova Roma. The East had been formed into a new empire, with a capital of its own. The political influence of that capital had raised its bishop from a suffragan, unknown to previous history, until he had become the greatest ecclesiastical personage of the East. A man of remarkable eloquence, who was brought, like St. Chrysostome, from Antioch, and was expected to equal his renown, had been placed by imperial favour in that most coveted see. He was the choice of Theodosius II. himself. He had begun his episcopate by assaulting the dignity of the Mother of God; the Church had met to judge him. He was deposed, and the sentence ran: "Compelled by the canons, and the letter of our most holy Father and Colleague, Celestine, bishop of Rome, we have with many tears come to this painful sentence. Our Lord Jesus Christ,

that of Constantinople in 381. He speaks of holding "the faith which was set forth by the holy Council at Nicæa, but confirmed at Ephesus".

whom he has slandered, decrees by this holy Synod that Nestorius be deprived of episcopal dignity and all sacerdotal communion."[1]

The letter of Celestine, thus referred to, was an act of plenary authority by the bishop of Rome, declaring the bishop of Constantinople to be degraded unless within ten days he acknowledged and abjured his error.

At the head of the council was St. Cyril, acting as the Pope's representative, together with other legates from Rome, who stated, in precise terms, that the Pope sat in the see and place of Peter : statements accepted without discussion by the council.

All, therefore, who receive the existence of the Church as a continuous corporate body must hold that by this, the first plenary council of the Church after the Nicene, the Pope's position, with all the claim made in the letters of the Popes as to the origin of their authority, was admitted by the Church as an existing thing, not a thing which the Church granted, but a thing which the Church acknowledged.

This condemnation of Nestorius had taken place in spite of all the opposition which the court party and the emperor himself could make to it. Theodosius had throughout been on the side of Nestorius. Eighteen years later he was to be equally on the side of Eutyches. And, in all the violence used by Dioscorus and his council, he was on the side of Dioscorus. On these several occasions he is believed to have been misled by the intrigues of his court, which did not allow the feeble

[1] Hefele, ii. 172.

spirit of the absolute prince to have a mind of his own.

Nine years therefore before the accession of St. Leo, the full position of the bishop of Rome, as Primate sitting in the See of Peter, had been acknowledged by an irrevocable authority. Rome, as a city, was living from hand to mouth. Its sovereign was usually seeking security between the marshes of Ravenna and the sea; he did not venture to dwell on the Palatine hill in the palace of Augustus. Its Bishop was acknowledged as sitting and ruling in the seat of Peter by episcopal descent from him: acknowledged by the East, in the bishops who were the subjects of the Eastern emperor, as well as by the bishops in the West, who, amid barbarian invasions, looked to the bishop of Rome as the sole remaining symbol of imperial power, but much more as the maintainer, champion, and standard of their episcopal authority, and of the Christian faith.

On the death of Sixtus III., in August, 440, Leo, a deacon, son of Quintianus, a Roman, was unanimously elected Pope, being then absent in Gaul, under a commission from the emperor. His age at this time can hardly have been less than fifty. He is believed to be the Leo who, in 418, is mentioned as an acolyte, the bearer of a decree from Pope Zosimus, as well as of a letter from Sixtus, then a priest, afterwards Pope, to Aurelius of Carthage. On this occasion, the future great Pope would come in contact with the greatest of the Fathers; and it is well to bear in mind that, for at least forty years, Leo and Augustine were contemporaries.

In the time of Pope Celestine, 422-432, he was archdeacon of Rome; and in this character was addressed by John Cassian, in dedicating to him the work on the Incarnation, as "My dear Leo, the honour of the Roman church and the divine ministry. You call upon me to raise my feeble hands against this novel heresy, this new enemy of the faith (that is Nestorius): I obey your entreaty; I obey your command."[1] During the pontificate of his predecessor Sixtus, 432-440, Leo was a man of great influence. St. Cyril addressed to him a letter against the design of Juvenal of Jerusalem to get for himself the rank of patriarch. Leo was recalled from Gaul, when engaged, as we have seen, in political matters of the utmost importance to the empire; and Prosper says: "More than forty days the Roman church was without a bishop, awaiting, with wonderful peace and patience, the arrival of the deacon Leo". On his arrival he was consecrated bishop, and mounted the throne of St. Peter at a time of extraordinary danger both to the empire and the Church. His first years were occupied in maintaining faith and discipline against the Manichæans, who had come in large numbers to Rome upon the capture of Carthage by Genseric the year before, and against Pelagians in Upper Italy, and Priscillianists in Spain. In the first ten years of his episcopate, besides the terrible deeds of Genseric by land and sea, who harried all that came within his reach with the ferocity of a Barbary pirate, the whole empire, both in the East and West, was

---

[1] Cassian, *de Incarnatione*; Preface, Migne, vol. l., p. 14.

held in panic by the immense hosts of Attila, who had joined under his single command the Scythian and the German tribes. He spread the most fearful havoc over the Eastern empire, from the Adriatic to the Black Seas, and Aetius with difficulty, aided by Visigoths and Franks, rescued the West, in 451, from an age of Scythian barbarity on the plains of Chalons.

These were the times in which St. Leo delivered at Rome those ninety-six sermons which have come down to us: some on the great festivals of our Lord; a good number on His passion; on the festivals of Rome's patron-saints, St. Peter and St Paul; on the anniversaries of his own consecration; on the fasts of the Church. Wherever he dwells on dogma or on devotion, on the several duties of Christian life, on the Person of our Lord, on the characters of His saints and martyrs, it is the voice of one speaking with consummate dignity, with the most finished theological accuracy, basing moral duties upon Christian mysteries. These sermons are acts of a ruler, whose mind is absorbed without effort or consciousness in the work of his office, to teach, instruct, support, as one who sits in the chair of the chief Apostle, and whose domain is the imperishable Church of God. Scarcely does he ever mention the secular troubles which made the Palatine hill no place for a degenerate emperor to occupy. The Rome of Leo is fenced by myriads of martyrs; and the earth over which he stands is full of the relics of saints. Of them and of their work, and of the Lord who bought them and made them, he speaks; and fear of the barbarism surging round him or of "change perplexing monarchs" is unknown to him.

He has left likewise a hundred and forty-three letters, of great importance for the history of his time. Some are dogmatic, some historical; some dwell on questions of canon law and discipline. They exhibit very distinctly the position which he held towards the imperial personages of his day: to Theodosius, Pulcheria, Marcian, in the East; to Valentinian, Galla Placidia, Eudoxia, in the West. They give his instructions to Julian, bishop of Cos, in whom he may be said to have instituted the race of nuncios. His language in them to various bishops, metropolitans, patriarchs, indicates, without arrogating, a supreme authority. They are instinct throughout with his own great character: we forget the author in the man; we know him as an author only because he was the ruler.

One of these letters, the 28th, is that in which he set forth to Flavian, bishop of Constantinople, the true doctrine of the Incarnation, when it was impugned by Eutyches. It was afterwards received by the metropolitans and bishops of the Church as the test of the true faith. Of all documents issued by the ancient Popes it remains the most famous. There is one thing in it specially remarkable. The division of the East and West, which became permanent upon the death of Theodosius, had put an end in great part to the knowledge of the Greek language, which had been cultivated for so many centuries in Rome; for Romans were no longer sent to hold great office among Greek-speaking populations. Greek is specially the language not only of poetry but of metaphysics and theology ; able by its almost infinite subtlety and variety to express whatever thought can conceive. St. Leo knew no Greek ; but in this dogmatic letter he has set forth the incomprehensible mystery on which is centred all the hope, the faith, and the love of Christians, with the clearness, accuracy, and simplicity of Athanasius or Basil ; and for once the language of Rome in the mouth of a Roman in the fifth century has equalled the language of Greece in the mouth of those who used it with the greatest effect.

The whole history of the Nestorian and Eutychean controversies shews the great danger in which these two opposing heresies, one arising from the perversion of the Antiochene school, the other from the perversion of the Alexandrine school, involved the Church. The great patriarchate of the East was shorn of its glory and finally shipwrecked by the one ; the great patriarchate which Athanasius and Cyril had ruled with such honour was lost in the other. Leo pointed out that each of these errors destroyed the very substance of the faith. In one passage of a letter[1] to the empress Pulcheria he has described in singularly few words the two aberrations which have been so fatal : " While Eutyches considers himself to have formed a more religious judgment upon the majesty of the Son of God, by not affirming that our nature was really in Him, he supposed that the whole of what is comprised in 'the Word was made flesh' belonged to one and the same substance. And far as Nestorius

[1] Ep. xxxi.

falls from the truth in asserting that Christ was born of His mother only man, equally far does he too deviate from the path of Catholic doctrine, when he believes that it was not our substance which was brought forth from the same virgin. His meaning is that that substance should be understood of the Godhead alone. So that what 'bore the form of a servant,' and what was like and conformable to us, was a sort of likeness of our nature, not its reality."

In these few words the Pope fathomed the whole abyss of error in the two opposing heresies, and shewed how each destroyed the Incarnation. Their subsequent history therefore is no wonder: that the one set up against the Body of Christ a false church from Antioch to China; the other tore Egypt from that same Body of Christ. The cause and the effect were adequate.

When Leo became Pope Cyril was in the last years of his episcopate, possessing the great consideration which his presiding at the Council of Ephesus had given him, over and above the rank of his see. He died four years afterwards, and was succeeded by his archdeacon Dioscorus. We have a letter[1] from St. Leo to Dioscorus, in which he certainly uses the language of a superior. He says that he writes to him "to confirm his beginnings": that as St. Peter had received from his Lord the Principate, and the Roman church remained constant to all which he had instituted, so it would be a crime to suppose that St. Mark, his disciple, and the first bishop of Alexandria, followed any other tradition: adding, "This

[1] Ep. ix.

we do not suffer," but "it is our will that you also should keep what has been handed down from our Fathers ". Nothing certainly but the possession of St. Peter's pastorship would justify such language used to the second bishop of the Church.

After the deposition of Nestorius, and the interval of Maximian's brief episcopate, St. Proclus had succeeded to the see of Constantinople, in which he sat with great dignity and renown for twelve years. He was in the middle of these twelve years at Leo's accession. It is astonishing how little the rank and influence of his see had been affected by the ignominious deposition of Nestorius. It would seem that when there is a close union between the civil and the spiritual powers, combined with an absolute monarchy, the influence which naturally attaches to the bishop of the capital, when the capital is also the monarch's residence, can not but continually increase. It is certain that, in the court of Theodosius, Proclus was eminent. He was succeeded in 446 by Flavian, who was scarcely seated when the aged and highly-considered abbot Eutyches began to stir up the heresy which bears his name. This was condemned by Flavian in his Resident Council in November, 448, but Eutyches did not submit.

The matter was reported to Rome both by Eutyches and by Flavian. The words of the latter to the Pope are : " The cause only requires your consolation and defence. Your consent will bring everything to tranquillity and peace. For thus the heresy which has arisen, and the disturbances which it has caused, will be most easily destroyed by the divine co-operation, through your most sacred letters. The council also, which is talked about, will be put aside, so that there may not be universal disturbances in the churches."[1]

When, seventeen years before, the heresy of Nestorius had been reported to Pope Celestine by St. Cyril, the Pope issued a letter of condemnation requiring Nestorius to retract within ten days or else pronouncing him to be deposed. This was the Pope's action in regard to the bishop of Constantinople, high in the favour of the emperor, who was the same then as now. In the present case of an abbot at Constantinople, whom likewise the emperor strongly supported, St. Leo, after first fully informing himself upon the whole matter, issued to Flavian the letter which he had asked for, and which is so renowned in the history of doctrine. No one, I think, can read this letter without astonishment at the power of language shewn by the Pope. He has to expose and destroy two heresies, and to exhibit in full proportion the divine and transcendent mystery which lies between them. Each sentence cuts through error like the clean sweep of a scimitar, and in so doing delineates the truth. I suppose that the power of antithesis is pushed to the utmost. But this document, received by all the bishops, and read for hundreds of years in churches, has put on St. Leo's head an imperishable crown : that of establishing for ever by the testimony of Scripture the force of Tradition and the authority of the Primacy exhibited in it, the Godhead

[1] Ep. xxvi.

and Manhood of his Lord in the work of human salvation. It was the completion of St. Peter's confession—" Thou art the Christ, the Son of the living God"; and the bishops at Chalcedon echoed their consent to it in the words—" Peter has spoken by Leo ".

But Eutyches had got the emperor Theodosius II. on his side, and, notwithstanding the words of Flavian to the Pope, that his letter would render a council unnecessary, a council was called at Ephesus, to which the Pope agreed to send his legates, though he thought it unnecessary, and only consented to it for the sake of peace.[1] "On the 8th August, 449, the council was opened in St. Mary's church at Ephesus. The previous imperial decrees had indeed given to understand that the chief occupation of the council would be to extirpate Nestorianism. But the negotiations shewed plainly that the Monophysite condemned in Byzantium, pluming himself on the reputation of Cyril and the council held eighteen years before in the same place, was bent on sitting in judgment upon the doctrine of the Two Natures, and would spare no violence in procuring a triumph. Dioscorus, who had already declared Flavian's judgment null and void, was made by the will of the emperor president of the council. The Roman legates were only able to be witnesses of a domination bearing down all before him. The fifth rank only was assigned to Flavian, in clear proof that Alexandria had not recognised the rank given to his see in 381. As Chrysostome had been treated by Theophilus, so he was now put as

[1] I take the following account from Hergenröther's *Photius*, i., p. 62.

an accused person, whose bitterest opponent was his judge. Dioscorus and his guard of soldiers, and fanatical monks, allowed themselves the grossest acts of violence. The Papal letters were not even read. Eutyches was heard, not his accusers. He was acquitted, they were condemned, Flavian among them. The doctrine of the Two Natures in Christ was formally proscribed, and many bishops compelled to subscribe the decrees of Dioscorus. The Roman legates had vainly protested against this tumultuous and illegal proceeding. One, the Deacon Hilary, fled to Rome, and gave an accurate account of it to Pope Leo. Flavian, also, had in vain appealed to Pope Leo and a council to be held in Italy. He died shortly afterwards, in consequence of the illtreatment received. The whole Eastern church fell into uttermost bewilderment. The majority of bishops yielded to the ruling party. The emperor who, with his want of understanding, was wholly in their hands, did not hesitate to set the seal of his imperial authority upon the unexampled violence of the Alexandrine patriarch.

"If ever the necessity of the Papal Primacy came out clearly it was at this moment. It alone would bring help to the Easterns even in such a case. The best of them had fixed their eyes upon it. Theodoret of Cyrus, whom the synod of Dioscorus had even in his absence deposed, as it had many others, appealed from the unrighteous sentence by letter and messengers to Rome, as the emperor forbade him to go thither in person. In this letter he points out how St. Paul, in the contest about the law, betook himself to Peter. So much more must he turn for help to the Apostolic See, to which in all things the Primacy belongs.¹ He describes the grandeur of Rome in eloquent words. It owes its highest glory to the Apostle Peter, and is especially distinguished for its unshaken faith. This has shewn itself afresh in the wonderful letter to Flavian. He then recounts the proceeding of Dioscorus and his own previous life. He assures the Pope that he waits for the decision of the Apostolic Chair, and desires to be informed whether he should accept or not his deposition. He will yield entire obedience to the Papal decision.

"The clergy and people of Constantinople and a majority of the bishops of the provinces of Pontus, Asia, and Syria sought for Leo's help."

This, then, is the precise moment of which Pope Nicolas I. speaks to the emperor Michael, who, four hundred years after this, was bringing about the Greek schism at the instance of Photius. Of this he uses words most remarkable in the mouth of a Pope: "If the great Leo had not been divinely moved to open his mouth, the Christian religion would have perished".²

But the Pope acted. "In October, 449, he held a council at Rome, 'against not the judgment but the violence' enacted at Ephesus, and rejected all the

---

¹ Διὰ πάντα γὰρ ὑμῶν τὸ πρωτεύειν ἁρμόττει.—Ep. lii. of St. Leo.

² "Religio Christiana penitus corruisset."—St. Leo's own words to the emperor about what was decreed in the Latrocinium are as strong—" Quoniam revera omne Christianæ fidei sacramentum, quod absit a temporibus vestræ pietatis, exscinditur, nisi hoc scelestissimum facinus, quod cuncta sacrilegia excedit, aboleatur "—Ep. xliv.

decrees passed under the presidency of Dioscorus. In his own name and that of this council he wrote to the emperor Theodosius II. On the one hand he urged his own supreme judicial authority, which after Flavian's appeal was bound to take effect according to the canons of Sardica; on the other he endeavoured to move the emperor to give up the Robber Council and consent to a council to be held in Italy. Until this all should remain in the condition in which it was before that assemblage had taken place. In the same terms he wrote to Pulcheria, whose interest with her brother he asked for. The deacon Hilary did the same. He had not been able to bring over to her the former letters of the Pope. He now informed her of the state of things, to obtain her co-operation in correcting what had happened. At the same time the Pope warned also his vicar, Anastasius of Thessalonica, against an incautious acceptance of an unjust judgment, and against every error from the true faith. He consoled Flavian under his bitter persecution, for he was not yet aware of his death, and assured him of assistance. He encouraged his Nuncio, bishop Julian, the abbots, monks, and people of Constantinople to remain firm in the faith, and to trust in God's help for the victory of the truth, on which he counted without fail. 'We must, therefore, hold what we held, and in the raging of a single tempest embrace the perfect tranquillity of faith, until the truth pours its rays on every side and consumes the darkness of unbelief.'[1] In this hope Leo used every effort to

[1] Ep. xlviii.

defend orthodoxy, to relieve the innocent who were persecuted, and to annul the influence of the Robber Council.

"Events in the Eastern empire tended to increase perplexity. The power of the violent bishop of Alexandria seemed to increase when an Alexandrine priest, Anatolius, who had been up to this time agent of Dioscorus at the court, was put in the place of the deceased Flavian in the chair of Constantinople, and consecrated by Dioscorus himself before the end of the year 449. By this the see of the capital seemed to be placed in a certain dependence upon the Egyptian patriarch. He took, moreover, a further step towards ecclesiastical supremacy; for Dioscorus, upon hearing that the Pope had annulled his synod, took upon him to issue an anathema against Leo himself, in a council of his adherents held at Nicæa. The emperor Theodosius, led by this party, seemed still less inclined to do justice to the Pope's demands. The Pope wrote again on the 25th December, 449, and assured him of his unalterable fidelity to the Nicene definition. The Monophysites were accustomed to represent their opponents as infringing this.

"In February, 450, the emperor Valentinian III. came to Rome with his mother Galla Placidia and his wife Eudoxia. The Pope, with the bishops about him, induced them to write to Theodosius II. in the same sense as the Pope had written. The Western emperor put forward specially the Primacy of the Papal See, which has the right and faculty of judging upon the faith and bishops, and he urged the appeal of Flavian. All the three letters,[1] and that of Eudoxia to Pulcheria, express most decidedly their conviction of the supreme authority of the Roman bishop. But Theodosius remained deaf to these representations also. He rests, in his reply, on the fact that peace has been restored by the punishment of the innovator Flavian ; that the Council of Ephesus was entirely free ; that its decrees were most orthodox ; that full account of them had been already sent to the most reverend patriarch Leo.[2] The Pope's zeal was comforted only by the steadfastness of Pulcheria, who wrote in assent to him, and that of the clergy, monks, and people of Constantinople. These the Pope encouraged by further letters."

"In the meantime great changes were about to take place at Constantinople. The eunuch Chrysaphius, the chief support of the Eutycheans, fell under imperial displeasure, and was banished. The empress Eudocia withdrew to Jerusalem. Pulcheria, as great in ability as zealous for the faith, recovered all her influence. Her brother fell from horseback and died suddenly, July 28th, 450 ; she succeeded to the throne, and raised to it with herself the general Marcian, one of the ablest men in the empire, whom she took for husband, with the condition that she should maintain her own virgin estate. The new rulers declared unreservedly

---

[1] Ep. lv.-lvii. Valentinian's words are "Quatenus beatissimus Romanæ civitatis episcopus, cui principatum sacerdotii super omnes antiquitas contulit, locum habeat ac facultatem de fide et sacerdotibus judicare".—Ep. lv.

[2] Ep. lxii.

Catholic intentions. They recalled the deposed and banished bishops. They brought back the bones of the confessor Flavian, and interred them in the church of the Apostles, the usual burying-place of bishops and emperors. Marcian forthwith announced his accession to Pope Leo, recommended his government to his prayers, and intimated his wish to restore peace to the Church by a council to be held under the authority of the Roman See. The Eastern emperor's words to the Pope are: "We have thought fit, in the first instance, to announce this to your Holiness, who holds the office of bishop and ruler over the divine faith".[1] On which the comment of Theodoret is: "Marcian and Pulcheria wrote to Leo, acknowledging in him the fulness of power". Marcian and Anatolius received with honour the Papal legates who had been sent to Theodosius II. Anatolius, if not from conviction, moved at least by the force of circumstances, accepted the Pope's dogmatic letter to Flavian, in a synod held before the end of November, 450, while he condemned Nestorius and Eutyches. The letter was sent to be subscribed by the Eastern metropolitans, as it had already been by the Western bishops. Many bishops who had followed Dioscorus testified repentance, and begged for the communion of the Apostolic See. The emperor and empress announced this happy change to the Pope, and

---

[1] τὴν τὲ σὴν ἁγιωσύνην ἐπισκοπεύουσαν καὶ ἄρχουσαν τῆς θείας πίστεως ἱεροῖς γράμμασιν ἐν πρώτοις δίκαιον ἡγησάμεθα προσειπεῖν.—Ep. lxxiii., edition Migne, p. 900. Theodoret, fragment, Migne, 86, p. 168: ἔγραψαν Λέοντι . . πᾶσαν αὐτῷ αὐθεντίαν παρέχοντες. Compare the words of the Eastern emperor with those of the Western, just cited: "principatum sacerdotii super omnes".

invited him to a council to be held in their empire. Anatolius sent three ecclesiastics to Rome, with letters bearing full attestation of his orthodoxy.

Thereupon Leo acknowledged Anatolius, accepted what had been done at his synod in favour of the repentant bishops, who should be contented for the present to be maintained in their churches. He ordered the names of Dioscorus, of Juvenal of Jerusalem, and Eustathius of Berytus, the heads of the Robber Council, not to be recited any more in the Diptychs.

The further correspondence of the Pope with the Eastern emperor discloses only one point of difference between them. Marcian considered a fresh council in the East desirable, and even necessary. Leo, who had before wished for a council in Italy, considered it now superfluous and inexpedient, as he had on a similar former occasion. For the memory of Flavian was restored. Most of the Eastern bishops had subscribed Leo's dogmatic decision, which amply secured the faith. Eusebius of Dorylœum, who was in Rome, enjoyed the communion of the Church. Theodoret of Cyrus was restored. The condemnation of those who had fallen was prepared. Then a new discussion on the dogmatic question seemed dangerous and unallowable, since the Church's decision, already issued without a general council, could not be reconsidered. All that remained was indulgence to those in fault, a matter entrusted to the new Papal legates together with Anatolius, in which Leo only reserved to himself the decision upon Dioscorus and the other heads of party. Moreover, the

Western bishops could hardly leave their dioceses through an incursion of the Huns. Under these circumstances, Leo desired at least a postponement of the council to a more suitable time. But, as the emperor had already, on the 17th May, convoked a council for the 1st September, 451, to Nicæa in Bythynia, before he had received the Pope's dissuading letter of the 9th June, Leo acceded to his appointment, in spite of the alleged and other difficulties. The emperor's zeal induced him to this, and, in addition to the already appointed legates, the bishop Lucentius and the priest Basil, he appointed Paschasinus, bishop of Lilybæum, and the priest Boniface, who, with Julian of Cos, should represent him at the council. Paschasinus was to preside. He only regretted, in a letter to Anatolius, of June 26th, that the short time appointed by the emperor would prevent the attendance of the Western bishops. He also wrote to the council a letter for his legates to deliver. He declined personal attendance on the ground of old custom, and the necessity of his presence in Italy. But he claimed decidedly, in virtue of his Primacy, the right of presiding for the legates who should represent him. He set himself earnestly to work, in order to efface the bad effects of the Robber Council, and to distinguish the innocent from the guilty; and gave to that end wise advice to the council. He enjoined especially not to reconsider what was already decided, and to maintain the old statutes of Nicæa. Further, to restore the bishops who had been unjustly condemned. The condemnation of Monophysitism should not assist the opposite extreme of Nestorianism. And he added a warning against ambitious transgressions of the ancient hierarchical order, which were not rare in the East, and doubly to be feared since the bishop of Constantinople had made a nomination to the Chair of Antioch.

"At the council of Chalcedon, to which place the council originally invoked for September at Nicæa had been transferred, the faith of the Church was solemnly pronounced against Nestorius and against Eutyches by condemnation of the Robber Council, and by an explicit dogmatic decision. It was the most numerous and brilliant assembly of bishops which the East had ever seen. And here it was that the rank and the supremacy of the Roman Chair came most clearly forth, in spite of various intrigues and petty struggles of the Eastern jealousy, sometimes breaking into tumult. At the demand of Leo's legates, who presided, Dioscorus had to give up his place among the bishops. His transgressions were brought to light. He was expressly censured for having attempted to direct a general council without being charged to do it by the Roman See : a thing which had never been permitted. He had suppressed Leo's letter, and not communicated it to the assembled bishops. He had even ventured to excommunicate the Pope. Dioscorus was punished with complete deposition. The partners in his guilt, Juvenal of Jerusalem and Thalassius of Cæsarea, were more mildly treated. Flavian and Eusebius were pronounced innocent ; Theodoret and Ibas restored to their sees.

Leo's dogmatic letter was received with loud acclamation as rule of faith. The bishops exclaimed, ' This is the faith of the Fathers; this is the faith of the Apostles; Peter has spoken by Leo '. It was only considered further to satisfy the doubts of certain less intelligent prelates. The Roman legates carefully maintained their right, and the council expressly recognised the Primacy of Rome by solemnly asking for the papal confirmation of its decrees.

" The words they use in their synodical letter to the Pope are: 'You are the interpreter to all of the voice of St. Peter; you attract to all the blessing of his faith; you are the originator of good; you lead us, as the head leads the members; you are he intrusted by the Saviour with the guardianship of the Vine'; and they end with the words—' we recognise in you the whole force of our acts, for their confirmation and establishment'."[1]

The synodical letter of the council of Chalcedon to Pope Leo stands as an imperishable witness of the Patristic Church to the Primacy of Peter. It is herein acknowledged by the East as well as the West. It is acknowledged in language which no heretical ingenuity can parry or cut through; for what *can* a council say to a Pope *more* than " you lead us as the head leads the members; you are entrusted by the Saviour with the guardianship of the vine"; in which the episcopal descent from Peter, with all its consequences, as claimed by the line of Popes down to St. Leo's time, is compre-

[1] Hergenröther, *Photius*, i. 70.

hended; and "we refer the whole of our acts for confirmation and establishment to you".

But among these acts referred to the Pope for his confirmation we must take note of the three canons, the 9th, 17th, and 28th. Leo, in his instructions to his legates, as read at the council by one of them, the Roman priest Bonifacius, had said: "You are not to allow the constitution of the holy Fathers to be violated or infringed by any rash aggression. But preserve in all respects the dignity of our Person in yourselves, whom we have deputed to represent us. And if, perchance, any, trusting in the splendour of their own cities, attempt an usurpation, reject it, with the firmness which becomes you."

The bishop, the clergy, and the court of Constantinople were, in fact, bent upon obtaining a legal sanction for the great authority and ever-increasing influence which had been wielded by the bishop of the capital since the time of the great Theodosius, and the canon of the 150 Fathers, passed at Constantinople in 381, but never accepted, nor even presented for acceptance, at Rome; never accepted at Alexandria, but bitterly resented by the successive patriarchs, Theophilus and Cyril. In spite of all this, the force of the Eastern absolute monarchy, and the identification of the bishop's influence with the sovereign's authority in the East over the bishops, had made that bishop, in the seventy years from 381 to 451, not only practically a patriarch, on an equal line with the patriarchs of Alexandria and Antioch, but by the continual action of the Resident Council at

Constantinople had given him opportunities, carefully used even by the best bishops, such as Atticus, Proclus, and Flavian, of interfering with episcopal causes even beyond the jurisdiction of the three great sees, of Ephesus, Cæsarea in Pontus, and Heraclea. Not only had he made for himself a patriarchate over these, but Anatolius, the newly-appointed bishop in succession to the martyred Flavian, had gone to the length of appointing Maximus to the patriarchal see of Antioch, in defiance of the old right of the metropolitans to elect to the great see of the East.

"Now, by the canons 9 and 17, it was first of all distinctly expressed, 'If a bishop or an ecclesiastic has an accusation against the metropolitan of his province, he shall appeal either to the exarch of the diocese, or to the chair of the imperial city, Constantinople, and be judged by him'. The see of Constantinople thus obtained the right of judging over all the Eastern exarchates, and even over the patriarchates of Alexandria and Antioch. It is true this was only facultative, as the right of option was granted to the complainant between the archbishop of Constantinople and the superior metropolitan. But it was a great privilege that a metropolitan not belonging to the Thracian diocese, the jurisdiction over which had been ceded by the archbishop of Heraclea to Constantinople, could be tried by the archbishop of the capital. At the same time his jurisdiction, and that of his standing council, up to that time customary, and originally one of arbitration, was confirmed and extended. Party spirit led to a frequent preference of it before that of the patriarch or exarch. But even this was only a prelude to the further step taken in the famous 28th canon, on the privileges of the church of Constantinople. Herein not only was the third canon of 381 at Constantinople, which had been received neither at Rome nor Alexandria, confirmed; but the church of Constantinople was made the second in rank, the first after the Roman, and distinguished with similar privileges. To mark the parity between them, the privileges of Rome were deduced from its being the capital of the empire. If the canon of 381 said the bishop of Byzantium shall hold the next rank after the Roman, because his city is New Rome, this canon said the Fathers gave its privileges to Old Rome because it was the imperial city. Secondly, the right to confirm and consecrate all metropolitans in the three exarchates was recognised to belong to the see of New Rome. These exarchates were thus entirely subjected to him. Further, the archbishop of New Rome was to consecrate all bishops in the countries occupied by barbarians.

"There can be no doubt that this canon, while it became in later times the great support of Byzantine claims, did not as yet give any equality with the Roman bishop as to the primacy of jurisdiction, but only expressed the primacy of rank. It had chiefly in view to confirm the rank already conceded to Constantinople, and to give him material support and a firm basis by the formal subjection to him of the three exarchates. But its wording was only too favourable to further claims. Aftertime used it for the most thoroughgoing deductions, according to which it was alleged not only against the two elder Eastern patriarchs, but against the Roman. It was attempted by means of it to derive his prerogatives only from the gift of the Fathers and the rank of capital. As Old Rome was no longer the residence of the emperors, the privileges of the capital passed to Byzantium. Photius drew this last conclusion. For the present no one attempted to put in question the higher jurisdiction of the Roman See. The greatest gain to the bishop of Constantinople was that he now obtained a chartered right to be the supreme metropolitan of the three exarchates. He was thus put on equal level as to jurisdiction with the patriarchs of Alexandria and Antioch. But by means of the precedence over them given to him, and the influence of his standing council, and the facultative right of judgment given to him within their jurisdictions, which they did not possess in his, he overshadowed and overshone them."[1]

"The time was most favourable for the success in the council itself of this scheme for the aggrandisement of the see of New Rome, urged on by the bishop, the clergy, the people, and the virtuous sovereigns, Marcian and Pulcheria. Dioscorus, the patriarch of Alexandria, had just been deposed, for his unheard-of misdeeds. The new patriarch of Antioch, Maximus, had been irregularly appointed by Anatolius, on whom he depended. Juvenal of Jerusalem had been for twenty years trying

[1] Photius, i. 74.

to get himself made a patriarch, and he succeeded now. The see of Ephesus was vacant. The archbishop of Heraclea was not present, and could hardly have offered opposition. The bishops present found nothing contrary to the custom under which they had grown up in the exaltation given to the see of the capital, or were in fear of deposition for the share they had taken in the Robber Council. All agreed, except the Roman legates, who had taken no part in passing these canons. Several bishops, especially the Illyrian, and Thalassius of Cæsarea, had not subscribed.

The legates obtained a fresh sitting on the 1st November, and attacked these canons passed the day before. The legate Lucentius said the 28th canon was against those of Nicæa, on which occasion were cited as from the acts of that council the words, "the Roman church always had the Primacy": words which the Greeks did not refuse. They denied that they had been compelled to pass the canon. They had done it freely and canonically. The bishop of the capital had long possessed these privileges, and the 3rd canon of 381 expressed them. The legates rejected this canon and the alleged custom. If those privileges were already valid, they required no confirmation; if they were not, they were to be rejected as an uncanonical innovation. Finally, the imperial commissioners declared, that the Primacy over all, and the highest rank, belonged to the archbishop of Old Rome; that similar rank should be allowed to the archbishop of New Rome, and the right to consecrate and confirm the metropolitans in the three exarchates.

The Eastern bishops agreed to this. The legate Lucentius demanded the rejection of the canons passed in the absence of the Roman legates; otherwise they protested and gave in their protest to the acts. With this protest the council concluded.

The synodical letter of the council, together with its canons and acts, were carried at once to Rome, and the assent of the Pope to the canons passed in favour of the bishop of Constantinople was hoped for in spite of the protestation put in against them by his legates. The letter pleaded that if the council had confirmed the old custom that the metropolitans of the Pontic, Thracian, and Asian exarchates should be consecrated by the bishop of Byzantium, it was not so much a favour granted to this see, as a provision made against disturbance being caused in the particular metropolis by the choice. They had also confirmed the canon of the 150 Fathers upon the rank of the see of Constantinople immediately after the Apostolic See of Rome, "in the confidence that you have so often extended to the church of Constantinople the radiance of your own apostolic dignity, because you impart without grudging a portion of your own goods to your household". "Be pleased, therefore, most holy and blessed Father, to give your consent to what we have determined for the removal of confusion, and the strengthening of good order in the Church. For the legates of your Holiness have warmly opposed these decisions, undoubtedly with the purpose that every good thing should proceed, in the first place, from your care; so that, as in matters of faith, so in discipline, all success should be ascribed to you. We are but carrying out the desire of our sovereigns, of the senate, of the whole imperial city, in giving this honour from the ecumenical council, as proceeding in the first instance from your Holiness, being well aware that all the good which happens to children is set down to the account of their parents. As we then have left the decision to the head (κεφαλή), let the head (κορυφή) also fulfil its part to the children. Thus our sovereigns will be obliged, who have made the decision of your Holiness a law of the State. The see of Constantinople will be rewarded for the zeal with which it has fulfilled the direction of your piety. To assure you that we have done nothing through favour or through enmity, but by guidance of the divine will, we have made known all our acts to you, for your confirmation and acceptance."

With this most flattering exposition to the Pope it was sought to win from him the approval which his legates had refused; since, without this, the privileges of Constantinople could never meet with general recognition. The letter of the council was also accompanied with a letter from the emperor Marcian, and one from Anatolius himself, carried by the bishop Lucian. Anatolius, in asking the Pope's confirmation of the privileges to his see, says, "The see of Constantinople has for its parent your own Apostolic See, having specially joined itself thereunto"; and expresses his confidence that "your Holiness will reckon as your own the honour done to the see of Constantinople, inasmuch as your Apostolic See has long treated it with affectionate care, and has imparted to it ungrudgingly assistance as it needed ".

"Anatolius was urgent. He hoped to reach his end before the see of Alexandria was filled up. He offered everything to gain Rome's consent. He had even got the Papal Nuncio Julian on his side, to intercede with Leo for him. Marcian and Pulcheria, whom Leo could hardly refuse, joined their requests to his, and many Eastern prelates whose interest was against this canon. Everything seemed to work in his favour, and the reiterated assurances of attachment to the Roman See calculated to set the Pope's mind at rest as to ulterior designs."

"But all this was unable to prevail on Leo to approve an innovation in the Church.[1] He perceived the point to which the efforts of the Byzantine bishops, too long endured, would lead in the end; what disadvantage they would bring to the peace of the Church; what a danger was prepared for the East in such a violation of the rights of its oldest and most illustrious sees. He absolutely declined the requests made to him. In his letters to the emperor, the empress, to Anatolius, and to Julian, dated 22nd May, 452, he set forth, in detail, the grounds which determined him to reject that augmentation of power in the see of Byzantium, so ardently desired at Chalcedon. First, Constantinople had no claim to such an exaltation of power and rank. It is an imperial residence; it is not an Apostolic See. Temporal precedence cannot furnish a basis for spiritual. Secondly, the canon directly contradicts the privileges of Alex-

[1] Photius, i. 80, translated.

andria and Antioch, as well as the rights of provincial primates, the sixth canon of the Nicene Council, and all the constitutions of the Fathers. Thirdly, the pretension of Anatolius could not be supported by the canons of Eastern bishops in 381, which had been by no means recognised. Fourthly, the whole decree was the result of ambition, and tended to the confusion of the Church. Fifthly, Anatolius, from the very beginning of his episcopate, had no reason to aim at any advance but that of virtue; and his pretension was so much the more blameable that he would not give it up even at the representation of the Roman legates; and he had already done too much against the canons for this new attempt to be allowed to pass uncensured. Sixthly, many bishops had been frightened and seduced into subscribing these decrees: except for this, it was impossible that they would have accepted them. Again, it was unjust to use the humiliation and vacancy of the see of Alexandria to infringe its rights, and a council assembled only on matters of faith for purposes of self-exaltation. It was a most dangerous example for the future. Imitation of it could only lead to the greatest perplexity. It was injurious to Anatolius himself, who risked losing what was his own in stretching after what did not belong to him. Lastly, the Pope was preserver and protector of the ancient law : he would be wanting to his holiest duties if he acceded to such an innovation or endured it. He could not, and dared not, prefer the wishes of an individual to the good of the whole House of the Lord."

In writing to the empress Pulcheria,[1] Leo says: "What desires the bishop of the church of Constantinople more than he has obtained? What will satisfy him, if the greatness and glory of such a city are too little for him? To attack the primacy of so many metropolitans, to bring a war of confusion into the provinces arranged in peace by the moderation of the Nicene Council, and to produce the consent of certain bishops, to which effect has been denied during so many years; for it is about sixty years since this connivance on their part is boasted of by him, but it avails him nothing for some one to attempt what no one has been able to gain. What has been obtained from the bishops, disregarding the rules of the Nicene Council, we annul by the authority of the Apostle St. Peter." While to Anatolius himself nothing can be more severe than the letter which he wrote censuring his arrogance and ambition. And he confirmed only the decrees of faith as passed in the council of Chalcedon. Thereupon Anatolius was so angry at the Pope's censure of himself, contained in this letter, that he would not promulgate it. In consequence, the Eutychians began to rumour that the Pope rejected the council. So the emperor Marcian, in a letter dated 15th February, 453, besought the Pope to confirm the council in a letter which should be read in all churches. This formal request of the Eastern emperor throws light upon the fact that the Nicene Council must have been confirmed by Pope Sylvester.[2]

Anatolius at last was obliged to excuse himself to

---

[1] Ep. cv. 　　[2] This is remarked by Hefele, i. 42.

Leo, in his letter, April, 454.[1] He was deeply troubled at the Pope's silence: he was quite innocent, as an individual, of any desire to aggrandise his see. It was the clergy of his church and the bishops in those parts who had been so eager for this; and even so the force and confirmation of their acts had been left to his Holiness.

The Pope replied to the emperor that he had already, in his letters, issued a confirmation of the dogmatic decrees of the council, which Anatolius had concealed, in order not to disclose his own shame; but that he would do this again, in order to dissipate every doubt as to his own mind. He did this in a letter to all the bishops who had been present at Chalcedon. In the first part he approved all the decisions of the council in matters of faith; while he rejected what had been passed against the canons of the Nicene Council, and he added to his letter a copy of the former letter to Anatolius, which had been suppressed by him.

It has been remarked that Leo found it harder to prevail over the pride of Anatolius than over the savage temper of Attila. But at last the full reception of Leo's decision by the emperor Marcian made him give way, and, as said above, he resumed his correspondence with the Pope.

In this great battle the Pope obtained a brilliant victory. The 28th canon seemed to be entirely given up. Down to the time of Photius it was not taken into the collection of canons. It had no legal force. But the

[1] Ep. cxxii.

principles which led to it continued to work on. The usual Byzantine employment of "accomplished facts" took place. Emperors less loyal than Marcian arose. The whole subsequent history justified the conduct of Leo, and shewed his penetration of the design fostered at Constantinople, by the plotting of future patriarchs from Acacius to Photius, by the tyranny of Byzantine monarchs, and the imitation of their Russian successors. Leo had detected, censured, and chained down for the time the spirit of schism.

Recapitulate the facts just passed in review.

At a great crisis in the history of the Church an Ecumenical Council had been legitimately called. Papal legates had attended it. A patriarch of Alexandria had presided. It acquitted the heretic abbot, and persecuted, even to death, the orthodox bishop who had brought him to judgment; and it established the heresy which denied the true faith of the Incarnation. As soon as this was reported to the Pope, by one of his legates who fled from the council, he annulled its decision by a plenary act of authority. The reigning emperor took part against him; but he died by a sudden accident. His sister, and the husband she had chosen for the good of the empire, succeeded him. They called a fresh council, which undid the wrong. This council accepted and subscribed the Pope's letter upon the great doctrine at issue. This letter of the Pope determined for ever the true expression of the Church's faith upon that very mystery in virtue of which the Church exists. The Council further addressed a synodical letter to the Pope, an act which expresses in the highest degree its own authority. In this letter it acknowledges the Primacy of the Pope as the authority of a father over his children, and as descending from the direct gift of Christ; and they are Eastern bishops who say this. But, besides, the Council beseeches the Pope to ratify certain canons which it has passed, the scope of which was to increase the authority of the bishop of Constantinople, on the ground that his see was the capital. The emperor and empress, the latter being that granddaughter of the great Theodosius who alone of his race inherited his genius together with his faith, beseech the Pope to consent. The senate, clergy, people of Constantinople join; the bishop professes himself his most humble servant; the other bishops of the Council are eager to exalt the chair of the capital over the sees of their ancient patriarchs, descending, like the Pope, from St. Peter.

What does the Pope? Declaring himself the guardian of that constitution which had come down from the beginning, and which was exhibited in the decrees of the Nicene Council, he replies that it is contrary to his duty to allow any such exaltation of a new see at the expense of the whole hierarchic order, which had subsisted from the time of the Apostles to his own. He refuses his consent, and the offending canons are expunged. The emperor, the empress, the bishops of the Council, the senate of Constantinople, and, last of all, the bishop himself, give way.

But by what power did Leo accomplish this? There

is only one possible answer. The Primacy, which the synodical letter of the Council acknowledges, was seated in the mind and heart of the Church at large. St. Peter Chrysologus wrote from the see of Ravenna to Eutyches, starting his heresy: "We exhort you, honoured brother, obediently to attend to the words of the most blessed Pope of the Roman city; for St. Peter, who lives and presides in his own see, grants the truth of the faith to those who seek for it". So Theodoret cried out from his see of Cyrus beyond Antioch to Leo: "I wait for the sentence of your Apostolic See, for it behoves you to have the Primacy in all things". So the Syrian church placed in its very devotions the words of its great teacher Ephraem: "Simon, my disciple, I have made thee the foundation of holy Church. I have already called thee the Rock, because thou shalt sustain my whole building. Thou are the bishop of those who build me a Church on earth. Through thee will I give all nations to drink." This belief was everywhere, and in virtue of this Leo annulled the Robber Council. In virtue of this he set forth the true faith of the Incarnation. In virtue of this he defended and maintained the true constitution of the Church, and censured the innovation of Greek despotism. In virtue of this he prevailed.

But we must also bear in mind what his own temporal position and that of Rome itself was. In this year, 451, of the council of Chalcedon, it hung as it were on a single thread, for Attila was expected. In the next year, 452, Leo had gone to Mantua to meet his advance upon Rome after he had destroyed Aquileia. All Rome's defence then lay in the prayers and the presence of her Pontiff. Even if it were only a poetic legend that the "Scourge of God," when Leo in his sacerdotal robes approached him, saw the two patron saints of Rome above his head, and therefore listened to his request to spare the city, it was Leo's act which obtained that result. Had Attila marched forward to Rome, there was none to stay him. Had he entered Rome it would have been a Mogul massacre and destruction, not a Gothic levying of blackmail. He would have left the city of Peter, not as it was after the three days' plunder of Alaric, or after the fourteen days of Genseric, but as he left so many cities of the West: Rome would have been as Babylon and Niniveh are.

Leo returned to Rome its saviour, in 452. In 455 he saved it again from Genseric. In the interval of these years he refused to give up to human ambition, pregnant with future schism, the original constitution of the Church; he refused to suffer "the vine entrusted to him by the Saviour Himself," in the words of the council, to be laid waste. And he did all this when the condition of that very Rome, in which he dwelt as the citadel of the Christian faith, was not safe for a day from barbaric threatening. The facts which took place in these years are frightful. In 454 Leo confirmed the doctrinal decrees of Chalcedon. In that same year the emperor Valentinian, as if he had been an assassin, plunged his sword in the body of Aetius, who had been for twenty years the support of the empire which remained to him.

He then brought about his own murder, by the vengeance of an outraged nobleman, who seized the throne, and compelled the widowed empress to accept him for her husband. She is said to have invited the Vandal Genseric to come from Carthage and avenge her dishonour. He came, and the emperor of two months was killed; while St. Leo saved his city from destruction, but saw it submitted to the plunder and cruelty of the Vandals during fourteen days. Thus in one year he witnessed the miserable end of the Theodosian line in Valentinian; the usurpation and murder of his successor, Maximus; the captivity of Eudoxia, a second time widowed, and with her daughters carried away to Carthage; and a new emperor, Avitus, who in the next year (456) was killed by Ricimer. St. Leo saw another emperor, Majorian, sent to Rome by the new emperor of the East, who succeeded Marcian in 457. His murder also, after four years' reign full of promise, St. Leo witnessed before he ended his own time of twenty-one years in 461. In the midst of such scenes St. Leo spoke and acted as if the peace of God ruled all around him. He legislated for the Church as for a kingdom set for ever. No mention is found in his works that he had twice saved Rome from destruction.

We are now in a position to review the whole four generations which passed from the Nicene Council to that of Chalcedon. In Pope Leo the Roman Primacy has become the Church's centre of gravity, the Church's centre of life. At Nicæa it stood at the head of the episcopate which had sprung out of its own bosom.

What were the causes, either of internal action, or of external events, or of both together, which produced this development? Was it aimed at by the Pope? Did it come to him through means which he had sought; by the force of events which he desired? Was it foreseen or unforeseen? Conscious or unconscious? The work of friends or of enemies? I shall proceed to give what I think will furnish some sort of answer to these questions.

First, I will take the great line of thought and doctrine in the Church.

During fifty years, which date almost exactly from the founding of Constantine's new capital, the Church was vehemently agitated by the Arian heresy and its offshoots. The Eusebian bishops, acting upon the jealous and tyrannical spirit of the emperor Constantius, moved him, at the time of the council of Sardica, against the Roman Primacy, and had well-nigh anticipated the division of the East and West. The Church was delivered from schism as well as heresy by the sudden death of that emperor, at the age of forty-four, in 361. During the whole period, the condition of the great Eastern sees had been calamitous. At Alexandria, Athanasius, hero and saint as he was, not only suffered five banishments, and was for years in peril of his life, but men of evil doctrine and evil life, a Pistus, a George, a Gregory, were successively thrust into his see, and at his death, in 373, he was succeeded by the heretic, Lucius. The ruin caused by these successive inroads in the diocese of the great confessor, and in the province over which it presided, cannot be expressed. It was worse still at Antioch, where, after the unjust deposition of Saint Eustathius in 330, first Euphronius, then Flaccillus, thirdly Stephanus, all of Arian opinions, were thrust into the third see of the Church. Stephanus was deposed even by Constantius for a scandalous act of villany perpetrated in Antioch upon a bishop, who was also an ambassador, bearing the decrees of the council of Sardica. Then came Leontius, another Arian, and of immoral life. He was followed by Eudoxius, who had come from the see of Germanicia, and went on to that of Constantinople. Thereupon the Arians made Meletius bishop, supposing him to be one of themselves. Finding out their mistake, they substituted Euzoius for him. As the orthodox elected Paulinus, Antioch had three bishops at once. Worse yet, if worse could be, was the history of the see of Constantinople from the death in 337 of its first virtuous bishop Alexander, whose prayer delivered the Church from Arius, to the time when St. Gregory, in 379, set up in a private room his small church of the Resurrection. During all that time it was the chosen home of heresy and faction. The whole recrudescence of the Arian heresy sprung from that Eusebius who was not satisfied with the see of Nicomedia when Constantius moved his court to the new capital. He succeeded in obtaining that see; then Macedonius, and thirdly Eudoxius made it infamous. Constantine found his deceiver, Constantius and Valens their worst instruments, in its bishops.

In the meantime a succession of men of highest

character sat in the Roman See: Sylvester, Marcus, Julius, Liberius, Damasus. When Theodosius terminated the course of official Arianism, he referred his subjects to the doctrine taught by Damasus at Rome, who continued the institution of the chief Apostle, and by Peter at Alexandria. In the strain of the Arian tempest, Rome had held fast to her moorings: Liberius upon his return had rejected the council of Rimini, and died reputed a saint by St. Ambrose, Pope Siricius, Theodoret. The result of the Arian heresy had been to re-establish with double force that Primacy which the bishops of the Eusebian party had done their utmost to disparage.

A generation later, the Pelegian heresy called out, as we have seen, in Africa, the efforts of two large councils, which condemned it, and sent their decrees for approval and confirmation to Pope Innocent. Thus in his later years St. Augustine was led naturally and unconsciously to delineate the special powers of that Roman Principatus which he had ever acknowledged. The like is the result of his long contest with the Donatist schism. By it he was led deeply to probe the nature of the Church's bond over her children: and to lay down in controversy with those schismatics principles which exhibit in the clearest light the Roman unity. Thus he shewed that the possession of the sacraments, and a valid succession to priesthood and episcopate by those who are in a state of schism, far from alleviating, intensified the guilt of the parties concerned. The Pelagian heresy and the Donatist schism served equally to bring into stronger light the functions and attributes of the see which presided over unity and truth.

At the same time another heretic, seated on the see of Constantinople, attacks the faith of the Church. He is supported by imperial favour at New Rome; he is struck down by the sentence of the bishop in Old Rome. A council, the second from the Nicene, sits. Composed entirely of Eastern bishops—subjects of the emperor who supports the heretical tenant of the see to which his own favour has exalted him—it acknowledges in express terms that Pope Celestine sits in the See of Peter. Thus it makes up for whatever has been lost by the non-existence of the acts of the first council. A child and his mother, not daring to occupy Rome itself on account of its insecurity, sit on the remains of the Western empire, while the great Eastern capital suffers the deposition of its bishop, whom all the private favour of the emperor is unable to save. The second see of the Church, an Eastern see, is prominent in acting under the guidance of the first see. The heresy of Nestorius illustrates the Petrine monarchy, as the stability of Rome, the Apostolic See, marks the inconstancy of imperial Constantinople.

Once more. A fourth heresy has its birth at Constantinople. The abbot Eutyches is reserved, in his old age, to produce from the new capital the opposite error to Nestorius. This time, strange to say, the great see of Athanasius and Cyril is involved in the guilt of a heresy which denies the Incarnation. The bishop of the new capital is martyred for his defence of it. The bishop of St. Mark's see takes strongest part against that of St. Peter; is ruined by his folly; he deals a blow thereby at the see which these two great Doctors made so illustrious—a blow from which it is destined never to recover. But the blow which he aimed at St. Peter's See results in causing its bishop to be proclaimed, by the largest council which ever sat in the East, as the father of the assembled bishops, as the man intrusted by Christ Himself with the guardianship of the Vine. And incidentally the whole scheme of exaltation devised by the bishops and emperors of New Rome, for the exaltation of its bishop, is brought forth to light, censured, and rejected.

What could be more opposed to the wishes and the efforts of the Popes during these hundred and twenty years than the several heresies and schisms, just mentioned? They combated them resolutely, and, by the help of God, overcame them. It is a collateral result that their own constancy in all this time worked upon the mind of the Church, and drew from her a deeper and larger acknowledgment of the power stored up in the See of Peter against the time of danger.

These are internal causes which I note, as tending to bring the Primacy into full action between 325 and 451 : they belong to the inward life of the Church, and betoken her progress as a spiritual kingdom.

I turn now to outward events, the fluctuations and transitions of temporal power.

The reigns of the sons and grandsons of the great

Theodosius witnessed not only the final division of Constantine's empire, but the dissolution in the Western half of the imperial power itself, as well as the exaggeration in the East of monarchic power, which we term the lower or Byzantine empire. By Leo's time Gaul and Spain, Illyricum and Africa, had been seized by various settlements of the Northern tribes. But the bishops in these various countries looked to Rome at once as the symbol of the empire, the last remaining link of the great civilisation which supported their natural life, and the origin and perpetual source of the spiritual discipline and doctrine in which they were bishops. The whole course of events in the West led its bishops to rally round the bishop of Rome : to seek, at his hands, for solution of all emerging questions of discipline or doctrine. Not only was there no see to compete with his, but his name expressed to their ears everything that was dear in religion and in country. The Arian Visigoth or Vandal was equally frightful as heretic or as barbarian. Again, Honorius and Valentinian were not masters in the West, as Arcadius and Theodosius II. were in the East. In the West the bishops advanced in freedom in the same proportion as they declined in the East. While Rome witnessed their involuntary emancipation from a weakened lord, Constantinople locked them up in an iron despotism. The bearing of the West and the East in the two councils of Ephesus and Chalcedon is strikingly different. There was no imperial *Comes* to affect Western minds, as he expressed the imperial pleasure to the bishops of the Eastern patriarchates: the Roman legates did not submit to his ordering.

This brings us to the most grievous alteration which the successors of Theodosius were bringing about in the Church's hierarchy. The wish to concentrate all power in Constantinople, for the purpose of banding their empire into one, against the Persian empire, threatening with a rival despotism on the East, and the Gothic or Hunnic thundercloud ever ready to burst from the North,—this real and ever-pressing danger led them, one and all, to increase the power and influence of the bishop in the capital. He was the first member of their court. They appointed him; they counted on him. The Alexandrine bishop was at the head of the most turbulent of cities, the most inflammable of peoples. The Antiochene bishop presided over eleven great provinces in the very neighbourhood of the Persian enemy. The emperor's hand could not be laid upon them, as it lay ever on the bishop of Constantinople. Thus St. Leo had reason to speak of that "connivance" in the seventy years preceding which had looked with indulgence upon a bishop building himself up on an illegitimate canon, making himself the body of a patriarch out of the subjected exarchates of Ephesus, Cæsarea, and Heraclea; finally deposing the two sees which ran up to Peter under the magnificence of the royal city, which dominated all the East, and took the place of Rome, twice captured and plundered. The alteration was indeed significant between the great position held at Nicæa by the bishops of Alexandria and Antioch, when the bishop of Byzantium was unnoticed, and the position of those bishops at Chalcedon: Dioscorus, patriarch of Alexandria, deposed; Maximus, the new patriarch of Antioch, fearful for his illicit ordination, by the hand of the bishop of the capital; while Anatolius was moving emperor, empress, senate, and bishops to get a charter for the encroachments of seventy years, sanctioned by an ecumenical council. In the first case, Rome, Alexandria, and Antioch stood at the head of a hierarchy, descending without break in its constituted order from the beginning. In the second, the See of Peter stood at the head as before, but over against him was the ex-suffragan of Heraclea, claiming the second place as bishop of Nova Roma, and aspiring to lead the East as Rome led the West. The key of the latter's position was that, while the bishop was named, the emperor was meant, and the Eastern bishops were ready to submit to the decision of the Resident Council in the capital, because the decision of the Council signified the favour of the emperor.

The temporal circumstances thus touched upon embrace six distinct but closely connected elements of change. They are:—

1. The weakening and at length overthrow of the imperial power in the West.

2. The barbarian, which are also Arian, settlements in Gaul, Spain, and most of all in Africa.

3. The uncertain and perilous position of the bishops in these several countries, over against the new princes.

4. The political peril and degradation of Rome, unsafe and exposed to danger as a city, while it continues the

sole point to which the bishops of the various provinces could look for support and guidance.

5. The position more and more assumed by the bishop of Constantinople, in which he stands as the leader of the whole Eastern episcopate.

6. The cowering of the Eastern bishops under the Byzantine despotism.

Not one of these changes but was the cause of anxious solicitude to the bishop of Rome. He had made no one of them. They were in his eyes the most terrible calamities. He struggled against them with his utmost power. But in like manner as the heresies and schisms first mentioned, so the collective effect of these external changes was to enhance the relative position and power of the Pope in the Church, and to make his see, as we have called it, the centre of gravity and action.

We have now noted an assemblage of internal and external causes independent of the action of any particular Pope, or of the collected action of the Popes, in the years which elapse between the two great councils of Nicæa and Chalcedon. In that period what may be termed the patriarchal constitution of the hierarchy is not only completed but terminated. The simple progress of events has shewn its insufficiency to meet the danger and necessity of the times.

One might say that Constantine's selection of a new capital, the division of the empire thence resulting, the Eastern jealousy which thenceforth enthroned itself on the banks of the Bosphorus, led to results which shewed this insufficiency in open light. Not only did the great sees of the East fall a prey to heresy and schism, so that the whole Eastern hierarchy, which had ranged itself so grandly in battle array at Nicæa, appeared in rout and disorder when Theodosius was raised to the throne, but Alexandria, Antioch, and Constantinople from that time further fell into continual rivalry with each other. The greater see, which was above all rivalry, was needed. And thus the course, both of internal and external events, without any intention or ambition of the Popes themselves, had in St. Leo's time fully revealed the power which the Divine Providence had put from the beginning in His Church. When the empire came into the Church it called into fresh and necessary action the bishop who presided in the Church as the emperor presided in the State. This was henceforth the normal condition of things. But then the rule of bad emperors, such as Constantius and Valens, and the rule of weak emperors, such as Arcadius and Theodosius II., made even more evident the need of a counterpoise in an equivalent power for good. It demanded at once the generative, moderating, also protective and defensive, authority of St. Peter ruling in his See. For as the emperor's power in the Church, accruing to him as a Christian, was universal, so it required to be balanced by a power not confined to a single patriarchate, but extending over the whole Church. And this is an important lesson which we learn from the history of the first century during which the empire came into union with the Church.

A few words must now be said on the particular qualities of the individual who was raised up to sit in St.

Peter's See at a time so exceptional as the twenty-one terrible years of St. Leo's pontificate.

First I would remark that St. Leo exercised no power which the whole line of his predecessors had not claimed before him. I have before touched upon the letters of the Popes, and drawn out from them sufficiently the nature of the authority which they set forth. Here, therefore, I need only say that the continuous series from Siricius, strictly carrying on what Damasus, Liberius, Julius, had written before him, and the first instance of which is found in the letter of Pope Clement, at the end of the first century, bases the authority of the Popes upon one, and only one, foundation. That foundation is the descent from Peter, sitting as bishop in the See of Rome, and the inheritance of Peter's universal Pastorship; his being the Rock on which the Church is built; his having the keys of the kingdom of heaven on earth placed in his hands to open or to shut; the perpetual office of confirming his brethren, which the Lord confided to Peter, and which the need of the Church made perpetual. This is what the Popes one and all wrote to the bishops all over the world; and the bishop is yet to be discovered who wrote back to them either of these two replies—Peter received no such charge, or you have inherited none such from him. Surely we may take the answer of the most eminent Father of the West as speaking for all: "The Apostolic See always had the Principate," and his delineation of that Principate in meeting the heresy of Pelagius as sufficient and accurate. And we may allow St. Cyril, the stoutest of Alexandrian patriarchs, being also himself the next in rank to the Roman bishop, to call St. Celestine, a Pope contemporary with St. Augustine, "archbishop of the world". It seems to me that, as to patristic authority, as to history, and as to the Church's voice pronounced at Ephesus in 431, at Chalcedon in 451, we may say, "Causa finita est". If there be in the whole world a man illogical enough to accept the doctrine declared at Chalcedon because of the authority of the Church pronouncing it, but to deny the Primacy acknowledged at Chalcedon, we can but leave such a man in his error, wherein it is clear that solicitude for truth does not guide him.

St. Leo maintained to the whole world, to the Eastern and Western emperors and empresses, to Theodosius II., who was indisposed to listen, though he did not venture to deny; to Marcian and Pulcheria, who were loyal and devoted; to the insolent Dioscorus, Cyril's unworthy successor; to the aspiring Anatolius, who suggested a future Photius; to all the bishops who would put up an imperial Constantinople in the face of an Apostolic Rome, that he inherited St. Peter's universal Pastorship. He claimed as much as this, and no more. So had his whole line claimed. But what the whole line had claimed, he was enabled by the force of things around him, by unexampled transitions of power, by terrible calamities, to exercise in the face of the whole world. His firmness of character, his great legislative spirit, his keen doctrinal accuracy of thought, his fearless and majestic demeanour and language, produced this result. In the interval between Attila and Genseric, when Rome trembled at the prospect of coming destruction, he asserted that Rome, by the gift of God alone, was the centre of the spiritual power which God had set up, and Constantinople in all the pride of empire, her princes, her senate, and the senate of the Church, acknowledged the truth of his assertion.

If he had not so acted, if he had failed in one iota of the power which he claimed and exercised, where would the Catholic Church have been? She would have been involved in fatal error at the Latrocinium, an error into which the Eastern emperor had plunged himself headlong. She would have submitted at Chalcedon to an usurpation, which, when partially effected four hundred years later, tore from her body a vast number of bishops, and has had for its ultimate result to make the city of Constantine the chief seat of the anti-Christian theocracy; wherein, moreover, the so-called successor of Anatolius exercises whatever authority he claims to possess as a Christian bishop, by grant of the mortal enemy of Christianity, who struck down Constantine's successor and put himself in his place. The tribes who were settling in the various provinces of the Western empire would have broken up such an episcopate as they chose to retain into as many petty jurisdictions as represented their own transitory power. Had this been effected, who would have made those tribes into nations? Who would have given cohesion to the ever-dividing Teuton? Where would have been either a Christian Europe or the world's actual civilisation? Where also would have been the kingdom of Christ, and the Stone cut without hands from the side of the mountain?

By Leo's vigour, his clear intellectual vision, his impassive moral courage, truth and unity were saved together. We possess them by inheritance from him: precisely in virtue of that succession which he maintained. And as the fourth council acknowledged all that he claimed when it welcomed his great dogmatic letter with the words, "Peter has spoken by Leo," so, fourteen centuries after his time, the universal Church exults when he who sits at the helm of Peter bears the name of all others in that unending line most renowned for fortitude and wisdom.

INDEX.

Alexandria, the second see, its bishop called to account by the Pope, 84, 94; degraded by the rise of Constantinople, 158; its position at the Nicene Council, 217; and at the council of Chalcedon, 543; its sufferings in the five banishments of Athanasius, 223

Alexandria and Antioch, their several schools, 452

Ambrose, St., his election, daily life, influence, writings, 432-5; acknowledges the Pope as the Doorkeeper and Shepherd of the Gospels, 329; deduces the whole order of the hierarchy from the Pope, 256

Anastasius, Pope, universal authority claimed in his single surviving letter, 330

Antioch, heresy and schism at, for fifty years, 220; deplorable state in 346; degraded by the rise of Constantinople, 158; its position at the Nicene Council, 217; and at the council of Chalcedon, 543

Athanasius, St., elected in 428 archbishop of Alexandria, 166; threatened by Constantine with deposition, 166; refuses to attend a council at Cæsarea, 167; attends a council at Tyre, and is deposed, 170; appeals to Constantine, and is banished to Treves, 171; returns, and is attacked by Eusebius, 179; flies to Rome, and is acquitted by Pope Julius, 179; returns in 346 after his second exile, 186; attacked by Constantius at the synods of Arles and Milan, 189; his judgment respecting Pope Liberius, 197; driven from Alexandria in the night attack, 200; declares the Church's independence of the empire, 202; an outlawed fugitive for five years, 203; returns by Julian's decree, 203; banished a fifth time, by Julian, but soon restored, 210; reverence of St. Basil for him, 211; his five banishments, and the sufferings of Alexandria, 223; his life, character, and style, 411; describes the virginal life, 317, 469; his first two treatises, 461, 399

Atticus, his episcopate, 306

Augustine, St., exponent of the union of Church and State, 289; his letter to Macedonius, 290; and to Count Boniface, 292; appeals to the actions of Jewish and heathen kings, 293; to the conversion of St. Paul, 296; welcomes the rescripts of Pope Innocent in 417, 335; six points in which the Principate of the Apostolic See is accepted by him, 337-341; draws the *City of God* from the fall of Rome, 361; his conversion, life, and works, 440-5; contrast of his life and writings with those of Theodore of Mopsuestia, 458

Banishment of Bishops by emperors, what it meant, 226

Basil, St., describes the persecution of Valens, 231; his homage to St. Athanasius, 211; his life and works, 421

Boniface I., Pope, expounds the Nicene Constitution, 66; defines the Roman Primacy at the fall of the city, 362

Celestine I., Pope, his Primacy completely acknowledged at the council of Ephesus, A.D. 431, 499-501, 312-315; his charge to his legates at this council, 311

Claudian surpasses Prudentius in style, 474; compared with Prudentius and Rutilius as to Rome's position, 481

Chrysostome, St. John, his birth, life, and writings, 429; parallel of his life with that of Theodore of Mopsuestia, 458

Church and State, their union set forth in the imperial letter of 430, 281; held unanimously by Fathers and emperors, 282, 286, 288; imperial power guardian of the union, 287; St. Augustine its exponent, 289-297; maintained by the laws of both powers, 298, 300, 302: produces a State-made patriarch in the East, 322; their reciprocal attitude to each other, 300-304; requires the equipoise of the Papacy for the safety of the Church, 544

Clement I., Pope, his letter, 96

Constantine, his position and design when sole emperor, 127; his legislation, 129-135, 265; his sovereignty, 136-145, 265; moves the imperial residence from Rome, 147, 160; consecrates Constantinople as Nova Roma, 149; oppresses the Church in his later years, 163-175, 216-217, 267; joined, originally, the empire of the world with the advocacy of the Church, 265; misled by Eusebius, 266, 163; frustration of his intentions in founding Constantinople, 271, 222; accepted the Church as the bearer of the one divine revelation, 287, 303, 145

Constantinople, rise of the see, 152, 305, 317; becomes at once the central field of heresy, 154, 253; in Arian hands for forty years, 221; exalted by every Byzantine emperor, 261, 322, 542; internal administration of the diocese, 319

Constantius I., his person and character, 187, 190; attacks Pope Liberius, 193; is denounced by Hosius and Athanasius, 202; receives clinical baptism from an Arian, and dies, 206

Council of Nicæa, an epoch in history, 29, 71; on six points, 383-7; aspect of the Church when it was convened, 34; viewed as proof of the Christian people, 36; viewed as a witness of the Church's previous history, 43; attests the whole system of the hierarchy, 56; meaning of the sixth canon, 61; marks the public introduction of monastic life, 386; and the first stadium of Theology, 400

Council of Constantinople in 381, its creed but not its canons received, 241; its third canon, 259

Council of Arles, A.D. 314, quoted, 33, 312

Council of Tyre, 170

Council of the Encænia, at Antioch, 180

Council of Sardica, 181, 185

Council of Ephesus, A.D. 431, 311-315

Council of Ephesus (Latrocinium), A.D. 449, 509; annulled by St. Leo, 511

Council of Aquileia, 256

Councils, General, how far and why convoked by emperors, 285

Cyril of Alexandria, St., his time, character, and works, 446; brings the heresy of Nestorius before Pope Celestine, 310; deputed by Pope Celestine to preside at Ephesus, 381

Cyril of Jerusalem, St., his life and catechetic doctrine, 426

Damasus, Pope, his letter to the Eastern bishops, 325; declares in synod, A.D. 369, that the Nicene Council was directed from Rome, 35, note

Decretal Letters of the Popes, lost from St. Clement to St. Julius I., 328; a continuous series from Pope Siricius, 328; part of the administration of Peter, 345; combine faith and discipline, 347; strengthen the "compages" of the Church, 348; nine characteristics of them in A.D. 385-440, 366-377

Dionysius, the Areopagite, works of the so-called theologian, 470

Dioscorus, Archbishop of Alexandria, conduct at the council of Ephesus, 509; addressed by St. Leo as one subordinate, 506; deposed and punished by the council of Chalcedon, 518

Ephraem, St., his life and writings, 417; his testimony to St. Peter's Primacy, 419; to the Eucharistic Presence, 420; to the seven sacraments, 420

Epiphanius, St., his life and witness, 428

Episcopate, the, its universality, completeness, subordination, and unity, 48, 56; maintained by willing obedience in times of persecution, 79; the Eastern, disorganised by Arianism, 237, 249

INDEX.   553

Eusebius, of Nicomedia, model of the court-bishop for after ages, 178; deposes Eustathius of Antioch, 164; leads Constantine to attack the hierarchy, 173; attacks Athanasius, 165, 179; his instrument in violating the Church's constitution, 237-9; a forerunner of Mahomet in doctrine, of Photius in government, 240

Factors, the three, which form the Apostolic Primacy, 15; their action in the eight periods of history, 26; in the period from A.D. 325-431, 381; between the Nicene Council and that of Chalcedon, 535-45

Gregory, St., the Great, makes the Church to be established on the solidity of the Prince of the Apostles, who has one see in three places, Rome, Alexandria, and Antioch, 53
Gregory of Nazianzum, St., his life and works, 423; on the faith of Rome and of Constantinople, 264; on episcopal councils on his time, 234; on the bishops at the council of Constantinople in 381, 235; describes the Arian tyranny, 236
Gregory of Nyssa, St., his life and works, 424

Heresy, promoting theology, 387, 393, 398, 484; bearing on the whole movement from Nicæa to Chalcedon, 482; its defeat a mode of the Church's advance, 275; corrupts the ideas which the Church magnifies, 485; recommends infallibility by confusion and unity by division, 486.
Hergenröther, Cardinal, his account of the Latrocinium, 509-513; of the council of Chalcedon, 514-519, 520-528; of the internal administration of the see of Constantinople, 319-322; his history of Photius, quoted *passim*
Hilary, St., his time of confession and work, 413; describes the councils of his time, 204
History, in patristic times, 470; great failure of it in fourth and fifth centuries, 471; how the Nicene Council makes up for its want in ante-Nicene times, 45, 56, 69, 71
Hosius, denounces the tyranny of Constantius, which cost him his life by cruel treatment, 201

Ignatius, St., of Antioch, alludes to St. Peter and St. Paul at Rome, 120
Infallibility demanded and exercised in the first centuries, 102
Innocent, Pope St., I., A.D. 402-417; on the see of Antioch, 54; bears witness to tradition, 89; his pontificate and letters, 330-333; creates an apostolic vicar over ten provinces, 342; letter to the patriarch of Antioch, 349

Jerome, St., his life and writings, 437; Erasmus on his style, 439
Julian, the twenty months of, 207
Julius I., Pope, A.D. 337-352; his great letter, 90-5, 181; to be considered with that of Pope Clement I., 96; obtains the council of Sardica, 182

Leo, St., the Great, sums up the history of 300 years to the bishops of Italy assembled at Rome, 110-115; his statement of his own office recognised by the council of Chalcedon, 8-10; bears witness to apostolical tradition, 87; the times at his accession in West and East, 492-497; the Papal Primacy at his accession, 498; elected during his absence as imperial commissioner in Gaul, 501; his writings the acts of a ruler who knows not fear, 503; they indicate supreme authority, 504; speaks in Latin as Athanasius or Basil in Greek, 505; speaks as a superior to the archbishop of Alexandria, 506: invited by the archbishop of Constantinople to terminate, by his letter, the heresy of Eutyches, 507; his great dogmatic letter censuring two opposite heresies, 308; necessity of his Primacy at the Latrocinium, 509; rejects a council œcumenical in its convocation, which would have destroyed the Church, 511, as asserted by Pope Nicolas I., 492; his Primacy at the council of Chalcedon, 518, 531-3; is entreated to sanction the 9th, 17th, and 28th canons, 525; he refuses his consent, 527; he annuls these canons in a letter to the empress, 529; the emperor Marcian beseeches him to confirm the council, 529; he confirms the dogmatic decrees, and rejects the three canons, 530; his

35A

confirmation and rejection accepted, 530; his Primacy exercised between Attila and Genseric, 533-5; it is become the Church's centre of gravity and life, 535; internal and external causes leading to this, 535-545; Leo exercised no powers but what his predecessors claimed, 546; what he did for his own and all succeeding times, 548

Letters of Fathers, a wonderful and still unexplored storehouse, 472

Liberius, Pope, A.D. 352-366, banished by Constantius, 196, 228

Litteræ formatæ, 73

Makarius the Great, St., 470

Monastic and Virginal Life, its public introduction, 386; universal praise of it by the Fathers, 462; and for its spiritual beauty, 467; its political importance unforeseen, 467; described by St. Anthony, 468; said by Athanasius to be created by our Lord in taking flesh of a Virgin, 469; ancient masters of it, 470

Mother and Daughter Churches, 74

Newman, Cardinal, quoted, 11, 13; the snow-penance of Napoleon, 16; the martyrs around their King, 393; on principles of interpretation in the ancient schools, 453; on Theodore of Mopsuestia, 455, 458; on the spread of the Nestorian heresy, 458; where he discloses the spiritual root of Arianism, 464; describes Tradition, 405; his notes on Athanasius contain a view of the Antenicene Church, 407; gives the character and writings of Athanasius, 411; identity of type in the Catholic Church, 483; all Christian ideas magnified in the Church, 485

Nicæa to Chalcedon, the intellectual movement, 481, 535-545; its history, by St. Vincent of Lerins, 487-491

Nicolas I., Pope, his letter to the emperor Michael, 63-67; declares that Pope Leo I. saved the Church from destruction, 492, 511

Papal Dignity, development of, in A.D. 325-381, 242-274; in 385-440, 366-382

Patriarchate, the triple Petrine, 49, 53

Patriarchates, the Eastern, inadequate to meet the imperial power, 544

Patristic Literature, its chief period, 388; makes a greater Hellas, and a greater Rome, 390; its unifying spirit, 392; called forth in part by heresy, 393; a continuous contest for life or death, 394-8

Periods, eight, in the history of the Church, 20-26

Peter, St., alone stands at the head of an episcopal line, 58; his Principate the fountainhead of ecclesiastical rule, 95

Primacy, a Divine institution founded on three words of Christ, 1-3; the three words cohere, forming one indivisible office, 4; effect of the three words through eighteen centuries, 5; the Church's recognition of a second Factor, 6-11; its third Factor, Divine Providence, as shewn through ages, 11-16; concurrent witness of three Factors, a proof of it beyond impeachment, 17-19; its sovereign action in the most divergent times, 26-28; evidence of it at the Nicene Council in the triple Petrine patriarchate, 49, 53, 63; in the sixth Nicene canon, 52, 61; in the rule of founding bishoprics followed by the Apostles, 58; the whole hierarchy drawn from it, 67-9, 95; its growth in the time of persecution a certain proof, 77; stronger even than in the case of the episcopate, 84; its exercise, proportionate to the condition of the Church, 98; how exercised in the first three centuries, 99, 123; the root, bond, and crown of the hierarchy from the first, 104, 109; recognition at the council of Ephesus, 312-314, 499-501; recognition at the council of Chalcedon, 8-10, 518-533; how understood by St. Augustine, 337-341

Proclus, St., his twelve years' episcopate and influence, 317, 507

Provincial Synods, 75

Prudentius, encomium of the Roman Peace, translated, 474-6; hymn to St. Laurence, 476; value as an historian, 478; description of the Day of the Apostles at Rome, 479; joins the Real Presence with the worship of reliques, 480; compared with Claudian and Rutilius, 481

Pulcheria, St., ascends the throne, and with her husband, Marcian, supports St. Leo, 514

Resident Synod, rise of, 155; chief instrument in exalting the bishop of Constantinople, 520, 523, 543

Reumont, attachment of the provinces to the empire, 481; Eastern emperor Oberherr of the West, 494

Rome, splendour of the city in 357, 243; stronghold of heathenism in Constantine's time, 248; spiritual life advances while temporal power decays, 246-8, 376-7; its political position very low before St. Leo's time, 490; living in 431 from hand to mouth, when the Pope's Primacy was acknowledged, 501, 314-5; the same in A.D. 451, in St. Leo's time, 534

Russia, its autocracy a transcript of Constantine's, in all its parts, 143

Scripture, universally studied by the Fathers, 4c4, 459; its key, the ecclesiastical sense, 406

Stilicho, the Western empire resting on him, 494

Theodoret, his life and works, 447; appeals from the Latrocinium to Pope Leo, 510

Theodosius I., made emperor, 213; his law of 380, 214; his difficulties, 277; condition of the empire in his reign, 351; gives Roman commands to barbarian chiefs, 353; his death, followed by the agony of the Western empire, 357

Theodosius II., reign and character, 495; on the side of Nestorius, 500; on the side of Eutyches, 500, 508; makes Dioscorus president of the Latrocinium, 509; supports him against Pope Leo, 513; falls from horseback and dies suddenly, 514; his letter of A.D. 430 convoking the council of Ephesus, 281

Tradition in doctrine, government, and life, the Church built upon it, 118-121; what it was which formed the basis of the patristic mind, 449-455; Scripture studied for its support, 404

Valens, his oppression, 209, 211; burnt to death, 212

Valentinian I., his government, 208

Valentinian II., murdered, mourned by St. Ambrose, 435

Valentinian III., fears to live in Rome, 501; his miserable end, 495, 534

Vincent of Lerins, his history of the Church's doctrinal progress in the first four centuries, 487-491

www.ingramcontent.com/pod-product-compliance
Lightning Source LLC
Chambersburg PA
CBHW031935290426
44108CB00011B/568